D1715831

CHINA'S LAW OF THE SEA

ISAAC B. KARDON

China's Law of the Sea

the Sea

THE NEW RULES OF MARITIME ORDER

Yale UNIVERSITY PRESS   NEW HAVEN AND LONDON

Published with assistance from the foundation established in memory of Calvin Chapin of the Class of 1788, Yale College.

Yale University Press books may be purchased in quantity for educational, business, or promotional use. For information, please e-mail sales.press@yale.edu (U.S. office) or sales@yaleup.co.uk (U.K. office).

Set in Scala type by Newgen North America.
Printed in the United States of America.

Library of Congress Control Number: 2022939257
ISBN 978-0-300-25647-5 (hardcover : alk. paper)

A catalogue record for this book is available from the British Library.

This paper meets the requirements of ANSI/NISO Z39.48-1992 (Permanence of Paper).

10 9 8 7 6 5 4 3 2 1

For my parents, with filial piety

CONTENTS

This study is the happy result of the author spending the better part of a decade studying the law of the sea treaty in China. I am grateful to many individuals (all of whom I could not possibly name) for helping me to pursue the experiences and knowledge that inform the book in your hands. Most fundamentally, I am forever indebted to the intellectual inspiration, generosity, and vital encouragement of Peter Katzenstein, without whom the dissertation that began this project would have been inconceivable.

This research is largely the product of direct observation and participation in China's academic and policy discourse on maritime disputes in the period 2012–2021. As a PhD student in 2012 I began a Foreign Languages and Area Studies fellowship at Tsinghua University in Beijing. During this time of intensive language study, I was invited by Jia Qingguo, dean of the Peking University School of International Studies, and Cornell University professor Xu Xin to present my first Chinese-language paper as the only non-Chinese participant in a Peking University workshop in Shandong Province. The workshop was an early effort in a continuing process among Chinese international law and international relations experts who are seeking to integrate the perspectives of their fields to better comprehend (and prosecute) China's roiling maritime disputes. That episode was the first in a series of extraordinary opportunities to observe and participate in the law of the sea discourse in China during a period of waning access for foreigners.

I found myself in the right place at the right time to observe the full expression of China's approach to the law of the sea. The year 2012 marked the beginning of a new administration under General Secretary Xi Jinping that has devoted ever-increasing attention and resources to China's maritime affairs. By 2013, the People's Republic of China (PRC) was embroiled in a seminal event for the development of China's law of the sea: an arbitral suit brought by the Philippines under Annex VII of the UN Convention on the Law of the Sea. This arbitration elevated maritime disputes from a peripheral and specialized issue to one of the most central and contentious issues in the foreign policy of the PRC.

The arbitral procedure stretched across the years 2013 to 2016 and galvanized a growing community of Chinese maritime specialists and practitioners. Riding a wave of meetings, workshops, conferences, classes, publications, advertising campaigns, media, and other advocacy on the arbitration, the Chinese maritime community intensified its efforts to explain and enact the PRC's positions on the "illegal arbitration." The surge of official and popular attention to the subject generated far-reaching discussions and new refinements to Chinese arguments about the law of the sea, PRC maritime strategy, and the complex international relations and questions of law attending the maritime disputes.

As a wide-eyed student of international law and international relations, I was able to observe and participate in many of these discussions. Several of these opportunities arose from the support of Zhang Xin-jun, Hong Nong, Yan Yan, and Wu Shicun, who facilitated my status in 2014 as a visiting scholar at the PRC National Institute for South China Sea Studies in Haikou, Hainan Province (itself an island in the South China Sea), where I was funded by the US Department of Education's Fulbright-Hayes Program. In 2015, I moved from the mainland to Academia Sinica in Taipei, where I was hosted by Song Yann-Huei and welcomed into Taiwan's lively debate on maritime disputes, newly intensified by the arbitration. This affiliation further yielded the rare privilege of a visit to the Spratly Islands in 2016 (to the sole feature under Taiwanese control, Itu Aba/Taiping). Later, as a professor at the US Naval War College's China Maritime Studies Institute since 2017, I returned regularly to the mainland and to Taiwan (until the pandemic years of 2020–2022) for conferences, workshops, and semi-official dialogues with Chinese maritime experts in government, academia, and think tanks.

Jerry Cohen's kindness and patient mentorship made possible so much of this remarkable access. Because of Professor Cohen's early, gracious advocacy for his "young colleague," I participated in countless fascinating meetings, conferences, and dialogues among some of the central players in China's maritime disputes—among them leading judges, diplomats, scholars, and lawyers from the PRC, Taiwan, the Philippines, Vietnam, and the United States. Through Professor Cohen's good offices and those of the US-Asia Law Institute at New York University School of Law and the National Committee on US-China Relations, I was also able to engage many of the key participants in China's UNCLOS arbitration, both in formal Track II dialogues and through frequent meetings and workshops. Peter Dutton has also been a steadfast champion of this book. I have benefited immeasurably from Professor Dutton's world-class expertise on the law of the sea and no less from his unstinting friendship and professional guidance. This work is also the product of the tutelage and incisive commentary of Iain Johnston and Tom Christensen, the co-directors of the Princeton-Harvard China and the World post-doctoral fellowship that supported my research and writing in 2017.

The book that you are about to begin is steeped in these experiences and relationships. My Chinese name even acquired a "海" (the character for ocean), and 孔适海 became my nom de guerre as I navigated China's dynamic maritime affairs discourse. Because of the political sensitivity of the subject in China, all references are to published or broadcast media sources. I did not conduct formal interviews with PRC scholars and officials, but the analysis here is grounded in and inspired by my extensive discussions with them. It is informed by my observations from countless hours in more than 150 maritime law and policy events in China and the United States through a decade of research.

As an American and now as a civilian employee of the US Navy (expressing, in what follows, only my own views, not those of the Department of Defense nor any other part of the United States government), I have continuously sought to maintain a critical, scholarly distance from the politicized turmoil surrounding China's maritime disputes. My intention has always been to listen patiently through the din of political rancor for the faint signals of the practical, empirical processes of rules being made and unmade in the waters of East Asia. Through this long-term effort to "sit firmly on my fishing boat" (稳坐钓鱼台) to wait out the storm, I aim to provide students of international law and order a comprehensive understanding of China's law of the sea.

ABBREVIATIONS

ADIZ   Air Defense Identification Zone
ASEAN   Association of Southeast Asian Nations
CCG   China Coast Guard
CCP   Chinese Communist Party
CIMA   Center for International Maritime Affairs
CLCS   Commission on the Limits of the Continental Shelf
CSIL   China Society of International Law
DOALOS   Division for Ocean Affairs and the Law of the Sea (UN)
DRM   Dispute resolution mechanisms
ECS   East China Sea
EEZ   Exclusive economic zone
ICJ   International Court of Justice
ILC   International Law Commission (UN)
ITLOS   International Tribunal for the Law of the Sea
LTE   Low-tide elevations
MCRM   Maritime Claims Reference Manual
MFA   Ministry of Foreign Affairs (PRC)
MLE   Maritime law enforcement
MND   Ministry of National Defense
MoA   Ministry of Agriculture (PRC)
MSR   Marine scientific research

NPC	National People's Congress
PCA	Permanent Court of Arbitration
PLA	People's Liberation Army
PLAN	People's Liberation Army Navy
PRC	People's Republic of China
ROC	Republic of China
SCIO	State Council Information Office
SCS	South China Sea
SOA	State Oceanic Administration (PRC)
SPC	Supreme People's Court (PRC)
UNCLOS	United Nations Convention on the Law of the Sea (1982, unless otherwise specified)
UNGA	United Nations General Assembly
UNSC	United Nations Security Council
UNTS	United Nations Treaty Series

CHINA'S LAW OF THE SEA

The Struggle for Maritime Order

FLYING LOW AT 5,000 FEET, I could just make out some tiny Spratly Islands through the small windows of a cavernous Republic of China Air Force C-130 transport aircraft. Sitting in the cargo bay with a gaggle of international scholars and our Taiwanese official hosts, we were making our descent to Itu Aba (Taiping) Island—but my binoculars were trained on the nearly completed 10,000-foot airstrip on Subi Reef some 35 nautical miles to the northwest, occupied by the People's Republic of China (PRC). Over the course of the preceding three years (2013–2016), Subi had undergone a radical transformation from a forgettable tropical reef, fully submerged at high tide, to a modern military base studded with radars and other signals intelligence sensors, hangars for fighter and bomber aircraft, surface-to-air missile batteries, electronic warfare arrays, and hardened fuel and power facilities. The entire American naval base at Pearl Harbor could fit inside Subi's sparkling lagoon.[1]

The outpost at Subi is one of three major facilities built by the PRC atop 3,200 acres of land reclaimed from dredged coral and sand in the southern reaches of the South China Sea, some 600 nautical miles from the Chinese mainland. Along with four other less-developed features, these remote bases are the most concrete expressions of China's claims to own and administer all of the Spratly Islands, or Nansha Archipelago

(南沙群岛). The rest of the vast expanse of water is dotted with hundreds of small islets, atolls, sandbars, and reefs ("maritime features"), some garrisoned with Vietnamese, Malaysian, Philippine, and (at Itu Aba) Taiwanese forces manning rudimentary facilities. The entire Spratly area has long been marked "dangerous ground" on international nautical charts because of the navigational hazards posed by its shallow reefs and cays. But it is the waters around them that pose the greatest danger.

The danger lies not only in conflicting ideas about what "the rules" are and should be in these waters but also in the practical actions and reactions to which these conflicting ideas give rise. The waters of the South China Sea (SCS)—as well as those of the East China Sea (ECS) and Yellow Sea—are the object of a tangle of disputes over the rules of the international law of the sea. China disputes most of these waters with all its maritime neighbors and with the United States (US) and several other maritime states that contest the PRC's distinctive claims to rights and jurisdiction across the East Asian littoral.[2]

China's maritime disputes are fundamentally about the rules of the international law of the sea, much of which is codified in the Third United Nations Convention on the Law of the Sea (UNCLOS, or "the Convention").[3] Beijing's efforts to prosecute its many maritime disputes are perhaps the clearest and most widely recognized case of the PRC's rising power and ambition coming into conflict with international order. Wielding substantial and growing maritime power, China has made clear in word and deed that the maritime order is a primary object of the nation's mission to "actively take part in revising existing international rules and setting new rules," in the words of the PRC's top foreign affairs official, Yang Jiechi, director of the Chinese Communist Party (CCP) Central Committee Foreign Affairs Commission.[4]

Chinese leaders' express intention to revise and create international rules raises fundamental questions of geopolitics and international law. Who decides on the rules of international law? How are international laws interpreted and applied, and through what processes? Which rules are at stake and what is their bearing on international order? If China intends to "actively guide the direction of change in the international order," as Yang instructed the most recent authoritative gathering of China's central leadership at the CCP 19th National Party Congress,[5] what are those actions, and what might the direction and magnitude of those changes be?

This study sets out with the general aim to understand whether and how China is indeed changing international order. The sheer theoretical abstraction of that order—whether conceived as "liberal," "rules-based," "post-war" or any other such formulation—inspires an analytical move to examine the concrete rules of international law. Such legal rules constitute a fundamental part of nearly all conceptions of order. At issue here is not whether China complies with the rules, however defined and interpreted.[6] Rather, the object is to learn how the Chinese party-state seeks to shape and use those rules, and to what practical effect. Through intensive focus on the treaty and customary rules of the international law of the sea, the book charts China's struggle to change international order in the maritime domain.

The maritime order is a likely arena for observing a changing order because it is the site of China's most legally explicit and politically contentious challenge to the rules. In this domain, the relevant rules are UNCLOS and customary international law, which comprise the basic elements of the maritime order. "China's law of the sea," as conceived here, represents Chinese leaders' vision for those rules as advanced by the PRC through its actions on, under, and above the world's oceans, in its domestic maritime law and policy, and in the global diplomatic arena. That distinctive vision of maritime order is most evident, most controversial, and perhaps most consequential in China's maritime disputes.

CHINA'S MARITIME DISPUTES

Pointed conflicts over specific rules of international maritime law are the basic substance of China's maritime disputes. These are distinct from China's disputes over territorial sovereignty to the many islands, rocks, and other features scattered across the South China Sea and East China Sea—namely, the Diaoyu/Senkaku Islands, the Paracel (Xisha) Islands, the Pratas (Dongsha) Islands, the Macclesfield (Zhongsha) Bank, and the Spratly (Nansha) Islands.[7] While territorial disputes over island sovereignty are more immediately accessible and tend to galvanize popular nationalism and media attention, they do not challenge the rules, per se.[8] The small, largely uninhabited islands have been disputed with varying

levels of intensity since the nineteenth century; these quarrels resemble
many other territorial disputes in that they boil down to a disagreement
on the facts, not the law: who occupies the land, when and how was it
occupied, and did anyone object?[9]

The proper objects of this study are instead the *maritime* disputes
over which rules govern the ocean space associated with those islands.
While the contested sovereignty of the islands is rightly regarded as
the historical origin of maritime disputes, China's claims and actions
deliberately and consistently sidestep the basic conflict of interest that
inheres in opposing claims to sovereign title. Instead, China claims,
"sovereignty is ours, shelve the disputes and pursue joint development"
(主权在我, 搁置争议, 共同开发), as former paramount leader Deng
Xiaoping instructed his comrades.[10] That formula has been applied by
successive PRC leaders as the fundamental policy for all of China's island sovereignty disputes.[11] When Deng issued that influential twelve-
character formula in 1978, he also told his Japanese counterpart, Prime
Minister Takeo Fukuda, that "we believe that it is wiser to avoid the issue [of sovereignty] if we cannot agree. . . . Our generation is not smart
enough. Our next generation will surely be smarter."[12]

Deng's prediction notwithstanding, the next generation led by CCP
General Secretary Xi Jinping has sustained his policy line of setting aside
the sovereignty question, at least in principle.[13] Xi and other Chinese
leaders have also dramatically augmented the attention and resources
channeled into consolidating PRC authority over the vast "blue territory"
(蓝色土地)—that is, the maritime space—surrounding the islands.[14] In
pressing its claims, Beijing's priority on "safeguarding rights" (维权) has
evidently come to outrank the desire for "safeguarding stability" (维稳).[15]
Xi's policy does not depart from the Deng-era guidance to shelve the sovereignty disputes, but it has brought about cumulatively more "assertive"
measures to safeguard China's putative rights.[16] While this approach has
not precipitated large-scale conflict, it has also not led to any meaningful
change to the status of island sovereignty disputes.[17] Maritime jurisdiction and resource rights, by contrast, have been arenas of active and persistent contestation and change.

China's conduct appears designed to remain below the threshold of
active conflict while consolidating its position in disputes. Hu Jintao and
Xi Jinping have presided over extraordinary efforts to build and employ

a capable civilian maritime law enforcement fleet and a sprawling bureaucratic enterprise to administer and manage ocean policy and law. They have nurtured the development of a People's Liberation Army Navy (PLAN) fleet that now contends with the US Navy (USN) as the region's dominant naval force.[18] Yet even with this impressive capability, China has hardly limited its repertoire to "gunboat diplomacy" (in the form of the naval warships bristling with weaponry that are most commonly associated with such coercive maritime conduct).[19] The PLAN has been a secondary or even tertiary player in the disputes, hovering over the horizon but seldom directly confronting opposing parties. Instead, Chinese practice is marked by the rapidly growing presence and activity of Chinese coast guard cutters, fishing and militia boats, oil rigs, survey ships, and marine scientific vessels, all patrolling, administering, surveilling, exploiting, or studying disputed waters.[20]

These practices are directly enabled by the substantial new facilities at Subi, Fiery Cross, and Mischief reefs, as well as the highly developed infrastructure on the Paracel Islands.[21] Those distant bases and the activities they support do not advance a PRC sovereignty claim—for that claim has been plainly asserted and long recognized.[22] Rather, they assert China's authority over maritime space. Through the practice of seeking to use and administer—and prevent others from using and administering—contested maritime space, Chinese official and quasi-official vessels strive to "embody China's sovereign rights and jurisdiction" with physical, practical presence.[23] In parallel with these muscular efforts, Chinese officials also strenuously assert that these and other maritime activities are lawful under the international law of the sea.

Underlying and enabling all of this activity is a more fundamental, if less immediately visible, tool of PRC maritime policy: the instrument of international law. Far from disregarding international law in its maritime disputes (as is often alleged), Beijing regards law as essential. Systematically, deliberately, and with growing sophistication, China's leaders seek to shape and use international law to their advantage. Operations on the water are undertaken expressly to advance China's definitions of "the rules" through actions portrayed as defending China's rights under international law.

The basic object and purpose of the international law of the sea is to define the legal status of maritime space. Similarly, the basic object and purpose of PRC maritime law is to define the legal status of the maritime space claimed under PRC jurisdiction. Through painstaking official endeavors, Chinese officials have brought certain elements of the international law of the sea into PRC law. China's domestic rules mostly mirror those of the law of the sea, adopting the Convention's basic structure of maritime zones of coastal state sovereign rights and jurisdiction. Those rules (in the form of national and provincial legislation, administrative regulations, departmental rules, and local measures) frequently borrow language from the UNCLOS treaty verbatim. In crucial areas, however, law of the sea rules internalized into China's system have been transformed in line with a clear political intent to assert the legality of controversial and sometimes indeterminate PRC claims.

These transformed rules are of great interest—politically to Chinese leaders and analytically to this study. They run the gamut from specific technical matters covering where to draw baselines around offshore islands, to legalistic parsing of the actions and vessels that may qualify for "marine scientific research," to raw political determinations weighing "the importance of the interests involved to the parties" (UNCLOS, Art. 59). With respect to each disputed rule, Chinese officials define their practices in terms of "China's law of the sea"—that is, framed in explicitly legal terms, implemented by domestic agents empowered by a domestic legal code that purports to uphold the law of the sea, but in service of the party-state's maritime objectives.

WHO MAKES THE RULES?

Asking whether China is "breaking the rules" does not leave us in much suspense when it comes to the international law of the sea. Like the positions taken by many other states, quite a few PRC claims and practices are unmistakably at odds with the black letters of UNCLOS. The more consequential questions concern whether and how China is *making* the rules. China's practice of certain law of the sea rules may change the maritime order and international order more broadly. Such changes may be more or less destabilizing. In the next chapter, we will consider the subject of order, detailing how it may change and to what effect. As a preliminary matter, though, the basic issues under inquiry have to do with how states may make or change rules of international law.

This study's primary aim is to analyze China's practical efforts to influence an important body of international rules.[24] Determining whether and how it has effectively done so requires close attention to the formal and informal processes by which law of the sea rules have changed. This rule-making process is well underway, and it can be analyzed empirically—even if the final end state of those rules remains uncertain. Orienting around the rules of the law of the sea, this study is positioned to inform our answers to certain vital academic and policy questions about China's rise. The payoff comes in the form of concrete observations about what, precisely, China intends the rules to be and how effectively it has put those intentions into practice.

While the full warp and woof of the "China challenge" surely exceeds any specific domain of inquiry, there are significant reasons to regard China's influence on the law of the sea as a leading indicator of its putative challenge to order. In the law of the sea, as in several other important domains, China has straightforwardly announced an intention to change the rules. In the words of Huang Huikang, former director-general of the PRC Ministry of Foreign Affairs (MFA) Department of Treaty and Law, current chairman of the MFA's International Law Advisory Committee, and a member of the UN International Law Commission (ILC):

> With the ever-increasing improvement of our comprehensive national strength and influence, China is gradually transforming from a mere "taker" or "follower" of international law toward a "participant" and "builder" of international law. . . . China has increasingly assumed the role of leader and shaper of international rules. The international community pays great attention to China's concept of international rule of law, and our participation in the game of international rules also needs to be guided by China's concept of international rule of law. . . . The reform of the global governance system and the international order is accelerating, and the struggle for institutional power and the dominance of the future order has become the main battlefield of the game between major powers.[25]

China's ability to achieve "dominance of the future order," in the words of the PRC MFA's leading international lawyer, thus hinges on the effective exercise of its power. China's explicit application of power to this "game of international rules" places the contest over making and shaping international law at the center of geopolitical competition with the United States and its allies. President Barack Obama warned that if the US does not rise to the challenge, "that void will be filled by China. . . . They will make the rules and those rules will not be to our advantage."[26] Such overt concern about "who makes the rules" has grown palpably in successive American administrations, in interaction with a Chinese leadership that likewise views the matter in starkly competitive terms. In the first senior-level meetings between the Biden administration and their PRC counterparts, American officials objected to Chinese actions that "threaten the rules-based order that maintains global stability."[27]

For Yang Jiechi and the party-state he represents, the basic principles and composition of that order are an object of explicit competition. "What China and the international community follow or uphold is the United Nations–centered international system and the international order underpinned by international law, not what is advocated by a small number of countries of the so-called 'rules-based' international order."[28] China's position on this issue of order and the rules composing it is plainly counterposed with that of the United States. However, this in itself does not make it a "challenge" to order. Indeed, as Alastair Iain Johnston has argued, when we consider China's relationship to international order in comparison to America's, the matter of which state is the greater revisionist is debatable.[29] Across a wide array of institutions and regimes usually regarded as part of the international order, China's record of compliance and integration compares favorably to America's. This "suggests that China is not challenging the so-called liberal international order as much as many people think," concludes Johnston.[30] When we further consider China's present orientation toward international order in light of its past, avowedly revolutionary approach, there is a distinct trend toward moderation.

Yet even if China's foreign policy is less revolutionary than before— and perhaps less revisionist than America's—we are still left with the brute fact of its markedly enhanced power to influence the rules in the twenty-first century. A China that has only marginally revisionist aims but employs substantially greater power to achieve them is more capable of changing the rules than a China with revolutionary ambitions but relatively little power to realize them. The degree of challenge may vary across different domains of order, but for the United States in particular, contending with growing Chinese power entails a "struggle" to make the rules.[31] We need not define international order as a function of American interests to recognize that direct conflicts between the US and China over the meaning and application of rules offer a rare analytical window into the question, "who makes the rules?"

The rules under contestation in China's maritime disputes raise this question quite starkly. The disputes highlight specific differences between China's preferred rules and those preferred by other parties. This circumstance allows the study that follows to adopt an altogether different tack than the normative question of "who is right?" or the conventional academic question of "who is complying with the rules?"[32] Instead, this book analyzes whether and how China is succeeding in its struggle to change the rules of the international law of the sea.

OVERVIEW OF THE BOOK

Chapter 1 develops a historical and theoretical framework for understanding the rules of the international law of the sea. It first conceptualizes rules of international law as fundamental building blocks of international order, however that order is characterized. It then reviews the primary sources of international law rules in custom and treaties, noting the processes by which these rules may formally change and situating them in the context of a specifically *maritime* order nested within international order.

Turning then to the historical dynamics of change and stability in the law of the sea, it details the specific ways that its rules have changed over time. While the 1982 UNCLOS codified much of the law of the sea, the meaning and application of its black letter rules have been subjects of continuous controversy and debate, making the law of the sea ripe for revision through the subsequent practice of states. These theoretical and historical considerations inform a practical method for observing and categorizing the ways China may effectively change or revise law of the sea rules. Changes may occur at the local, regional, and/or global level, and they may be observed in China's "state practice" in interaction with that of "specially affected states." The rules under inquiry are those actively contested in China's maritime disputes:

(1) geographic rules, (2) resource rules, (3) navigation rules, and (4) dispute resolution rules.

Chapter 2 explores China's evolving attitudes toward international law, focusing on contemporary beliefs about the law of the sea and expectations for how China can change it. First, it summarizes both ideological and instrumental elements of this attitude toward the "weapon of international law" since China's fateful encounters with British gunboats and European treaties in the first part of the nineteenth century. Tracing the legacy of this experience into the contemporary PRC, it then unpacks PRC participation in international legal processes and its role in the development of the 1982 UNCLOS treaty. The chapter ends with an overview of the domestic maritime legal and administrative apparatus that has evolved to internalize the law of the sea in the PRC and promote the programmatic aim of becoming a maritime power.

Chapter 3 analyzes the geographic rules of the law of the sea, which regulate the spatial extent of state authority in the maritime domain. The contested geographic rules in China's maritime disputes concern entitlements, baselines, and maritime boundaries. Chapter 3 first examines these rules as they manifest in PRC practice—that is, in its laws, regulations, official pronouncements, and administrative and law enforcement activities—to draw a preliminary conclusion about the consistency and uniformity with which the PRC promotes a particular interpretation or application of geographic rules. Then it analyzes the responses of the states most affected by China's practice. These "specially affected states" may object, acquiesce, or adopt China's preferred rule; the responses will determine whether that rule may be emerging as a legal norm in the region and beyond.

Chapters 4 through 6 follow this same method of identifying the specific rules under contestation, evaluating China's practice for uniformity and consistency, and assessing the specially affected states' responses to determine whether China's preferred rule may have wider normative effects. Chapter 4 applies this method to resource rules, which assign rights and jurisdiction over marine resources. Chapter 5 treats navigation rules, which establish the rights and freedoms of "flag states" and the coastal state's authority to limit them in and above their claimed jurisdictional zones. Chapter 6 takes up dispute resolution rules, which determine how legal institutions may be brought to bear in settling differences over other rules and their application to specific cases.

A concluding chapter synthesizes the practices analyzed throughout the study, recapping evidence that China has promoted the development of uneven regional norms that are unlikely to be effective as rules of international law. Based on the patterns of practice observed in the four contested sets of rules, the potential for China to change legal rules at a global or universal level is generally limited. However, there is accumulating evidence of an inchoate East Asian maritime order in which UNCLOS is not the only significant source of rules. The practice of China and many specially affected states shows a distinct trend toward deference to the supremacy of coastal state sovereignty (China's in particular) and toward weakened institutions for formal dispute resolution. Finally, by further widening the aperture to consider the cumulative effect of China's maritime practices on international order more broadly, the chapter considers whether "China's law of the sea" is more likely the exception or the rule in other domains of international politics.

CHAPTER ONE

Order, Rules, and Change in the Law of the Sea

The relations and interests of nations can only be coordinated
through rules and institutions; you cannot just listen to whom-
ever has the strongest fist. Great powers should take the lead as
advocates and defenders of the international rule of law, keep
their promises, refrain from exceptionalism, abjure double
standards, and never distort international law to infringe on the
legitimate rights and interests of other countries nor undermine
international peace and stability in the name of rule of law. But
for unjust and unreasonable international rules and institutions, we will advance reforms and promote changes to global
governance.
—*Chen Yixin, Director-General of the CCP Central Committee
Political and Legal Affairs Commission*[1]

IF CHINA IS INDEED CHANGING the rules, how would we know? By
what process would such changes occur? Have China's actions caused
specific changes to the law of the sea? What would it take for those
changes to constitute a challenge to international order? This chapter
takes up those questions by proposing a framework for studying China's
law of the sea. If we want to understand whether and how China is
changing the rules in any domain, we will need a basic theoretical and
practical grasp of what the rules are and some account of the mechanisms through which they may change. Then we may assess the extent
to which the rules of the international law of the sea are changing in line
with China's preferences. We take up these conceptual and historical
matters in three steps.

First, international orders may be conceptualized both from the
top down and from the bottom up. Looked at from either vantage, rules
are basic elements of order, and changing rules provide indications of
a changing order. Rules of international law provide unique informa-

tion about the character of any order. They connect the highly abstracted "international order" and its governance to certain concrete, specified, and agreed rules. Many of the most significant rules are customary international law, the product of the historical patterns of purposive state behaviors that crystallize into a binding rule—one which may change as those patterns of behavior shift. Description of the processes by which rules of international law may be formally and informally modified is a helpful first step in recognizing a changing order.

Second, a distinct maritime order is recognizable as a part (or sub-order) nested within the wider international order. The rules of the international law of the sea are one of its defining components, and they have been the object of several rounds of major revision in the last century. The maritime order, in turn, has undergone a great transformation. Where coastal states long enjoyed maritime rights only as far as they could enforce them, a new legal regime of broad sovereign rights and jurisdiction over maritime space came into force over the last few decades of the twentieth century. Coastal states now exercise new, legalized forms of authority over radically more maritime space than was ever before subject to state control. In juxtaposition, the enduring interest of strong maritime states in maintaining the freedom of the seas has tempered these changes and forged an uneasy balance in the maritime order. Important aspects of that balance are codified in international treaties, the 1982 UNCLOS most of all. Yet even in this widely accepted "constitution for the oceans," ratified by more states than any multilateral treaty other than the United Nations Charter, there remain vast gulfs between states about the correct interpretation and application of the black letters of the treaty instrument.[2] China's maritime disputes are the most consequential front in the struggle over what kind of maritime order UNCLOS prescribes.

Third, a practical method for recognizing China's influence on law of the sea rules starts with its "state practice"—that is, in sustained patterns of formal declarations, domestic legislation and regulation, and operations of central and local party-state organs and agents. In concert, these practices express China's preferred rules, permitting assessment of their substance and application. How China puts these preferred rules into practice is only the first consideration, however, because the interactive practice of other states is also necessary for that rule to have wider effect. Most relevant are those states in direct disputes over rights and jurisdiction with China. Their practices determine the minimum neces- sary threshold for a rule to change under some rudimentary and uncon- troversial standards drawn from jurisprudence.[3] Finally, holistic consid- eration must be given to the cumulative effects of individual changes to rules and how they may contribute to a changing order.

THE STRUGGLE FOR ORDER

The question of whether and how China is changing international order is often answered with reference to a familiar typology of "status quo" versus "revisionist" rising powers: China either accepts (and perhaps even supports) the order, or it rejects and contests it (in whole or in part).[4] The first problem that such designations always encounter is reason- able disagreement about what this abstract theoretical notion of "order" is and how it may be supported or contested. We must first adequately define what we mean by order before we can make sense of the struggle among states to revise or sustain it.

Two seemingly opposed models of order will help us conceptualize the process of changing rules. The first is a top-down, structural view in which rules are meaningful only in the context of the political order in which they operate. As the order changes, those rules change in a sys- tematic way, registering the prevailing configurations of power and au- thority within the order. The second model is a bottom-up, process-based approach in which rules emerge as properties of sustained international interactions. States' patterned behaviors and beliefs or agreements about the rules governing those interactions constitute the order in a given do- main. Specific rule changes will accumulate to form the characteristics of that order. Despite their inverted relationships with the rules, these two models can be complementary.

The theoretical problem hinges on whether we think of order as a cause or an effect. Put simply, does the order make the rules, or do the rules make the order? The former proposition conceives order as a func- tion of (hegemonic) power in the international system.[5] Alastair Iain Johnston distills the basic claim from this vantage: "international order comprises an array of institutions, rules, and norms that more or less reflect the dominant state's interests."[6] With such a conceptualization in mind, the logical way to analyze a "challenge" to order is to assess a rising state's "cooperation with the hegemon" in the form of its compliance with the rules.[7] This, Johnston argues, is a highly problematic way to operationalize a challenge because it categorically excludes the possibility that the dominant state may itself not comply with—and may even seek to revise—the order (which is circularly defined in terms of that dominant state's own power and interest).[8]

This critique of the top-down model prompts further consideration of what a challenge to order would properly entail. If rules are simply "the pattern of ruler practices" that set the parameters of what is prudent for weaker actors,[9] then any change to the rules not caused by the ruling state(s) is by definition a challenge to order. This conception assumes that the dominant state has articulated a clear set of rules that it generally follows itself, such that other states may be held to that standard.[10] It further requires that those rules generally cohere with one another, such that acts to uphold one rule do not violate another rule.[11] These assumptions are especially hard to sustain with respect to the law of the sea, where the United States remains outside the main rule-making treaty (UNCLOS). Even if the maritime rules that the US seeks to uphold are generally accepted, in this mode we are hard-pressed to "recognize the difference between conflicts of interest between the United States and China, on the one hand, and conflicts between China and 'international order,' on the other."[12] Avoiding this common conflation of order with the dominant state's interests will demand more precision in defining *which* order we have in mind and how it is composed.

The bottom-up approach in which rules determine order gives the theoretical problem a different cast. Order may be separated from any one dominant state's interests, but it then becomes difficult to put any unified order in focus. Here "cooperation with the hegemon" can be incidental, because once rules (and institutions that coordinate them) exist, they function independently (at least to some degree) to shape state behavior.[13] Viewed bottom-up, order is a more "diffuse and shared system of authority," in Ikenberry's rendering.[14] He treats "an international order [as] a political formation in which settled rules and arrangements exist between states to guide their interaction," such that revisions to the rules logically change the order.[15] The character and substance of those rules reveal the nature of the order. The existence of mostly liberal rules, for example, gives rise to a mostly liberal order.

But do the qualities of individual rules scale to the level of order? Whether rules are conceived as rational solutions to functional problems or socially constructed "ensembles of intersubjective beliefs, principles, and norms," the jump from a collection of rules to the more abstract notion of order is disorienting.[16] What type and degree of change to the rules is sufficient to produce a change to order? If order is an emergent property of patterned interactions among states whose behaviors are guided to greater or lesser degree by rules, norms, and institutions, it has no conceptual boundaries and prescribes no objective way to decide which state or states decide which rules are fundamental to a given order.[17] The fact that there are mutually contradictory rules and principles across a given order further complicates the idea that the whole is the sum of its parts. We trade off a vision of the whole order when we choose to focus exclusively on the character of individual rules.

This study treats the theoretical problems sketched above as a conceptual minefield best left to the theorists.[18] But sidestepping it without damaging the coherence and validity of our conclusions requires finding the lowest common denominator that unites the various conceptions of order: the rules. Order may still be determined by the hegemon in greater or lesser part, such that the "primary foundation of rights and rules is in the power and interests of the dominant groups or states in a social system."[19] In that same order, weak and strong states alike may also engage in patterned practices that effectively bind them in rules and institutions that are costly, difficult, or inappropriate to breach.[20] However order is conceived, its character depends on its rules. Change may come from the top down or the bottom up—or, more realistically, both. Common conceptual ground may always be found in the notion of rules (however created, sustained, modified, or destroyed) as fundamental to any international order.

Global, Regional, and Functional Orders

Before turning to the question of which rules matter and how they may change, we will also need to specify their operative domain. Where and what is the order (or orders) in which the rules are in effect? Does it make sense to speak of a universal international order, "liberal" or otherwise, such that a rising state could plausibly "change the rules governing the [entire] international system," in Gilpin's broad rendering? Or is order better analyzed by differentiating it by function or by region? Geographically defined order is probably the historical norm, whether manifested in continental or maritime empires, spheres of influence, or regional alliance structures.[21] The payoff for this study lies in finding the right scope for observing dynamics in a specifically *maritime* order.

Some rules, like those associated with the principle of sovereignty, plainly operate at a universal level (if unevenly).[22] Others are specified in particular functional domains. There are plausibly distinct, "issue-specific" orders or regimes concerning trade, finance, military matters, the environment, the oceans, and so on.[23] Take tariff barriers, for example, which are regulated by rules in various treaties and organizations that bear only on matters of international trade. Still others have a defined geographic valence. The European Union promulgates rules for only its members. More abstractly (and pertinently to this study), East Asia may have a particular normative architecture that generates and sustains rules—for example, through the Association of Southeast Asian Nations (ASEAN) and associated organizations, or Confucian culture—that apply only among regional states.[24]

While this question about the nature of order(s) is usually styled as a theoretical conundrum, careful empirical attention to the substance and scope of the rules themselves yields some insights that should inform which level of analysis is appropriate for a given inquiry. These distinctions between universal, functional, and geographic are often more analytical than actual. States and their agents are simultaneously engaged in practice across these putative orders, which intersect and nest within one another in myriad and shifting ways. In proposing "a world of regions," Peter Katzenstein conceives of "porous" regional orders shaped by American power and purpose, as well as by forces of globalization and internationalization that circulate rules and norms from outside the region.[25] States are simultaneously actors in any number of different orders, operating at universal, regional, and local levels, and in functionally differentiated arenas of international practice.

Considering the "international order" requires recognition of various nested sub-orders.[26] The international legal order is one such analytically distinct sub-order, but it is also one which both permeates the wider international order and forms central institutions and rules within other sub-orders. The trade, financial, human rights, and environmental orders, for example, function on the basis of rules whose import derives in whole or in part from the international legal order. Maritime order likewise rests heavily on international legal order for its major characteristics. Thus the reductive move adopted here: interrogating specific rules of international law.

Rules of International Law: Building Blocks of Order

International law is not the only source of rules in international relations, but it is the dominant mode of recognizing, interpreting, and applying them in the contemporary era. It also provides a rigorous language and doctrinal foundation for making sense of rules. These qualities recommend inquiry into rules of international law as a necessary, if not sufficient, set of observations to form any judgment about whether, when, and how maritime order is changing. Such observations will not tell us *why* the change occurred, but they will capture it with the precision and practicality that define the domain of law.

At the unit-level of the rule, we can observe whether a specific rule (or set of rules) is applicable only in particular functional or geographic orders, or if it obtains universally. Because rules may evolve or fall out of practice over time, tracking them individually allows more confident judgments about where, when, and to what degree they are in play. This reductive approach is nonetheless informative in describing change at the structural level. Gilpin attends only to effects at the level of the international system, but he still posits that "as its relative power increases, a rising state attempts to change the rules governing the international system."[27] Changing individual rules, then, are necessary even in that spare rendering of order as a function of raw material power. Knowing the status and dynamics of important rules yields dividends whatever the level of analysis at which we seek to understand their effects.

But which rules matter? Any reasonable designation of important rules will prominently include those written down and agreed upon in treaty form; it may also include norms, customs, common social practices or usages, ethical codes, and other informal elements of international politics. This study limits the scope of its inquiry to rules of international law.[28] In the post-war international order, international law is the source of "the most important rules influencing interstate behavior."[29] These rules of international law register the basic political arrangement of the contemporary system. "Although the rights and rules governing inter-state behavior are to varying degrees based on consensus and mutual interest," Gilpin writes, "the primary foundation of rights and rules is in the power and interests of the dominant groups or states."[30]

Further refining this blunt characterization, we may consider that the international law governing specific domains reflects those domi-nant states' capacities to express their power toward specific purposes.[31] Those domains in which two or more dominant states seek conflicting international legal arrangements are thus sites to observe a challenge to order. By bringing to the foreground the specific rules (or interpretations of rules) preferred by different states, such disputes over rules provide a laboratory for observing the dynamics of change in a given order.

Rules of international law arise from varied sources. The statute cre-ating the International Court of Justice (ICJ) is the most authoritative statement on the matter, describing four "sources" of international law: first, "international conventions, whether general or particular, establish-ing rules expressly recognized by the contesting states" (that is, treaties); second, "international custom, as evidence of a general practice accepted as law"; third, "the general principles of law, recognized by civilized na-tions; fourth, "the judicial decisions and the teachings of the most highly qualified publicists of the various nations as subsidiary means for the de-termination of rules of law."[32] Of these, treaty and custom are generally regarded as most significant and will be the primary focus of this study.[33]

Treaty Rules

Treaties are readily conformable to our common-sense understand-ing of rules as "black letters" written on paper. The states party to the treaty have ratified it, thus formally consenting to the legal instrument as binding—at least in theory. In practice, of course, states sometimes interpret all or part of a treaty in different ways or simply fail to honor their obligations under the treaty. They are no less rules for manifesting mixed records of compliance.

In fact, it is precisely those rules that are *not* followed in uniform and widespread fashion that give rise to the disputes of greatest interest. Even treaty rules hammered out over the course of long negotiation may be prone to vagueness and indeterminacy, which makes them liable to change over time (UNCLOS provides a fine example, examined below).[34]

Ultimately, the sovereign usually enjoys discretion to make a final determination about the scope and nature of its own obligations.

For some legal scholars, such "auto-interpretation" is not so problematic because properly drafted laws and properly trained lawyers and judges will constrain more reckless or opportunistic efforts to distort legal obligations.[35] The scope of indeterminacy is relatively narrow and "discretion is 'relative' because its limits are assumed to be set by law."[36] Those critical of the coherence and efficacy of this "epistemic community of international lawyers," however, argue that such exercises of discretion "cannot be detached from the conditions of political contestation in which they are made."[37] Reasonable analysts may differ about whether the entire legal edifice is indeterminate, or only select rules.[38] Whatever that judgment, in the absence of supranational authority, it is clear enough that the legal outcome in cases of indeterminacy is seldom determined solely by impartial recourse to legal rules.[39]

A treaty duly ratified by sovereign states constitutes a set of rules binding on those states, though their meaning and application are not immutable. Each treaty prescribes its own mechanisms for formal change or amendment of the rights and obligations it confers.[40] Each is also subject to interpretation through "subsequent agreements" among the parties to a treaty and their subsequent practice, following the terms of the widely recognized Vienna Convention on the Law of Treaties.[41] Such subsequent state practice helps to "strike a balance between the core concepts [of a treaty] and the contemporary norms that have emerged since its inception, in other treaty regimes and in the realm of custom."[42] The meaning of a treaty's black letters may change as states interpret and apply them in varying ways.

Customary Rules

Customary international law (or custom) is the second significant body of rules to consider and the most prone to change through political contestation. Custom is "unwritten law deriving from practice accepted as law," according to the conclusions of the International Law Commission (ILC) following a lengthy study culminating in a United Nations General Assembly (UNGA) resolution in 2018.[43] Customary rules form over the course of time and are presumed to be binding on all states in the international legal community. While the proliferation of treaties in the twentieth century has overshadowed the customary foundations of international law, custom remains the dark matter of the international legal universe. It presumably accounts for the greatest number and widest variety of international legal rules, yet it cannot be inventoried or comprehensively described.[44]

Custom is regarded as "a primitive source of law because it lacks clear rules of change" and remains notoriously difficult to describe and analyze concretely.[45] With some notable exceptions, it falls out of most work on international politics.[46] Yet "customary international law *is* norms . . . with powerful behavioral effects," explain Martha Finnemore and Katherine Sikkink, noting that international relations scholars researching norms have essentially been speaking in prose all along about customary law.[47] Custom is the stuff of contention that animates so much of the study of international politics, and it warrants closer attention as a constituent part of order.[48]

While there is no consensus over how custom is to be properly identified and applied, there is little controversy over its components: state practice and *opinio juris sive necessitatis* ("opinio juris"). State practice is often termed the "objective" element: it comprises "the conduct of the state, whether in the exercises of its executive, legislative, judicial or other functions."[49] It thus captures policy, law, court decisions, administrative rules, and other official actions undertaken by states and their agents.[50] Opinio juris is the "subjective" element: "the practice in question must be undertaken with a sense of legal right or obligation."[51] The ICJ has consistently reasoned that these "two conditions must be fulfilled" for courts to recognize a customary rule.[52] Parallel reasoning should apply to making an empirical and political assessment of custom.[53]

But exactly how much state practice and opinio juris is required for a customary rule to "crystallize" or become recognizable? The ILC has determined that "the practice must be general, meaning that it must be sufficiently widespread and representative, as well as consistent."[54] Further, "custom is to be distinguished from mere usage or habit."[55] This construction "does not lend itself to exact formulations" and thus can only be answered authoritatively on a case-by-case basis.[56] It nevertheless provides a helpful standard. Even if there is no set number of states or formula for determining whether a custom exists, this standard enables basic judgments that may quickly exclude those state actions that are plainly not widespread and representative.[57]

Of critical importance to this study of contested rules, "specially affected States" must participate in a practice for it to be considered "general practice accepted as law."[58] Furthermore, the state practice in question must be "both extensive and virtually uniform [to be considered] a settled practice."[59] Thus custom may not form solely by one or more states acting ad hoc in ways that they consider to be in their interests: the practice and belief in its legality must be undertaken with intention, by a sufficient number of states affected by the practice, and in a virtually uniform way in order for customary international law to form.

Special Custom

Customary practices that are not uniform across the entire international system may nonetheless become part of international law as "special" or "particular" customary international law.[60] Rules of this type are formed by a more limited number of states in a specified domain through the familiar elements of state practice and opinio juris. Special customs "deal with non-generalizable topics such as title to or rights in specific portions of world real estate"; these may be described as "regional customs."[61] Customary practices that are neither widespread nor representative across the globe may nonetheless become binding rules on certain states. This is critically important to the question of China's influence on rules, which appears likely to have a strong regional valence.

The narrower scope of such special rules, however, imposes a higher standard for their recognition. In theory, *all* of the specially affected states must consent to the formation of rules of special custom, as opposed to some merely representative and widespread subset of states.[62] Various special customary rules have been defined by the ICJ as applying within a specific geographic scope: "particular to the Inter-American system,"[63] "limited . . . to the African continent,"[64] "particular to Latin-American States,"[65] or even binding only among two states.[66] This standard allows that customary rules may arise in East Asia and bind only East Asian states or may operate only within a distinct sub-region like Southeast Asia or the East China Sea.

While there is debate as to what combination of practice and opinio juris will be sufficient for the recognition of a customary norm, every formula for such changes prominently (or exclusively) highlights the state practice of specially affected states as a *necessary* element.[67] There is some support among legal scholars for the notion that opinio juris is not altogether necessary or is perhaps derivative of practice.[68] How much and precisely what kind of practice is a case-specific question that requires close attention to the facts and circumstances attending any particular rule. Little can be said a priori about the exact sufficient conditions for practice in any particular case, but a large body of international jurisprudence has found it necessary in any case to ascertain a "virtually uniform" practice. This does not mean that some inconsistencies and contradictions exclude the possibility that the practice may generate a norm. The practice need not be "in absolutely rigorous conformity with the rule"—rather, it "should, in general, be consistent with such rules."[69] Practice that is non-uniform or inconsistent in some degree may still be dispositive, but it is weaker evidence of a customary norm.[70]

Conflict Rules

The process by which international legal rules may be changed presents a practical dilemma. Former US Attorney General William Barr, following the "state of exception" reasoning championed by the Nazi legal theorist Carl Schmitt, puts it this way: "the only way to change international law is to break it."[71] Unless a domain of practice is completely devoid of applicable rules, states must breach an existing rule to effectively generate a new customary rule. Anthony D'Amato explains the reasoning: "When a state violates an existing rule of customary international law, it undoubtedly is 'guilty' of an illegal act, but the illegal act itself becomes a disconfirmatory instance of the underlying rule. The next state will find it somewhat easier to disobey the rule, until eventually a new line of conduct will replace the original rule by a new rule."[72]

This process, however, presumes the existence of a rule that is sufficiently determinate as to prescribe clearly lawful practice(s) and to make any deviation readily identifiable. This is not always the case—and particularly so when we consider some of the contested rules of the law of the sea. Such big, complex, multilateral treaties, according to international law scholar Phillip Allott, may be nothing more than "a disagreement reduced to writing."[73] Considerable scope exists for change at the margins of interpretation without practices occurring in unequivocal breach of a rule.[74]

Properly understood, rules of international law give rise to both cooperation and conflict. The "cooperation thesis" at the heart of so much theorizing about international law fails to adequately comprehend the role of legal rules as prominent sites of contestation and struggle.[75] Explicitly or implicitly, many students of international law take as an article of faith that its rules necessarily serve to "reduce friction and controversies among states . . . by prescribing how controversies may be avoided, mitigated or resolved."[76] Monica Hakimi urges the field to consider disagreements over rules not as a failure or limitation of international law but rather as an essential feature: "conflict is part of what international law is for."[77]

In international relations, a related faith in cooperation is implicit in what might be described as the "compliance paradigm." Questions about international law are often rendered in terms of whether its rules successfully generate compliance.[78] Conceptualized in terms of its association with cooperative behavior, international law (and its related institutions) appears to exist "outside of politics, either neutral among political disputes or defending goals that are so universally held that they are not subject to political contestation."[79] This "enchanted view of law" treats rules as functional only insofar as they facilitate cooperation.[80] A more empirical attitude, adopted here, makes no such assumption. Rules may equally be the catalysts of conflict. Customary rules in particular typically do not fit a "rulebook" model for rigid application in all cases; instead it is the conflict over whether and how to apply the law that establishes a contingent rule for a specific case.[81] The following examination of how the customary and conventional law of the sea has changed over time will demonstrate these cooperative and conflictual currents (Figure 1).

UNCLOS: A CONSTITUTION FOR THE OCEANS

What sort of an order is the contemporary maritime order and what are its mechanisms of change? To begin with, the UNCLOS treaty is the centerpiece of this order. Tommy Koh, the president of the United Nations

FIGURE 1. **Conceptualizing China's Maritime Disputes Within the International Order** (Illustration by author.)

conference that developed the new Convention, announced at the close of treaty negotiations that "we succeeded in adopting a convention covering every aspect of the uses and resources of the sea . . . [and] achieved our fundamental objective of producing a comprehensive constitution for the oceans which will stand the test of time."[82] The notion of the 1982 UNCLOS as a "constitution for the oceans" indicates its framers' aspirations for a treaty of universal scope and legitimate status as the primary body of rules governing human activities in the world's oceans. The Convention formally binds its 168 parties to rules that aim to supersede the "morass" of incompatible maritime claims across the globe.[83]

While this "constitution" does not formally bind non-ratifying states, even those few states outside of the treaty are in principle subject to the maritime rules it prescribes to the extent that they now represent customary law.[84] The United States is the most conspicuous non-party.[85] Most of the treaty's rules are reckoned universal because "they have passed into custom as a result of State practice" or because, as the US argues, the treaty largely codifies pre-existing custom.[86]

The treaty instrument further and expressly accommodates the customary international law that comprises the traditional law of the sea, "affirming that matters not regulated by this Convention continue to be governed by the rules and principles of general international law."[87] The only elements of the treaty that may not be customary are its formal organizations: the International Seabed Authority (ISA), the International Tribunal for the Law of the Sea (ITLOS), and the Commission on the Limits of the Continental Shelf (CLCS). (These regulate the exploitation of deep sea resources, provide compulsory dispute resolution, and evaluate continental shelf claims, respectively.)

By design, UNCLOS is a "package deal" in which states may not opt out of any particular rules (as is permitted in some treaties). Instead, the Convention rejects any reservations that "purport to exclude or modify the legal effect of the provisions of this Convention in their application to that State" (UNCLOS, Art. 310). "Thus," Koh argues, "it is not possible for a State to pick what it likes and to disregard what it does not like."[88] A state's orientation to the treaty—within it (as is China) or outside it (as is the United States)—has especially significant bearing on dispute resolution. It is only compulsory for parties to the treaty. This distinction is explored at length in chapter 6, but it should preliminarily be regarded as an exception that proves the rule: in general the UNCLOS treaty accounts for the major rules of the international law of the sea.

The package deal reflects a hard-won compromise of competing interests represented at the Conference: 160 states participated in the negotiations from 1973 to 1982, ranging from the world's premier maritime powers to tiny, landlocked developing states. As many as 120 of these states caucused together as the "G-77," which consisted mainly of the decolonized states of Latin America, Africa, and Asia. China's leaders defined this broad group as "the Third World," identifying itself as one of these developing countries sharing a "common struggle against the hated enemies," the "superpowers."[89] Ironically, the US and the USSR found a rare common cause in resisting the numerically advantaged G-77 group and its "revolt against the West."[90]

At the heart of the contestation was the Third World drive to allocate resource rights and jurisdiction to coastal states and protect the "common heritage of mankind" from maritime powers who would otherwise "monopolize" the economic and strategic value of the oceans. The maritime powers, meanwhile, advocated the continuation of the traditional doctrine of "freedom of the seas," and they fought back efforts to enclose maritime space under coastal state jurisdiction.[91] Ultimately, "the G-77 got much of what they seemed to want at UNCLOS III—but in watered-down fashion." By virtue of their numbers, "they often dominated the creation of the formula notion, but usually had to fall back on critical details. They compromised on almost every issue."[92] This perception was shared by the Chinese delegation, which recognized that the final product "reflected a great deal of compromise, particularly on the part of developing countries."[93]

The substance of this delicate compromise is of signal importance to this study because UNCLOS rules are notoriously ambiguous on several critical matters. They often "paper over the cracks of unresolved disagreements" from the Conference, in the words of one judge who has ruled on several UNCLOS cases.[94] The primary disagreement was (and remains) between the principles of *mare liberum* (free seas) and *mare clausum* (closed seas), a debate that has been raging since the seventeenth century.[95] Mare liberum implies a liberal conception of maritime order, in which most uses and resources of the seas remain unregulated.[96] Mare clausum emerged as a counterweight, prescribing a "doctrine of the sovereignty of the seas" that espoused a more territorialized order in which those uses of the sea fell under the jurisdiction of sovereign states.[97]

Over the course of the twentieth century, this tension came to a head. By the 1960s, "it could fairly be said that the old legal order had collapsed and the world was faced with a plethora of conflicting claims for jurisdiction and resources by coastal States. Instead of order, we had chaos."[98] In striking an indeterminate balance between these competing principles, UNCLOS represents a "revolutionary change in the law of the sea"—especially in its creation of the exclusive economic zone, which combines coastal state jurisdiction and "flag" state (that is, vessels flagged by foreign states) high seas freedoms in a sui generis regime.[99]

As in other revolutions, the problem of establishing a stable order was left to the next generation. Notwithstanding the triumph of reaching a comprehensive treaty agreement, states interpreted the black letters of UNCLOS to prescribe quite different behaviors.[100] Even if those rules provide a constitutional framework, the age-old struggle to define and shape order on the world's oceans persists.

The rules of contemporary maritime order embody the competing political, economic, and strategic interests of states. Their indeterminacy on several important matters has given rise to a host of maritime disputes and an active competition to determine which version of the rules will predominate, if any. China's particular struggle to make maritime rules must be recognized in the context of how the law of the sea was already changing when Beijing first dipped its toes into the water. This complex history need not be recited here.[101] What bears some discussion is how powerful and weak states alike have shaped the law of the sea's development over the past century.

With the rise of new technologies, resources, and governments with bureaucratic capacity to wield them, state authority over ocean space expanded "with a speed and geographic scope that would be the envy of the most ambitious conquerors in human history."[102] This move toward a more "closed" maritime order is not without irony. Most law of the sea scholars date the "effective start of this process [to] President Truman's claim to the continental shelf in 1945."[103] With what became known as the Truman Proclamations, the United States laid claim to the natural resources of the seabed and subsoil of the continental shelf as "appertaining to the United States, subject to its jurisdiction and control."[104]

With the stroke of a pen, the leading defender of the freedom of the seas ushered in an era of "ocean enclosure" and "creeping jurisdiction" that would soon be embraced most enthusiastically by the developing world. Latin American and African states, in particular, moved to establish explicit, legal norms and rules recognizing exclusive state authority over ever-wider tracts of ocean space.[105] This "contraction and dismemberment of the freedom of the high seas" proceeded through gradual expansion of the scope and deepening of the content of state authority.[106] States mounted ambitious new claims to rights for fishing and resource exploitation, and they established new patterns of practice by enforcing those rights when other states objected or interfered.[107]

The newly formed United Nations convened two conferences on the law of the sea, held in 1958 and 1960 (UNCLOS I and UNCLOS II). Only the first of those sessions produced any laws, in the form of the four Geneva Conventions on the Law of the Sea.[108] The direct catalyst for a new round of law of the sea negotiations came in November 1967, in the form of a speech in the General Assembly by the UN representative from

Malta, Arvid Pardo. He introduced his remarks in explicit opposition to the maneuvering of the United States to keep his "premature proposal" off of the floor.[109] His speech gave publicity to the notion of the "common heritage of mankind" in the world's oceans beyond the limits of national jurisdiction. Pardo's stirring words precipitated the formation of a thirty-five-nation UN Ad Hoc Committee to Study the Peaceful Uses of the Sea-Bed and Ocean Floor to consider the question of how to utilize the resources of the high seas.[110]

Despite American and Soviet efforts to keep the ocean enclosure movement from gathering momentum, the ad hoc committee garnered widespread support throughout the developing world and ultimately became a permanent, forty-two-member "UN Seabed Committee" whose work gave rise to the Conference.[111] These discussions initially dealt with the deep seabed *beyond* state jurisdiction, which required a concomitant effort to determine the limits of state jurisdiction. Although they did not draft articles in advance (as had been done by the ILC prior to the first two UNCLOS conferences), the Seabed Committee established certain core norms for the Convention that would follow.

The push for a new oceans regime culminated in a series of declarations from the Third World that spilled out of the Seabed Committee and into the complex and contested arena of international oceans politics. By 1970, Argentina, Brazil, Chile, Ecuador, El Salvador, Nicaragua, Panama, Peru, and Uruguay circulated a call for the UN member states to recognize that "any norms governing the limits of national sovereignty and jurisdiction over the sea, its soil and its subsoil, and the conditions for the exploitation of their resources, must take account of the geographical realities of the coastal States and the special needs and economic and social responsibilities of developing States."[112] This statement crystallized a sentiment that some form of jurisdiction over a vast space beyond the territorial sea would be under coastal state authority.

Following the work of the Seabed Committee from 1968 to 1973, the UNGA went on to authorize a third attempt to codify and develop the law of the sea "in response to the advance of technology, to the demand, especially by the developing countries, for greater international equity, and by the new uses of the sea and its resources."[113] International relations scholars heralded the Conference as a watershed in "the politics of rule-making in oceans" in which the "major maritime countries no longer control the process."[114] Others characterized the political movement that produced UNCLOS III as "the Third World against global liberalism."[115]

For China, then hardly a maritime power, this upending of US and Soviet dominance was a welcome development. The US opted to withhold its signature upon the treaty's completion in December 1982, and the Soviets signed while professing misgivings.[116] The CCP's official newspaper, the *People's Daily*, touted the achievement: "The adoption of the Law of the Sea Convention is a victory in the long-term struggle of the Third World countries for equal maritime rights against the superpowers' maritime hegemony."[117] Wang Shuguang, the director of the PRC's State Oceanic Administration (SOA), later described the treaty as having "spawned the formation of a new international maritime order."[118] China was hardly the originator of this broad-based effort to redefine the ocean order, but it plainly embraced and joined the movement.

For all the excitement about the creation of a new treaty, the struggle to define the practical meaning of its black letters was only beginning. Law of the sea "developments must come incrementally and interstitially through State practice."[119] If China is indeed "changing the rules" of the law of the sea, it will be evident in its practices and, necessarily, those of the other coastal states of the world.

A PRACTICAL APPROACH TO STUDYING CHINA'S LAW OF THE SEA

The waves of change to the law of the sea over the last century have washed over the shores of every coastal nation, China's among them. The periodic codification and continuous development of these rules have yielded far broader geographic enclosure of maritime space under state authority, among other major changes. That authority is manifest in jurisdiction for states to govern vast and formerly ungoverned geographic zones and to regulate functional matters like scientific research, environmental conservation, and deep-seabed mineral exploitation. While most of these changes are now enshrined in the Convention, the practical meaning of certain of its important rules, norms, and principles remains in flux.[120] The scope and substance of recognized state authority at sea—that is, the rules of the maritime order—are now the object of geopolitical and legal contention, not least among the great powers.

The principal mechanism by which states may contest and (potentially) change rules of international law is through their practices. While the black letters of the rules are themselves fixed unless and until amended or superseded by another legal instrument, the subsequent practice of coastal states provides the necessary (and perhaps sufficient) conditions for change to law of the sea norms.[121] Universal change will only occur to the extent that some "widespread and representative" group of states puts the innovation into "general and consistent" practice.[122] Local and regional rule changes require less extensive practice; only the specially affected subset of states' practice is dispositive.

State Practice of China and Specially Affected States

Virtually uniform and consistent state practice is required for customary rules to change. Yet however uniform and consistent China's own practice of the law of the sea may be, it is also necessary to analyze the corresponding practices of "specially affected states" to determine whether and in which respects a norm has changed. Structured, focused comparison of Chinese and specially affected state practices constitutes the primary evidence for observing China's desired rules and probing the plausibility of their wider adoption in the region and beyond. This method, unpacked below, can establish whether a necessary threshold has in fact been crossed for the recognition of new rules of international law.[123]

States may be "specially affected" by dint of their geographic proximity, the opposability of their claims, or any other mechanism by which their interests are directly affected by the emergence of a norm. Chinese jurists emphasize that "the health of the international legal system depends on the efforts of those States who are specially affected," lest the interests of non-Western states be underweighted.[124] As with all matters of state practice, there is no off-the-shelf formula to determine which states should count as specially affected, so determinations must be made on a case-by-case basis.

A two-part analysis is therefore a jumping off point for examining the extent to which the PRC has put its preferred norms into practice in a way that may lead to changes to the rules: (1) Is China's practice virtually uniform and reasonably consistent? (2) Do specially affected states object to China's practices, acquiesce to them, or adopt similar practices?

Further specification of these questions is required to address the status and trajectory of specific, contested law of the sea norms. China's maritime disputes provide a set of scope conditions to identify those particular rules that may be subject to changes relevant to the maritime order.

Scope Conditions and Case Selection

China's maritime disputes are a crucible for normative change of the type most relevant to international order. They pit China's desired rules against those of specially affected states—a group that necessarily includes those states with which China has an active maritime dispute. At the heart of each dispute is one or more conflicting claims about the meaning of specific norms in the UNCLOS treaty and in customary maritime law. In many cases, the disputes center on the issue of which body of rules is applicable: does UNCLOS or customary international law (or both) govern a particular question? In other cases, it is a question of how the agreed rule should be interpreted: does a particular norm prescribe these rights?

The disputes frame these controversies by highlighting certain consequential differences between China's claims and those of the other disputants. These differences are most pronounced on questions of boundaries, resources, navigation, and dispute resolution. Each of those four issues has been an explicit concern for PRC leaders at least since China ratified UNCLOS. In depositing its instrument of ratification in 1996, the PRC submitted a statement to the UN that formalized its delegation's prior complaints about "shortcomings and even serious defects in the provisions of quite a few articles in the Convention"[125] The statement affirmed China's claims to sovereignty, but it also proposed a distinctive interpretation of four sets of rules.[126] These are formal stances on China's proposed interpretations of (and exceptions to) UNCLOS rules, and they provide the core objects of analysis for the four empirical chapters of this book. The rules in question are as follows:

1. *Geographic Rules.* These rules define the scope of maritime order, allocating rights and jurisdiction that determine the spatial extent of state authority. China has no settled maritime boundaries with any of its neighbors and thus no agreement as to where China's rights and jurisdiction end and those of other states begin.[127] These

geographic disputes implicate at least three connected sets of rules: (i) the type and extent of maritime entitlements due to land territory, (ii) the nature of baselines around islands, and (iii) the delimitation of maritime boundaries that map the outer limits of jurisdiction from opposing continental shelves and exclusive economic zones (EEZs).

2. *Resource Rules.* Within the boundaries of maritime jurisdiction, the law of the sea grants coastal states sovereign rights over resources and jurisdiction to manage them. Disagreement over the proper allocation of specific rights and jurisdiction over fisheries, hydrocarbons, minerals, and other resources is a fairly common variety of maritime dispute worldwide. Despite a handful of fishery and survey agreements among the claimants, competition over marine resources is especially acute in China's near seas. These disputes can also be rendered as the product of three interrelated sets of rules: (i) the applicability of the customary regime of historic rights, (ii) the allocation and enforcement of rights to fisheries, and (iii) the allocation and enforcement of rights to hydrocarbon resources.

3. *Navigation Rules.* Navigational rights are foundational elements of maritime order. The freedoms of the seas (that is, various navigational rights) are in constant tension with the authority of coastal states to regulate the navigation of "flag" or "user" states' vessels and aircraft. This is the principal object of Sino-American contestation, and this similarly revolves around three rule-sets: (i) the right of foreign vessels to conduct "innocent passage" through the territorial sea; (ii) the rights of warships and other government vessels to operate in foreign EEZs; and (iii) the freedoms of overflight above the EEZ.

4. *Dispute Resolution Rules.* This final cluster of related rules bears on each of the substantive areas of dispute, defining the processes by which they may resolved—both within and without the treaty architecture. Disputes over how disputes themselves should be resolved present a special kind of problem for order, and they find expression in China's maritime contests in the form of another three distinct sets of rules: (i) the jurisdiction of compulsory dispute resolution mechanisms within the UNCLOS framework; (ii) the use of alternative, non-compulsory (including non-legal) dispute

resolution procedures; and (iii) the determination of whether a dispute exists to be resolved.

Each of these four rule-sets is a bundle of functionally connected norms that prescribe certain rights and jurisdiction in a key functional area of the law of the sea. Each is an arena of direct contestation between China and some combination of its maritime neighbors, the United States, and a handful of other states, depending on the norm in question. These disputes are the only observable domain in which China's preferred rules—its desired building blocks of maritime order—are directly tested against the competing preferences of other states.

This study addresses exclusively these active and specific disputes because they center on rules that are explicitly contested. Such "selection on the dependent variable" would be inappropriate if this study aimed to explain *why* China had maritime disputes (or why it had disputes about some rules but not others). It would be insufficient to survey how China influenced the progressive development of the law of the sea regime as a whole. After all, in several other functional areas of the law of the sea, China has not confronted such concerted resistance to its preferences. In fact, it is likely China has exercised substantive influence on rule-making bodies and organizations like the International Seabed Authority in the exploitation of deep-seabed minerals and in the Intergovernmental Conference on Biological Diversity Beyond National Jurisdiction, where large permanent Chinese missions and delegations have been exceptionally active participants.[128]

This selection of actively disputed rules allows focused analysis of the *politics* of international legal change. In the broader arena of the law of the sea and oceans governance, there are many processes of normative change underway concerning which it makes little sense to analyze a Chinese challenge to order. The wider phenomena of creeping jurisdiction and ocean enclosure were occurring before the PRC took any active interest in the law of the sea. Since the treaty entered force, environmental degradation and technological advances have driven normative changes to rules governing ecological protection, mineral exploitation, fisheries management, and many more. Yet while China likely does affect how these norms develop, only its active disputes define parameters of the political struggle to determine the rules of maritime order. If the scope of the inquiry is expanded to cover all the many facets of the law of the sea, uncontested norms will distort the analysis by including changes that do not conduce to any plausible challenge to maritime order.

Another important set of rules excluded from this inquiry are those concerning territorial sovereignty. China's maritime disputes should be analyzed separately from its sovereignty disputes, which concern title to the hundreds of small islands and other features dotting the South and East China Seas.[129] The question of which state rightly holds sovereign title is, in principle, governed by the international law of territorial acquisition.[130] But these customary rules lie outside the law of the sea, which addresses rights and jurisdiction flowing from a recognized sovereign title. The rules of territorial acquisition also rest on relatively stable normative ground, in that there is no basic disagreement on the applicable rules among the various claimants—only on the facts underlying their particular claims to sovereignty. In the highly unlikely event that two or more disputing states were to consent, the ICJ would in principle be able to adjudicate these claims without contemplating any of the law of the sea rules that China contests. Far more likely, the sovereignty disputes will not be settled, and the fundamental conflict will remain over who controls the water space.

Disputed law of the sea rules, then, present a rare political arena to observe a genuine and specific competition over fundamental questions of the rules at the heart of international order. China's practices and those of the specially affected states are the necessary elements of any putative change to rules governing boundaries, resources, navigation, and dispute resolution.

How Will We Know Whether China Is Changing the Rules?
China's ratification of UNCLOS in 1996 announced its official consent to be bound by the treaty's rules. In the same breath, however, PRC leaders announced a formal challenge to the way those same rules are to be interpreted and applied. This official declaration staked out China's preferred interpretation of the treaty and its applicable scope, laying down clear markers on several of the norms that the PRC still contests today.[131] How can we observe whether and to what extent China has been able to remedy these "serious defects" in UNCLOS?

There are few formal mechanisms through which this may be confirmed. These are limited to the amendment to the UN Convention on the Law of the Sea (UNCLOS, Arts. 312–317), the creation of an additional multilateral treaty instrument or "implementing agreement" (UNCLOS, Art. 311), or an authoritative judgment by an international court (UNCLOS, Part XV).[132] Importantly, arbitration under UNCLOS—and indeed international adjudication in general—is binding only on the parties to the procedure itself (UNCLOS, Art. 296). There is no doctrine of *stare decisis* in international law such that court decisions establish rules that apply to other parties in other cases. Courts and arbitral panels consider prior rulings but are not bound in any legal sense by prior judgments.

Absent such formally recognized change, any meaningful revision to the norms underlying the law of the sea will be evident only in the normal patterns of behavior by states—that is, by watching to see which rules best fit the observed actions of states. Of course, alterations in behavioral patterns may be attributable to many factors beyond China's influence. Indeed, the "progressive development of international law" (as described in the Preamble to UNCLOS and in the UN Charter, Art. 13) to change and encompass new domains has been remarkably swift and consequential in the law of the sea.[133] The entrance of new actors in the international legal arena, the introduction of new technologies, and the discovery of new resources are among the prominent factors driving these developments. China's practice must be considered against this baseline of existing trends of normative change in the law of the sea.

Treaty and/or Customary Pathways

Rule change may manifest through two pathways: (1) a new interpretation or application of UNCLOS rules that reflects China's preferred norms; and (2) revised customary international law that reflects China's preferred norms. These pathways often overlap and generally implicate the same practices. They may lead to converging endpoints. That is, the emergence of a customary rule may effectively modify the treaty's interpretation or application; alternatively, a modified treaty interpretation or application may effectively displace a customary rule.[134]

In practice, treaty and customary pathways may be indistinguishable—especially as regards Chinese disputes with the United States, which is not a party to the UNCLOS treaty. The US regards itself as "a leader in developing customary and conventional law of the sea," and even from its position outside the Convention it follows the policy that it is legally obligated under those treaty provisions that "generally confirm existing maritime law and practice."[135] Nonetheless, for analytical purposes we can distinguish them to better articulate the practice requirements that would make a rule change possible.

The key difference between the conventional and customary pathways is whether a changed norm is recognized within the treaty framework or outside of it as a part of the general, customary body of the law of the sea. Changes within the treaty necessarily have a global quality—that is, they affect treaty rules that apply universally. Such modifications must be reflected in interpretations or applications of the treaty rule by a widespread and representative group of states party to UNCLOS. Customary rules, however, have several thresholds for change because a "special custom" may arise at the local or regional level, without giving rise to a global rule. A local custom will only be reflected in the practice of the specially affected states (that is, those with specific disputes with China), whereas regional custom must be evident among a representative group in the region, and global custom will need to meet the same "general and consistent" standard required of a revised treaty interpretation or application.

Virtual Uniformity and Consistency in PRC Practice

The key similarity of the pathways is that both require *virtual uniformity* and *consistency* of China's practice. What standard should be employed to assess these qualities? The uniformity requirement means that the same practices should be evident across all cases where the rule is in play—that is, they should not vary by geographic setting. In the context of China's maritime disputes, this amounts to a question of whether China's (1) maritime laws and regulations (to include PRC judicial interpretations of those rules) prescribe a clear rule; (2) official statements (to include speeches and press conferences by senior officials) and formal submissions to international bodies express that same rule; and (3) state organs implement the rule nearly uniformly across different geographic areas of dispute.[136] For each disputed rule we will ascertain each of these factors to come to a rule-specific determination. Failing this test is sufficient to severely undermine the wider applicability of the rule.

The consistency requirement means that the practice should be sustained over time. There is no particular duration of practice that will suffice to meet this standard—and indeed, even the possibility of "instant custom" cannot be ruled out.[137] Nonetheless, we may expect that for a practice to be recognizable as such, it must be repeated. China's rapidly developing domestic maritime legal and regulatory apparatus adds an additional consideration that the practice may become more consistent over time, an explicit goal of Chinese policymakers. While an inconsistent practice falls short of the mark, growing consistency over time suggests that the implicated rule may "ripen" or "harden" in the future.[138] Thus a virtually uniform practice that is *becoming* more consistent may give rise to a changing rule. If it is inconsistent without evidence that consistency is improving over time, this undermines its potential to become a more widely applicable rule. Both virtual uniformity and (growing) consistency are necessary for there to be a recognizable, reasonably coherent rule that might realistically bind other states.

Specially Affected State Responses to China's Practice

However uniform and consistent China's practice in its disputes, there is no viable pathway to changing or creating a recognizable rule without the interactive practice of specially affected states.[139] These states may explicitly object, in word and deed, to China's preferred rule, they may acquiesce to it, or they may adopt or share the same view of the rule. Their individual opinio juris is beyond the scope of this inquiry, which takes their state practice alone to be a necessary condition.[140]

If all specially affected states expressly object to China's rule, there is little potential for it to be more broadly applicable. Acquiescence, by contrast, makes it plausible for the rule to be considered a local or, with wider participation, a regional rule. If those specially affected states themselves adopt China's preferred rule, it is likely to become at least a local or regional custom—and perhaps even a general customary rule, if a widespread and representative group of states also share the practice. This latter possibility is not excluded by the mere existence of a dispute because not all rules are implicated in each dispute, nor can we neglect cases where disputants apply China's preferred rule elsewhere, outside of the context of their dispute with China.

Which states are "specially affected" varies based on the disputed rule. Boundary questions specially affect only those states with active disputes with China over boundary delimitation. Disputed resources, by contrast,

TABLE 1

PATHWAYS OF RULE CHANGE IN UNCLOS

Rule type	Practice requirements	Potential for rule change
Treaty law	Virtually uniform (over geographic space) and consistent (over time) practice at widespread and representative international level (among states party to the treaty) or Formal amendment procedure / additional implementing agreement	Interpretation and application of a treaty rule changed for all UNCLOS parties
Customary law	(1) Virtually uniform and consistent practice at local level or (2) Virtually uniform and consistent practice at representative regional level or (3) Virtually uniform and consistent practice at widespread and representative international level	(1) Rule of local custom or (2) Rule of regional custom or (3) Rule of international (global) custom

implicate all states with opposable claims to resource rights. Navigation disputes bear on another class of specially affected states, namely those who routinely seek to exercise navigational rights in disputed areas. Finally, dispute resolution affects those states with active disagreements over any of the substantive rules just addressed (Table 1). By any reasonable accounting, Taiwan is specially affected by China's practices across each of these domains; however, the island's ambiguous legal status under international law and the many ways in which its own maritime claims are intertwined with those of China render its practices both impossible to categorize and unnecessary to this analysis.[141]

This analytical method is inductive. It relies exclusively on empirical observation of China's practices and the corresponding practices of specially affected states to draw conclusions about the actual or potential degree of change to a specified rule. The method is also designed to establish *necessary* conditions for a rule change, as opposed to making a conclusive pronouncement on the status of a rule (an authoritative judgment that is properly left to a court or arbitral body). While there are and will remain many competing formulations of what type and extent of practice is sufficient to produce a rule change, this one focuses on the near-universally shared criteria of virtually uniform and consistent practice.[142] The quality of China's practice is the first-order consideration, because failing that test renders moot the question of any broader rule change. The second-order consideration is how specially affected states respond to Chinese efforts to promote its preferred rule, again providing a threshold of necessity for wider rule change. If those states do not at least acquiesce to China's practice, there is little possibility for it to gain wider applicability.

This final step returns us to the question of whether and how the overall maritime order is changed by China's desired rules. In making this "top down" determination, there is a risk of committing the fallacy of composition.[143] Any international order is more than the sum total of discrete rules, even if those rules are among its fundamental building blocks.[144] Analysis at the level of the maritime order therefore requires a more holistic assessment of the overall consequence of China's promotion of its distinctive vision of the rules. This net assessment is left to the concluding chapter, when the full empirical weight of observed practice can be brought to bear. To begin to understand that wider effect, we turn now to the question of how Chinese leaders formulate and direct their practice in the law of the sea.

CHAPTER TWO

International Law and China's Maritime Power

Actively participate in the formulation of international rules;
promote the handling of foreign-related economic and social
affairs according to the law; strengthen our country's discourse
power and influence in international legal affairs; and use legal
methods to safeguard our country's sovereignty, security and
development interests.
—*Chinese Communist Party Central Committee, "Decision on
Comprehensively Governing the Country According to Law"*[1]

China's participation and contribution in the field of international law is not only a process of integration into the international system, but also a process of continuous innovation and
development that is leaving a growing Chinese imprint. In this
process, we have used the weapon of international law to safeguard and expand our national interests, while at the same time
making contributions to all of humanity. Our efforts on all fronts
have earned the respect of the international community.
—*Xu Hong, Director-General of the Ministry of Foreign Affairs
Department of Treaty and Law*[2]

Peace-loving countries will definitely use UNCLOS as a weapon
to defeat maritime power politics.
—*Wang Shuguang, Director of the PRC State Oceanic
Administration*[3]

WHEN PRC LEADERS invoke "the weapon of international law," what
do they mean? How have Chinese officials and agencies employed the
international law of the sea, and for what purposes? This chapter explores
China's maritime rule-making agenda through inquiry into the domestic
platform of ideas, policies, and organizations concerning PRC maritime
disputes. We discover a party-state system that channels and transforms

norms from international law into domestic institutions. The party-state has internalized law of the sea norms in the form of domestic maritime law and policy, which is continuously adjusted to "perfect" PRC practice in the law of the sea. The way in which that practice, in turn, may be sufficient to re-form the international rules will be the object of analysis in the succeeding chapters.

By attending here to the basic organizational question of *how* China puts its preferred maritime rules into practice, we come to understand the specific and programmatic goals underlying that practice. Prominent among these is the goal for China to become a "maritime power" (海洋强国) capable of making and shaping international rules.[4] Since CCP General Secretary Jiang Zemin elevated this "important historical task" to the central leadership agenda in 2000, numerous domestic policy initiatives, laws, and regulations have been implemented across the party-state's burgeoning maritime affairs apparatus.[5] Subsequently, Xi Jinping has directed a concerted effort to achieve more specific goals deemed necessary to "build maritime power," advocating a "transformation" of China's economic, technological, administrative, and military capabilities in the maritime domain to "safeguard China's maritime rights and interests" (维护海洋权益).[6] Far beyond simply building naval capability, this is a comprehensive program to excel in all facets of maritime activity.[7]

This domestic process affords considerable insight into how China's current leaders conceive of international law, maritime rules, and their bearing on China's interests. The analysis thus illuminates China's opinio juris on law of the sea matters as a first step toward evaluating its state practice. What are the basic beliefs and ideas that animate China's approach to "the rules"? How have these ideas been expressed in China's contemporary attitudes toward the law of the sea? These attitudes bear examination as products of China's long history of struggle with the "Western" international legal order and as a basis for the corresponding commitment to re-order it to China's advantage.

This chapter first unpacks the party-state's approach to questions of international (maritime) law. China's approach is instrumental by design. Past and present Chinese officials have sought to wield international law as a "weapon to protect and expand China's national interests," stripped of Western presumptions of normativity.[8] We then turn to the domestic legal and political processes by which the international law of the sea has taken effect within the PRC. By tracing China's participation in the negotiation of UNCLOS and its subsequent decision to ratify that treaty, we gain insight into the PRC's official understanding of what the agreed rules were and how they might evolve. A final section analyzes the evolving domestic maritime legal and administrative apparatus mobilized to promote and enforce China's preferred rules in practice.

CHINESE ATTITUDES TOWARD INTERNATIONAL LAW

China's relationship to the law of the sea is a defining part of the larger story of China's encounter with international law. In this story, the enduring legacy of China's long "century of humiliation" at the hands of foreign powers plays a seminal role. The PRC's official account of this traumatic period begins in 1839, when British gunboats pried open Chinese markets to the opium trade. The First Opium War was the result, ultimately forcing the Qing imperial court to sue for peace and accept the first of a series of humiliating treaties imposed under international law. The Treaty of Nanking was signed 29 August 1842 aboard a British Royal Navy frigate anchored in the Yangtze River over two hundred miles inland. Other British vessels, some built of iron and powered by steam, had devastated the Qing's fleet of wooden junks. They penetrated China's major riverine systems, exploiting weak coastal defenses to deliver highly unfavorable terms in this first of China's "unequal treaties."[9] This episode lends crucial insights into the purposes toward which Chinese leaders today employ the "weapon" of international law.

The official Chinese story of the century of humiliation gives prominent play to maritime threats. "During and after the Opium War," Xi Jinping told the CCP Central Committee Politburo, "most of the invasions of our country by Western powers came from the sea."[10] Cadres, officials, and students are taught that "the sufferings of China in contemporary times mainly originated from the ocean."[11] With the exception of the formidable Ming fleet of the fifteenth century, successive Chinese dynasties focused their strategic attention and resources on the continent. Chinese maritime defenses were rudimentary, with decentralized control over minimal resources and ancient technology dedicated mostly to passive defense-in-depth.[12] This posture is often summarized by the idea that China "emphasized the land while neglecting the sea" (重陆轻海), remaining tethered to a terrestrial strategic outlook. A strengthening

China has sought to rectify this imbalance by pursuing its "transformation" into a maritime power over recent decades.[13]

Officials and scholars lament China's historical continental orientation as a strategic mistake, counting some 470 seaborne invasions of China, which compelled its rulers to accede to foreign demands in what came to be called the "unequal treaty system."[14] The "unequal treaties of the nineteenth century and the failure to recognize the People's Republic of China for much of the twentieth century encouraged a perception that international law was primarily an instrument of political power."[15] Righting the wrongs of these unequal treaties has been a nearly continuous nationalist project since the early twentieth century. While the historiography of this narrative may be challenged, this is a standard national history of maritime weakness informing policy discussions underway in China well into the twenty-first century.[16] Achieving greater control of China's vulnerable maritime approaches—through legal and other means—has become a basic element of the PRC's approach to maritime order.

International Law as a Tool of Western Hegemony
A key element of this narrative is that the West has used international law to abet its domination of a weak China.[17] Yet today, China's leading foreign affairs official Yang Jiechi touts the PRC's "more than 25,000 bilateral treaties, more than 500 multilateral conventions, and a significantly increased voice and influence in the field of international law."[18] This is a complete role reversal. Where the 1,000 or more reviled unequal treaties came to epitomize the West's weaponization of its international legal rules, the PRC is now a self-proclaimed "defender, practitioner, and contributor of the basic principles of international law."[19] China's contemporary rulers position themselves as champions of the international legal system, with central officials like Yang Jiechi deliberately wielding "the important weapon of international law" to advance Chinese interests (and, at least rhetorically, those of the developing world).[20]

Students in the PRC learn that this role reversal is due primarily to development of China's power. Prior deficiency in this crucial attribute allowed other nations to impose international law to Chinese disadvantage. The mainland's most eminent international law scholar, Wang Tieya, concluded that "[t]he unequal treaty regime thus formed was essentially based on force. Force was symbolized by gunboats and naval vessels on the rivers, in the ports and along the coasts."[21] PRC historiography appears unanimous in the view that "[t]he reality of history is that trade followed gunboats, not contracts."[22] Those contracts and treaties came only under the duress of superior Western firepower. For John King Fairbank, "the early treaties in themselves did not remake the Chinese view of the world. To China they represented the supremacy of Western power, but this did not convey the Western idea of the supremacy of law. When Western diplomats extolled the sanctity of the treaties, their Chinese listeners could see the treaty documents as written compacts, but not the institution of law that underlay them."[23] The application of the international law under which these unequal treaties were sanctified appeared to rest on force alone.

The succession of military defeats and unequal treaties made it necessary for the court to accept foreign diplomats and trade legations on the basis of unfamiliar rules of international law. The Chinese response to these external pressures included the creation of a new foreign office on the European model in 1861, the *Tsungli Yamen* (总理衙门). The officials in this new diplomatic organization studied foreign texts on international law and advised the court on the unfamiliar foreign practice of conducting relations on equal footing with other states.[24] Remarking on an influential text in circulation among Chinese intellectuals in the 1860s, Wheaton's *Elements of International Law,* representatives from the new foreign office told the Qing emperor that "your ministers find that although this book on foreign laws and regulations is not basically in complete agreement with Chinese systems, it nevertheless contains sporadic passages which are useful."[25] No longer able to magnanimously accept tribute from Western potentates, Chinese rulers adjusted their practice to "bridle and rein in" the "powerful sea barbarians" with the barbarians' own instruments.[26]

The first commonly cited example of such instrumental use of international law involves the customary international law of the sea. After a Prussian warship seized Danish vessels in the harbor at Tianjin in 1864, Qing diplomats invoked the concept of China's "territorial sea" to deny Prussia's prize, secure the release of the vessels, and claim compensation for China due to the violation of its maritime rights.[27] In registering their complaint with the Prussian envoy, the Qing ministers stated that "[t]he various oceans under China's jurisdiction have, as a rule, been specifically stipulated in all her peace treaties with the foreign nations, and in the peace treaty with your nation [Prussia], there is such a term as 'Chinese ocean.'"[28] Those same treaties that denied China equal rights were now invoked to vindicate its maritime claims.

In their subsequent memorial to the court, the ministers noted the surprising utility of international law in advancing China's claim: "For instance, in connection with Prussia's detention of Danish ships in Tianjin harbor this year, your ministers covertly used some statements from that law book [Wheaton's *Elements of International Law*] in arguing with [the Prussian minister]. Thereby, the Prussian minister acknowledged his mistake and bowed his head without further contention. This seems to be proof of its usefulness." International law was introduced into Chinese curricula by 1879, when the Beijing College of Foreign Languages opened the first school for legal education and enrolled nine students to specialize in international law. Chinese law students learned to treat international legal agreements as a "defensive weapon," a weak substitute for powerful diplomacy but still "the only way to maintain 'peace' with Western powers and protect its interests."[29]

In the Republican era (1911–1949), Chinese leaders took up the nationalist cause of revoking the unequal treaties. By 1926, an "International Commission on Extraterritoriality" was formed, composed of officials from the United States, Japan, the United Kingdom, and nine other European states holding extraterritorial rights in China. The commission recommended a phased dismantling of the unequal treaty regime. Their conditions for doing so effectively made China a "probationary" member of the international community of sovereign equals, linking renegotiation of extraterritorial rights with institutionalization of legal and judicial procedures sufficient to protect the rights of foreign nationals and business interests in China. If the Chinese achieved "reasonable compliance with all the recommendations" under this "progressive scheme," the parties "might consider the abolition of extraterritoriality" on an ad hoc basis.[30]

The American government was the last to conclude a treaty renouncing extraterritorial privileges, signed in 1943.[31] This was a belated effort to support a beleaguered wartime ally and delegitimize a system that had lately accrued only to the benefit of the invading Japanese.[32] Generations of Chinese students have learned that the Western renunciation of the unequal treaties was not undertaken in good faith, nor even fully completed.[33]

International Law as a Tool of Chinese Socialism
Chinese elites developed a particular conception of the function and purpose of international law in consequence of this protracted "dismemberment" of China's sovereignty.[34] At a minimum, international law appeared potentially useful as an instrument of statecraft to fend off further depredation. This attitude differed from the outright repudiation of international law by some post-colonial states, in part because China was only "semi-colonized."[35] Instead, continued engagement with foreigners and their international legal practices led to the gradual institutionalization of methods to "use the barbarian to check the barbarian"—that is, borrowing from the West's repertoire of international law and using it as an instrument to limit their domination over Chinese society.[36] While rejecting "unequal" extraterritorial agreements that had carved up Qing China among the British, French, Americans, Japanese, and others, the modern PRC renegotiated terms agreeable to its own interests.[37] China's leaders came to believe that "international law could be useful as a device for defending China's interests."[38]

China now wields "the important weapon of international law" with growing confidence and purpose. Ideologically, at least, there are straightforward reasons for this attitude. Yang Jiechi and other leading cadres take the Marxist-Leninist position that international law is "a product of the development of human society and international relations to a certain historical stage, with a political, class, and contemporary nature."[39] Regarded in terms of historical materialism, international law is a part of the "superstructure" of the international system, which is determined by the fundamental economic and social "substructure" of dominant capitalist societies.[40] This unchallenged orthodoxy in the modern PRC implies that international law should now better reflect China's position of power and wealth in the global order.[41]

For the Chinese party-state, following Lenin, law represents "an expression of the will of the ruling class," the formal "registration of power relations."[42] Whatever the theoretical reasoning, the practical imperative dictated by this view has been to limit the degree to which international legal agreements may infringe upon China's sovereign autonomy. "International law," explained the CCP's mouthpiece newspaper in 1957, "is one of the instruments for settling international problems. If this instrument is useful to our country, to the socialist cause, or to the cause of peace of the people of the world, we will use it. However, if this instrument is disadvantageous to our country, to the socialist cause, or to the cause of peace of the people of the world, we will not use it and should create a new instrument to replace it."[43] Instrumentality is a feature, not a bug, in this conception of international law. It becomes more useful as China's underlying economic, social, political, and military power grow.

A signal moment in the evolution of China's instrumental attitude toward international law came with PRC accession to the United Nations Security Council (UNSC) in 1971. During the prior twenty-two years in which the PRC was excluded from the United Nations, Chinese observers viewed the organization as "an instrument of American aggression against and intervention in the affairs of other states."[44] It could be easily dismissed as an illegitimate source of international rules. The PRC's near-total exclusion from the international legal order made its opposition to the binding force of international legal norms inevitable. Yet with its newfound position of recognition and universal veto power in the UNSC, China adopted new, more complex attitudes toward international law, and its international legal practice took on greater consequence. China had consistently advocated for greater deference to sovereign autonomy in the international legal system, but it has become steadily more capable of reinforcing and expanding that norm.

This emphasis on sovereign autonomy is among China's Five Principles of Peaceful Coexistence, the rhetorical centerpiece of the PRC's modern diplomacy on international law.[45] Each of the five principles is a variation on the theme of defending sovereignty: mutual respect for sovereignty and territorial integrity, mutual non-aggression, non-interference in each other's internal affairs, equality and mutual benefit, and peaceful coexistence.[46] Developed over the course of treaty negotiations with India and Burma during the early 1950s, the Five Principles represent a diplomatic response to an international legal system that "include[d] many obligations which obviously encroach upon the sovereignty of other states, invade other states' domestic jurisdiction, and are detrimental to other states' interests."[47] The Five Principles are the ideological bridge connecting China's rejection of international law to its instrumentalization of international law. Their tenets are "faithful to Lenin's policy of peaceful coexistence, and have creatively developed it" beyond the Soviet rendering of two wholly separate international legal orders, one capitalist and one socialist.[48] China's leaders recognize a single international legal order in which they have a voice and exercise growing influence.

Western scholars observe that China has staked out a position on sovereignty as the central rule in international legal order, and it views the UN as its central institution. Alastair Iain Johnston describes Beijing's "hyper-sovereigntist" tendencies, while Jessica Weiss and Jeremy Wallace argue that "[r]ather than being a frontal challenge to the existing international order, greater Chinese influence will likely shift the international order in a more Westphalian direction, as Beijing continues to support the principles enshrined in the UN Charter of state sovereignty, equality, and non-interference." Allen Carlson unpacked certain "historically-conditioned sovereignty-centric values" that have shaped China's approach to order.[49]

Chinese leaders generally confirm these arguments. Xi Jinping has often championed a UN- and sovereignty-centric orientation toward order, stating that "the Five Principles are widely recognized and supported by the international community and have become the basic norms of international relations and the basic principles of international law. . . . We must take advantage of the trend and firmly safeguard the international order with the purposes and principles of the UN Charter as the core."[50] Yang Jiechi further elaborated this idea, exhorting diplomats to "actively participate in the reform and construction of the global governance system, strengthen the application of international law, firmly maintain the international order and international system with the purposes and principles of the UN Charter as the core, actively participate in the formulation of international rules."[51] Wang Yi, the Minister of Foreign Affairs, has stressed that (the Republic of) "China was the first country to put its signature on the UN Charter. . . . [T]he UN remains the best-equipped institution and platform in the international system, international law remains the most authoritative framework of rules governing state-to-state relations, and the purposes and principles of the UN Charter remain the overarching signpost toward global peace and development."[52]

China's ideological line is evidently to struggle from within a unified international legal order centered around the United Nations. In this struggle, China is "a Westphalia fundamentalist," a fierce defender of the inviolability of sovereignty—in principle, if not always in practice.[53] Elements of that extant order evidently offend Chinese sensibilities and are perceived to contravene PRC interests, so international rule-making has become an explicit goal.[54] The first opportunity to do so as a permanent UNSC member arose immediately upon the People's Republic of China's accession to the UN, in the form of the unfolding negotiations over a new multilateral treaty for the law of the sea.

CHINA NAVIGATES THE TREATY PROCESS

The PRC delegation to the Third United Nations Conference on the Law of the Sea ("the Conference") arrived in New York City in December 1973. Not one of the delegates was trained as an international lawyer, nor would such training in Cultural Revolution–era China have imparted a positive view of "hegemonic" international law. Whatever their personal beliefs may have been, the Chinese delegates to the Conference were obliged to express the party's disdain for the "bourgeois" membership and hypocritical principles of the international legal order—even as they set out to negotiate the largest multilateral treaty in that system other than the UN Charter.

Among many radical and destructive acts of the Great Proletarian Cultural Revolution (1966–1976) was the disestablishment of China's system of higher education. International law was among the most reviled disciplines. Ideological attacks on law "led to the spread of legal nihilism of despising the law, negating the legal system and ignoring legal education."[55] Law schools were shuttered and used as psychiatric hospitals, storage for vegetables, and military barracks. Law professors and practitioners were "sent down" to the countryside for "reeducation" and menial labor. Diplomats were recalled en masse from their postings abroad.[56] By the time the PRC took its seat in the UN in 1971, UN Ambassador Huang Hua did not have any politically viable legal experts to place on the UN's Sixth Committee (for legal matters). For that role, he appointed his wife, He Liliang, who was trained as an economist.[57] The following year, the diplomat Ling Qing declined an initial appointment to lead the PRC negotiation efforts for UNCLOS because he "had never before researched the law of the sea."[58]

PRC delegates to the Conference represented a set of Chinese preferences for the rules articulated in a series of three working papers submitted to the Seabed Committee.[59] The substantive positions laid out in those papers have remained largely intact for the last half-century, and each is examined in detail in subsequent chapters. Their unifying theme, however, is a thoroughgoing deference to the discretion of the coastal state. This preference maps onto China's broader political objective to press a broader Third World struggle, centering on the sovereign autonomy of states.

A PRC representative to the Seabed Committee aligned China with the "struggle of Asian, African and Latin American countries in defense of their national rights and interests and state sovereignty against the maritime hegemony of the superpowers." He further railed against the superpowers' efforts "to cook up and impose on others 'resolutions' and 'conventions' designed to strengthen their hegemonic position on the seas and oceans and put a 'legal' cloak on their encroachment upon the sovereignty and plunder of the resources of other countries. . . . Can this be 'international law'! It is a crude violation of the principle of state sovereignty. It is imperialist logic, pure and simple."[60]

This rhetorical bluster and steady advocacy for the Third World continued throughout the UNCLOS negotiations. A PRC delegate announced to an early plenary session that "the central issue of the Conference was whether or not superpower control and monopoly of the seas should be ended and the sovereignty and interests of small and medium sized countries defended. . . . [China] firmly opposes any attempt by the superpowers to impose on others the outdated legal regime of the sea based on hegemony."[61] The head of the PRC delegation further explained that China identified categorically with this Third World group:

> The new legal regime of the sea should accord with the interests of the developing countries and the basic interests of the peoples of the world. The superpowers [are] trying to exploit certain differences among the developing countries in order to control, dominate and plunder them. All developing countries, although they

might differ on specific issues, must unite against hegemonist policies. The fundamental and vital interests of developing countries [are] closely linked, and unity [will] bring victory in the protracted and unremitting struggle. China [is] a developing socialist country belonging to the Third World. Its Government [will], as always, adhere to its just position of principle, resolutely stand together with the other developing countries and all countries that [cherish] independence and sovereignty and [oppose] hegemonist policies, and work together with them to establish a fair and reasonable law of the sea that [will] meet the requirements of the present era and safeguard the sovereignty and national economic interests of all countries.[62]

Codified Disadvantages

China's ideological commitment to sovereignty and Third World solidarity sat at cross-purposes with its material interests regarding the substantive terms of the Convention. By virtue of China's geography, the expansion of coastal state jurisdiction (that was the central ambition of the developing world) put it at a disadvantage. As the 200 nautical mile (nm) limit emerged as the breadth of the new "economic zone" of coastal state jurisdiction, Chinese negotiators recognized that China's oceanic frontage—on the Yellow Sea, the East China Sea, and the South China Sea—looked out on "semi-enclosed seas."[63] These narrow bodies of water would inevitably become a tangle of overlapping jurisdictional claims. The basic structure of the new UNCLOS jurisdictional zones ensured that China would not enjoy the full 200nm entitlements.

Ling Qing reported discussing the 200nm exclusive economic zone with delegates from other states and reaching the conclusion that it was indeed disadvantageous to China. Still, he recognized that "we had no choice but to accept it if [we] wanted to ensure solidarity in the group of developing nations. Afterward I revisited this issue in a discussion with the Chinese delegation . . . [some of whom] believed I was wavering in my politics and not resolute in supporting the 200nm rule."[64] That 200nm rule further intensified China's maritime disputes and granted expansive new coastal state jurisdiction such that Chinese vessels and warships seeking to exit China's semi-enclosed seas would necessarily navigate through other states' jurisdictional zones (that is, "zone-lock").

Even as delegates came to recognize that the rules endorsed by the PRC were not in its material interest, there was no shift of diplomatic tack. One Chinese law of the sea specialist later lamented that "the EEZ and new continental shelf, which have been said to be able to expand China's jurisdiction, have actually become a true 'soft underbelly' or 'troublemaker' for China. . . . It is precisely because of the new system of expanded maritime jurisdiction in the Convention that China and its neighbors are having disputes over the delimitation of the EEZ and continental shelf. . . . Thus, the argument that the provisions of the Convention and China's claims will expand the maritime space under China's jurisdiction to 'three million square kilometers' has become a purely theoretical deduction that ignores the reality of China's geography."[65] However appealing this extended jurisdiction appeared, China's geopolitical aims to use the treaty to struggle against "maritime superpowers" won out.

Yet for all the Chinese delegation's vitriol against "superpower maritime hegemony," these maritime powers were not similarly constrained by the new Convention on several issues of keen interest to the PRC. Ling Qing recalled that the "big maritime powers" all benefited handsomely from the 200nm EEZ, which granted the United States the world's second largest EEZ entitlements (after France with its many overseas island territories). He expressed further dismay that the Convention allowed the "Japanese to think they are the fourth biggest country in the world."[66] PRC scholars still lament this pattern of "control and domination in the formulation of the law by a few Western developed countries" who exercise undue influence on "international maritime legislation."[67] Even in a treaty that was forged in the face of their protests, the maritime powers maintained certain traditional advantages.

These problems were well known as the PRC prepared to sign the treaty at the Conference's close in December 1982. A Chinese delegate to the closing ceremony announced that "there are still shortcomings and even serious defects in the provisions of a few articles in the Convention. The Convention is not entirely satisfactory to us."[68] Upon ratification in 1996, the PRC National People's Congress (NPC) issued a signing statement that reflected China's clear dissatisfaction, stressing four points:

1. China reserved the right to delimit a 200nm EEZ as described in the Convention.

2. China implicitly denied the compulsory jurisdiction of dispute resolution bodies in UNCLOS Part XV, electing to solve the inevitable delimitation problems that would arise from 200nm entitlements "through consultations" only.[69]

3. China claimed sovereignty over the many islands and "archipelagos" under dispute.

4. China reaffirmed its opposition to the "innocent passage" regime established in the Convention, which lacked the PRC's preferred stipulation that "innocent passage through the territorial sea shall not prejudice the right of a coastal state to request, in accordance with its laws and regulations, a foreign State to obtain advance approval from or give prior notification to the coastal State for the passage of its warships."[70]

Each of these points has been the object of subsequent PRC practice in the law of the sea. The rules China formally contested in this statement are among the rules at issue in its maritime disputes. Yet on balance, PRC leaders concluded, the "defects" were surmountable. To assuage concerns, Vice-Foreign Minister Li Zhaoxing cited four principal reasons for ratification to the Standing Committee of the Eighth PRC National People's Congress: (1) to preserve and protect PRC "maritime rights and interests" and to "enlarge PRC maritime jurisdiction"; (2) to maintain "pioneer investor status" in deep-seabed mining; (3) to benefit from participation in UNCLOS by bringing the PRC role in global maritime affairs into full play; and (4) to shape a good image for the PRC.[71]

This reconciled view of the Convention won out over its known "defects." The PRC had helped create a new multilateral treaty that marshaled the voting power and voice of the developing world against the Soviets and Americans. The disadvantageous terms of the treaty were not seen as immutable. Indeed, PRC's maritime expert community has expressed confidence that the treaty will change, recommending that China simply practice the law of the sea according to its lights. Gao Zhiguo, a former PRC judge on ITLOS and leading maritime official, also notes that China "must continue to make efforts" to reform the various "imperfections and shortcomings" of the treaty by asserting its preferred rules in practice.[72] Xu Guangjian, another former ITLOS judge, assessed that the black letters of UNCLOS were not determinate in key respects and "did not forbid coastal states from formulating their own laws. . . . In other words, countries could do as they choose."[73]

One of the key mitigating judgments among Chinese law of the sea experts is that the Convention is not, in fact, a constitution for the oceans. The black letters of the treaty are not exhaustive of the law of the sea, which they see as rooted in and still composed largely of customary international law. Zhang Haiwen, a senior PRC maritime official, asserts that "the UNCLOS is a component of the international law of the sea, which in turn is subordinate to international law."[74] Another senior official, Ma Xinmin, a former deputy director-general of the MFA's Treaty and Law Department, writes that "China insists that the UNCLOS and general international law [that is, customary international law] are in parallel. . . . The UNCLOS has established a basic legal framework for the modern law of the sea regime. But it is far from covering all matters concerning maritime rights and obligations."[75] PRC insistence on the validity of general or customary international law, even in conflict with the treaty, has been a defining theme within its official and scholarly maritime community.

The PRC decision to join the Convention in spite of these disadvantages reflected a more basic political priority. Beijing championed this act of "international legislation" (国际立法) against the will of the superpowers.[76] PRC maritime officials still take credit for significant "contributions to the formulation of UNCLOS," which created "a just and reasonable order for the world's oceans." Because this new maritime order was inchoate, it allowed PRC maritime officials to maintain that "important articles and clauses are still ambiguous in the Convention," producing conflicts over rules in which "both answers are justifiable."[77] China has justified its favored answers about the law of the sea in the process of translating the treaty instrument into PRC domestic law and policy. This internalization process transforms the law of the sea into an administrative tool to implement the Chinese interpretation of the rules. The status of UNCLOS within PRC domestic law must be understood in light of these domestic processes, which nominally apply to all treaties.

The Status of Treaties in the PRC
The process by which treaties take effect in the PRC offers insights into China's willingness to accede to a seemingly disadvantageous treaty.

There is no clearly defined status for treaties in the Chinese legal system and no expectation for determinate relationships to be established in future amendments. The party-state eschews formalistic procedures for incorporating treaties, valuing the political discretion to interpret and apply international law according to sovereign prerogatives.

The PRC Constitution is all but silent on the subject of international law.[78] In 138 articles, it addresses international law in only three.[79] The text does not define "treaties" or "agreements," nor does it stipulate any specific procedure by which international law bears on domestic law or creates any type of binding legal obligation for the state.[80] The only statute that aims to deal systematically with the question was not enacted until 1990, in the form of the PRC Law on Treaty Procedure. This law is "applicable to bilateral or multilateral treaties and agreements and other instruments of the nature of a treaty or agreement concluded between the People's Republic of China and foreign States," restating the constitutional ambiguity on the subject of what, properly, may be considered a treaty.[81]

Xue Hanqin, the PRC's sitting judge on the International Court of Justice (and previous ICJ vice-president), explains that "[u]nder Chinese law, there is no statute that explicitly regulates the forms or modalities for implementing treaty provisions at the domestic level or in national courts. . . . [A]s is obvious, treaties vary in terms of their status and legal effect on the domestic legal system; *not all treaties constitute part of [China's] domestic law.*"[82] Instead, Chinese legal scholars suggest that PRC "domestic legislation is increasingly drawing on the mature and reasonable parts of international treaties"—that is, selectively incorporating and transforming treaty law, but dismissing those elements that are not "mature" or "reasonable" from the perspective of PRC leadership and in light of its political priorities.[83]

The upshot of this indeterminate process is that when the PRC accedes to treaties, the international legal norms prescribed in those treaties do not necessarily manifest in domestic law. This does not mean that treaties do not engender certain effects, legally and politically—only that these effects are contingent on leadership preferences and decisions. China is hardly unique in acting strategically or instrumentally with regard to treaty rules.[84] But China's rulers are exceptional in their command of a centralized domestic political-legal system that can transform international legal norms from treaties to suit programmatic objectives.

The Effect of the Party-State on Treaties

This basic ambiguity about the status of treaties in PRC law affords considerable discretion to the party-state in deciding when, where, and how rules of international law may be internalized and put into practice. The CCP is the sole organization with the authority to make law practically meaningful: "the party-political system controls and promotes the transformation of 'law in text' to 'law in action,'" explains a PRC legal scholar.[85] Consensus from key party stakeholders must be achieved outside of the legislative arena.

For legal issues in which the party perceives a political interest, the state's legislative (National People's Congress) and executive (State Council) organs have no practical authority to legislate or regulate. This arrangement amounts to a preemptive veto for central party authorities over any normal state procedure. That veto is held by the office of the president as an enumerated power, but that president is also (and more consequentially) the party's general secretary. The party's hierarchical control creates the ever-present possibility of veto or modification of any international legal process in the PRC.[86]

This institutional model is a principled choice, and it has been repeated and reinforced at various crucial junctures. Its clear hierarchy reflects the overriding emphasis Chinese leaders place on the party's monopoly on political authority. One expression of this is the party's sole authority to interpret China's sovereign autonomy, protecting the CCP's sole authority on vital matters of state. Rules of international law do not restrict that sovereign prerogative; indeed, they must conform to it. A leading PRC international law scholar, Jia Bingbing, argues that this design is deliberate and blessed by the international legal system: "Whatever shape international law will assume, its implementation largely remains national—within and specific to each and every State that fully respects its authority. The rule of law at the international level ultimately boils down to its realization at the national level."[87]

Lenin's Legal Legacy

The central party interest in sovereign autonomy and discretion on matters of international law is manifest in a series of reforms to PRC legal institutions since the 1990s. The March 2018 amendment of the PRC Constitution to recognize "the leadership of the CCP" only formalizes the party's well-established authority over "political-legal affairs."[88] Operating outside and hierarchically above the domestic legal framework, the party has embraced legalized rules and institutions as mechanisms for transmitting orders from central leadership and monitoring their implementation.[89]

The leaders of the Chinese Communist Party today value this instrument of law for the same reasons Lenin did: it is a vital tool of governance. The Leninist vision of law differs fundamentally from the liberal emphasis on individual rights enforceable against a state. For Lenin, legal institutions are refined instruments for transmitting orders and seeing to it that they are implemented: "For the center not only to advise, persuade, and argue (as has been the case hitherto), but really *conduct* the orchestra, it is necessary to know exactly who is playing which fiddle, and where and how; where and how instruction has been or is being received in playing each instrument; who is playing out of tune (when the music begins to jar on the ear), and where and why; and who should be transferred, and how and where to, so that the discord may be remedied, etc."[90]

For party theorists, the utility of legal mechanisms for coordinating the sprawling PRC governance apparatus is apparent: "The party-state system creates strong political momentum in the form of special tasks to transmit signals from the political [that is, party] system to the administrative [that is, state] system according to the real needs of the country. . . . This method gives full play to the party's organizational and mobilizational advantages, allowing state institutions to quickly detect and identify the political momentum released by the party-political system."[91] The legal reform process serves to consolidate and channel these party "organizational and mobilizational advantages" toward state implementation of the desired rules and policies.

A steady diet of party-led reforms to the PRC legal system has substantially realized this Leninist vision of a party that monopolizes control over the bureaucratic state.[92] A 1991 CCP circular entitled "Certain Opinions on Strengthening the Party Leadership over the State Legislative Work" marked a first formal indication that the CCP's Central Committee Political Bureau (or "Politburo," the most powerful party organ) would intervene directly in legislative processes on matters of political importance.[93] Since then, successive generations of party-state leaders have pursued reforms to enable them to "rule the country by law" (依法治国).[94] By the March 2018 constitutional amendments, the CCP also opted to formally replace the constitutional language of "rule of law" (法制) with "rule by law" (法治).[95] Such measures advance Lenin's vision of a central party "conductor" at the head of the state orchestra, directing its entire executive, legislative, judicial, and administrative apparatus.

Rule by International Law

This objective to rule the country by law has defined implications for the international legal "work" of the party-state. At the Fourth Plenum of the Eighteenth Party Congress in October 2014, Xi Jinping elevated "ruling the country by law" to one of the party's four highest governance objectives, that is, the "Four Comprehensives" (四个全面).[96] Among the priorities identified in the Fourth Plenum "Decision" issued by the CCP Central Committee was a redoubled commitment to improve China's use of international law to advance political aims: "Strengthen foreign-related legal work. Adapt to the incessant deepening of opening up to the outside world, perfect foreign-oriented legal and regulatory systems. . . . Vigorously participate in the formulation of international norms, promote the handling of foreign-related economic and social affairs according to the law, strengthen our country's discourse power (话语权) and influence in international legal affairs, use legal methods to safeguard our country's sovereignty, security and development interests."[97]

The party has continued positioning itself to use international law as a means of achieving defined interests and objectives. In 2020, the Central Committee issued a follow-on "Plan for the Construction of Rule By Law in China," stressing the importance of "foreign-related legal work . . . [to] comprehensively use legislation, law enforcement, and judicial means to carry out the struggle to safeguard national sovereignty, dignity and core interests."[98] Wang Chen, a Politburo member and secretary-general of the NPC Standing Committee, wrote an authoritative interpretation of Xi's legal agenda for the *People's Daily* in April 2021. He explained this domestic program's relationship to the party-state's international law work: "In accordance with the deployment requirements of the Party Central Committee, we must accelerate the strategic layout of foreign-related legal work, strengthen legal thinking, apply the rule of law, and comprehensively use legislation, law enforcement, and judicial methods to carry out foreign-related struggles to effectively respond to challenges and prevent risks."[99]

This ongoing political-legal reform process has continuously refined the instrumentality of law in the hands of the party-state. That legal instrument appears to be especially favored in the campaign to prosecute China's maritime disputes. The disputes have given rise to a host of party-directed "special tasks" for PRC maritime agencies to put the party's political priorities into legal practice. In this light, programmatic party-state goals, like building maritime power, are not so much independent of international law as *enabled* by it. The international law of the sea, in the form of UNCLOS or custom, establishes the legitimate basis for China to claim certain maritime rights. The party sees to it that those rights are compatible with its evolving maritime interests, mobilizing and providing resources and guidance to an increasingly sophisticated state apparatus for putting maritime law into international practice.

MOBILIZING FOR MARITIME POWER

In building a rule-by-law system, China's central leadership has progressively articulated its objectives on maritime affairs, channeling resources and guidance into an expanding party-state maritime apparatus. This mobilization may be understood to improve the PRC's capacity to consistently and uniformly shape "the rules" in China's favor. China's maritime disputes play a catalytic effect in this process because they implicate the PRC's sovereignty and territorial integrity, imbuing law of the sea issues with intense political salience reserved only for "core interests" (核心利益).[100] The centrality of maritime issues to the party-state is manifest in the CCP's campaign to transform China into a strong maritime nation.[101]

Jiang Zemin first announced the aim for China to become a "maritime power" in 2000, and his two successors as CCP general secretary substantially developed this central objective.[102] Hu Jintao called on cadres "to resolutely safeguard maritime rights and interests and build China into a maritime power."[103] Xi Jinping has further mobilized the nation to take programmatic "countermeasures to safeguard our nation's maritime rights and interests" and "step up efforts to build China into a maritime power."[104]

Safeguarding China's maritime rights and interests has been a prominent party-state goal since at least the landmark PRC Territorial Sea and Contiguous Zone Law (Territorial Sea Law) in 1992.[105] Fusing the legal concept of "rights" (权利) to the political concept of "interests" (利益), the compound word 海洋权益 neatly expresses their inextricable connection in China's political-legal system. China's specific maritime rights and interests remain formally undefined, but they essentially circumscribe the contested legal rights and various economic, strategic, and social interests at stake in its maritime disputes.[106] Party-state planning documents, official white papers, newspaper editorials, and scholarly works embark from the premise Chinese maritime rights and interests are under foreign threat and must be defended.[107] They are also a centerpiece of the campaign to mobilize and organize two broad groups playing critical roles in China's practice of the law of the sea: China's maritime law enforcement and naval forces, and its international law and diplomatic community.

Mobilizing Operational Maritime Forces

In keeping with the hierarchical structure of the party-state, a top-down impetus drives various central, provincial, and local party organs to further articulate the maritime power program as it bears on practical issues. Officials in the state apparatus then interpret that political guidance and promulgate measures to carry it out in practice. Rules and practices that have bearing on China's maritime disputes take on special urgency because of the perceived threats to China's maritime rights and interests. According to Liu Kefu, then director of the PRC State Oceanic Administration (SOA) East China Sea Branch, this means that "the most important prerequisite for the building of a maritime power is to . . . protect the nation's maritime rights and interests from being violated. If our nation's core maritime rights and interests cannot be effectively protected, there is no way to talk about building a maritime power."[108]

The substance of those rights and interests is expressed in PRC law and practice (analyzed in detail in the subsequent chapters). Putting those rights and interests into practice consistently and uniformly, however, relies first upon the capacity of China's maritime law enforcement (MLE) and naval forces. These organizations are charged with the operational task of asserting China's claimed rights on the water.[109]

Liu Cigui, then SOA director, elaborated on some of the resources and processes required for MLE forces to properly "control the
ocean" (管控海洋):

> Comprehensive management and control of the ocean is an impor-
> tant support for building maritime power. In addition to having
> maritime defense forces compatible with national conditions, a
> pattern of management and control should be formed in which
> administrative, legal, economic, and other means are integrated;
> central and local governments are integrated; and government
> leadership coordinates social actions. . . . [China must] establish
> maritime administration and maritime law enforcement systems
> that are consistent, authoritative and highly efficient, have fairly
> concentrated functions, and have uniform responsibilities; that
> can perform overall planning for both internally oriented admin-
> istrative law enforcement and externally oriented rights protection
> law enforcement; and that can provide organizational support for
> efforts to build China into a maritime power. . . . [China should
> seek] continued improvements to the modernization of rights pro-
> tection law enforcement equipment and facilities, and continued
> construction of polar icebreakers, oceanic scientific research ships,
> and marine surveillance ships.[110]

A more consistent, uniform, and capable MLE force devoted to
"rights protection law enforcement" (维权执法) has been the result. That
rights protection mission has grown to encompass virtually all activities
of the newly consolidated China Coast Guard (CCG). Created over a series of reforms and reorganizations of a sprawling maritime bureaucracy
and nine separate MLE agencies, the unified CCG was formed in 2013
and placed under a solely military chain of command in 2018 to replace
its former dual civilian-military structure. It is commanded by a People's
Liberation Army Navy (PLAN) rear admiral, and it fields over 130 vessels displacing more than 1,000 tons, including several retired PLAN
destroyers and frigates.[111] It is easily the world's largest coast guard by
tonnage, boasting large, oceangoing cutters (some displacing as much as
12,000 tons, larger than all but the biggest warships) that conduct often
coercive "rights protection" operations across China's disputed waters.[112]
The CCG is a paramilitary force with a hierarchical organization that

reaches down from central to local levels, now wielding legal authorization to use coercive and even lethal force to "safeguard" China's maritime claims.[113]

These MLE forces are "the primary instrument of rights protection in peacetime," but their organization had been haphazard until recent reforms.[114] Senior CCP leadership has long recognized the "dysfunction" and "insufficient capacity" of this ad hoc apparatus and has persistently sought to reform it toward achieving "comprehensive administrative control" of China's claimed sea areas.[115] Administrative organizations like SOA, which formerly operated one of China's several MLE agencies, have been reshuffled into an increasingly centralized maritime policy structure led by top party officials on the Central Committee, including Xi himself and his top foreign affairs lieutenant, Yang Jiechi.[116] This standing body "strengthens overall party leadership . . . and ability to direct the activities, set policies, and promote reforms" across the maritime enterprise, integrating it into China's wider foreign policy goals.[117]

Among the results of this central coordination is growing integration of MLE with the PLA Navy. Together with China's "third sea force," a risk-prone maritime militia, they act as the "tip of the spear" in China's practical efforts to press its maritime claims and preferred rules.[118] China's navy plays a role in the "rights protection" mission as a backstop to the frontline MLE forces.[119] PLA leadership recognizes maritime rights and interests as China's core interest on which "there can be no compromise: not an inch of blue national territory can be surrendered," according to the deputy chief of PLA General Staff, Qi Jianguo.[120] Xi has provided ample resources and support for the development of a "powerful modern navy" to serve as "a strategic support for building a maritime power and an important part of realizing the Chinese dream of the great rejuvenation of the Chinese nation."[121]

The PLAN is arguably the principal beneficiary of the "maritime power" program.[122] It maintains some limited law-enforcement functions but has set its sights on more wide-ranging military missions as the steady build-up of civilian and paramilitary MLE forces relieves it of constabulary duties.[123] Beginning in 2006, at the behest of the PLA Navy East Sea Fleet commander, PRC Premier Wen Jiabao directly authorized "regular rights-protection patrols" (定期维权巡航) in jurisdictional waters surrounding the Diaoyu Islands.[124] This regularization has continued at a rapid pace to the point where MLE forces are able to sustain operations throughout the expanse of China's claimed jurisdictional waters. Those waters are increasingly well-defined and subject to elaborate regulation on management and law enforcement.[125]

While the PLAN has long considered itself the "basic force for protecting the state's maritime rights and interests," it has gained a powerful auxiliary in the increasingly potent MLE force.[126] In consequence, the PLAN has steadily modernized to take on missions like "far seas protection" beyond claimed PRC jurisdiction, employing resources that would otherwise be dedicated to a "near seas" constabulary role.[127] The significant capabilities of the MLE force allow a division of labor in the near seas, with the PLAN in the supporting role in "strategic cooperation" with civilians.[128] PLAN leadership has been coordinating with their MLE counterparts on matters of "administrative control" (管控) since 2009, conducting regular joint exercises, establishing a joint command structure, sharing intelligence, and mutually supporting fuel and other logistical needs.[129] Operating just "over the horizon" from the white-hulled frontline MLE forces, the gray-hulled PLAN fleet has added impressive firepower and symbolic weight to PRC rights protection missions at several critical junctures, examined in detail in subsequent chapters.

Mobilizing the Lawyers and the Bureaucrats

Maritime law enforcement of course presumes the existence of maritime laws to be enforced. The party-state has duly proliferated a large corpus of maritime-related domestic legislation, administrative regulations, departmental rules, local measures, judicial interpretations, and sundry other official normative documents and circulars.[130] The process of joining UNCLOS and claiming the various new jurisdictional authorities and sovereign rights it entailed has generated extraordinary activity in the field of maritime law in China. This sprawling field is comprised of the bureaucrats tasked to "rule the country by law," the academics in and out of government who develop and propagate China's interpretations of maritime and international law, and the professional diplomats who defend China's maritime law (which has substantial international implications due to disputes) in the international arena. Each bears attention as an agent of the domestic mobilization process that "builds maritime power" to put China's preferred rules into practice.

China's lawyers and law-administering bureaucrats work in concert based on the central guidance laid out above. The director-general of the MFA's Department of Treaty and Law, Xu Hong, described the centralized coordination of diplomatic, bureaucratic, and academic actors as follows:

> [T]he development of Chinese international law is the result of the unity and joint efforts of the government, academia and research community. The MFA has always received strong support and assistance from the academic community, and the exchanges with the academic community have become closer and closer in recent years. In addition to the mechanisms of the Chinese Society of International Law, the International Law Advisory Committee of the MFA, and the invitation of young and middle-aged scholars to the MFA for short-term exchanges, we have established a joint research mechanism for all major topics of international law, and all major achievements include the efforts and dedication of the academic community. Whether it is the response to the South China Sea Arbitration case, the submission of comments in the advisory process of the ICJ, or contributing to China's proposals on the negotiation of important treaties, we have the strong support of a team of legal scholars behind us. I would like to take this opportunity to express my heartfelt gratitude. Many scholars and professors have devoted themselves to the work in question, without seeking fame or reward, because they all share a common goal: to work together to make the cause of international law stronger in China.[131]

These various modes of official-academic cooperation and coordination have substantial bearing on China's practice of the law of the sea. China's efforts to effectively wield international law in the maritime domain are rooted in this unfolding domestic political process, wherein the party-state directs and organizes the maritime law "work" within and without government. Political imperatives in the form of leaders' speeches, major party "decisions" and documents, and state planning directives collectively define tasks for the maritime law community. Xu Hong stresses the urgency of these tasks, noting that China "faces the pressure of the West's attempt to use one-sided interpretations and applications of international law to establish new mechanisms and rules to contain us."[132] China's legal experts are duly tasked to develop one-sided interpretations and applications of international law as a "counter-measure" (对策).

Maritime Bureaucrats

Over the course of the 1990s, the pending effectiveness of UNCLOS (1994) and later PRC ratification (1996) gave rise to a series of political documents defining the various maritime-related legislative, administrative, and diplomatic tasks on the horizon.[133] "In order to protect maritime rights and interests," explained a leading UNCLOS expert from the Chinese Academy of Social Sciences, "we must have national mechanisms that are organized according to the law—specifically, domestic law. . . . In designing and implementing a perfect legal system for the oceans, UNCLOS will play a fundamental role."[134]

Prominent among these documents was China's "Oceans Agenda 21," a planning framework promulgated by the NPC in 1996. Drafted by the leading State Council organ with maritime responsibilities, the SOA, it identified the Convention with an expansion in the scope of China's maritime rights and interests: "UNCLOS has brought opportunities for the development and exploitation of the oceans over a wider area." The Oceans Agenda further noted that UNCLOS provided a legitimate basis for establishing state authority over this broad area, having "established a formal international legal basis for comprehensive management of the oceans, defense of maritime rights, and protection of maritime environment and resources . . . [in an area of] approximately 3 million square kilometers of waters." The agenda refers to "maritime rights and interests" eight times, in five instances accompanied by the imperative that party-state agencies "undertake consistent action to defend" them.[135]

The party-state elite consensus codified in this document was that extant legal rules governing maritime issues failed to take into account China's political interest "in the ocean as a whole."[136] Maritime affairs have since come to prominence in all manner of party-state planning documents, to include the authoritative central "Five-Year Plans" (5YP) formally approved by the NPC. The most recent 13th and 14th 5YPs announced the imperative to "promulgate a 'Basic Maritime Law'" (海洋基本法) that unifies China's sprawling and inconsistent maritime legislation.[137] China's maritime claims and evolving political goals in the maritime domain have yielded a patchwork of rules in different functional arenas. The secretary of the Party Committee of the China Institute for Maritime Affairs within the Ministry of National Resources Legal, Jia Yu, advocates for this basic law to "govern maritime strategy, planning, policy, and management . . . and reflect the national strategy of building a maritime power and playing a greater role in making the rules for the world's oceans."[138]

The Courts

PRC courts are among the groups called upon by central leadership to make this maritime legal system more uniform and internationally influential. China's judicial system is obliged to "incorporate party and state policy factors into judicial considerations."[139] With no presumption of judicial independence, PRC courts openly serve to advance the policy goals associated with maritime power.[140] Because the party has placed such weight on maritime matters, its political inputs have been readily observable. Zhou Qiang, the president of the PRC Supreme People's Court (SPC), announced in 2016 that the courts are tasked to "provide powerful judicial services and guarantees for the strategy of building maritime power" and "protect maritime rights and interests and safeguard the security of China's blue territory."[141]

PRC courts have delivered several rulings and interpretations that promote China's maritime rights and interests and align with maritime power goals. A pair of SPC provisions in 2016 resolved ambiguities about the scope of jurisdiction for China's maritime courts, announcing the validity of Chinese maritime law for cases originating anywhere within undefined "sea areas under our country's jurisdiction."[142] At lower levels, the Xiamen and Shanghai maritime courts have ruled on cases originating in territorial waters near the Diaoyu in 2014 and near the Scarborough Shoal in 2016, thus asserting China's sovereignty and "adjudicative jurisdiction" in waters subject to international dispute.[143] The courts' actions contribute to more uniform practice in China's jurisdictional waters, and they further "form evidence of the consistent exercise of 'judicial sovereignty'" (司法主权) in support of China's claims.[144]

When Chinese courts try cases involving disputed maritime areas, they intend to "give full play to China's judicial voice in the formulation of international maritime rules," in Zhou Qiang's authoritative rendering.[145]

A 2015 SPC opinion on maritime commercial trials offered an explicitly "international vision to stand at the forefront of international maritime judicial theory and practice . . . [and provide] effective judicial guarantee for building maritime power."[146] By 2016, the SPC announced the establishment of an "international maritime judicial center," conceived as a maritime judicial system that influences international maritime law through the sheer scale of its caseload (the world's largest) and its judges' consistent and uniform application of China's preferred rules.[147]

These judicial processes are domestic, but they "realize the two-way interaction between the domestic rule of law and the international rule of law."[148] China's domestic interpretations of the rules are intended to influence international interpretations of those same rules. The court's leadership actively seeks to "try cases with international influence" that bear on disputed international maritime law issues, according to a sitting SPC judge, Wang Shumei: "China has taken a key step forward from learning and borrowing international maritime rules to leading the development of those rules."[149]

Legal Academia and Think Tanks

International law scholars in China play a meaningful role in developing and propagating China's preferred rules. PRC leaders have sought to cultivate "international legal talents" who will "be good at using international law as a weapon to safeguard our national interests and national dignity, to promote international justice, and firmly grasp the initiative of international cooperation and struggle," in Jiang Zemin's words.[150] Through outreach to these specialists, the party-state aims to "establish foreign-oriented rule of law talent teams who thoroughly understand international legal rules and are good at dealing with foreign-oriented legal affairs," according to a 2014 CCP Central Committee Decision.[151]

The scholarly community is financially incentivized and politically rewarded for pursuing particular research tracks on maritime issues. Party-state institutions like the CCP Central Committee on Politics and Law, the State Council's National Social Science Fund, the Ministry of Education, and the Ministry of Justice offer scholarships and awards on a wide range of maritime rights–related subjects like "Studies on the Legal Strategy for Protecting China's Sovereignty Over the Nansha Islands

Under New Circumstances" and "The Legal Order of the Sea Under the New Type of Major Power Relations Between China and the United States: Interest Coordination and Cooperation."[152]

Professional associations like the Chinese Society of International Law serve as quasi-official touch-points for the party-state to mobilize and direct this community, according to the director of MFA's Department of Treaty and Law.[153] With ample funding, elite universities have established dedicated training and education centers for these "talents" in maritime law and strategy. Such institutes are envisioned as pipelines into government as well as platforms for Chinese legal academia to become more sophisticated and internationally influential.[154]

The line between the party-state and private academia is necessarily blurred due to significant central control over education. The MFA and Ministry of Education directly run the China Foreign Affairs University; state research institutes like the Center for International Maritime Affairs (CIMA, now under the Ministry of Natural Resources) publish scholarship as well as official reports. CIMA leadership has briefed CCP Central Committee Political Bureau on maritime rights.[155] State think tanks often work directly under the supervision of one or more agencies, including MFA and SOA, producing work for internal circulation as well as external publication.[156]

University research centers have been established under State Council programs in major universities. For example, Nanjing University's Collaborative Innovation Center of South China Sea Studies enjoys partnerships and resources from the MFA, Hainan Province, SOA, and the PLA Naval Command College, among other sources of "government support."[157] Increasingly, Chinese scholars are publishing on maritime legal issues in English-language law journals and periodicals, reaping professional rewards for helping develop the legal arguments underlying China's maritime rights and interests.[158]

Central CCP leaders take direct interest in the development of this cadre of Chinese international law specialists in private academia. For example, Wang Chen, a CCP Central Committee Political Bureau member and president of the Chinese Law Society, exhorted the "9th National Outstanding Young Jurists Award Ceremony" to follow "Xi Jinping Thought on the rule of law," explaining that "it is necessary to actively participate in foreign-related legal struggles, counter suppression (反制打压), and make better use of the rule of law to respond to international challenges."[159]

Diplomats

Collaboration between academics and diplomats on international law of the sea matters has equipped Chinese practice with a more potent "weapon" for advancing its claims and vision of the rules. The MFA plays a coordinating role but has itself been mobilized and resourced to engage in diplomacy on behalf of China's maritime claims and maritime power objectives. MFA's most senior leaders issue official statements and participate in a variety of diplomatic forums related to the law of the sea, drawing expertise and manpower from specialized MFA branches like the Department of Treaty and Law (条约法律司) and Department of Boundary and Maritime Affairs (边疆与海洋事务司).

The direction of this specialized cadre of international lawyers enables some of the most readily recognizable PRC state practice in its maritime disputes.[160] The scholarly community tracks and supports the MFA's various activities in the "practice of international law," cataloging it in academic journals and routinely bringing specialized expertise to bear on complex issues like "historical rights" and boundary delimitation.[161] Yang Jiechi has advocated "exchanges and consultations on legal work concerning foreign affairs [to] allow think tanks and experts to play their due role."[162] International lawyers and scholars are recruited by the diplomatic corps for "capacity building in the application of international law," furnishing ready legal arguments and justifications for the political decisions that drive China's maritime policy and law.[163]

The Philippines' January 2013 initiation of a claim against China under the terms of UNCLOS Part XV triggered even greater integration of diplomacy and international law academia. Over three years while the procedure played out without formal PRC participation, the MFA drew heavily on an already mobilized cadre of PRC international law scholars and practitioners to state its case. Drawing on talent from across the think-tank and university maritime research ecosystem, China's international spokespeople developed a series of specific positions on the inadmissibility of the case. In their statements and position papers, these officials participated in the international struggle over the suit, if not in the formal legal procedure.

The party-state sets the terms and direction of Chinese contributions to the proxy academic war fought in the trenches of law journals, international conferences, and the media.[164] The struggle to persuade foreign scholarly audiences of the invalidity of the "South China Sea Arbitration" continues to the present. The consistency with which Chinese diplomats, academics, and maritime experts have presented the PRC's arguments has clarified important aspects of China's claims and practices.

Over the course of sustained domestic reform and mobilization, China has sharpened its "weapon of international law." PRC leaders especially prize this potent political instrument in contentious circumstances, like China's maritime disputes. Where the "unequal treaties" once served as instruments of foreign coercion against a weak China, the modern PRC strives to seize control of that instrument for its own purposes. Diplomats, lawyers, judges, scholars, and maritime officials are tasked to "make [China's] voice heard" and leave a distinctly Chinese imprint on the major treaties of the day.[165]

Yang Jiechi voices this intention in regard to the law of the sea, vowing Chinese "resolve and determination to safeguard territorial sovereignty and maritime rights and interests. . . . We will never give up our legitimate interests. No country should expect us to trade our core interests away or swallow the bitter consequences of our sovereignty, security and development interests being undermined. The Chinese government and people will remain united and act resolutely to safeguard every inch of our land and every swath of our waters."[166]

Sovereignty is sacrosanct in the PRC's international legal practice, and especially so in its maritime disputes. Facing disadvantageous rules—like those UNCLOS articles with officially noted "defects" and "shortcomings"—Beijing rests its appeal on sovereign autonomy. The party-state's discretion to interpret and apply maritime law is near-absolute under PRC law. It has exercised this prerogative with the clear intent and purpose of prosecuting China's contested maritime claims. Employing a centralized and increasingly well-organized set of maritime tools, Xi Jinping directs the party-state to "coordinate its work on domestic rule by law and foreign-related rule by law . . . [in order to] protect maritime rights and interests."[167]

China's central party leaders see the utility of international law to meet the geopolitical moment. China under Xi increasingly seeks to "take an active part in reforming and developing the global governance system."[168] By "building maritime power" at the domestic level, China positions itself to be more active and influential in rule-making for the maritime order: "These great changes unseen in a century entail the turbulent reconstruction of the world order. The 'rise of the East and the fall of the West' (东升西降) in world power is bringing about modern transformation of the international rule of law."[169]

This perception of an order primed for changes inspires an all-hands-on-deck program to augment and channel China's maritime law enforcement, naval, economic, bureaucratic, and even legal academic capabilities into PRC practice. The MFA's former director-general of the Department of Treaty and Law, Huang Huikang, writes that "this new situation requires China's international law community to closely follow the latest theoretical and practical development of the law of the sea, continuously improve the ability to use the law of the sea to serve the goal of building a maritime power, enrich and strengthen the legal basis for China's maritime rights and interests claims, and strive to promote the construction of a more fair and reasonable international maritime legal order."[170]

China's law of the sea is thus a product of this domestic mobilization and coordination, positioning the nation for protracted struggle over rules of maritime order. China's leaders have allocated considerable resources and political attention toward purposeful practice in maritime disputes. With roughly half the PRC's claimed 3-million-square-kilometer area of maritime jurisdiction under active dispute with other countries, shaping the rules that define the geographic scope of maritime jurisdiction is among the most urgent objectives in China's state practice.

CHAPTER THREE

Geographic Rules

More than half of the 3 million square kilometers of maritime
jurisdiction claimed by China faces overlapping maritime claims
and jurisdictional disputes with neighboring countries. Our work
to safeguard maritime rights and interests is facing a very complicated and severe situation.
—*Xi Jinping, General Secretary of the Chinese Communist Party,*
Speech to the CCP Central Committee Political Bureau[1]

REGULATING THE GEOGRAPHIC extent of state authority is a primary function of international law.[2] The international law of the sea performs this role in the oceans by providing rules for projecting maritime
zones and delimiting the maritime boundaries between coastal states.
UNCLOS establishes black letter rules to determine where one state's
maritime jurisdiction and sovereign rights end and another's begin.
China's disputes over all of its maritime boundaries have significant
bearing on how this rule-set is understood and practiced.

The determination of how far away from its shores a state may le-
gitimately impose its jurisdiction is a foundation of the law of the sea
regime, first enshrined as the "cannon-shot rule" of state control over territorial seas within the range of its coastal artillery.[3] The basic established
principle is that "the land dominates the sea" (*la terre domine la mer*): lawful claims to maritime jurisdiction arise only from sovereign territory.[4]
Counterposed against the principle of freedom of the seas, this terrestrial
grounding for maritime jurisdiction is one pole of the delicate and evolving balance between a closed and an open maritime order.[5] As detailed
in chapter 1, striking an ambivalent balance between the control rights
of coastal states and the navigational rights of flag states was among the
most important compromises embedded in the 1982 UNCLOS.

The scope of a state's maritime authority begins with the maritime "entitlements" that a coastal state may claim from sovereign land territory—be it islands, rocks, or mainland coastline. An entitlement is a state's right to claim a defined breadth for the maritime zones projected from coastal baselines. Entitlements are a separate determination from boundary delimitation, but in practice they are tightly linked. Boundary delimitation is fundamentally a question of overlapping entitlements, so recognition of such entitlements must precede any delimitation.[6] Baselines are the aptly named geographic baseline from which entitlements originate. Altogether, these three interlinked sets of rules determine the geographic scope of state authority at sea.[7]

Contests over these same rules about where and how to draw the line between one state's jurisdiction and another's lie at the heart of China's maritime disputes.[8] Indeed, not one of China's maritime boundaries has been fully settled, in essence because China's neighbors do not accept China's rules for delimiting such boundaries, and vice versa.[9] Where, exactly, do China's claims and practices regarding the scope of its own maritime rights and jurisdiction (that is, its entitlements, baselines, and boundaries) come into conflict with those of other states? Are China's claims and practices uniform and applied consistently in such a way that they constitute a recognizable rule in China's claimed waters? How universal are China's preferred rules on entitlements and boundaries—that is, how generally are they represented or opposed in the claims and practices of other states?

This chapter addresses those questions through analysis of the following sets of rules governing the spatial extent of coastal state maritime jurisdiction: (1) entitlements for islands, rocks, and other maritime features; (2) baselines around mainland coasts, offshore islands, and archipelagos; and (3) outer limits of coastal state jurisdiction (that is, the breadth of exclusive economic zones and continental shelves). In each case, we first examine the specific rules prescribed in PRC law and policy and ask whether PRC agencies have put them into practice in a consistent, virtually uniform way. Secondly, we analyze the extent to which the states most directly affected have acquiesced or objected to China's practices. In combination, these two factors allow for a preliminary judgment about whether and to what extent the underlying norms are changing in line with China's preferred rules on the geographic scope of state authority at sea (Figure 2).

FIGURE 2. **PRC Geographic Claims**
The EEZ claims and Nansha/Spratly territorial sea baseline claims depicted here are
hypothetical because the PRC has yet to issue a formal claim. They derive from the
strict reading of PRC rules claiming straight baselines around offshore archipelagos
and full 200nm EEZ projections from all baselines. (Data from PRC MFA, "Declaration on the Baselines of the Territorial Sea"; Asia Maritime Transparency Initiative,
"Reading Between the Lines"; CLCS, "Submission by the PRC Concerning the Outer
Limits of the Continental Shelf." Map design by Paul Franz | Data: Mapcreator and
openstreetmap.org.)

RULES FOR MARITIME ENTITLEMENTS

The first and most essential determinant of a coastal state's maritime boundaries is its sovereign territory. Claims to maritime jurisdiction begin on terra firma. As the ICJ ruled in the 1951 *Anglo-Norwegian Fisheries* case, "it is the land which confers upon the coastal State a right to the waters off its coasts."[10] The legal status of the dry land from which maritime zones are projected is thus the first consideration in determining any coastal state's geographic entitlements.

Under UNCLOS, even very small or remote islands may be entitled to very large zones of maritime jurisdiction and sovereign rights. The determination as to which types of land forms rate which maritime zones is addressed concisely in the "regime of islands" in Part VIII of the Convention: "(1) An island is a naturally formed area of land, surrounded by water, which is above water at high tide. (2) Except as provided for in paragraph 3, the territorial sea, the contiguous zone, the exclusive economic zone and the continental shelf of an island are determined in accordance with the provisions of this Convention applicable to other land territory. (3) Rocks which cannot sustain human habitation or economic life of their own shall have no exclusive economic zone or continental shelf" (UNCLOS, Art. 121).

A separate UNCLOS rule governs "low-tide elevations" (LTEs), defined as "a naturally formed area of land which is surrounded by and above water at low tide but submerged at high tide" (Art. 13.1). LTEs are not themselves sovereign territory, but they may be used as basepoints for territorial sea baselines under certain conditions (Arts. 7.4, 13.2). This spare set of rules has led to a variety of interpretations and practices regarding which land features rate which zones.

China's undelimited maritime boundaries are in part a result of disputes over which features are "islands" entitled to claim EEZs and continental shelves, which are "rocks" that do not rate an EEZ or a continental shelf, and which are LTEs that project no entitlements and should only affect the drawing of baselines. The PRC island-building campaign in the Spratlys, in particular, has created new facts on the water and challenged Article 121's "naturally formed area of land" requirement. This question of entitlements was also the core claim in the Philippines' arbitration against China, which hinged on the severability of entitlement claims from maritime boundary delimitation, over which the court lacked jurisdiction.[11] The SCS Arbitration merits award of 12 July 2016 rendered a straightforward (if controversial) judgment on the matter, pointedly rejecting Chinese claims that boundary delimitation was necessarily implied by the Philippines claim and marking a new, more acute phase in the contestation over the basic rules governing the spatial scope of state maritime authority.

A second major determinant is the existence of opposable claims of other states. Because the distance between territory under the sovereignty of different states is often less than the maritime entitlement that territory may generate unopposed, consideration of the entitlements due to "opposite or adjacent" coastal areas is a crucial matter for delimitation (UNCLOS, Arts. 15, 74, and 83). Both islands and mainland territory may generate entitlements, so the opposability of such claims introduces another site of contestation over how to prescribe maritime entitlements.

PRC Practice on Entitlements

China's 1992 Territorial Sea and Contiguous Zone Law (PRC Territorial Sea Law) sets out the PRC's claims to project a 12nm territorial sea and 24nm contiguous zone from its coastal baselines.[12] The law claims maritime entitlements from all of the PRC's sovereign territory—naming the mainland as well as the disputed Diaoyu/Senkaku Islands, the Paracel (Xisha) Islands, Spratly (Nansha) Islands, the Pratas (Dongsha) Islands, "and other islands belonging to the PRC" (Art. 2), thus implicitly incorporating the Macclesfield (Zhongsha) Bank. The 1998 PRC Exclusive Economic Zone and Continental Shelf Law (EEZ Law) declares that an EEZ and continental shelf likewise extend 200 nautical miles from baselines and potentially further for the extended continental shelf.[13] These legislative acts establish China's basic rule: wherever China has territory, it claims maritime entitlements extending from its baselines.

Those two laws are broadly consistent with PRC practice regarding entitlements since 1958, when China issued an official "Declaration on the Territorial Sea," providing for a 12nm territorial sea maritime entitlement from "all territories of the PRC including Chinese mainland and its coastal islands, as well as Taiwan and its surrounding islands, the Penghu Islands, the [Pratas] Dongsha Islands, the [Paracel] Xisha

Islands, the [Macclesfield Bank] Zhongsha Islands, the [Spratly] Nansha Islands and all other islands belonging to China which are separated from the mainland and its coastal islands by the high seas."[14]

Island/Rock/LTE Entitlements

No official statement or legal instrument excludes any PRC territory from generating 200nm entitlements. In principle, then, China claims the full panoply of maritime zones extending from over 18,000 kilometers of continental coastline and from the additional 14,500 kilometers of coastline surrounding the approximately 11,000 maritime features over which the PRC claims sovereignty.[15] Jia Yu, the party secretary of the Ministry of National Resources Center for International Maritime Affairs, contends that 7,300 of these have an area of more than 500 square meters.[16] The 2012 PRC State Oceanic Administration (SOA) "National Island Protection Plan" notes that these islands have a total land area of nearly 80,000 square kilometers, and some 70 percent of them lie within 10 kilometers of the mainland coast, such that they may serve as basepoints for territorial sea baselines. The Island Protection Plan also states that "*some* islands have significant bearing on rights and interests, national defense, resources, and ecology," implying that perhaps only some of them generate entitlements.[17]

The key determinant for entitlements is the island/rock/LTE status of the relevant features. The threshold of five hundred square meters in PRC statements is arbitrary, if reasonably consistent across official statements. No size requirement elsewhere in China's maritime code is associated with attaining "island" status.[18] We should keep in mind UNCLOS Article 121's only criteria for the status of maritime features that generate entitlements: they are naturally formed and above water at high tide. Those that "cannot support human habitation or economic life of their own" do not rate a 200nm EEZ or continental shelf entitlement. The principal PRC legal instrument on the subject, the 2009 Island Protection Law, defines islands according to the UNCLOS standard requirement that they are naturally formed and above water at high tide; they may be inhabited or uninhabited (Art. 2).[19] The law does not address whether the size of the feature has any bearing on potential entitlements.

The Island Protection Law defines an LTE as "a naturally formed area of land which is surrounded by and above water at low tide but submerged at high tide" (Art. 57.3), mirroring the standard in UNCLOS (Art. 13.1). It does not stipulate to the additional language in that same article limiting the LTE's role in entitlements: "Where a low-tide elevation is wholly situated at a distance exceeding the breadth of the territorial sea from the mainland or an island, it has no territorial sea of its own" (UNCLOS, Art. 13.2). No other instrument of PRC law or regulation speaks to the question of whether and how LTEs are to be treated with respect to entitlements. A set of two SOA measures to implement the Island Protection Law from 2016 and 2017 detail regulatory requirements for naming and utilizing uninhabited islands, but they explicitly include LTEs with uninhabited islands in their application of the measures.[20] The MFA's 2014 "Position Paper" on the South China Sea Arbitration maintains this ambiguity, arguing that "whether LTEs can be appropriated as territory is in itself a question of territorial sovereignty, not a matter concerning the interpretation or application of the Convention."[21] China's practice thus does not exclude LTEs from sovereign appropriation or from generating entitlements; it treats the matter as a question of sovereignty outside the scope of UNCLOS.

The status of China's reclaimed islands atop LTEs and submerged features in the South China Sea raises further possibilities for "artificial islands" as the source of entitlement claims. A body of PRC law and regulation has formed around artificial islands, channeling resources into their administration and establishing their function as platforms for marine environmental protection. This was one of the earliest areas of maritime law development in China, beginning with the 1982 Marine Environmental Protection Law and 1982 State Council Regulation on the Exploitation of Offshore Petroleum Resources in Cooperation with Foreign Entities.[22] In these and other regulations, such man-made features are not treated as islands that warrant entitlements, in line with the general international rule. A 2007 SOA "Opinion" on artificial islands and the 2021 PRC Coast Guard Law similarly address artificial islands.[23] These instruments also give no indication that such installations themselves generate entitlements—though the possibility cannot be excluded, based on the indeterminate text of these documents. In principle, at least, there is a uniform and consistent standard in China's practice that naturally formed features are entitled to maritime zones—but only from established baselines.

Baseline Requirements

This baseline requirement is a major source of non-uniformity in China's practice. The PRC first demarcated some of its baselines in the 1996 "Declaration on the Baselines of the Territorial Sea," covering the mainland coastline and surrounding the Paracel (Xisha) Islands in the northern SCS.[24] In 2012, a "Statement on the Baselines of the Territorial Sea of Diaoyu Dao" officially claimed baselines around Diaoyu/Senkaku "and its affiliated islands."[25] No other baselines have been formally declared, leaving the disputed Spratly, Macclesfield, and Pratas Islands, as well as the several thousand other non-disputed coastal features, without any domestic legal basis for entitlements.

However, China evidently intends to draw further baselines. An April 2011 MFA *note verbale* to the UN secretary-general stated that "China's Nansha [Spratly] Islands is fully entitled to Territorial Sea, EEZ, and Continental Shelf."[26] Subsequent MFA statements beginning in 2016 claimed that China "has" the full slate of entitlements, including EEZ and continental shelf, "based on the Nanhai Zhudao (南海诸岛)," a still-wider geographic construct that comprises all four "island groups" that China claims in the SCS.[27]

Ministry of National Resources official Jia Yu describes Spratly "archipelago" as "chiefly consisting of, inter alia, Taiping Island, Nanwei Island, Zhongye Island, the Zhenghe Reefs, and Wan'an Shoal. According to the Standard Names for the Islands of the South China Sea (24 April 1983), a document produced by China's Committee on Geographical Names, the Nansha Islands consist of 14 archipelagos (群岛) and islands (岛屿), 6 sandbanks (沙洲), 113 submerged reefs (暗礁), 35 shoals (暗沙), and 21 hidden shoals (暗滩). At four degrees latitude, James Shoal (曾母暗沙) represents the southernmost extent of Chinese territory."[28] These are presumably the features around which China intends to draw baselines. Jia Yu wrote in 2019 that "the Chinese government will also delineate and announce the remaining territorial sea baselines. . . . In legal principle, Taiwan and its affiliated islands, the [Pratas] Dongsha Islands, the [Macclesfield Bank] Zhongsha Islands, and the Spratly [Nansha] Islands, which belong to China, also have their own internal waters and territorial seas."[29]

There has been no further clarification as to whether these statements mean that each island group is individually entitled to all maritime zones. At a minimum, the Spratly (Nansha) Islands are the object of such a claim and a likely candidate for announced baselines. One plausible set of hypothetical Spratly baselines connecting all of China's claimed features with straight lines is represented in Figure 2.[30] Absent defined baselines or any further announcement of entitlement claims, there is a notable lack of uniformity in China's practice on this matter. Certain islands have not been assigned entitlements, while others have, without any clear rule dictating when and why. However, the trend is evidently toward greater uniformity and consistency in this practice as the PRC declares additional baselines and accompanying entitlements. The characteristics of several individual features will further illuminate PRC practice on the island issue and illustrate its non-uniformity.

Relevant Individual Features

Scarborough (Huangyan/黄岩岛) Shoal. Scarborough Shoal is a part of China's Macclesfield Bank (Zhongsha) claim, though it sits isolated some 170 nautical miles east of that group of submerged features.[31] The "Sailing Directions" of the PLA Navy's Navigation Guarantee Department describe the reef as "the only atoll among [the Zhongsha] islands to be exposed above sea level" and note two features of the "isosceles triangle-shaped" reef as having a surface area of approximately 10 square meters.[32] It is among the most controversial features in the South China Sea because its seizure by the PRC in 2012 precipitated the Philippines' claim against China in the SCS Arbitration.[33] The PRC issued its first major statement on the subject in 1997, in which it rejected the Philippines' claim to jurisdiction over Scarborough, asserting that "under a situation where there is an overlapping of EEZs among concerned countries, the act of a country to unilaterally proclaim its 200[nm] EEZ is null and void."[34] That statement implies a Chinese EEZ entitlement covering Scarborough Shoal, though it does not specify whether that entitlement derives from Huangyan alone or from its tenuous status as a distant part of the Macclesfield Bank (Zhongsha). However, both the MFA and a study by the quasi-official China Society of International Law following the 2016 award indicate that Macclesfield (Zhongsha) Bank and Scarborough are to be treated "as a unit" for the purposes of generating entitlements.[35]

James (Zengmu/曾母暗沙) Shoal. At 4 degrees north latitude, James Shoal is China's southernmost claimed territory.[36] It sits only 24 nautical miles from the Borneo coast of Malaysia and some 133 nautical miles from the nearest feature above water at high tide, Louisa Shoal. The shoal itself is approximately 20 meters underwater.[37] This shoal has been the site of periodic presence by official vessels, beginning at least when a Type-051 PLAN destroyer dropped anchor there in 1983.[38] Hainan Province sent a "visiting mission" to the reef in 1992, dropping "seven sovereign steles" into the waters above.[39] James Shoal was also the site of several well-publicized oath-taking ceremonies by sailors aboard PLAN vessels in 2013 and 2014.[40] China Coast Guard ships and official research vessels now routinely operate near Luconia Shoals, just north of this feature.[41] The PRC has never issued a specific claim to entitlements from this feature, but its designation as an integral part of the Spratly (Nansha) island group indicates that it will be surrounded by a PRC baseline and granted entitlements.

Mischief (Meiji / 美济礁) Reef. The aptly named Mischief Reef is another critical case for PRC entitlement practice. The naturally submerged feature is roughly 130 nautical miles from one of the Philippines' main islands, Palawan, well within the Philippines' claimed continental shelf entitlement. It was seized by the PRC in 1994–1995 and now features 1,379 acres of reclaimed land and one of the PRC's three large facilities in the Spratlys (along with Fiery Cross Reef and Subi Reef).[42] The PLAN "Sailing Directions" describe it as "an enclosed, independent atoll" some 62 nautical miles from the nearest feature and thus not within the 12nm territorial sea of any high-tide feature.[43] The "Sailing Directions" also identify "dozens of reef rocks" that "can be exposed during half-tide," implying that China regards the feature as an LTE.[44] In a note verbale to the UN, the PRC officially claimed that "China has sovereignty over Nansha Qundao [Spratlys], including Meiji Jiao, and their adjacent waters and airspace."[45] In explicitly claiming sovereignty to a feature that its own government organ (the PLAN) classifies as an LTE beyond 12 nautical miles from any high-tide feature, China confirms that its rule permits LTEs to generate entitlements even if they lie beyond the territorial sea of a rock or island.

Ieodo (Suyan / 苏岩礁) Rock. Another feature relevant to assessing China's entitlement practice is Ieodo (Suyan) Rock, claimed by both China and the Republic of Korea (ROK). This submerged feature is not the object of a territorial claim by either state. Instead, each state regards it as part of its entitlement to an EEZ or continental shelf in the East China Sea.[46] The feature sits almost 5 meters underwater at low tide and thus is not an LTE.[47] In 2003, Korea erected the Ieodo Ocean Research Station on top of this submerged feature. A PRC MFA spokesperson stated that the ROK's "unilateral actions cannot produce anything of legal validity," describing the feature as "located in the overlapping area of EEZ" between the two countries.[48] SOA Director Liu Cigui described Suyan alongside the Diaoyu/Senkaku, Scarborough (Huangyan), and Spratly (Nansha) islands among "waters under China's jurisdiction" and thus the object of regular "rights patrols" but not itself sovereign territory.[49] China's practice regarding Suyan is arguably not uniform given its practice on James Shoal, because it does not claim entitlements from the feature despite its comparable characteristics. One difference appears to be that Suyan is not associated with a group of islands to which China stakes a sovereignty claim.

Okinotori (沖之鸟) *Island.* Okinotori is a small feature to the southeast of Japan's main islands from which the Japanese government claims EEZ and continental shelf entitlements. It is not the object of a territorial dispute, but PRC officials have repeatedly objected to Japan's entitlement claim on the grounds that "Okinotori Reef is less than 10 square meters above the water surface at high tide. It is clearly a rock as stipulated in the Convention, and therefore should not have an EEZ or a continental shelf, and the construction of artificial facilities cannot change its legal status."[50] Set against Scarborough (Huangyan), which likewise has no more than 10 square meters protruding above water at high tide, the PRC evidently has a non-uniform standard for determining which features may be considered full-fledged islands. China has consistently affirmed this position in several subsequent notes verbales to the UN secretary-general: "Okinotorishima Island is in fact a rock as referred to in Article 121(3) of the Convention" and consequently "shall have no exclusive economic zone."[51]

China evidently objects to EEZ and continental shelf entitlements from isolated small features—but only when they are controlled by other states. China's own practice, as we shall explore in the subsequent section, tends to cluster small features into "archipelagos" or island groups, from which entitlements may be claimed. In 2014, the MFA clearly stated for the first time that "in order to determine China's maritime entitlements based on the Nansha [Spratly] Islands under the Convention, all maritime features comprising the Nansha Islands must be taken into account."[52] Rather than treating small or submerged features as individually rating entitlements, it appears that these entitlements depend on baselines drawn around sprawling island groups.

In summary, PRC practice on the question of entitlements from specific features shows consistency over time. However, it lacks a measure of uniformity in its application to different features, due largely to the requirement for baselines. China is permissively silent on the question of whether LTEs may generate entitlements, an issue that arises especially in the context of baseline rules (examined below). Because China has yet to delimit baselines around certain features (which alone in Chinese law are the origin of entitlements), and because of its own objections to other states' claims to generate entitlements from small features, China has not practiced uniformly on the matter. Nonetheless, the claim is set to become more uniform and consistent as China declares baselines around more features. The key issues on entitlement rules revolve around the potential zones projected from disputed islands in the Spratlys, which must be investigated further in the practice of states with opposable claims (Table 2).

TABLE 2

PRC PRACTICE OF ENTITLEMENT RULES

PRC-preferred rule	Uniformity (geographic)	Consistency (over time)	Detail
200nm entitlements may be projected from any PRC-claimed baselines	No	Yes	No baselines around several offshore islands; objections to other states' 200nm entitlements from claimed islands
Any maritime feature may be granted maritime entitlements	No	Yes	LTEs are not excluded from sovereign appropriation or from generating entitlements; regarded as question of sovereignty outside the scope of UNCLOS

Specially Affected State Responses to PRC Entitlement Practice

For China's proposed rules on entitlements from its offshore features to generate a local or regional norm, the other states claiming zones in the South China Sea would need to acquiesce to the PRC's claim to the full panoply of extended maritime zones from its offshore islands. The practice of states specially affected by Chinese entitlement claims is critical to the question of whether the PRC's entitlement rules, while not entirely uniform, may nonetheless have wider applicability. The PRC's actual and likely baselines around offshore islands and those of its maritime neighbors are generally within 400 nautical miles of one another. As a result, China's claims to the full entitlements of a 200nm EEZ (or extended continental shelf beyond 200nm) result in overlapping entitlements with Vietnam, the Philippines, Malaysia, Indonesia, and Brunei.[53]

Two legal processes have drawn out a series of official statements from claimants (and other interested parties) that demonstrate nearly uniform opposition to China's practice of claiming 200nm EEZ entitlements from its offshore island groups in the South China Sea. The first of these processes arose from the May 2009 official deadline under UNCLOS (Annex II, Art. 4) requiring a large majority of coastal states to submit at least preliminary extended continental shelf claims to the Commission on the Limits of the Continental Shelf (CLCS).[54] This deadline generated a flurry of submissions that significantly clarified the specially affected states' respective positions on entitlements from disputed islands.

Vietnam and Malaysia delivered a Joint Submission to the CLCS on 6 May 2009 that declared EEZ and continental shelf entitlements extending solely from their coastal baselines.[55] In denying the Spratly Islands any effect on those entitlements (claimed in whole by Vietnam and in part by Malaysia), these states each affirmed that those features do not generate an EEZ or continental shelf. Vietnam then submitted an individual CLCS claim to areas further north, also pointedly excluding the Paracel Islands (which it claims in full) from being the source of any entitlements.[56] Other SCS claimants quickly issued a series of notes verbales to the UN secretary-general.[57] The first was China's now-infamous submission of the PRC's "dashed-line" map, which implied that the Joint Submission was invalid because it overlapped Chinese entitlements.[58] Vietnam subsequently protested against China's entitlement claims beyond those allowed under UNCLOS Article 121.[59]

Thus, Malaysia and Vietnam have directly objected to China's practice of claiming full entitlements from SCS islands.

The second important process yielding clear state practice on entitlements was the SCS Arbitration from 2013 to 2016. The Philippines' claim initiating this case was based on an argument that the Spratly features under dispute were "rocks" or LTEs under UNCLOS Article 121.[60] According to the arbitral tribunal, in objecting to China's entitlement claims to specific features, "the Philippines has in fact presented a dispute concerning the status of every maritime feature claimed by China within 200 nautical miles of Mischief Reef and Second Thomas Shoal [two main features implicated in its claim], at least to the extent of whether such features are islands capable of generating an entitlement to an exclusive economic zone and to a continental shelf."[61] Philippines Secretary of Foreign Affairs Albert Del Rosario further contended in a statement before the arbitration that "China's recent massive reclamation activities cannot lawfully change the original nature and character of these features."[62] The arbitral tribunal's merits award validated the Philippines' claim, finding that "none of the high-tide features in the Spratly Islands generate entitlements to an exclusive economic zone or continental shelf."[63] Subsequent Philippines official statements confirm its categorical rejection of entitlements beyond the tribunal's interpretation of UNCLOS Article 121.[64] This categorical ruling against any of the Spratly features rating status as a fully entitled island furnished the authoritative (if disputed) basis by which the Philippines and others object to China's practice of claiming full entitlements.

Alongside the Philippines, both Indonesia and Vietnam affirmed this judgment in stating with greater specificity that no individual Spratly island generates EEZ or continental shelf entitlements. In 2020 Indonesia issued a note verbale maintaining that its 2010 note verbale (cited above) "has been confirmed by the Award of 12 July 2016 [the SCS Arbitration] . . . in which no maritime features [sic] in the Spratly Islands is entitled to an EEZ or continental shelf of its own."[65] Vietnam submitted an official position paper to the arbitral tribunal declaring that none of the Spratlys "can enjoy their own exclusive economic zone and continental shelf or generate maritime entitlements in excess of 12nm since they are LTEs or 'rocks' under Article 121(3) of the Convention."[66] Vietnam later asserted that "LTEs or submerged features are not capable of appropriation and do not, in and of themselves, generate entitlements to any maritime zones."[67]

Malaysia has not publicly affirmed the SCS arbitral award, but its practice supports the tribunal's substantive findings. In particular, Malaysia's CLCS submissions deny any entitlements to Spratly features. Further, Malaysia's UN mission issued a note verbale in 2020 stating that the PRC claims to "sovereign rights or jurisdiction . . . exceed the geographic and substantive limits of China's maritime entitlements under the Convention."[68] Brunei has maintained a studied silence on the issue, offering only anodyne expressions of commitment to "peace, stability, and prosperity."[69] Japan has not objected directly to China's entitlement claims from offshore islands, but it notably rejects China's efforts to prevent the CLCS from considering its continental shelf entitlement submission from Okinotorishima, arguing in a note verbale that China (and Korea which likewise objected) had no standing to do so because it has no dispute over the territory nor any prospect of overlapping entitlements.[70]

Among specially affected states, Vietnam, the Philippines, Indonesia, and Malaysia have officially lodged objections to China's entitlement

TABLE 3

SPECIALLY AFFECTED STATE RESPONSES TO PRC ENTITLEMENT PRACTICE

	200nm entitlements from all islands	LTE entitlements
Brunei	Acquiesce	Acquiesce
Indonesia	Object	Object
Japan	Adopt (from Okinotori)	N/A
Korea	Object (to Okinotori)	Adopt (from Ieodo)
Malaysia	Object	Object
Philippines	Object	Object
Vietnam	Object	Object

rules, citing UNCLOS rules on entitlements and (for all but Malaysia) the SCS arbitral award's interpretation and application of those rules. At a minimum, practice in the Southeast Asia region does not support the norm of full entitlements from "rocks" and LTEs that China prefers. This, however, does not foreclose the possibility that comparable practices are widespread and representative elsewhere (Table 3).

RULES FOR BASELINES

Coastal states draw baselines around their coastlines as the starting point for projecting their claimed entitlements. Seaward of the baselines are the various maritime zones to which a state may be entitled, and landward are its fully sovereign internal waters. There are three types of baselines in the law of the sea. The first are "normal baselines," defined by "the low-water line along the coast" (UNCLOS, Art. 5).

A second category of "straight baselines" may be employed "where the coastline is deeply indented and cut into, or if there is a fringe of islands along the coast in its immediate vicinity" (UNCLOS, Art. 7.1). Such straight baselines connect basepoints drawn at "appropriate points" (that is, the fringe of nearby islands, or as closing lines across deep indents in the coastline, like bays). Those basepoints may not be LTEs "unless lighthouses or similar installations which are permanently above sea level have been built on them or except in instances where the drawing of baselines to and from such elevations has received general recognition (UNCLOS, Art. 7.4).

A third type is "archipelagic baselines," which may be drawn by "archipelagic states" to connect "the outermost points of the outermost islands and drying reefs of the archipelago" (UNCLOS, Art. 47.1). Closer inquiry into how baselines have been put in practice by the PRC, and how other states have responded, will allow a preliminary judgment about the extent to which the PRC's baseline rules may have wider impact on the law of the sea.

PRC Practice on Baselines

China's substantive practice on baselines began with its 1958 "Declaration on the Territorial Sea," which announced that "China's territorial sea along the mainland and its coastal islands takes as its baseline the line composed of the straight lines connecting basepoints on the mainland coast and on the outermost of the coastal islands" (Art. 2). However, China promulgated no basepoints or baselines for nearly forty years afterward. The Declaration initiated the practice of calling China's South China Sea island claims "archipelagos" (群岛), with the exception of the Penghu Islands in the Taiwan Strait, which were categorized as an "island chain" (列岛). The Diaoyu/Senkaku in the East China Sea are not mentioned (though not necessarily excluded). The 1992 Territorial Sea Law is broadly consistent with the 1958 Declaration, stating that "the PRC's territorial sea baselines are designated by the method of straight baselines and consist of straight lines between adjacent basepoints" (Art. 3); the law also includes "Taiwan and the various affiliated islands including Diaoyu Island" (Art. 2). It does not mention normal baselines, which UNCLOS prescribes as the default practice, nor does it designate any basepoints for drawing baselines.

On the eve of its UNCLOS ratification, China announced specific basepoints and baselines in the 1996 "Declaration on the Baselines of the Territorial Sea." This instrument established straight baselines from 49 separate basepoints along the coast of the mainland and Hainan Island, and it showed 28 additional basepoints surrounding the Paracel Islands. The document further announced that the PRC would later declare its "remaining territorial sea baselines." This task was partially accomplished with the 2012 PRC "Statement on the Baselines of the Territorial Sea of Diaoyu Dao and Its Affiliated Islands," which draws straight baselines from two separate sets of basepoints, twelve around Diaoyu Island and five around Chiwei Islet (see Figure 2).

These three instruments compose the framework of PRC law on baselines, and they are basically consistent from 1958 to 1996 to 2012. To date, no PRC baselines have been drawn around the disputed Spratly (Nansha), Macclesfield Bank (Zhongsha), or Pratas (Dongsha) islands, though in principle under PRC law they will be (and indeed must be drawn in order to officially claim maritime entitlements from them, as addressed above).[71] Two features of this basic framework are of most consequence for analysis of PRC practice on baselines. First is the universal application of straight baselines instead of normal baselines; second is the enclosure of groups of offshore islands within a single set of baselines.

"Universal" Straight Baselines

Beginning near the shores, the PRC rule of straight baselines around mainland territory is observably uniform and consistent since first put into practice with the 1996 baseline declaration. UNCLOS prescribes "normal baselines" unless there are fringing islands or indentations. Nevertheless, China chose to apply straight baselines to every coastal area, whatever its geographic characteristics; this is a clear expression of its preferred rule of universal straight baselines.

Further offshore, however, China's practice of drawing straight baselines is strikingly non-uniform. Of the five groups of disputed offshore islands, only two—the Paracel (Xisha) Islands and the Diaoyu/Senkaku Islands—have established baselines to date. Furthermore, the PRC's mode of applying baselines to the two groups is non-uniform. In the Paracels, China has linked the outermost points of the whole group of islands, even though they are geographically clustered in two separate groups, the Amphitrite Group in the northeast and the Crescent Group roughly 50 nautical miles to the west. In the Diaoyu/Senkaku, two separate sets of straight baselines enclose two clusters of islands that are likewise roughly 50 nautical miles apart. No official explanation for this varied practice has been offered, nor has there been any formal specification as to precisely how the Spratlys (Nansha), Pratas (Dongsha), or Macclesfield Bank (Zhongsha) would be surrounded by one or more sets of straight baselines (Figure 2 projects hypothetical straight baselines around these features). The purposes of these baselines are in line with Chinese rules on entitlements—that is, they are part of the process for "relevant Chinese departments to exercise jurisdiction . . . based on territorial sea baselines, and carry out regular surveillance and monitoring," according to a leading PRC maritime official, Jia Yu.[72]

Straight Baselines Enclosing "Outlying Archipelagos"

The signature element of China's baseline practice is its use of straight baselines to enclose "outlying archipelagos," or "island groups." This is most geographically consequential in the case of the Spratlys, regarding which the MFA has claimed: "The Nansha Islands comprises many maritime features. China has always enjoyed sovereignty over the Nansha Islands in its entirety, not just over some features thereof."[73]

In stating this preferred rule to fully enclose groups of islands, the PRC seeks an exception from the UNCLOS rules for "archipelagic states . . . constituted wholly by one or more archipelagos" (UNCLOS Art. 46), which "may draw straight archipelagic baselines joining the outermost points of the outermost islands and drying reefs of the archipelago" (UNCLOS Art. 47). China has not claimed status as an archipelagic state (nor could it, given its continental landmass), but it interprets the Convention's lack of an express prohibition as validation for the customary status of its practice of enclosing its claimed "outlying" (远洋) or "mid-ocean" (洋中) archipelagos inside straight baselines. This rule evidently applies to the various groups of offshore islands beyond the mainland territorial sea. It is thus the most distinctive and potentially rule-altering element of PRC baseline practice.

As noted above, only two of the five such outlying archipelagos claimed by China are currently surrounded by straight baselines. However, the 1996 baseline declaration asserts that China intends to use the straight method around all of its claimed coastal territories. To date, no particular instrument of PRC law or regulation has established a uniform method for doing so, leaving only the two extant cases, which differ in either unifying distant clusters of islands (at the Paracels) or splitting them into separate groups (Diaoyu/Senkaku). PRC officials like Ma Xinmin, former deputy director-general of the MFA's Department of Treaty and Law and a leading figure in China's diplomacy on its maritime disputes, explain China's position as follows:

> [China] insists that the regime of continental States' outlying archipelagos exists in general international law. China considers that this regime is [a] matter not regulated by the UNCLOS as indicated in its Preamble, and should be governed by the rules and principles of general international law. China constantly claims that Dongsha [Pratas] Islands, Xisha [Paracel] Islands, Zhongsha [Macclesfield Bank] Islands and Nansha [Spratly] Islands are China's outlying archipelagos. Various islands, rocks, low-tide elevations, "interconnecting waters" and "other natural features" in each archipelago constitute its integral parts. China consistently maintains territorial sovereignty and maritime entitlements based on each Islands [sic] as a unit. The legal status of each archipelago

and its maritime entitlements should be considered in perspective of the Islands as a whole, rather than in view of its constituting part[s]—the individual island, rock and low-tide elevation.[74]

This position minimizes the scope of UNCLOS and rests Chinese claims on norms of customary international law (alternately referred to as "general" international law). The purported custom of establishing outlying archipelagos is also the object of a growing body of research and advocacy within the PRC's official and semi-official law of the sea community, which has consistently highlighted a pattern of general state practice that they argue constitutes a customary rule permitting the enclosure of outlying archipelagos.[75]

The first Chinese exposition of this category of outlying archipelagos appeared in a 1995 law review article by Zhao Lihai, a professor at Peking University and one of China's leading law of the sea experts at the time. In 1996, he went on to become China's first judge on ITLOS, the standing UNCLOS arbitral body. Describing "mid-ocean islands" (大洋中的群岛) as a critical question "bound up in China's sovereign rights in the SCS islands," Zhao offered an argument based on state practice and the insufficiency of UNCLOS, concluding that such island groups may be regarded as "a single unit" for the purposes of drawing baselines and claiming entitlements.[76] He also cites earlier Chinese practice, in the form of the 1973 PRC "Working Paper on Sea Area Within the Limits of National Jurisdiction," which states that "an archipelago or an island chain consisting of islands close to each other may be taken as an integral whole in defining the limits of the territorial sea around it."[77]

These arguments continue in a series of articles written by government and academic specialists in subsequent years.[78] Like Zhao Lihai, these authors tend to focus primarily, if not exclusively, on the status of the Spratlys. Chinese studies also typically discuss the negotiations of UNCLOS, during which this issue was debated and China's position was not adopted in treaty. "Matters that were not regulated by the Convention," reason two authors from China's National Marine Data and Information Service regarding this question, "should be determined by general rules or custom formed by state practice."[79] A pair of Hainan University maritime law specialists further hold that "the political unity of the archipelago cannot be severed[;] otherwise it would mean 'splitting' the territorial integrity of states, because the sovereignty of the state is 'uniform' over all its territory, without any distinction of degree of strength or effectiveness."[80]

While still undetermined in PRC law, the rule implied in Chinese practice appears consistent since before ratification—and consistently justified on the grounds of customary rather than UNCLOS rules.[81] China's practice explicitly does not conform to the UNCLOS rule for archipelagos, which not only excludes China from "archipelagic state" status but further states that the "archipelagic waters" circumscribed by archipelagic baselines require a land-to-water ratio between 1:1 and 9:1 (UNCLOS, Art. 47.1). The Paracels have a land area of roughly 665 square kilometers, with 17,375 square kilometers of water enclosed inside their baselines, yielding a ratio of 26.1:1.[82] In the Diaoyu/Senkaku, the ratio around the Diaoyu Island cluster is 27.1:1, while the ratio in the smaller cluster around Chiwei Islet is less than 1:1.[83] Notably, however, China's official statements on the Diaoyu/Senkaku Islands typically do not refer to the group as an archipelago (群岛), calling them instead "Diaoyu Island and all the islands appertaining thereto."[84] There is no official explanation for this non-uniform method for classifying and grouping offshore features.

None of these practices conforms to the UNCLOS rule, but neither do they conform to any uniform rule evident in PRC practice. The pending decision on how to draw Spratly baselines will be a critical test of China's practice. The Spratlys comprise only about 5 square kilometers of dry land dispersed over 410,000 square kilometers of maritime space, meaning that a single set of baselines would yield a water/land ratio of 82,000:1 (see Figure 2 for a visual representation).[85] Suggestions from academics for Spratly baselines have ranged from a single set of baselines (like the Paracels), two clusters (like the Diaoyu/Senkaku), to twelve separate "blocks" (区块) surrounding smaller groupings of features.[86] Each method would enclose some or all of the "archipelago" within straight baselines.

The PRC's impending claim to enclose the Spratlys as an integral unit is now evident in a series of official and semi-official statements. The MFA's 2014 "Position Paper" refers to China's "sovereignty over the Nansha Islands in its entirety, not just over some features thereof," and further emphasizes "the legal status of low-tide elevations as components of an archipelago."[87] An MFA spokesperson decried that "some countries ignore this basic fact and split the Nansha Islands into their constituent parts in an attempt to deny the holistic integrity and maritime rights and interests of the Nansha Islands, which is inconsistent with generally accepted international law."[88] A study issued by the China Society of International Law (CSIL) adds that, historically, China has "made no distinction between islands and sea areas," claiming that this practice is in line with customary international law.[89]

The analysis above shows a consistent PRC claim to treat outlying archipelagos as a unit for the purpose of drawing baselines. However, its application in practice has been non-uniform due to the lack of such baselines around some island groups and the different methods of drawing baselines applied to the Paracels and Diaoyu/Senkaku. Some uniformity may, however, be assessed if the underlying rule applied is interpreted loosely as permitting states to draw baselines around outlying archipelagos in ad hoc fashion. The wider influence of such a rule will depend in the first place on the acquiescence or objection to China's baselines conveyed by the states that claim all or some of those islands or the maritime space around them (Table 4).

TABLE 4

PRC PRACTICE OF BASELINE RULES

PRC-preferred rule	Uniformity (geographic)	Consistency (over time)	Detail
Straight baselines around all territory	No	Yes	Undeclared baselines around Nansha, Zhongsha, Dongsha Islands
Straight baselines enclosing "outlying archipelagos" as a single unit	No	Yes	Some island groups lack baselines; Diaoyu employs different method than Xisha

Specially Affected State Responses to China's Baseline Practice
PRC practices on baselines specially affect those states that also claim territorial sovereignty over the features around which China has (or intends to) draw baselines: Japan, Malaysia, the Philippines, and Vietnam. Indonesia is not a territorial claimant, but the PRC's claim to Spratly straight baselines and entitlements infringes on Indonesia's claimed EEZs, rendering it a specially affected state as well. While drawing baselines implicates a variety of rules (to include those governing appropriation of LTEs), these states' responses regarding the PRC's baselines are the elements of their practice dispositive to this analysis of whether or not the PRC's proposed rule of straight baselines around all claimed territory may gain wider acceptance.

The basic PRC practice of employing straight baselines as a rule, rather than an exception, has met little opposition. Indeed, Japan and Vietnam themselves each employ straight baselines as a rule.[90] Malaysia's South China Sea coastline employs straight baselines as well, as illustrated in the charts accompanying its 2009 "Joint Submission" to the CLCS, though its domestic legislation also includes provisions for normal baselines.[91] The Philippines and Indonesia (which is not a territorial claimant) are each declared archipelagic states with archipelagic straight baselines. No specially affected state has drawn any baselines surrounding disputed features.[92] Vietnam also objects to (part) of China's mainland baselines, rejecting the PRC baseline segment east of Leizhou (points 31 and 32) for its violation of UNCLOS rules on straight baselines (Art. 7) and on straits transit passage (Art. 38). In "so drawing, the PRC has turned a considerable sea area into its internal water[s]."[93] South Korea has likewise objected to some of China's baselines in the southern Yellow Sea, including its use of LTEs as basepoints, though not in the context of a territorial dispute.[94]

China's actual and projected baselines for its island claims, by contrast, have met consistent objection from nearly all specially affected states. With regard to the Paracel Islands, Vietnam is the sole other claimant (excepting Taiwan) and thus properly regarded as the only state specially affected by this aspect of China's baseline practice. Shortly after China's promulgation of Paracels baselines in 1996, Vietnam lodged a formal complaint with the UN, stating that China had "violated the provisions of the 1982 UNCLOS by giving the Hoang Sa archipelago [Paracel Islands] the status of an archipelagic state to illegally annex a vast sea area into the so-called internal water of the archipelago."[95] Though calling the Paracels an "archipelago," Vietnam has persistently objected to the Chinese practice of enclosing it within straight baselines and has not done so itself. A 2012 Vietnamese legislative act seeking to conform its domestic laws to UNCLOS, including its baselines, declared that UNCLOS (or other treaties in which Vietnam is a party) "shall prevail in case there are differences."[96] In 2014, Vietnam objected again in the context of a disputed oil rig, noting its prior objection to China's Paracel baseline claim and adding that "a baseline incompatible with international law cannot be used as the basis for a maritime claim."[97]

China's formal baseline claim to the disputed Diaoyu/Senkaku Islands specially affects only one state, Japan. Japan deposited charts with the UN in 2008 depicting a 12nm territorial sea around "Senkaku-Shoto," but it has not promulgated specific baselines from which they are projected.[98] When China declared two separate sets of baselines around Senkaku/Diaoyu in 2012, Japan formally objected to the UN that the "deposit of a chart and a list of geographical coordinates of [base] points made by the PRC with regard to the baselines of the territorial sea of the Senkaku Islands . . . has no ground under international law including the UNCLOS."[99] Japan has not objected to the specific PRC method of drawing two sets of straight baselines around the rocky features. This technical question is moot, in Japan's view, because of its official position that all PRC "unilateral action" is legally invalid. The government of Japan maintains that "[t]here exists no issue of territorial sovereignty to be resolved concerning the Senkaku Islands."[100]

Still more protest from specially affected states has arisen in response to China's projected baselines around the Spratlys and the Macclesfield Bank (including Scarborough Shoal). While China has stated officially that the Spratlys are a single unit entitled to EEZ and continental shelf from straight baselines, it has yet to designate these baselines. Several states have nonetheless formally protested this implied rule and its hypothetical application. Vietnam (which also claims sovereignty over all of the Spratlys) submitted a note verbale to the UN asserting that "the baselines of the groups of islands in the East Sea [SCS], including the Hoang Sa [Paracel] and the Truong Sa [Spratly] Islands, cannot be drawn by joining the outermost points of their respective outermost features. . . . Viet Nam opposes any maritime claims in the East Sea [SCS] that exceed the limits provided in UNCLOS."[101] In its affirmation of UNCLOS rules on baselines, Vietnam rejects the Chinese appeal to customary law for a separate "outlying archipelagos" regime.

The Philippines has joined Vietnam in this specific objection to China's baseline rule and rejection of its possible customary status. While claiming sovereignty over Scarborough Shoal as well as thirty-three Spratly features, the Philippines has revised its archipelagic baselines to conform to UNCLOS and excluded any disputed features from that baseline system.[102] In 2009, the Philippines passed Republic Act No. 9522, which states that these additional baselines will be established separate from the archipelagic baselines surrounding the main Philippine islands and "shall be determined as 'Regime of Islands' . . . consistent with Article 121 of UNCLOS." This replaced the Philippines' former practice enclosing its "Kalayaan Island Group" (the thirty-three features it claims in the Spratlys) within straight baselines and treating the space within as fully sovereign waters.[103]

The Philippines asserts that UNCLOS rules supersede any purported customary rule for outlying archipelagos. This objection crystallized on the subject of baselines in its arbitral suit against China. Although the Philippines has declined to comment extensively on the award out of concern for its bilateral relationship with China, its Department of Foreign Affairs ultimately embraced the award on its fourth anniversary in 2020.[104] The Philippines further submitted a note verbale to the UN rejecting as unlawful China's "assertion that the Spratly Islands should be enclosed within a system of archipelagic or straight baselines, surrounding the high tide features of the group, and accorded an entitlement to maritime zones as a single unit."[105]

Indonesia has likewise affirmed the SCS Arbitration award's rejection of straight baselines around the Spratlys. While its statements focus on the jurisdictional entitlements China claims from those baselines, it has also objected since 2010 to China's "use of uninhabited rocks, reefs and atolls isolated from the mainland and in the middle of the high sea as a basepoint." Indonesia's 2020 note verbale emphasized that its position on this matter was "confirmed by the [SCS] arbitral tribunal award"; that note went on to deny China's specific claims from the Spratlys, for which "the Government of the Republic of Indonesia sees no legal reasoning under international law, particularly UNCLOS 1982."[106] Indonesia's affirmation that UNCLOS provides the controlling rules contradicts China's claim and denies its purported effects on maritime boundary delimitation.[107]

In summary, specially affected states have issued near-uniform and explicit rejections of China's baseline claims around the disputed island groups in the South China Sea and East China Sea. Only Malaysia has declined to object specifically to this proposed PRC rule, focusing instead on China's sovereignty and historic rights claims. However, in arguing that China's claims are "contrary to the Convention and without lawful effect," Malaysia joins its fellow claimants in objecting to the possibility of a customary rule permitting China's practices on outlying archipelagos.[108] With the exception of Vietnam, however, China's mainland straight baselines have met no objection from specially affected states. Both these elements of China's baseline practice therefore warrant further inquiry in the general practice of coastal states (Table 5).

TABLE 5

SPECIALLY AFFECTED STATE RESPONSES TO PRC BASELINE PRACTICE

	Straight baselines as default	Enclosure of "outlying archipelagos"	LTEs as basepoints beyond 12nm
Indonesia	N/A (archipelagic state)	Object	Object
Japan	Adopt	N/A	Object
Korea	Object	N/A	Object
Malaysia	Adopt	Object	Object
Philippines	N/A (archipelagic state)	Object	Object
Vietnam	Adopt[a]	Object	Object

[a]Vietnam employs straight baselines but also objects to PRC's Leizhou-Hainan straight baseline.

RULES FOR MARITIME BOUNDARY DELIMITATION

Maritime boundary delimitation "presupposes an area of overlapping entitlements," which themselves originate from baselines.[109] Thus the entitlement and baseline practices analyzed above combine to inform the full geographic extent of China's claims, evident in its maritime boundaries. By virtue of EEZ and continental shelf entitlements claimed from all its baselines—including those baselines actually and hypothetically surrounding the disputed island groups of the South China Sea and East China Sea—China's claimed maritime zones overlap those of its maritime neighbors.

Such overlapping boundaries usually entail delimitation disputes, which are quite common. Less than half of the world's roughly four hundred potential maritime boundaries are even partially delimited.[110] The 1982 UNCLOS brought about a huge seaward extension of coastal state maritime zones, creating vast new areas of potentially overlapping jurisdiction and sovereign rights.[111] China is especially affected by this enlarged scope for boundary disputes because it is bordered by semi-enclosed seas, with less than 400 nautical miles between most adjacent and opposing coastal territory. While these overlaps are not the origins of China's maritime disputes, they have introduced new problems and result in the present circumstance in which all of China's maritime boundaries are under dispute, and none are fully delimited.

The customary and UNCLOS rules for determining boundaries where entitlements overlap are "virtually void of substantive content . . . [and] of next to no practical utility at all for those seeking to better understand how to delimit a boundary."[112] That is, there is no set formula for determining where to draw the line separating maritime zones projected from opposite or adjacent coasts. Such delimitation disputes may be resolved between the affected sovereign states in any mutually agreed manner they choose. UNCLOS prescribes that delimitations between opposing entitlements are to be "effected by agreement on the basis of international law, as referred to in Article 38 of the Statute of the ICJ, in order to achieve an equitable solution" (UNCLOS, Arts. 74.1, 83.1), a standard widely recognized as customary international law.[113] This lack of a fixed standard is often considered to be a virtue of these rules, in the sense that "equitable solutions" accommodate the many and varied geographic, legal, and other circumstances that attend different maritime boundaries.

"It is axiomatic that States are free to agree upon the course of the maritime boundaries between themselves in any way they wish."[114] Unsurprisingly, disputes over boundaries are often very difficult to resolve through diplomatic negotiations.[115] In consequence, "maritime boundary delimitation has given rise to more cases before the ICJ than any other single subject," and it is likewise a major element of ITLOS jurisprudence.[116] Two basic methods have emerged in that jurisprudence. The first is the application of a provisional "equidistance" median line between opposite or adjacent coastlines. This has been the starting point in many negotiations and judicial procedures.[117] The second method also starts with an equidistance line "unless there are compelling reasons preventing that" and then proceeds to make adjustments to "achieve an equitable result."[118] In deciding that this "three-stage" equidistance method should not be "applied in a mechanical fashion," several recent cases have stressed that "it will not be appropriate in every case to begin with a provisional equidistance/median line."[119] These are fine differences between "equity" and "equidistance," but they bear major implications for delimitation.

In any event, maritime boundary delimitations turn in essence on "generating a line separating the overlapping entitlements of States," which in turn originate from baselines.[120] As such, this area of practice compounds the disputes over those rules examined in the prior two sections, and it introduces a new set of considerations at the outer limits of China's claimed jurisdiction.

PRC Practice on Maritime Boundary Delimitation

The PRC's first significant practice on maritime boundary delimitation came with its 1958 "Declaration on the Territorial Sea," which described the territorial seas surrounding China's claimed offshore islands as "separated from the mainland and its coastal islands by the high seas." This statement does not match the PRC's current practice, which has evolved to include the EEZ and continental shelf claims that have emerged along with UNCLOS.[121]

As the EEZ norm emerged in the 1970s, China adapted its practice to absorb this vast new maritime space. By 1973, the PRC's UN mission was already embracing the new zone in its "Working Paper on Sea Area Within the Limits of National Jurisdiction": "A coastal state may reasonably define a [200nm] exclusive economic zone . . . in accordance with its geographical and geological conditions, the state of its natural resources and its needs of national economic development."[122] The working paper further describes "the principle that the continental shelf is the natural prolongation of the continental territory, [which] a coastal State may reasonably define, according to its specific geographical conditions."[123] Regarding both zones, the working paper proposes that delimitation of boundaries "shall be jointly determined through consultations on an equal footing" and "on the basis of safeguarding and respecting the sovereignty of each other."[124] Conducting bilateral "consultations" on the basis of the above rules remains an accurate portrayal of the PRC's official stance on how its overlapping jurisdictional zones are to be delimited.[125]

When ratifying UNCLOS in 1996, China further specified that the PRC "will effect, through consultations, the delimitation of boundary of the maritime jurisdiction with the States with coasts opposite or adjacent to China respectively on the basis of international law and in accordance with the equitable principle."[126] In the "equidistance versus equitable principle" debate, China has consistently affirmed in practice its preference for application of the equitable principle as a rule. The 1998 Exclusive Economic Zone and Continental Shelf Law likewise appeals to the "principle of equity" as the basis for negotiating conflicting claims to either zone (Art. 2). There is no determinate content to "equity," but the PRC invokes the principle with regard to all of its maritime boundaries.

The Sino-Vietnamese Partial Boundary

China and Vietnam mutually invoked the equitable principle in their negotiations from 1993 to 2000 over their maritime boundary in the Gulf of Tonkin (Beibu), which established a 506km boundary in December 2000 (effective June 2004).[127] The delimitation rules on which the parties agreed in private have not been disclosed but may be inferred from the boundary line they delimited. Where most maritime boundary delimitations would have given some weight to any prior boundary agreement over the relevant area, China rejected the application of the line drawn in an 1887 border treaty between France and China.[128] Wang Yi, currently the PRC foreign minister, led the negotiations and described their result as aligned with the "principle of equity" as applied to the delimitation of "the overlapping areas of China's and Vietnam's rights and interests."[129] The agreement produced a single line delimiting the Sino-Vietnamese territorial sea, exclusive economic zone, and continental shelf boundaries. The parties did not appear to start with a provisional equidistant median line in drawing this boundary, which marginally favors Vietnam.

This non-equidistant boundary allows further inference about the rules that the PRC has employed for offshore island entitlements in boundary delimitation. The southernmost point of the agreed boundary is just over 200 nautical miles from the northwesternmost basepoint of China's claimed baselines around the Paracel (Xisha) Islands, thus eliminating any potential effect of entitlements claimed from those disputed islands.[130] Within the Gulf, however, the entitlements of several small islands were a factor. They were accommodated by assigning 25 percent effect to Bạch Long Vĩ (Bai Long Wei) Island and 50 percent effect to Con Co Island.[131] In applying these "partial effects," the agreement granted Vietnam 53.23 percent of the Gulf's maritime area (and 46.77 percent to China).[132]

In this negotiation at least, China agreed to apply the rule that small offshore islands will generate lesser entitlements than mainland coastline due to their disproportionately small size.[133] It is remarkable that Vietnam benefited in the final delimitation due to effects from an island that the PRC formerly occupied (Bai Long Wei) but had restored to Vietnam's sovereignty in 1957 (the lone case of compromise in any of China's island sovereignty disputes).[134] This single, partial delimitation is China's only formally agreed application of maritime boundary rules, so its adjustment of the boundary to account for only partial effects from islands is a significant practice.

The "Nine-Dash Line" Potential Boundary in the SCS

Elsewhere along its maritime periphery, China's boundary practice is considerably more difficult to describe. This is in part due to the Chinese "nine-dash line" claim that appears to encompass some 80 percent of the sea area of the South China Sea. It has no published coordinates, so the area circumscribed is necessarily approximate. At a minimum, however, it represents a claim to sovereignty over the islands within the line.[135] Beyond that, the line's meaning is ambiguous in Chinese practice.

At a minimum, the nine-dash line has never been officially claimed nor renounced as China's provisional maritime boundary. There are several authoritative voices in the PRC who nonetheless argue that it may indeed be a provisional maritime boundary line. Gao Zhiguo, then a sitting ITLOS judge and leading PRC maritime official, wrote in the *American Journal of International Law* in 2013 that "the nine-dash line is in the nature of a potential maritime boundary between China and the opposite states." Judge Gao and his co-author Jia Bingbing cite "authoritative atlases" describing it as a "national boundary," some of which include a tenth dash to the east of Taiwan.[136] Chinese officials from the former Republic of China (ROC) Ministry of Internal Affairs Department of Geography have also claimed that "the dotted national boundary line was drawn as the median line between China and the adjacent states," perhaps reflecting an idiosyncratic interpretation of emerging rules for the continental shelf inspired by the US Truman Proclamations in 1945.[137] PRC maritime officials have referred to it as China's "dashed national boundary line in the SCS."[138]

The nine-dash line is more meaningful as an element in China's claim to historic rights (examined in chapter 4), but it nevertheless has had significant bearing on China's boundary practices. The crude dashed lines sketched on the map extend deep into the claimed entitlements of the SCS states. Three of the lines are apparently beyond 200 nautical miles from any high-tide feature claimed by the PRC, and six of them lie significantly closer to the undisputed territory of another state than to any PRC-claimed feature.[139] These would not constitute an equidistance/median line under any circumstances—and especially so if proportional effects were granted to the long mainland coastlines that sit opposite the tiny SCS features, as was China's practice in the Gulf of Tonkin agreement.

The PRC has not formally published any claims as to the extent of its continental shelf and EEZ claims in the South China Sea, so in the absence of any disconfirming practice, it is reasonable to treat the dashed line as China's unilateral provisional maritime boundary. Importantly, that function would not be inconsistent with the more certain claim to historic rights. Apart from that claim, China's actual practice on boundary delimitation in the SCS is quite limited. There have been no formal boundary delimitation talks between China and any of its SCS neighbors since the conclusion of Sino-Vietnamese negotiations in 2000.

China has additionally undertaken to exclude itself from compulsory dispute resolution procedures on maritime boundaries under UNCLOS, exercising its right under UNCLOS Article 298.[140] Under this circumstance, China has invoked UNCLOS Articles 74 and 83 to seek "provisional arrangements of a practical nature" for delimiting these zones.[141] Those arrangements have largely been abortive joint development deals, accompanied by unilateral assertions and actions to demonstrate China's claimed rights and jurisdiction over waters within the nine-dash line. Because the rules of boundary delimitation are so short on substantive content, these practices are best approached according to rules regarding resources and navigation, analyzed in chapters 4 and 5.

The Natuna "Carveout"

China's practice regarding its maritime boundary dispute with Indonesia in the far southwest corner of the South China Sea provides rare information from which to draw an inference about the delimitation rule it seeks to employ. Indonesia's Natuna Islands are not subject to a sovereignty dispute, and they project a 200nm EEZ entitlement into the nine-dash line (see Natuna "Carveout" in Figure 3). It is a unique circumstance that neutralizes the confounding question of sovereignty and surfaces only the entitlement and boundary issues. The "carveout" area is beyond 200 nautical miles from any high-tide Chinese-claimed feature, but it is still treated by the PRC as an area of overlapping entitlement. This confirms that China's nine-dash line claim entails more than projected entitlements from the features within it, representing maritime claims with no terrestrial linkage.[142]

While Indonesia refuses to acknowledge China's claim to an overlapping entitlement and consequent boundary dispute, the PRC has steadily maintained that there is a boundary delimitation between the two countries. In 1995, China's MFA spokesman, Chen Jian, rebuffed Indonesia's protest that there was no shared maritime boundary between them, and he pronounced China's willingness to "hold talks with Indonesia on the demarcation of their common sea boundary."[143] This conflicting position remained in 2020, but the specific boundary issue was omitted in a PRC note verbale to the UN asserting that "China and Indonesia have overlapping claims over maritime rights and interests in some parts of the South China Sea."[144] This invocation of the familiar, undefined "maritime rights and interests" does not necessarily imply that China's claimed boundary overlaps with Indonesia's. That inconsistency with prior practice further implies a non-uniform rule applied to boundary delimitation along the rest of China's disputed maritime periphery.

Natural Prolongation in the Yellow and East China Seas

Disputed islands are a significantly less influential factor in China's boundary delimitation practice in the Yellow Sea and East China Sea. In the former, there are no island sovereignty disputes between China and either Korea. In the latter, the disputed Diaoyu/Senkaku Islands lie at the far southern end of a long undelimited China-Japan maritime boundary stretching north some 650 nautical miles. Even if China asserts full entitlements from these features, their effect on the whole of the boundary would be relatively small.[145] The principal disputed rules in China's practice in this area therefore concern the limits of the continental shelf and how the continental shelf relates to the EEZ regime.

The PRC has consistently taken the position that it is entitled to draw its continental shelf boundary in accordance with the principle of "natural prolongation." The 1998 Law on the Exclusive Economic Zone and Continental Shelf defines China's continental shelf as extending "throughout the prolongation of its land territory to the outer edge of the continental margin, or to a distance of 200 nm from the baselines from which the breadth of the territorial sea is measured where the outer edge of the continental margin does not extend up to that distance" (Art. 2). This claim is consistent with one of the two modes prescribed in UNCLOS for defining the continental shelf, with China opting for "the outer edge of the continental margin" over a "distance-based" 200nm shelf, irrespective of the physical nature of the seabed (UNCLOS, Art. 76.1). Both modes are valid under UNCLOS, but in this case they are in contradiction with one another because the distance between Chinese and Japanese opposing coastlines is less than 400 nautical miles.

China consistently claims that its entitlement to an extended continental shelf (beyond 200 nautical miles) on the basis of natural prolongation supersedes Japan's claim to a distance-based 200nm shelf.[146] In 2009, China submitted preliminary information to the CLCS regarding its intent to claim an extended continental shelf in the ECS in accordance with Article 76 of the Convention. The submission "established that the outer limits of China's continental shelf that extends beyond 200 nautical miles in the East China Sea locate on the axis of the Okinawa Trough."[147] The Okinawa Trough is a depression in the seabed with depths of 894–2,719 meters running roughly 650 nautical miles north to south in the ECS. Its axis is significantly closer to the Japanese archipelago than to the Chinese mainland (see Figure 2).[148]

The PRC's formal outer continental shelf claim came in September 2012, with a CLCS submission to an area of the ECS 206 nautical miles north of the northernmost disputed Diaoyu/Senkaku feature and thus beyond any of their possible entitlements.[149] It consists of a proposed partial boundary line 209 nautical miles in length, drawn from ten fixed points established at the "maximum water depth points of the Okinawa Trough."[150] The executive summary accompanying this technical document implies there will be future formal submissions to other portions of China's claimed maritime boundary, noting that it comes "without prejudice to any future submission by China on delineation of the outer limits of the continental shelf in ECS and other seas."[151] China further contends that its scientific data demonstrate that "the geomorphologic and geological features show that the continental shelf in the ECS is the natural prolongation of China's land territory, and the Okinawa Trough is an important geomorphologic unit with prominent cut-off characteristics, which is the termination to where [sic] the continental shelf of the ECS extends. The continental shelf in [the] ECS extends beyond 200 nm from the baselines from which the breadth of the territorial sea is measured."[152]

The PRC proposes a boundary that would, in effect, "significantly deprive Japan of its 200nm EEZ and distance-based continental shelf."[153] Under UNCLOS, continental shelf entitlements exist ipso facto and ab initio—that is, those rights "do not depend on occupation, effective or notional, or on any express proclamation" (UNCLOS, Art. 77.3). Therefore China and Japan each automatically enjoy some continental shelf rights. EEZ rights and jurisdiction, by contrast, must be explicitly claimed. China's claim to an extended continental shelf, in effect, prioritizes one valid rule in UNCLOS over another, favoring one of the possible continental shelf rules (natural prolongation) over the distance-based formula and, further, dismissing Japan's appeal to its EEZ entitlement as inferior to China's continental shelf entitlement. If China's rule were to prevail, the result would be a substantially truncated set of entitlements for Japan.

China has also consistently employed the natural prolongation rule in the Yellow Sea and ECS where its entitlements overlap those of North and South Korea. In the case of North Korea, their overlapping entitlements lie in the northern part of the Yellow Sea, which is as narrow as 100 nautical miles at points. Neither China nor North Korea has established territorial sea baselines in their areas of opposing coastline (north of the Shandong Peninsula) nor have they delimited their claimed EEZ and continental shelf in the area.[154] The secrecy with which these nations conduct their bilateral diplomacy makes it unclear which rule China seeks to employ for this maritime boundary. However, negotiations have reportedly been underway since 1997, in which China invokes "equitable principles" and rejects North Korea's desire to employ a median line.[155]

Further south, China and South Korea have a boundary dispute based on overlapping entitlements in the southern Yellow Sea and northern ECS, which are also less than 400 nautical miles in breadth. In the ECS, China's 2012 partial CLCS submission substantially overlaps that of South Korea, submitted only two weeks later. Both claimed natural prolongation of their continental shelf to the Okinawa Trough (albeit with different fixed points, based on their respective national scientific data).[156] The parties held a series of inconclusive maritime boundary negotiations from 1996 to 2008; in 2014 they agreed to resume talks, with no result to date. One complicating issue arising in these negotiations is the effect of Ieodo (Suyan) Rock on the overlapping entitlement claims. Again, China appeals to the natural prolongation of the continental shelf as the controlling rule, against Korea's claim to an EEZ that would be delimited by an equidistance line.[157] This practice roughly mirrors China's practice with Japan in the ECS.

In the Yellow Sea, there is no physical continental margin to which natural prolongation of an extended continental shelf might be applied. Instead, the PRC claims a maritime boundary based on the "silt line" that purportedly divides the seabed, with silty sediments from China's Yangtze River on one side, and those from South Korea's Hwang Ho River on the other.[158] Effecting a delimitation based on China's silt line would place some two-thirds of the Yellow Sea on the PRC side of the border. China's practice in these two separate boundary negotiations with South Korea is consistent in claiming natural prolongation, yet the rule as applied manifests in non-uniform fashion: China claims a maritime boundary based on a silt line in the Yellow Sea and a continental margin in the East China Sea.

China's boundary practice has been generally consistent—yet it is non-uniform, applying different rules to different potential boundaries. Some part of this non-uniformity must be attributed to the non-uniform geography of the SCS, ECS, and Yellow Sea. Different rules may be more appropriate to the distinct geomorphology of the continental shelves and the different distributions of islands and coastlines that may generate entitlements. In support of this position, Judge Gao Zhiguo wrote a separate opinion in the 2012 *Myanmar v. Bangladesh* delimitation case before ITLOS, asserting that every boundary delimitation is unique and arguing against the uniform application of the equidistance (or any other) rule "in disregard of the fact that Nature has made the geographical circumstances of the coasts of the world case-specific."[159]

Indeed, the varied circumstances attending China's boundaries may make uniform application of a single rule inappropriate. The ECS has a distinct depression at the Okinawa Trough that provides a geomorphological rationale for natural prolongation. The geomorphology of the SCS precludes an extended continental shelf claim based on natural prolongation, as it lacks a pronounced break like the Okinawa Trough. Its basin generally lies in the center of the body of water, within 200 nautical miles of the disputed island groups and most coastlines. Some speculate that the nine-dash line is drawn approximately at the "200-meter isobath," the water depth sometimes used to determine the limits of the continental shelf; however, this rationale has never been presented by any PRC official source or declaration.[160]

The effect of islands on delimitation introduces yet another non-uniform element into China's practice. The disputed Spratly features crowd the coastlines of the Philippines, Malaysia, Brunei, and Vietnam, leading to a distinct pattern of overlap due to China's unique claim to entitlements from all of them and its nine-dash line. In contrast, the putative entitlements from the Diaoyu/Senkaku would only influence a small portion of the potential China-Japan boundary in the ECS. Finally, the Yellow Sea has no interruption in its shelf, nor any major islands that project overlapping entitlements. Recognizing the objective geographic

TABLE 6

PRC PRACTICE OF BOUNDARY RULES

PRC-preferred rule	Uniformity (geographic)	Consistency (over time)	Detail
Equitable principle over equidistance	No	Yes	Claims the "natural prolongation" of extended shelf outweighs opposing 200nm EEZs
Full effects from islands facing mainland coastline	No	Yes	Agreed to partial effects in Gulf of Tonkin (2000)
Provisional boundary based on nine-dash line	No (varied across SCS, no comparable claim elsewhere)	No	No formal claim as provisional boundary; Natuna "Carveout" implies line (not territory) generates entitlements

sources of this variation, China's non-uniform practice does not necessarily diminish the influence of the rules it invokes in those specific sectors against specially affected states. This geographical uniqueness renders the wider application of these rules a practical impossibility (Table 6).

Specially Affected State Responses to China's Boundary Practice
China's claimed maritime boundaries overlap those of Vietnam, Indonesia, Malaysia, Brunei, the Philippines, Japan, and both Koreas. These are the states specially affected by China's practice of its preferred boundary rules. None of these states has fully delimited its maritime boundaries as a result of disputes with the PRC (and, in some cases, with one another as well). None of the claimants' maritime boundary delimitation talks with the PRC have borne fruit, save for the partially agreed China-Vietnam boundary in the Gulf of Tonkin. Each of these states has responded in practice to PRC claims in ways that allow for preliminary

assessments about the potential normativity of the two principal rules China has employed to delimit boundaries, namely, the nine-dash line and natural prolongation.

Relevant Objections to the Nine-Dash Line

The littoral states of the South China Sea have with near unanimity rejected the possibility that the nine-dash line may serve as even a provisional maritime boundary. Vietnam and Malaysia have put this objection into its most formal practice, in the form of individual and joint submissions to the CLCS for parts of their extended continental shelf claims in the SCS. These submissions, in 2009 (Vietnam and Malaysia) and 2019 (Malaysia), directly counter China's entitlement claims and protest the boundaries implied by the nine-dash line. While neither state has issued official charts or lists of coordinates showing the outer limits of its EEZ, their joint submissions delimit a 200nm EEZ projection from coastal baselines, with no effect granted to any of the disputed islands.[161]

The CLCS will not formally consider these submissions—nor any of China's—because the maritime areas to which they refer are in dispute. Yet the simple existence of these contradictory claims represents a significant hurdle for China's presumptive national boundary based on the nine-dash line. Both states have subsequently specified that they do not accept any potential boundaries generated by the line or the disputed islands of the SCS, citing UNCLOS as the controlling body of law against China's appeals to custom.[162]

Indonesia has issued several of the most strenuous objections to China's boundary claims in the SCS. Anticipating the entry into force of UNCLOS, the long-standing SCS island sovereignty disputes produced a tangle of new overlapping entitlements. Recognizing this emerging problem by 1990, Indonesia brokered a series of maritime dialogues among the SCS claimant states' diplomats and law of the sea specialists.[163] It was during these meetings in 1993 that China first promoted its perplexing nine-dash line claim in a diplomatic note to Indonesia. Indonesia was initially reticent to respond. "We didn't want to make a big fuss out of it," according to an Indonesian spokesperson, because "repetition of an untruth will ultimately make it appear as the truth." Indonesia's Foreign Minister Ali Atalas further downplayed China's nine dashes as "an illustrative map and not a real one," dismissing the "necessity to have a sea border delimitation. China is too far away to the north."[164]

Once the nine-dash line map was formally published in China's 7 May 2009 note verbale, Indonesia issued a clear response targeting that claim: "The so-called 'nine-dotted-lines map' . . . clearly lacks international legal basis and is tantamount to upset the UNCLOS 1982."[165] In a subsequent submission, Indonesia reiterated this statement verbatim and added that the SCS Arbitration had "confirmed" its position: "Indonesia sees no legal reasoning under international law, particularly UNCLOS 1982, to conduct negotiation on maritime boundaries delimitation with the PRC."[166] That statement denies the validity of China's claim to any overlapping entitlements with Indonesia, rejecting the PRC's offer "to settle the overlapping claims through negotiation and consultation with Indonesia."[167] Indonesia formally rejects rules China applies to its potential boundary with Indonesia as untenable under UNCLOS and unsupported in customary practice.

The Philippines has also rejected China's ostensible rules for maritime boundary delimitation.[168] These objections came to the fore as the Philippines lodged its SCS Arbitration suit in 2013. In a bilateral diplomatic note early in the arbitral process, the Philippines Department of Foreign Affairs announced that the Philippines "strongly objects to the indication that the nine-dash lines are China's national boundaries" and further stated that the line "has no basis under international law, in particular the 1982 UNCLOS."[169] The core premise of that arbitral suit was that China did not enjoy any lawful entitlements that overlap with those of the Philippines, thus eliminating the need for any maritime boundaries to be delimited in the procedure.[170] Against China's repeated official assertions that "there exists an issue of maritime delimitation between the two States," the Philippines has refused to accept the premises underlying China's boundary claims.[171] Specifically, the Philippines objected to PRC entitlements projected from disputed features as breaching UNCLOS rules.[172]

Regional Responses to Natural Prolongation

In the East China Sea and Yellow Sea, China has relied on a less ambiguous appeal to the rule of "natural prolongation" as the equitable solution.

This boundary practice has met consistent and direct opposition from both Japan and South Korea. Japan has rejected natural prolongation outright, protesting China's (and South Korea's) application of that rule to the Okinawa Trough, which would reduce Japan's entitlements in the ECS to less than 200 nautical miles. As an alternative, Japan's 1996 Law on the Exclusive Economic Zone and the Continental Shelf claims a 200nm EEZ and continental shelf, adopting a median line equidistant between the opposite coastal baselines of China and South Korea as a provisional boundary.[173] Rejecting out of hand China's sovereignty and entitlement claims from the Senkaku (Diaoyu) Islands, Japan has refused to consider these islands as a factor in maritime boundary delimitation.[174]

Japan appeals to two UNCLOS rules that contradict China's application of natural prolongation as the "equitable" way to delimit their boundary. Claiming 200nm limits for its own EEZ and continental shelf, Japan consistently cites its lawful entitlement to an EEZ (UNCLOS, Art. 56) and the alternative continental shelf entitlement provided in UNCLOS (Art. 76.1) that automatically grants coastal states rights over a distance-based continental shelf.[175] An official Japanese position paper from 2015 states this rule conflict plainly:

> Both Japan and China are entitled to EEZ and continental shelf up to 200nm from their respective territorial sea baselines. . . . While China claims the natural prolongation of its continental shelf to the Okinawa Trough, it does not clarify the specific boundary line which it considers desirable. It should be pointed out that the natural prolongation theory is an idea which used to be adopted under international law in the past. . . . [T]he relevant provisions of the 1982 UNCLOS and subsequent international jurisprudence show that there is no room to apply the natural prolongation theory to the boundary delimitation of maritime areas where the distance between two opposite states is less than 400nm. In addition, the geographical feature of the Okinawa [T]rough (minor gap of seabed) cannot be interpreted as having any particular legal implication. China's claim for the entitlement of continental shelf up to the Okinawa Trough is therefore baseless in light of international law today.[176]

It is unnecessary to determine here whether Japan is correct on the geomorphological facts of the Okinawa Trough, because its objection targets the validity of China's application of a specific rule. Whether Japan is correct that the natural prolongation rule is inapplicable or defunct is a jurisprudential question that has not been decisively resolved.[177] What is certain from Japan's practice, though, is that it maintains a long-standing objection to a specific Chinese boundary practice: the PRC claim that the natural prolongation of an extended continental shelf can supersede the distance-based EEZ or continental shelf entitlements of another state— even to the extent that it deprives that state of a full 200nm entitlement. Japan rejects the validity of the purported Chinese rule that permits application of an extended shelf claim in a body of water less than 400 nautical miles in breadth.

By contrast, South Korea evidently shares China's position on this particular conflict of rules: "Nothing in the text of UNCLOS supports the suggestion that the establishment of the outer limits of the continental shelf beyond 200nm in an area where the distance between States with opposite coasts is less than 400nm cannot be accomplished under the provisions of the Convention."[178] Korea's specific and official affirmation of China's preferred rule is important, establishing it as the "majority" opinion among the specially affected states in the ECS boundary delimitation. The formal Korean position on the natural prolongation versus distance-based rule is that "neither basis is afforded priority over the other under the Convention. Japan, therefore, cannot use its entitlement based on the distance criterion to negate Korea's entitlement based on geomorphological considerations, or to block the Commission from issuing recommendations with regard to the existence and limits of the continental shelf in the ECS." The fact that Korea employs an equidistance formula in its boundary dispute with China over the Yellow Sea demonstrates that its support for China's preferred rule is not uniform: it is apparently conditional on the geography of the ECS (and its own self-interest).[179]

In summary, China's varied boundary claims across these three bodies of water yield non-uniform objections among the specially affected states. In the SCS, all of the claimants save Brunei have explicitly rejected the ostensible PRC boundary rule. While their precise expressions have varied, each rejects the premise that China's claimed islands or nine-dash line may generate overlapping entitlements. In the Yellow

TABLE 7

SPECIALLY AFFECTED STATE RESPONSES TO PRC BOUNDARY PRACTICE

	Equitable principle over equidistance	Full effects of islands opposing mainland coastline	Nine-dash line as a (provisional) boundary
Brunei	Acquiesce	Object[b]	Object[b]
Indonesia	N/A	N/A	Object
Japan	Object	N/A	N/A
Korea	Object[a]	N/A	N/A
Malaysia	Object	Object	Object
Philippines	Object	Object	Object
Vietnam	Object	Object	Object

[a]The Korean objection is itself non-uniform, however, and should be somewhat discounted because Korea employs a similar equitable principle in its boundary dispute with Japan.

[b]Brunei has not made public statements objecting, but in practice it maintains EEZ and continental shelf claims that deny the PRC-preferred rule.

Sea, both Koreas object to China's specific interpretation of natural prolongation as the "silt line," claiming equidistance as the controlling rule. In the East China Sea, by contrast, the specially affected states are split 50–50, with Japan opposed and South Korea in support of China's application of the natural prolongation rule against Japan's 200nm EEZ and continental shelf. Given this pattern, the potential for China's preferred rules to be recognized as local or regional custom is limited to that latter circumstance in the ECS (Table 7).

China's semi-enclosed seas and claims to islands close to foreign shores make inevitable that its entitlements overlap those of neighboring (and not-so-neighboring) littoral states. Delimitation disputes arising from such circumstances are quite common, explaining the "profoundly incomplete nature of the maritime political map of the world in contrast to its terrestrial counterpart."[180] This maritime political map is likely to remain incomplete, because East Asia is the site not only of garden-variety overlapping claims but also of fundamental disagreement about the rules to be applied in the mapping. China's appeal to several conflicting rules beyond UNCLOS introduces a critical normative challenge.

With respect to entitlements, the PRC's claims to 200nm zones from all territory—including small features close to long opposing coastlines—severely limit the potential entitlements of the littoral states of the South China Sea, East China Sea, and Yellow Sea. The projections depicted on Figures 2 through 4 show the fullest possible projection of 200 nautical miles from China's hypothetical baselines around the Spratlys. These are not plausible EEZ boundaries, but they demonstrate the incompatibility of China's desired rules with the existence of EEZs for other coastal states in the South China Sea. These states have predictably rejected China's preferred entitlement rule, seeking to realize the fullest possible breadth of their UNCLOS-derived zones. This conflict is most extreme in the case of the nine-dash line, which is expressly conceived and applied beyond the scope of UNCLOS. A near second is the enclosure of "outlying archipelagos" with straight baselines, a practice which also sets aside UNCLOS and relies instead on customary international law as the source of the PRC-preferred rule. In response, the states that dispute (and even partially occupy) these features appeal to the black letters of the Convention in defiance of China's practice.

The dynamics in the East China Sea are more subtle. The lack of an extraordinary dashed-line claim and the absence of disputed islands abutting opposing coastlines make the key issue the equity of using "natural prolongation" for delimiting the continental shelf. UNCLOS provides for both natural prolongation as well as a distance-based 200nm shelf as equally valid modes of claiming these seabed resource rights, hewing to a "fundamental norm" in the treaty of "emphasis on equity and the rejection of any obligatory method."[181] Korea's common cause with China in proposing natural prolongation against Japan's 200nm EEZ and shelf gives additional weight to the application of the rule in the region. However, because "each case is unique and requires special treatment," the general applicability of any boundary rule is confined to its ad hoc interpretation in a given geographic circumstance.[182] UNCLOS does not provide a rule of resolution applicable to every boundary, leaving states considerable discretion to find mutually agreeable, equitable means to settle their disputes.

China emphasizes customary international law as the solution to geographic rules in UNCLOS that do not accrue to its benefit. Jia Bingbing, a leading international law scholar at Tsinghua University, explains why: "As the UNCLOS cannot cover all rules and practices in international law, customary law on related subject-matters will come to the aid of those States parties who find themselves in a void of law in maritime disputes."[183] This view is on official display in a 2020 PRC note verbale: "China treats UNCLOS with a rigorous and responsible attitude and opposes using UNCLOS as a political tool to attack other countries. UNCLOS does not cover everything about maritime order."[184] The fundamental argument is that the scope of UNCLOS is not comprehensive, so maritime order admits of many opposing rules. China, of course, intends for its preferred rules to prevail.

Among the interests driving China's insistence on its extra-UNCLOS geographic claims are the economic benefits bestowed by control over maritime space. The PRC's steady advocacy for its version of the law of the sea rests in part on its perception that China's entitlements under UNCLOS are inequitable, unfairly truncated by its geographic confinement in semi-enclosed seas. "Even under the provision in the law most favorable to it," the director of the PLAN Naval Research Institute writes, "the maritime space over which China has jurisdiction is relatively small compared to that of its neighboring nations and bestows on it limited benefits."[185] The next chapter takes up those limited benefits by analyzing rules about the allocation of marine resources, where China's determination to rectify its disadvantaged geography is put into practice on and below the water.

CHAPTER FOUR

Resource Rules

For complicated historical reasons, my country's surrounding waters, especially in the South China Sea, are among the regions in the world with the most island sovereignty disputes, the most acute maritime delimitation issues, the most intense competition for resources, and the most complicated geopolitical situation in the world. . . . The ocean is an important base for strategic resources, and the world's ocean resources have huge development potential. In the 21st century, mankind has entered a period of large-scale development and utilization of the ocean. The ocean's role in the country's economic development pattern and opening to the outside world is more important; its role in safeguarding national sovereignty, security, and development interests is also becoming more prominent. . . . If the country organizes the development of land and ocean resources in a unified manner, the country can become prosperous and strong.
—Xi Jinping, *General Secretary of the Chinese Communist Party, Speech to CCP Central Committee Political Bureau*[1]

ALLOCATING RIGHTS TO MARINE resources is one of the primary functions of the international law of the sea. That law has accommodated the steady creep of coastal state rights over ever-wider tracts of maritime space and codified vast new jurisdictional zones in the 1982 UNCLOS. These dramatic changes have already revised the maritime order—particularly as it pertains to the natural resources of the world's oceans and seabed. China's potential influence on these resource rules today must be set against a background of the long-standing trend toward ocean enclosure, a historical wave on which China's current practices ride.

The present historical moment in the development of the law of the sea shows the cumulative effects of centuries of change. States have employed improving scientific and administrative technologies first to exploit the wealth of their near shores and then to advance further seaward. Until the twentieth century, states limited their exclusive resource claims to a narrow band of territorial sea, typically no more than 3 nautical miles. With the Truman Proclamations of 1945, the dam broke and the world's oceans became a patchwork of coastal state jurisdictional zones stretching out to 200 nautical miles beyond.[2] The fisheries of the former high seas and mineral wealth of the deep seabed were subjected to state ownership. Trends of global population growth, emerging technologies, and scientific discovery have combined to transform the oceans from a seemingly inexhaustible pool of common resources to a domain whose fundamental dynamic is competition under scarcity.[3] Some 87 percent of the world's known seabed hydrocarbon resources and over 90 percent of global fish stocks are now under coastal state jurisdiction.[4] Both are decidedly finite resources.

Acute international competition for fish, seabed minerals, and offshore oil and gas generates frequent disputes and sometimes conflict. China's maritime disputes are of a piece with this broader global phenomenon of resource contention, but they present distinctive characteristics due to the PRC's unique claims and the region's special political geography. The eight states surrounding the narrow semi-enclosed seas around China also prize the economic value of their coastal waters, and they have fought to preserve their UNCLOS entitlements against PRC claims. China has engaged these claimant states in decades of talks—and especially talks about further talks—regarding joint development of the waters and seabed of the South China Sea, East China Sea, and Yellow Sea. Practical cooperation, however, has been rare, narrowly targeted, and fleeting. Instead, the norm across the region has been to encroach on the marine resource rights of other states. China has been the most energetic participant in this contentious practice. Fielding the region's (and, with few exceptions, the world's) largest marine industries and its strongest maritime law enforcement fleet, China has been singularly capable and willing to press its resource claims in practice.

This chapter analyzes those practices in depth, with an eye toward discerning the underlying rules that the PRC prescribes and enforces to realize the economic potential of its claimed sovereign rights to natural resources (Figure 3). China's indeterminate claims of precisely where, geographically, its rights and jurisdiction exist is a practically (and

FIGURE 3. **PRC Resource Claims**
The EEZ claims and Nansha/Spratly territorial sea baseline claims depicted here are hypothetical because the PRC has yet to issue a formal claim. They derive from the strict reading of PRC rules claiming straight baselines around offshore archipelagos and full 200nm EEZ projections from all baselines. (Data from China National Offshore Oil Company, "Notification of Part of Open Blocks"; PRC MFA, "Declaration on the Baselines of the Territorial Sea"; Asia Maritime Transparency Initiative, "Reading Between the Lines"; CLCS, "Submission by the PRC Concerning the Outer Limits of the Continental Shelf." Map design by Paul Franz | Data: Mapcreator and openstreetmap.org.)

analytically) challenging element in its practice. Tracing China's preferred rules through its practices will allow us to evaluate the degree to which those PRC practices are accepted by specially affected states. This, in turn, will help us determine the degree to which China's preferred resource rules are taking hold.

RULES ON HISTORIC RIGHTS

The architects of UNCLOS regard the treaty as a "constitution for the oceans" that "succeeded in adopting a Convention covering every aspect of the uses and resources of the sea."[5] This view found substantial support in the SCS Arbitration, which ruled that "the system of maritime zones created by the Convention was intended to be comprehensive and to cover any area of sea or seabed."[6] Yet for the PRC, those UNCLOS rules are not exhaustive: "the Convention is *not* the sole legal source of maritime rights," according to Ma Xinmin, formerly the deputy director-general of the MFA Department of Treaty and Law.[7] Yang Jiechi, China's most senior foreign affairs official explained that position as rooted in historical claims: "China's territorial sovereignty and maritime rights and interests in the South China Sea have been formed over the course of over two thousand years. They are fully backed by historical and legal evidence. Under no circumstances can they ever be negated by a so-called award that is full of nonsense. The award can neither change historical facts nor deny China's claims of rights and interests in the South China Sea."[8]

From China's perspective, the UNCLOS aspiration to constitutional status is nothing more than "an inspiring slogan."[9] Chinese officials and scholars assert the PRC practice is validated by customary international law, arguing that the Convention does not extinguish historically grounded rights. The extent to which this interpretation of the rules is indeed supported by wider general practice is debatable and taken up in this book's conclusion. What is no longer debatable is the specific Chinese claim to "historic rights," evidently throughout the waters enclosed by the nine-dash line, and its steady practice to realize those rights against the protests of its neighbors.

On paper, at least, the Convention furnishes a comprehensive framework for allocating coastal state jurisdiction over economic activities and "sovereign rights" to explore and exploit the natural resources within each state's EEZ and continental shelf (UNCLOS, Arts. 56, 77).[10] Those sovereign rights are not equivalent to sovereign title, which a state enjoys only on land and in its internal waters and territorial sea. Instead, they are a concept first employed in the codification of the continental shelf in the first UNCLOS negotiation in 1956, which enumerated a set of defined, exclusive rights to the coastal state—well short of the full bundle of rights and jurisdiction conferred by sovereign title.[11]

Alongside creating the new category of sovereign rights to marine resources of the waters and seabed, the other main component of the EEZ regime grants new modes of jurisdiction to the coastal state. These are defined as limited jurisdictional competencies, covering only specified activities in that zone: "(i) the establishment and use of artificial islands, installations, and structures; (ii) marine scientific research; and (iii) the protection and preservation of the marine environment" (UNCLOS, Art. 56.1.b). Rather than allocating property rights, these provisions assign competence to the state to both prescribe and enforce its domestic law on those defined activities.[12] The broad interpretive meaning that may be assigned to each of these categories of jurisdiction has been especially consequential in PRC practice on law of the sea resource rules. Close analysis of that practice will illuminate precisely what rules the PRC seeks to enforce and promote with respect to historic rights to marine resources.

PRC Practice on Historic Rights
The PRC's first substantial official act on marine resource rights was the 1958 "Declaration on the Territorial Sea." Stating that China's claimed offshore islands "are separated from the mainland and its coastal islands by the high seas," the Declaration does not propose any exclusive PRC resource rights in the water space beyond those islands' territorial seas. However, the EEZ regime that grants such rights was not widely reflected in general practice until the 1970s, so this omission is logical and inconsequential for subsequent claims to that entitlement (see chapter 3). However, the omission of any reference to the historic rights that the PRC now claims long predate that Declaration *is* a fundamental inconsistency in Chinese practice on this matter.

It was not until the 1998 Law on the Exclusive Economic Zone and Continental Shelf (EEZ Law) that the PRC formally enacted a claim to "historic rights." This key piece of legislation largely restates the sovereign rights and jurisdiction set out in the Convention and then adds that "the provisions of this Act shall not affect the historic rights [历史性权利] of the PRC" (Art. 14).[13] No prior PRC legal instrument proposes any such historic rights, nor are they elaborated in the EEZ law. The claim did not appear again in an official document until China's official statement the day of the SCS arbitral award, 12 July 2016: "China has exclusive economic zone and continental shelf, based on Nanhai Zhudao [the SCS islands]. China has historic rights in the South China Sea."[14]

These two declarative statements provide the most authoritative account in PRC practice regarding the nature of the rules it prescribes for marine resources in the EEZ. The first establishes that all four of the claimed island groups (the "four shas") in the SCS, either individually or in combination, generate EEZ and continental shelf entitlements.[15] The second adds an important detail to the 1998 EEZ Law's broad statement—namely, that China claims historic rights in the SCS that are not abridged by UNCLOS entitlements.[16] The 2016 statement does not name the nine-dash line, but that map evidently describes geographic space in which China's claimed historic rights are in effect.

The Nine-Dash Line as a Historic Rights Claim

Although maps do not, in themselves, constitute evidence of sovereignty or jurisdiction, the map China attached to its 7 May 2009 note verbale is the most notorious representation of the PRC's historic rights claim.[17] The language in the note is spare; it does not ascribe any clear meaning or purpose to the map nor even list any geographic coordinates: "China has indisputable sovereignty over the islands in the SCS and the *adjacent* waters, and enjoys sovereign rights and jurisdiction over the *relevant* waters as well as the seabed and subsoil thereof (see attached map). The above position is consistently held by the Chinese Government, and is widely known to the international community."[18] The claim to rights and jurisdiction over "relevant waters" invokes China's claimed EEZ and continental shelf entitlements under UNCLOS. The "adjacent waters" must refer to the territorial sea and internal waters around the islands, over which the PRC claims sovereignty. "Adjacent waters" and "relevant waters" are not terms of art in UNCLOS, and nowhere does the note verbale mention any historical basis for the PRC's assertions. Only the map speaks to the historic rights claim.

Geographically, at least, the map makes a remarkable statement. Beginning in the northwest, the first "dash" is sketched about 85 nautical miles west of the westernmost PRC basepoint in the Paracels (Xisha) at Triton Island and only 35 nautical miles east of Vietnam's A10 basepoint south of Danang.[19] The lines then arc down to a southernmost point just beyond 4 degrees north latitude, some 900 nautical miles from the nearest undisputed Chinese territory of Hainan, only 24 nautical miles from Malaysia's Borneo coast. The U-shaped pattern then continues northeast, hugging the Malaysia, Brunei, and Philippines coastlines, with the last line in the Luzon Strait between Taiwan and the Philippines' northernmost point at Y'Ami Island.[20] Although the lines are discontinuous, they enclose an enormous volume of water space—some two million square kilometers, nearly the size of the Mediterranean Sea.[21] The only other lines on the minimal map are the territorial boundaries between the countries of southeast Asia, which are demarcated with the same dot-dash style. Yet those boundaries are linked together without any discontinuities, deepening the ambiguity still further.[22] The map does not display a legend or other interpretive guide to its symbology.

The original map on which the 2009 map is based was produced for internal use by the Republic of China's Interior Ministry in 1947; it was then published in a commercial atlas in 1948.[23] The ROC map consisted of eleven dashed and dotted lines circumscribing some 80 percent of the water space of the SCS. Two lines were removed by bilateral agreement with Vietnam in 1953, an adjustment that reinforces the notion that the map depicts a provisional boundary line as well as a claim circumscribing historic rights.[24] Senior PRC officials describe the map and its associated historic rights claim as "a complex inheritance from the Republic of China"; they have made no formal efforts to define its specific meaning.[25]

Because the Guomindang (KMT) Party, now in Taiwan, was the author of this claim, its practices are pertinent to understanding the basis for the PRC claim. The Taiwanese government adopted "South China Sea Policy Guidelines" in 1993 indicating that "the SCS area within the *historic water limit* is the maritime area under the jurisdiction of the Republic of China (ROC), in which the ROC possesses all rights and interests."[26] The ROC's Legislative Yuan later considered including "historic rights" in its Law on the Territorial Sea but dropped this claim on a second reading of the draft legislation.[27] Bill Hayton traces the process within Taiwan over the period following its original development of the "Location Sketch Map of the SCS Islands" (南海诸岛位置略图) in 1946, noting the efforts of certain entrepreneurs in Taiwan and on the mainland who ultimately failed to introduce "historic rights" (or "historic waters," which approximate full sovereignty) into ROC legislation.[28]

These historically based proposals had migrated across the Taiwan Strait to the mainland by the 1990s. In 1996, discussing the PRC EEZ Law in draft form, NPC Chairman and Vice-Foreign Minister Li Zhaoxing announced that the proposed language on historical claims was not in conflict with UNCLOS because, he alleged, the treaty "contains special regulations on historic waters."[29] Li emphasized the importance of developing domestic law to reinforce that interpretation: "In order to protect my country's sovereign rights and jurisdiction over the exclusive economic zone and continental shelf, and to safeguard my country's maritime rights and interests, it is necessary to adopt the form of domestic legislation to specifically implement the international maritime legal system stipulated in the Convention."[30] Li further referenced the now-infamous "nine-dash lines which have long been marked and delineated in the Chinese map of the South China Sea" as the embodiment of this claim.[31]

Yet the purported historical rights referenced in the 1998 EEZ Law and presumably illustrated in the map are still nowhere specified in PRC law—nor even fixed at any particular geographic location.[32] Even those lines, dots, and dashes have been rendered in a variety of ways and in a variety of locations in different Chinese official and semi-official maps.[33] A set of regulations issued in 2017 by the Ministry of Natural Resources calls for inspections of "problem maps" with "serious problems that endanger national unity, sovereignty, and territorial integrity," among which are included "representation of the discontinuous lines in the SCS [南海断续线] that do not comply with relevant national regulations."[34] This particular document, however, is the only national regulation that makes explicit reference to the nine-dash line.

Gao Zhiguo (the ITLOS judge and PRC maritime official) has argued that China's nine-dash line claim is based in customary international law, which "supplements what is provided for under UNCLOS."[35] Its "legal purpose and status" is to confirm China's sovereign title over the features within the line and to claim "historic rights, which preceded the advent of UNCLOS" and therefore cannot be extinguished by the new law of the sea.[36] This legal argument does not attempt to establish the factual basis of China's effective control over the resources, only that there is a colorable legal claim that PRC rights to those resources exist independent of UNCLOS.[37] Substantiating those factual claims has become a cottage industry of research within the PRC law of the sea community.

Claimed Content of PRC Historic Rights

The most detailed explanation from a PRC official about the content of historic rights claimed within the nine-dash line came in a 2015 law journal article by Jia Yu, party secretary of CIMA. She offers the clearest public account by a PRC official to date regarding the scope and content of China's claimed historic rights:

> Historic rights include historic title, traditional fishing rights, and historic navigational rights. Historic ownership of historic waters by coastal states is a sovereign right, and traditional fishing rights and historic navigational rights are part of historic rights. Historic rights cannot generally be claimed and acquired over non-living resources on the continental shelf. The history of China's development and control of the South China Sea and China's practice show that China has territorial sovereignty over the islands in the South China Sea and enjoys historical rights in the waters within the South China Sea discontinuous line [断续线], including historical ownership of historical waters such as the Qiongzhou Strait, traditional fishing rights, and historical navigational rights. The South China Sea discontinuous line thus represents China's territorial sovereignty over the islands in the South China Sea and its historical rights in the South China Sea.[38]

This statement clarifies three substantive aspects of China's historic rights claim: (1) it is rooted in a claim to sovereign title over the SCS features; (2) it includes traditional fishing and historic navigation acquired through long-standing practice, and (3) the nine-dash line encompasses the waters in which these rights apply. The fuller meaning of the nine-dash line must be inferred from the consistent PRC practice of asserting resource rights within the waters it encloses, often well beyond the "relevant waters" within 200 nautical miles of PRC-claimed features. The map does not, in itself, describe any legible rule that might be applied or enforced.

This informal explanation aside, other PRC officials have yet to render any formal, positive account of the substantive rights or functional jurisdiction depicted by the line. They have only asserted that it, at a minimum, composes part of China's historical evidence of sovereignty over the features within the lines and that some type of "traditional" or historic Chinese rights to resources exists within it.[39] Logically, such historical usage excludes exploitation of oil and gas and other uses that emerged only in the twentieth century, well after the supposed establishment of its historic rights.

Some more recent archival work has offered further clarity. A 2018 "Catalogue of Evidence" funded by the Chinese government lists the following historical practices as substantiating China's historic rights: "declarations of sovereignty" (主权宣示), "navigation management" (航行管理), "law enforcement rights" (执法权), "military utilization" (军事使用), "commercial development and operation" (开发和经营), "marine scientific research" (海上科学研究), "conservation and use of living resources" (生物资源的养护利用), "construction and management of artificial islands, facilities, and structures" (人工岛屿，设施和结构的建造与管理), and "rights protection" (维权).[40] These historical usages are based on closed archival records and cannot be independently confirmed. However, even taking them at face value, China engaging in all of those practices cannot rule out the simultaneous historical usage of these same resources by other states. The historical utilization of these disputed waters by any of the littoral states would falsify the Chinese claim to have developed an exclusive privilege to them through historical practice.

"Other Sea Areas Under PRC Jurisdiction"

China's claimed historic rights are also potentially included in a body of domestic law governing "other sea areas under PRC jurisdiction" (中华人民共和国管辖的其他海域), a term first employed in the 1982

PRC Marine Environmental Protection Law.[41] This indeterminate jurisdictional claim has since been applied to 198 PRC legal instruments tasking central, provincial, and local agencies to administer and enforce laws, typically last in a list of the UNCLOS-prescribed maritime zones—namely, the territorial sea, the contiguous zone, the EEZ, and the continental shelf. Many pieces of maritime legislation creating new functional responsibilities for state agencies contain this language, which then reappears in lower-level implementing regulations, measures, and departmental rules intended to specify the practical duties of the relevant actors.[42]

The undefined "other sea areas" complicate the PRC's efforts to coordinate administration and enforcement of domestic maritime law. With no specified geographic scope in which PRC agencies are authorized to exercise jurisdiction, PRC practice manifests some notable confusion and inconsistency. In 2003 the Supreme People's Court (SPC) issued an interpretation of the 1999 Special Maritime Procedure Law that awkwardly avoids the question of which "other sea areas" are indeed under PRC jurisdiction: "The phrase 'the sea areas under jurisdiction' as prescribed in Item 3 of Article 7 of the Special Maritime Procedure Law refers to the contiguous zones, exclusive economic zones, continental shelves, and other sea areas that are under the jurisdiction of the People's Republic of China."[43] This circular reasoning is also present in a pair of 2016 SPC "interpretations" on the question of the jurisdiction of specialized PRC maritime courts.[44] There the court makes no explicit connection between historic rights and these "other sea areas," but that linkage is the most reasonable inference about jurisdictional zones claimed beyond the entitlements granted by UNCLOS.

In a study commissioned by the Ministry of Foreign Affairs to critique the SCS arbitral award, the China Society of International Law offers some clarification, stating that "China's historic rights in the SCS have a scope much greater than those to the living and non-living resources, and the bases for China's historic rights include much more than navigation and fishing. . . . [T]he maritime zones under the jurisdiction of China comprise not only the maritime ones that China is entitled to under the Convention, but also those areas in which China has historic rights."[45] In support of this assertion, this officially sanctioned rebuttal cites the "consistent" administrative actions of the state to put the rule into practice. These practices alone are insufficient, however, for a custom to form. Thus the second important element of the CSIL argument concerns the acquiescence of specially affected states. China's May 2009 note verbale (CLM/18/2009) asserts that its claim "is widely known to the international community," which by implication, has had ample opportunity to object since its obscure publication in 1948. CSIL carries this further, singling out the Philippines as a relevant case in which "an acceptance or acquiescence obviously exists" because it had not objected to the nine-dash line when it was first published, nor had it rejected China's 1998 EEZ Law claiming historic rights.[46]

Overall, PRC practice on its "historic rights" claim shows a gradually emerging consensus on what they entail. Its consistency has increased over time, especially since the 1998 EEZ Law. Since then, China's official statements have claimed historic rights with greater specificity, making clear their application to fisheries and navigation at a minimum. There is no evident claim to such rights elsewhere, nor is one necessary for the Chinese claim in the SCS to itself be virtually uniform. At any rate, the uniformity of China's practice to exercise and enforce these

TABLE 8

PRC PRACTICE OF HISTORIC RIGHTS RULES

PRC-preferred rule	Uniformity (geographic)	Consistency (over time)	Detail
Custom-based "historic rights" are superior to UNCLOS-based sovereign rights	Yes (within SCS)	No	Ostensible boundary claim comes to include resource and navigation rights
Coastal states may exercise jurisdiction and enjoy rights over "other sea areas" beyond UNCLOS entitlements	Yes	No	Undefined scope: nine-dash line in SCS, unknown in ECS

Note: The 1998 EEZ Law marks the beginning of official claims to some historic rights and "other sea areas," which have since grown more specific and consistent in PRC practice.

claimed rights within the nine-dash line is unobservable in formal legal instruments. To develop a fuller understanding of the nature of the rule the PRC implements to govern historic rights, the next section evaluates the reactions of specially affected states to the economic practices of Chinese firms and individuals (Table 8).

Specially Affected State Responses to China's Historic Rights Practice
China's historic rights claims appear incompatible with exclusive sovereign rights that UNCLOS bestows on the other main claimants in the South China Sea: Vietnam, Malaysia, Indonesia, Brunei, and the Philippines. Each of these countries asserts its right to a 200nm EEZ; Vietnam and Malaysia have further submitted extended continental shelf claims within the area circumscribed by the nine-dash line. They are thus each specially affected by PRC claims to historic resource rights within those entitlements.

Vietnam began objecting to China's historic rights claim as soon as it was codified in the 1998 EEZ Law. In a diplomatic note to the UN, Vietnam declared that it "shall not recognize any so-called 'historical interests' which are not in consistence with international law."[47] After the 2009 publication of the nine-dash line, Vietnam further protested the legitimacy of the PRC's sovereignty claims to the SCS islands and their "adjacent waters," dismissing them and the nine-dash line map as having "no legal, historical or factual basis" and being "therefore . . . null and void."[48] In 2011, at a meeting of States Parties to UNCLOS, Vietnam's deputy minister of foreign affairs and head of its UN delegation spoke to "reiterate our consistent position that all claims of national sovereignty or sovereign rights and jurisdiction over maritime spaces that are not in accordance with the provisions of the UNCLOS, such as the nine-dotted line in the SCS, illustrated in the map presented by the PRC to the Secretary-General of the UN on 7 May 2009, are totally illegal and unacceptable."[49] Finally, Vietnam weighed in again in 2020, notifying the UN that "Viet Nam opposes any maritime claims in the East Sea [SCS] that exceed the limits provided in UNCLOS, including claims to historic rights; these claims are without lawful effect."[50] Vietnam, like the other claimants, evidently sharpened its objections to the rule as China sharpened its specific historic rights claim.

For the Philippines, objection to China's historic rights claim figured centrally in its arbitral suit. Prior to filing for arbitration, Manila had struggled with the ambiguity of the claim implied in the nine-dash line map, stating in 2011 that it would be illegal *if* it claimed rights beyond UNCLOS.[51] The Philippines' January 2013 Notification and Statement of Claim for arbitration requests a finding that "China's claims based on its 'nine-dash line' are inconsistent with the Convention and therefore invalid." This formal submission further asserts that "the Philippines has consistently expressed the view to China in bilateral meetings and diplomatic correspondence that it is entitled to an exclusive economic zone and continental shelf of 200nm from its archipelagic baselines, and to the *exclusive* enjoyment of the living and non-living resources in these zones."[52]

By 2020, the Philippines had fully and formally embraced the award: "The Tribunal conclusively settled the issue of historic rights and maritime entitlements in the SCS. The Tribunal ruled that claims to historic rights, or other sovereign rights or jurisdiction that exceed the geographic and substantive limits of maritime entitlements under UNCLOS, are without lawful effect. It further ruled that UNCLOS 'superseded any historic rights, or other sovereign rights or jurisdiction, in excess of the limits imposed therein.'"[53] Bolstered by the SCS arbitral award, the Philippines has expressed an unequivocal rejection of the validity of any resource rights claims, historical or otherwise, to waters eligible for UNCLOS entitlements.

Prior to the SCS arbitral award in 2016, Indonesia had been the most enthusiastic objector to the Chinese historic rights claim. As the broker of a series of talks among claimants beginning in 1990, Indonesia's initial position had been to avoid acknowledgment of the Chinese claim represented in the map that it began referencing in these dialogues in 1993.[54] With China's formal publication of the nine-dash line map in 2009, Indonesia reciprocated in 2010 with formal opposition to the claim: "Indonesia also follows closely the debate over the above mentioned map which has also been referred to as the so-called 'nine-dotted-lines map.' Thus far, there is no clear explanation as to the legal basis, the method of drawing, and the status of these separated dotted-lines. It seems that those separated dotted lines may have been the maritime zones of various disputed small features in the waters of the SCS . . . the so-called 'nine-dotted-lines map' . . . clearly lacks international legal basis and is tantamount to upset the UNCLOS 1982."[55] A decade later, Indonesia formally leveled its objection again, but with greater specificity: "No historic rights exist in Indonesia's EEZ and continental shelf vis-à-vis the PRC. Should there be any historic rights existing prior to the entry into force of UNCLOS 1982, those rights were superseded by the provisions of UNCLOS 1982."[56] Indonesia has officially rejected China's historic rights claim in its particulars but also in its general status as a rule that would derogate from coastal state entitlements under UNCLOS.

Malaysia has likewise made a formal objection to PRC historic rights claims and, further, has opposed the general viability of the PRC's proposed rule. During an exchange of notes following Malaysia's 2019 CLCS submission, its government issued a note verbale stating that "the Government of Malaysia rejects China's claim to historic rights, or other sovereign rights or jurisdiction, with respect to the maritime areas of the SCS encompassed by the relevant part of the 'nine-dash line' as they are contrary to the Convention and without lawful effect to the extent that they exceed the geographic and substantive limits of China's maritime entitlements under the Convention."[57]

With the sole exception of Brunei, which has been conspicuously silent on disputes, all the states specially affected by China's historic rights

TABLE 9

SPECIALLY AFFECTED STATE RESPONSES TO PRC HISTORIC RIGHTS PRACTICE

	PRC historic rights supplant UNCLOS
Brunei	Acquiesce
Indonesia	Object
Malaysia	Object
Philippines	Object
Vietnam	Object

claims have mounted consistent objections—not only to China's purportedly unlawful infringement on their claims, but on the validity of the
Chinese rule under UNCLOS. From the perspective of one leading PRC
official, Jia Yu, the Philippines, Malaysia, Vietnam, and Indonesia "have
not questioned or denied the existence of China's nine-dash line. These
countries not only did not express objections in the years after the nine-
dash line was first made public; they've always tacitly accepted its existence."[58] The evidence presented above flatly contradicts this argument.

By China's own standard for historic rights, its claim lacks a necessary element of acquiescence of other states—in particular those specially affected. Facing widespread opposition among specially affected
states, it is implausible that China's desired rule is progressing toward
acceptance as a customary norm (Table 9).

RULES ON FISHERIES

States have long exercised exclusive fishing rights in their fully sovereign
internal waters and territorial seas. Until the advent of the EEZ, seaward
of that narrow coastal band of water, no state enjoyed any exclusive fishing rights, nor any jurisdiction over fishing activities except over vessels bearing their flag. In establishing a zone of exclusive coastal state
sovereign rights and jurisdiction over resources and their use, UNCLOS
Part V created a new set of rules, the EEZ regime, to govern fisheries
practices over roughly one third of the world's water space. The remaining two thirds remain high seas in which no exclusive or even preferential fishing rights exist. A fundamental dispute about equity is already
baked into the marine resource rule-set: the very origins of the EEZ concept lie in the demands of developing states that sought to secure their
own fishing rights against their usurpation by developed maritime states
with distant-water fishing fleets operating at regional and global scale.[59]

The state practices most relevant to this particular class of sovereign
rights are the state's official acts to manage and regulate fishing activities
by its nationals operating within its jurisdictional waters and beyond.
The basic contention over fisheries rules arises from the scarcity of the
resource and the interdependence of various state practices in managing
and conserving fish stocks and ecosystems, largely undertaken by state
maritime law enforcement (MLE) organizations. Because of the "fugi-
tive" nature of some fish stocks that straddle or migrate through dif-

ferent states' jurisdictional waters, issues within a state's jurisdictional waters are ecologically connected to those in the high seas and in the jurisdictions of other states.

The EEZ regime is the locus of fishing rules that are of most consequence in China's maritime disputes. No state has yet fully defined its EEZ in the South China Sea, East China Sea, and Yellow Sea. The obligation to reach "provisional arrangements of a practical nature" (UNCLOS, Art. 74.3) has yielded a few defined areas of cooperative fisheries practice in the region. However, China's historic rights claims introduce additional complexity into regional disputes over fisheries resources well beyond the garden-variety cases of illegal, unreported, and unregulated (IUU) fishing, a clear violation of the rules that China officially condemns (though does not effectively regulate).[60] Rather, the disputed rules in question concern the extent of China's jurisdiction and resource rights, especially as it applies to the notion of "traditional fishing rights" and whether they may supplant the exclusive resource rights granted by the EEZ.

The Convention provides for only one form of such traditional fishing rights: "archipelagic States . . . shall recognize traditional fishing rights and other legitimate activities of the immediately adjacent neighboring States in certain areas falling within archipelagic waters . . . [as] regulated by bilateral agreements between them" (UNCLOS, Art. 51.1). Widening this very narrowly construed role for traditional fishing rights is among the most notable elements of PRC practice in this domain. This section addresses these and other fisheries practices of the PRC in which disputed rules—not mere illegal use of scarce resources—are in play.

PRC Practice on Fisheries

China's practice to assert its preferred fisheries rules manifests mainly as fisheries law enforcement. Domestic PRC laws, regulations, and rules in this sector deal primarily with issues of usage rights, determining the type and volume of fishing activities permitted in various zones under claimed PRC jurisdiction. Secondarily, they assign competencies to various agencies for managing and enforcing the lawful exercise of those usage rights. Because those claimed usage rights and maritime law enforcement jurisdiction are so often applied in areas of disputed entitlements, they have given rise to significant friction with neighboring states. It is these problem areas, rather than the large body of technical regulations or the constant IUU fishing, that are of most interest.

Competition for increasingly scarce fisheries resources is a fundamental driver of these practices. Some significant part of that scarcity is due simply to China's scale. Since 1990, China has fielded the world's largest fishing fleet and has become the world's largest fish producer, accounting for 35 percent of global fish production in 2018 according to the Food and Agriculture Organization of the UN, more than the rest of Asia combined.[61] China's Ministry of Agriculture estimated in 2019 that the PRC supplied 40 percent of the world's total fish production, including "over two thirds" of its aquaculture output, lauding its own success in "achieving the legislative purpose of promoting the development of fishery production and meeting the needs of people's lives."[62] Those needs prominently include increased protein consumption.

Since 1985, China has met these needs by expanding the scope of sanctioned fishing activities beyond its claimed jurisdictional waters.[63] This shift is partly a consequence of the rapid depletion of China's coastal fisheries over the last several decades. Total catch in the SCS is now between 5 percent and 30 percent of levels in the 1950s due to overfishing and pollution, and it is worse in the northern sector closest to China.[64] This stress on fisheries has produced high rates of unemployment in the sector, underutilization of the fishing fleet, and a corresponding push by commercial and private fishermen to expand the space in which they exploit these diminishing resources.[65] This bottom-up driver catalyzes the top-down practices that characterize China's enforcement of its preferred fisheries rules.[66]

The banner piece of national legislation in this sector is the 1986 Fisheries Law, which has been revised and amended at intervals as China's fisheries administrative apparatus has matured.[67] Its main amendment occurred in 2000, incorporating the 1998 EEZ Law by extending fisheries provisions to formally cover the EEZ as well as "other sea areas under PRC jurisdiction." Among the enabling legal instruments for this law are the 1987 Regulations for the Implementation of the Fisheries Law of the PRC, which were twice revised by the State Council in 2020 but still feature the undefined "other sea areas under PRC jurisdiction."[68] The document directs fisheries authorities at the provincial and municipal level to determine areas for enforcement of domestic law "through consultation" with the central government, but otherwise it grants them discretion in implementing the Fisheries Law with "approval" by those same local-level departments. This flexible system may yield advantages for management and administration, but it also introduces challenges to the uniformity and consistency of China's state practice.[69]

Until the late 1990s, provincial and local agencies under the Ministry of Agriculture were empowered to "lay down implementation measures of national laws according to the circumstances of their respective administrative regions. The fisheries authorities at all levels drew up local measures and rules to strengthen fisheries management."[70] But beginning in 1998, Beijing began to exercise considerably greater centralized guidance over fisheries matters.

A Fisheries Law Enforcement Command (FLEC) was established under the Ministry of Agriculture in 1998 in order to "adapt to the implementation of the new international maritime regime" whose most salient feature for fisheries was China's newly claimed EEZ.[71] FLEC soon received authorization from the State Council to build fourteen mid- to large-sized cutters, adding substantial capacity to enforce China's fisheries laws in practice.[72] An NPC "inspection" of China's implementation of the Fisheries Law later that year counts a total of 2,679 fisheries administration agencies at all levels of government, 2,581 fishery administration vessels of various types, and 27,400 licensed law enforcement officers across the country.[73]

The duties of this sprawling fisheries law enforcement apparatus range from routine patrols and permits to extremely sensitive "rights protection" missions in disputed waters. According to Liu Cigui, then-director of SOA:

> We will maintain the law enforcement patrols that have become normalized to safeguard rights and interests in the waters of the Diaoyu Islands. We will show our jurisdictional claims externally through ongoing patrols of the waters of the South China Sea under Chinese jurisdiction. We will move ahead in areas including selection of the scope of protection for territorial sea basepoints, management of place names in the South China Sea, research to determine the extent of the continental shelf extending beyond the

200-nautical-mile limit, and the naming of seabed places. We will move further ahead with comprehensive administration, and we will strike a "combination blow," the main elements of which will be legal, administrative, and maritime activities and public opinion propaganda. We will undertake systematic deepening of research and external propaganda on hot issues of maritime rights and interests.[74]

This comprehensive set of efforts—including active enforcement and propaganda work—has direct implications for the fisheries rules applied in PRC practice.

Summer Fishing Bans

China's summer "seasonal fishing bans" (伏季休渔) are the clearest top-down measure in this vein. These measures ban most types of fishing for most species in designated maritime areas during defined periods, ostensibly in the name of fisheries conservation. They were initiated in the ECS and Yellow Sea in 1995 and then applied in the SCS beginning in 1999.[75] The Yellow Sea ban has been fixed above 35 degrees north latitude; the ECS ban has remained between 35 degrees and 26 degrees 30 minutes north latitude, covering the area just north of the disputed Diaoyu/Senkaku to the mouth of the Yellow Sea. The SCS ban has been less uniform, creeping gradually southward. Since 2009, it has covered all waters north of 12 degrees north latitude, south of which lie the Spratly (Nansha) Islands.[76] The dates of the ban's implementation have also varied, from ten weeks to sixteen weeks from May/June to August/September.[77] These annual bans cover large areas that lie within the claimed entitlements of the eight other littoral states.

Enforcement of the ban entails significant PRC actions against foreign fishing vessels.[78] By 2019, senior officials from the Ministry of Agriculture reported that PRC fisheries law enforcement had conducted 2,225,000 nautical miles of "inspection" on the water, an increase of 70 percent over 2017.[79] The precise locations of these patrols are not recorded, but the large increase in activity over the course of those two years suggests that full coverage of the banned water space has historically been beyond the capacity of fisheries law enforcement to continuously monitor. Instead, the Fisheries Law Enforcement Command distributes law enforcement in "key areas" of the summer fishing bans in the SCS, ECS, and Yellow Sea on the basis of monthly inspections. The vice-minister of agriculture, Yu Kangzhen, described cracking down on illegal fishing practices as "like cutting leeks; you cut and cut and they still may grow back."[80]

While the specialized FLEC is the chief enforcer of fisheries law, the paramilitary China Coast Guard is increasingly playing a key role. The CCG's official WeChat account reported its annual activities to date in September 2020: "Jointly with local fishery administration departments, we have carried out special operations against foreign fishing vessels, continuously increased boarding, inspection and detaining, driving away foreign fishing vessels 1,138 times, including 73 boarding and inspection, and detaining 11 foreign fishing vessels and 66 persons. [These actions] strongly protect our fishing interests and maritime rights."[81] According to PRC diplomats, these "clear and consistent" enforcement actions are "regular administrative measures taken by China to protect living marine resources in the relevant waters and a proper act to fulfill China's international obligation and responsibility . . . in waters under China's jurisdiction."[82] Such actions are particularly intense against Vietnamese fishermen near the Paracels, where reports of harassment, arrest, and even kidnapping and ransom by Chinese maritime law enforcement were prominent in the period 2005–2012.[83]

North of 12 degrees north latitude, the seasonal bans represent China's application of its interpretation of its obligations to conserve and manage its fish stocks under UNCLOS. This includes both disputed and undisputed waters but is largely water space in which China's jurisdiction is uncontested. South of the 12 degree line, however, lie the waters surrounding the Spratly (Nansha) Islands, for which a separate and non-uniform regime has emerged. These "special fishing activities" (专项捕捞行为) are to be strictly supervised under a separate set of rules.[84]

PRC Fishing South of 12 Degrees North Latitude

No Chinese fishing was permitted south of 12 degrees north latitude until 1985, when the CCP Central Committee and the PRC State Council issued "Instructions on Relaxing Policies and Accelerating the Development of the Fisheries Industry."[85] Central and local authorities subsequently directed fishermen in Hainan and Guangdong provinces to begin operating in these disputed waters.[86] By 1988, China had seized the first of several Spratly features in a small-scale naval conflict with Vietnam and later established rudimentary facilities on a number of unoccupied features.[87] These are now significantly improved by the well-developed facilities at Subi, Fiery Cross, and Mischief reefs that enable sustained Chinese fishing (and law enforcement presence) throughout the southern tier of the SCS.

This "revival of production in the Spratlys" brought about specialized regulations for fishing in ten designated fisheries zones covering the whole Spratly area, where PRC fishermen are incentivized to "catch sovereignty fish" (捕主权鱼).[88] From the perspective of the Ministry of Agriculture SCS Fisheries Bureau director, Wu Zhuang, "the development of fisheries near the Spratly Islands involves questions of sovereignty over China's Spratly Islands. Development equals presence, presence equals occupation, and occupation equals sovereignty."[89] In 1994, diesel fuel subsidies were made available to owners of vessels fishing in the Spratlys; by 2003, the Ministry of Agriculture had issued a set of specialized regulations solely for Spratlys fisheries production that established an organized licensing and fuel subsidy system.[90] These regulations allowed the central state to manage and direct PRC fishing vessels to utilize disputed resources and thereby "maintain a conspicuous presence," thought to provide "the primary method [to] show control of sovereignty in the Spratlys."[91] Special Spratly fishing licenses are now managed at the provincial level in accordance with central regulation.[92]

The terms of the 2003 Spratly regulations reflect an expectation that such fishing will be dangerous: the regulations provide compensation for losses due to incidents and mandate installation of China's "Beidou" satellite positioning and communication equipment on Spratly-going vessels.[93] Beginning in 2009, PRC fisheries law enforcement cutters started to escort Chinese fishing vessels on their Spratly voyages. Wu Zhuang, the chief official overseeing these actions, describes the operations as designed to "rescue our fishing boats caught by neighboring country's law enforcement." Wu notes that "our fishermen have often been attacked and detained by force by neighboring countries. So far [to 2013], nearly 400 of our fishing boats have been arrested and attacked by neighboring countries in Nansha."[94]

Another relevant state practice in fisheries below 12 degrees is that of the PRC maritime militia. This large auxiliary force of nominally civilian fishing vessels is administered by the central National Defense Mobilization Commission and overseen by the PRC State Council and the PLA Central Military Commission.[95] While the members of these forces are ostensibly private actors, they may be mobilized and placed under military chain of command. These militias are active throughout China's coastal areas, and they have participated in various centrally organized efforts since the 1950s. At least eighty-four of the vessels operating out of the Paracels have been purpose-built with reinforced hulls, water cannon, and rails for "shouldering." They have participated in many of the signal conflicts in the SCS, including the PRC's seizure of the western Paracel Islands in 1974, the occupation of Mischief Reef in 1995, various encounters with US Navy vessels from 2009 to the present, a blockade of the Philippines' garrison at Second Thomas Shoal in 2014, the envelopment of the Philippine-claimed Sandy Cay in 2017, and amassing at Whitsun Reef in 2020–2021.[96] As the instruments of state policy, the maritime militia have played a large part in China's assertion of its fisheries rights in disputed zones.

Traditional Fishing Rights

In addition to UNCLOS-based sovereign rights and jurisdiction over fisheries, China has begun to include "traditional" fishing rights. Since 2015, PRC officials have argued that customary international law accommodates such rights:

> The early practice of the international community recognized the exclusive fishing rights of coastal States in their coastal waters on the one hand, and emphasized the traditional fishing interests of other States in those waters on the other. The fact that other States have long been engaged in customary fishing activities in areas that were formerly part of the high seas and are now within the exclusive fishing domain or jurisdiction of the coastal State has given them a historical right to fish. . . . With the entry into force of the Convention, the international community has emphasized the sovereign rights of coastal states over the living resources of the EEZ, resulting in the weakening and marginalization of traditional

fishing rights. However, as an important component of historic rights, traditional fishing rights are related to the livelihoods of many fishermen and their families. Coastal states should respect the long-established traditional fishing rights of other countries, give priority to traditional fishing rights in the allocation of surplus allowable catch, and grant access to countries whose nationals habitually fish in their EEZs, subject to their own laws and regulations. . . . The argument that the Convention's creation of exclusive jurisdiction implies the overthrow of traditional rights is not only unconvincing, but also conceptually and legally flawed.[97]

The fishing activities are here described as historical, but provenance of the claims themselves is relatively recent. Some form of traditional fishing rights was contemplated during China's ratification process in 1996, when Vice-Foreign Minister Li Zhaoxing spoke to the NPC about the challenge posed by EEZ rules, observing that "PRC fishermen have long been conducting traditional fishing activities in the Spratly Islands. UNCLOS contains special regulations on historic waters."[98] No Chinese legal instrument has yet expressly claimed such traditional rights, though leading officials have publicly endorsed the concept; for example, SCS Fisheries Bureau Director Wu Zhuang put it this way: "The waters of Nansha have always been our country's traditional fishing grounds, and the homes of our fishermen's ancestors who have farmed the sea and fished for generations. However, since the 1970s, the Nansha waters have been restless because surrounding countries invaded and occupied our Nansha islands and reefs."[99] Reversing this purported invasion is among the rationales underlying China's subsequent fisheries practice.

These "countermeasures" have become more consistent and uniform over time. A 2015 State Council "National Marine Functional Zoning Plan" names "52 traditional fishing grounds along the coast of our country, covering most of the sea areas under our jurisdiction." These include the aforementioned ten zones in the Spratlys, areas near Pratas (Dongsha), and several zones near the Paracel (Xisha) Islands and Macclesfield Bank (Dongsha). Diaoyu is not evidently one of the areas designated for traditional fishing. No map or coordinates accompany the list of traditional fishing grounds, but they cover "most" of China's claimed jurisdictional waters and thus overlap and extend beyond those zones China claims under UNCLOS.

The clearest case of PRC traditional fishing claims extending beyond any UNCLOS entitlement involves the "Nansha Southwest Fishing Ground" (南沙西南部渔场) and the "Nansha South Fishing Ground" (南沙南部渔场). Indonesia claims parts of these two areas within its 200nm EEZ extending from the Natuna Islands. The nine-dash line claim overlaps the Natuna EEZ in an area of 94,000 square kilometers, at least 33,000 of which are beyond 200 nautical miles from Spratly Island, the nearest PRC-claimed high tide feature (see Figure 3, Natuna "Carveout").[100] Chinese diplomats have protested that their vessels were "operating normally in China's traditional fishing ground in the Spratly waters when they were seized by Indonesia's fisheries law enforcement."[101] A series of encounters among Chinese and Indonesian fisheries law enforcement vessels in this area began in spring 2010, when PRC vessels forced their Indonesian counterparts to release a Chinese fishing vessel from the Nansha Southwest Fishing Ground.[102] Chinese and Indonesian sources report that, prior to this, Indonesian law enforcement had routinely arrested and detained PRC vessels fishing in the Natuna EEZ but, beginning in 2010, were prevented from doing so by the Chinese law enforcement "escorts" that began to protect Chinese fishing vessels and assert the PRC's rights in the area.

PRC fisheries law enforcement vessels prevented Indonesian law enforcement actions several times that spring and summer, at times soliciting diplomatic support from the MFA to negotiate the release of Chinese vessels and crews.[103] By the end of 2011 Chinese media noted that more than ten PRC fisheries law enforcement vessels had carried out "close-in escorts" for Chinese fishermen, confronting twenty-two "armed vessels" from Indonesia, the Philippines, and Vietnam and rescuing twelve Chinese fishing boats and more than one hundred fishermen seized by neighboring countries.[104] One remarkable instance of this practice came in March 2016, when the CCG confronted an Indonesian Ministry of Marine Affairs and Fisheries vessel with a Chinese fishing vessel under tow and then rammed it to free the detained Chinese vessel.[105]

These and similar episodes preceded the first specific PRC statements—in a series of comments from MFA spokespeople in 2016 and 2017—invoking "traditional fishing" in these waters lying beyond any possible Chinese entitlements under UNCLOS.[106] Chinese fishing in these waters has continued episodically, with a series of incidents in 2019–2020 leading an MFA spokesperson to describe China's actions as consistent with its "sovereign rights and jurisdiction over relevant waters near the Nansha Islands. In the meantime, China has historical rights in the SCS. . . . Chinese coast guard vessels have been performing normal patrols in the waters under China's jurisdiction."[107] Similar comments by PRC diplomats in the Philippines accompanied the 2012 struggle for control of Scarborough (Huangyan) Island and subsequent activity in that area.[108] These areas are presumably part of the "West and South Zhongsha Fishing Ground" named in the 2015 functional zoning plan. They figure in the SCS Arbitration award, and they are analyzed below as part of the Philippines' response as a specially affected state.

In summary, China's fisheries practice has not shown consistency over time nor uniformity over maritime space. The shift in 1985 to promote fishing south of 12 degrees north latitude, however, marks an important move toward uniformity by beginning the assertion of PRC fishing rights throughout its areas of claimed jurisdiction. The substance of those claims has been more consistently expressed only since 2015, when the locations of PRC "traditional fishing grounds" were designated. There has also been growing consistency in PRC efforts to enforce those presumed traditional fishing rights since the beginning of escort patrols in 2009.[109]

Improving central coordination is likely to reinforce the uniformity and consistency of this PRC claim, though such irregularity in a historical claim damages its coherence. Furthermore, no official statement has expressly defined traditional fishing "rights" and announced how they are meant to relate to sovereign rights under UNCLOS, except to imply that they are a class of "historic right." Even in this ambiguous form, however, China's practice illuminates its desired rule and its relationship to the EEZ regime: opposing the exclusivity of the sovereign rights over marine resources granted under UNCLOS, China claims some evidently non-exclusive historic rights to certain fisheries (Table 10).

Specially Affected State Responses to China's Fisheries Practice
The group of states specially affected by China's fisheries claims includes each of the states with boundary and entitlement disputes with

TABLE 10

PRC PRACTICE OF FISHERIES RULES

PRC-preferred rule	Uniformity (geographic)	Consistency (over time)	Detail
Traditional fishing conferring non-exclusive rights in foreign jurisdictional zones	No	No	Traditional rights undefined until 2015; lag in enforcement in southern part of SCS; unclear if/when rights are exclusive
Exclusive fishing rights in all "sea areas under PRC jurisdiction"	No	No	Distinct difference north and south of 12 degrees; growing consistency since summer fishing bans (1999 to present)

China—namely, the eight states surrounding the SCS and ECS. These littoral states face the most acute expressions of China's rules on historic rights and traditional fishing. China's practice implies, at a minimum, that littoral states do not enjoy *exclusive* sovereign rights and jurisdiction over their UNCLOS maritime entitlements. The other nations' stance on this implied rule may be observed in the way they have responded to Chinese fishing in areas of former high seas that now constitute areas of their EEZs.[110]

The historic rights controversy examined above demonstrated uniform and consistent opposition to the general assertion that China possesses resource rights that derogate from other coastal states' UNCLOS entitlements. These categorical statements apply also to fisheries and need not be retread. However, the conflict of rules comes to a head in the fisheries law enforcement practices of other states against Chinese fishing vessels, which warrant further attention. The critical consideration is whether these states have objected by way of law enforcement against PRC fishing practices and enforcement actions in disputed jurisdictional resource zones. These objections need not predate the practical efforts by the PRC to exercise its claimed rights, though consistent acquiescence in such usage significantly undermines the strength of the objection to counter the PRC rule.[111] Additional insights into these specially affected states' positions on China's preferred fisheries rules may also be gleaned from the cooperative pattern of fishing agreements and joint law enforcement within the region. If such agreements tacitly recognize Chinese rights beyond UNCLOS, they may be interpreted as acquiescence to the rules underlying PRC claims.

Foreign Enforcement Against PRC Fisheries Activity

PRC fishing vessels are frequent targets of foreign law enforcement action across the disputed waters of the South China Sea, where China's historic rights and traditional fishing overlap the littoral countries' UNCLOS entitlements. In the East China Sea and Yellow Sea, Japanese and South Korean law enforcement have also taken frequent actions against Chinese fishing vessels—but generally not as a result of any dispute over jurisdiction. The law enforcement in these cases does not surface any conflict of rules because it is typically responding to Chinese vessels' illegal, unregulated, or unreported (IUU) fishing rather than Chinese assertions of resource rights. In the absence of Chinese historic rights claims within overlapping EEZ entitlements, there is little contention over which rules govern resource rights in those northern waters.[112]

Vietnam's law enforcement practice against PRC fishermen has been vigorous, particularly in the near coastal waters of the Gulf of Tonkin prior to the 2004 Sino-Vietnamese boundary agreement discussed in chapter 3. Elsewhere in the SCS, Vietnam has consistently defied China's summer fishing bans, issuing frequent protests and continuing to permit and protect Vietnamese fishing according to its domestic law.[113] Its fisheries law enforcement practices have rarely been observed against Chinese or other vessels fishing in disputed Spratly and Paracel waters, despite consistent formal objections to those rights. Lacking the capacity to sustain patrols in those waters, Vietnam has found other mechanisms to sustain its rights claims. In this regard, Vietnam mirrors its communist neighbor the PRC by emphasizing party centrality in determining fisheries policy and "propagating the domestic law on fishing and . . . IUU fishing."[114] Like the PRC, Vietnam has elevated its coast guard to an armed service, garrisoned and built up its Spratly reefs, and employed aggressive maritime militia forces.[115]

The Philippines has similarly objected to assertions of Chinese historic or traditional fisheries rights in its jurisdictional waters. As in the Vietnamese case, these objections crystallized in response to the PRC's fishing bans. When the banned area was extended to 12 degrees north latitude in 2012, encompassing Philippines-claimed waters around Scarborough Shoal, the Philippine government announced: "Our position is we do not recognize China's fishing ban in as much as portions of the ban encompass our EEZ."[116] The Philippines' objections have also manifested in various ways through its arbitral suit. In particular, the Philippines contested Chinese efforts to prevent Filipino fishing near various disputed features. These official responses are observable since at least 1995, when China seized Mischief Reef and sought to prevent Philippine fishing around that submerged feature over Philippine protests that the waters "are part of the Philippines' EEZ," a complaint also lodged regarding Second Thomas Shoal, another LTE.[117]

Philippine law enforcement has frequently arrested Chinese fishermen, but this has typically occurred in undisputed waters in which the Chinese are conducting IUU fishing rather than trying to exercise resource rights.[118] Prior to PRC "escort" patrols for the Chinese fishing fleet, the Philippines also periodically cracked down in waters surrounding disputed Spratly features. Philippine officials have invoked their UNCLOS entitlements in those instances, as they did in 2011 when maritime police, enforcing Philippine laws, arrested eleven Chinese fishermen at Half-Moon Shoal in the southeast Spratlys.[119] The "Scarborough Shoal Incident" of 2012 was precipitated by a Philippines' law enforcement action in which a naval vessel, the BRP *Gregorio del Pillar* (itself a decommissioned US Coast Guard cutter, transferred to augment the low capacity of Philippines maritime law enforcement), attempted to detain Chinese poachers. The rapid arrival of Chinese maritime law enforcement to prevent the arrest of these fishermen was the first instance of an effective PRC "counter–law enforcement" action against the Philippines, and it initiated a standoff that culminated in PRC control of the feature.[120]

The Philippines Department of Foreign Affairs has also objected to China's "traditional fishing" claims at both Scarborough Shoal and Whitsun (Julian Felipe) Reef, announcing of the latter that it "rejects China's assertion that Julian Felipe Reef and its waters are their 'traditional fishing grounds.' Tradition yields to law whether or not it is regarded as traditional fishing. The UNCLOS—to which both the Republic of the Philippines and China are parties—and the final and binding 12 July 2016 Award in the South China Sea Arbitration are clearly the only norm applicable to this situation."[121]

In the case of Scarborough Shoal, the Philippines has asserted its own traditional fishing rights within the territorial sea of that feature. In light of China's "de facto control" of the feature and its surrounding waters, the Philippines has maintained its sovereignty claim while seeking to continue fishing in the area in accordance with "a general rule of international law that requires a state to respect long and uninterrupted fishing by the nationals of another state in its territorial sea."[122] In so doing, they employ the same historical reasoning that animates the Chinese claim, though they limit it expressly to the territorial sea. This amounts to acquiescence, in principle, to the Chinese position that traditional fishing rights are compatible with UNCLOS. However, it is also a rejection of the superiority of such rights over UNCLOS entitlements and of the PRC practice of applying them beyond the territorial sea.[123]

Indonesia has likewise maintained a categorical opposition to any Chinese fishing rights that are not derived from UNCLOS entitlements. Its foreign ministry has objected in particular to the illegitimacy of China's extension of resource rights into Indonesian jurisdictional waters: "The PRC's historical claim on the [Indonesian] EEZ on the grounds that Chinese fishermen have long been active in these waters is unilateral, has no legal basis, and has never been recognized by UNCLOS. This argument has been discussed and countered by the SCS Tribunal's 2016 award. Indonesia also rejects the term 'relevant waters' claimed by the PRC because this term is not well-known and is not in accordance with UNCLOS."[124] As in the Philippine case, the Indonesians do not recognize any form of traditional fishing rights (nor any PRC jurisdictional zone) that derogates from its exclusive sovereign rights.

Indonesian law enforcement has been active against Chinese (and other) fishing in its Natuna EEZ, sometimes seizing and sinking offending vessels.[125] Such seizures occurred regularly prior to 2009, but since then China's fishing fleet has sometimes been accompanied by law enforcement "escorts" that have periodically interfered with Indonesian law enforcement and prevented it from seizing vessels and making arrests.[126] The southwesternmost PRC outpost at Fiery Cross Reef has been vital to resupplying and sustaining these increasing Chinese law enforcement activities across the southern tier of the SCS. These actions in turn enable a growing Chinese fishing presence and overwhelm the limited Indonesian capacity to enforce its laws. Indonesia has resorted to a significant upgrade of its military presence and capability in the area, and it now deploys major surface combatants from an upgraded base at Natuna Besar.[127]

The increasingly southerly thrust of PRC enforcement of its fishing rights has similarly challenged Malaysian maritime law enforcement. Where Malaysia had periodically arrested Chinese fishermen in the southern section of the Spratlys within its EEZ claim, these actions have more recently been stymied by the presence of larger Chinese fishing fleets with armed government escorts.[128] The first reported incident occurred in April 2010, when a Chinese fisheries law enforcement vessel was challenged by the Royal Malaysian Navy as it escorted Chinese fishing boats around Swallow Reef.[129] Malaysian officials began openly criticizing Chinese "intrusions" into this area in 2013. By 2015, Malaysia's National Security Minister Shahidan Kassim publicized the presence of CCG vessels at the South Luconia Shoals and announced upgraded law enforcement efforts to counter "the movement of illegal foreign fishermen there."[130] He told foreign press that "this is not an area with overlapping claims. In this case, we're taking diplomatic action."[131] In response, China's diplomats denied knowledge of Chinese vessels in the area, thus downplaying their claimed resource rights in the area.[132] In 2020, the Malaysian government published a report documenting six diplomatic protests to the PRC in the period 2016–2019, at least one of which specifically objected to China's claim to fishing rights at South Luconia Shoals on the basis of Malaysian sovereign rights in the area.[133]

China's imposition of seasonal fishing bans in the SCS has occasioned repeated diplomatic protests from Vietnam and the Philippines, whose claimed entitlements fall within the restricted areas. The bans have not specially affected Malaysia, Indonesia, or Brunei, whose claims all lie south of 12 degrees north latitude.[134] These littoral states on the southern tier (with the exception of Brunei) have objected instead to the persistent presence of PRC fishing vessels and law enforcement in their claimed EEZs. Indonesia's law enforcement has had several direct confrontations with their PRC counterparts; Malaysia has kept a lower profile but nonetheless has operationally and diplomatically contested Chinese fishing and fisheries law enforcement.[135] Within the southeast Asian region overall, there is observable and consistent opposition to China's claims to fisheries rights within EEZs claimed by other states.

Fisheries Cooperation with the PRC

The highly contentious law enforcement dynamics in the South China Sea are less prevalent in the East China Sea and Yellow Sea. Without PRC historic or traditional fishing rights claims in the disputed areas, and with only the Diaoyu/Senkaku Islands the source of sovereignty disputes, Japan and South Korea have joined China in cooperative fisheries and law enforcement arrangements covering most of their overlapping EEZ claims. In the SCS, the only such agreement is with Vietnam in the Gulf of Tonkin (Beibu). The terms and implementation of these agreements are important indicators of the degree to which these specially affected states acquiesce to PRC fisheries claims.[136]

Japan and China both ratified UNCLOS in June 1996, and their mutual intent to declare EEZs led to the negotiation of a fisheries agreement between the parties covering much of those newly overlapping entitlements. The 1997 Sino-Japanese Fisheries Agreement (effective 1 June 2000) defined three areas of agreed fisheries rules, the largest of which concerned the uncontested EEZ claims of each country.[137] The smaller "joint" fisheries area is the "Provisional Measures Zone" (PMZ, 暂定措施水域) defined by ten points covering the main area of their overlapping 200nm claims in the ECS.[138] A Joint Fisheries Commission meets annually to determine catch and vessel quotas and other relevant management measures in the area, which should also "take into account the impact on traditional fisheries" (Art. 7.2). The parties exercise "flag state jurisdiction" in the PMZ, policing only their own vessels (Art. 7.3). The area south of the PMZ is exempted from the agreement (Art. 6). These are the waters within 200 nautical miles of the Diaoyu/Senkaku Islands, in which the parties could not agree to any fisheries arrangements "in view of the sensitivity of the Diaoyu Islands and Taiwan issues."[139] Although much bilateral fishing controversy has also occurred around the Diaoyu/Senkaku, the dispute concerns sovereignty rather than resource rights.

The parties also agreed that their nationals could be licensed to fish the other's undisputed EEZ according to the "relevant laws and regulations of the other contracting party" (Art. 2).[140] Each state determines the number of vessels of the other state permitted, their catch quotas and species, required conservation measures, and other operating conditions—that is, each state enforces its own EEZ laws. Notably, those determinations may include "traditional fishing activities" (传统渔业活动) (Art. 3). In an annex to the agreement, the parties affirmed that they would "respect the existing fishery activities, and consider the traditional operations of the other contracting party."[141] Further specifying these activities, an attached codicil from the PRC ambassador to Japan affirms that the parties agreed that "Chinese squid fishing vessels should be able to operate in the Sea of Japan and the EEZ of Japan in the N. Pacific without paying license fees." There is no corresponding concession of such privileges to Japanese fishermen in Chinese EEZs.

Japan thereby acquiesced to certain Chinese traditional fishing practices within its UNCLOS-entitled EEZ. While the terms of the instrument do not accord a "right" to these fishermen, they acknowledge that existing patterns of Chinese fishing in areas beyond claimed PRC jurisdiction should be given consideration. This protocol differs significantly from the conflictual circumstances in the SCS, because PRC fishing in Japan's EEZ is *non-exclusive* of Japanese fishing and indeed allowed only with Japan's prior consent. That this consent has been granted is significant, but the agreement does not bind Japan to continue the practice. In subsequent meetings of the Joint Fisheries Commission, China has agreed to reduce the number and catch of squid fishing boats in Japan's EEZ.[142] In further contrast to the South China Sea, PRC law enforcement has not escorted or otherwise protected its nationals when they fish in Japan's undisputed EEZ in the Sea of Japan and the north Pacific.

The China-Korea fisheries relationship has produced frequent strife involving Chinese fishing vessels in the Yellow Sea and northern ECS.[143] Each year, Korean fisheries law enforcement seizes (and releases on bond) hundreds of Chinese vessels and makes thousands of arrests, but these incidents largely concern IUU fishing in the uncontested South Korean EEZ.[144] Overlapping EEZ claims after UNCLOS led the parties to conclude the Sino-Korean Fisheries Agreement in 2001.[145] The agreement mirrors the Sino-Japanese instrument in its main contours: a "Provisional Measures Zone" in the center of the Yellow Sea with uncontested EEZ on either side, in which a Joint Fisheries Commission meets annually to determine procedures and limits for the year.

In contrast to the Sino-Japanese deal, the parties are not required to recognize the other's traditional fishing, though they may consider their own traditional fishing as a factor in determining measures in the EEZ areas outside of the PMZ (Art. 3). Further distinguishing the agreement on this matter, the bilateral commission is not obliged to consider this factor, as it is in the Japanese case.[146] Korea thus does not acquiesce to any PRC traditional fishing, treating all of the waters pending boundary delimitation in accordance with sovereign rights under UNCLOS. The parties have allocated even numbers of vessels and volumes of catch in their respective EEZs, with no evident preferential rights awarded to either state in the other's EEZ.[147]

The PRC's final fisheries agreement was completed along with its maritime boundary agreement with Vietnam in the Gulf of Tonkin. It establishes a "Common Fisheries Zone" (CFZ, 共同渔区), which extends 30.5 nautical miles on either side of the agreed boundary (Art. 3). Within this area, as in the PMZs with Japan and Korea, the two parties implement a joint scheme for licensing and managing fisheries (Arts. 6–7, 13). Yet unlike those zones in the ECS and Yellow Sea, which lack an agreed maritime boundary, the parties in the Gulf of Tonkin exercise exclusive jurisdiction on their side of the maritime boundary and often enforce their laws against the other nation's vessels in that zone.[148]

The lack of any provisions regarding traditional fisheries is an important omission in this agreement. China claims two traditional fishing grounds in the Beibu Gulf, one north of the CFZ, the other to the south off the coast of Hainan.[149] Meanwhile, China has long rejected Vietnam's claim to a "historic bay" in the Gulf of Tonkin entailing exclusive fishing rights. An MFA official argued that among the factors disqualifying Vietnam's claim were the lack of PRC acquiescence and the demonstrated usage by foreign fishermen of supposedly exclusive waters and resources.[150] If China's proposed rule on historic rights to traditional fishing were uniformly applied, its own claims would be disqualified according to these conditions.

In the Tonkin (Beibu) Gulf, the PRC has quietly dismantled its traditional fishing practice, agreeing to a four-year "transitional arrangement" north of the CFZ that gradually phased out "existing fisheries activities" (Art. 11). The PRC undertook an intensive campaign to prevent Chinese fishermen in Hainan from breaching the agreement. Wu Zhuang, director of the SCS Fisheries Bureau, told reporters that "in order to make the masses of fishermen, fisheries management departments, and wider community understand [that their traditional fishing rights were being phased out], we have organized large-scale, long-term propaganda, education, and training work."[151] These official efforts to suppress PRC traditional fishing have not prevented Chinese fishermen from conducting IUU fishing in those areas. Still, the agreement relinquishes roughly one third of China's claimed traditional fishing grounds in the gulf; one specialist projected 12,000 Hainanese fishermen abandoned their livelihood as a result.[152]

In its three standing fisheries agreements, China has relinquished different aspects of its claimed fishing rights, accepting in practice that sovereign rights in recognized EEZs prevail over traditional rights—but only by agreement. In the Gulf of Tonkin, China established a boundary and accepted exclusive Vietnamese rights on its side that barred its own traditional fishing practices. In the Yellow Sea, China did not sustain any traditional fishing claims in Korea's claimed EEZ. In the East China Sea, China negotiated for Japan to "consider" and "respect" these rights, but it tacitly accepts exclusive Japanese jurisdiction in its uncontested EEZ. In interaction with these specially affected states, the PRC has agreed to dismantle aspects of its historic rights claims to fisheries, revealing a non-uniform practice in enforcing its supposed rule.[153]

In the Spratly area, however, China's traditional fishing claims are increasingly consistent and uniform. Beijing directs fishing activity to the southern reaches of the South China Sea and provides increasing law enforcement support for the exploitation of living resources within other states' claimed EEZs. These practices are distinct from the garden-variety IUU fishing that so often embroils Chinese fishermen in controversies in foreign EEZs.[154] They are a clear expression of the preferred Chinese rule, which prescribes traditional fishing rights arising from historic rights and sovereignty over the disputed features. The

TABLE 11

SPECIALLY AFFECTED STATE RESPONSES TO PRC FISHERIES PRACTICE

	Traditional fishing	*Seasonal fisheries ban*
Brunei	Acquiesce	Acquiesce
Indonesia	Object	N/A
Japan	Acquiesce (regulated by Japan)	N/A
Korea	N/A	Object
Malaysia	Object	N/A
Philippines	Object[a]	Object
Vietnam	Object	Object

[a]The Philippines has not objected to PRC traditional fishing practices in disputed territorial seas.

specially affected states, however, have repeatedly objected in formal and operational manner to China's assertion that this rule supersedes their sovereign rights under UNCLOS (Table 11).

RULES ON HYDROCARBON DEVELOPMENT

Between a quarter and a third of the world's hydrocarbons are now produced offshore, with natural gas a particularly fast-growing segment of that production as new technologies make it more readily exploitable.[155] Since offshore oil was first drilled in 1947 off the Louisiana coast, disputes over rights to exploit it have been proliferating. East Asia is no exception. A 1968 geophysical survey conducted by the International Committee for Coordination of Joint Prospecting for Mineral Resources in Asian Offshore Areas confirmed the presence of oil and gas resources in the SCS and ECS, with potentially significant reservoirs in the ECS near the Okinawa Trough.[156] China and other East Asian states swiftly mobilized to expand and reinforce their resource claims, abetted by the continental shelf regime codified in the 1958 Geneva Convention on the Continental Shelf, which did not establish a fixed breadth for coastal state claims but conferred exclusive rights to the resources of the seabed.[157] The 1982 Convention codified the EEZ, providing an additional, overlapping set of law of the sea rules pertaining to the same areas. As it does for living resources, the Convention allocates exclusive rights to the non-living resources to the coastal state; it also confers the right to build "artificial islands" required for offshore energy drilling (UNCLOS, Art. 56).

China has an especially acute interest in the resource potential of regional waters. As a net importer of foreign oil (since 1993), China depends on energy shipments from the Middle East, Russia, and Africa to meet overwhelming growth in domestic demand. PRC leadership thus perceives acute threats to China's energy security and especially prizes any domestically owned hydrocarbons. Resources developed under PRC jurisdiction are presumably less vulnerable to disruption.[158] Although the UNCLOS "provisional measures" doctrine applies to disputed non-living resources, China has not reached any significant cooperative agreements on oil and gas within disputed zones. Its practices in claiming and enforcing rights to these resources are a potential pathway for changing resource rules.

PRC Practice on Hydrocarbon Development
The geographic scope of China's claims to hydrocarbon resources is determined firstly by its declared entitlement claims to continental shelf and EEZ. These are the "natural prolongation" of the continental shelf into the Yellow Sea and ECS as well as the vague claim to EEZ and continental shelf from the SCS islands, perhaps defined by the nine-dash line. Because there is no historical or traditional practice of exploiting oil and gas, the PRC does not clearly appeal to any additional rules in support of these claims.[159] China has explored but not actively exploited any seabed hydrocarbons from disputed seabed. Instead, the PRC has practiced a rule of denying other states' rights to exploit those resources within their entitlements claimed under UNCLOS.

The first PRC sector opened to foreign investment in "Reform and Opening" was offshore oil, initiated in the 1982 Regulation of the PRC on the Exploitation of Offshore Petroleum Resources in Cooperation with Foreign Enterprises.[160] These regulations apply to petroleum resources "owned by the PRC" in "the internal waters, territorial sea, continental shelf, and other waters under PRC jurisdiction" (Art. 2). This is the first formal PRC claim to rights deriving from a continental shelf.[161] Amendments in 2001, 2011, and 2013 have not included EEZ rights or jurisdiction in defining the scope or substance of the claim; this is consistent with the PRC's emphasis on the continental shelf natural prolongation rule so prominent in its ECS and Yellow Sea boundary delimitation disputes. According to the 1986 Mineral Resources Law, the PRC State Council "exercises the state's ownership of all mineral resources" in the undefined area of maritime jurisdiction in which purportedly exclusive PRC resource rights obtain.[162] This is a uniform and consistent standard, though it leaves considerable ambiguity about the geographic scope of China's claimed rights. These must be assessed in its operational practice to utilize—and prevent others from utilizing—these oil and gas resources.

Efforts to Exploit Disputed Offshore Oil and Gas

China's hydrocarbon activity in disputed offshore waters has consisted mainly of surveys, diplomatic objections, and operational "countermeasures" (对策) to interfere with the survey and production activities of other claimant states (and the various foreign firms licensed under those states' domestic law). In the South China Sea, the three principal disputed oil and/or gas fields in which these activities have occurred are at Vanguard Bank (万安滩), Luconia (Sarawan) Shoals (南/北康暗沙), and Reed (Recto) Bank (礼乐滩), all south of 12 degrees north latitude. In the East China Sea, the most acute area of hydrocarbon contention is the Xihu/Okinawa gas fields, which lie within the overlapping zone of Japanese and Chinese entitlement claims (see Figure 3).[163]

In the ECS, China's efforts to develop resources in disputed zones began with a 2003 China National Offshore Oil Corporation (CNOOC) joint venture with Royal Dutch Shell and Unocal to develop gas at the Chunxiao (Shirikaba) field (in "Xihu Gas Fields," Figure 3). Japan objected quickly to China's unilateral exploration at Chunxiao, where they had commissioned a survey and determined that the gas reservoir had geological features that likely extend to the Japanese side of its claimed median line.[164] Both of China's foreign partners withdrew in 2004, but CNOOC continued seismic surveys while the MFA rebuffed Japan's complaints about the activity, refusing to share any of the seismic data on the basis that the survey was conducted based on sovereign rights within the PRC exclusive economic zone. Reiterating those same exclusive grounds, PRC officials criticized Japanese surveys on the Japanese side of the median line conducted later that year. CNOOC continued surveys in the area into 2005; its survey vessels were escorted on occasion by PLAN destroyers and MLE vessels that warned off Japanese vessels and aircraft.[165] At least fourteen other PRC oil or gas platforms are clustered in this area nearby the provisional median line. These practices are consistent with China's claim to natural prolongation of its continental shelf in the area, though they reveal a de facto sensitivity to the existence of the unrecognized median line.

In the SCS, China began surveying as early as the 1980s. "Comprehensive surveys" conducted by China Academy of Sciences vessels from 1984 to 1986 observably trace the contours of the nine-dash line claim, indicating the desired scope of PRC resource rights in the SCS, even though no specific, official linkage between hydrocarbons and historic rights claims has been made.[166] Some forty years after those initial surveys, however, China's SCS hydrocarbon production remains solely in the undisputed northern tier.

Beginning in 2019, however, PRC survey and law enforcement vessels began operating more conspicuously in the southern tier, engaging in more assertive operational behaviors with previously unhindered Malaysian and Indonesian hydrocarbon exploration and drilling vessels.[167] In December 2021, the PRC issued its first publicly reported formal objection to Indonesian drilling in an area of long-standing, uncontested Indonesian oil and gas production.[168] This development marks a notable expansion in the evident scope of China's claims to resource rights. It adds a measure of uniformity to its claim across the SCS—albeit at the expense of its consistency over time. By and large, China had avoided clearly asserting resource rights in this remote area, but it has begun to match its operational practice to its notional diplomatic claim to resource rights throughout the nine-dash line.[169] The likeliest explanation for this inconsistent position is the PRC's increased capacity to operate and sustain MLE and survey vessels in the far southern reaches of the SCS, not least because of the facilities at nearby Fiery Cross Reef.

Several prior PRC efforts to develop resources in disputed zones further south have floundered, beginning with the first PRC concession to a disputed oil and gas block in 1992, in Vanguard Bank at Wan'An Bei-21

(WAB-21). The large, 25,000-square-kilometer block is drawn in such a way that it infringes only on Vietnam's claimed entitlements, not those of Malaysia or Indonesia.[170] A small American firm, Crestone Energy, won the lease with apparent support from the US State Department and with assurances from Beijing that the project would be protected by PLA naval might.[171] Over Vietnamese objections that the area lies on its continental shelf, China justified its action as an exercise of its territorial sovereignty but did not invoke specific resource rights.[172] Crestone proceeded to conduct seismic surveys and began drilling exploratory wells, even as Vietnam leased out an overlapping block to a consortium including Mobil Oil Corporation and began surveying operations. The Crestone exploration did not yield promising results, and the firm sold its lease in 1996 to another American firm (Benton Oil and Gas), which by 2014 opted to sell those rights to the current leaseholder, the PRC firm Brightoil.[173]

From the Crestone controversy onward, China periodically objected to Vietnamese, Philippine, and Malaysian oil exploration and active production along the southern and eastern tier of the SCS.[174] Vietnamese joint ventures to explore blocks along the west side of the SCS drew special focus from the MFA, which issued some eighteen protests in 2006–2007 alone, marking the beginning of a more assertive posture on long-standing commercial production.[175] Some of these Vietnamese zones clearly lay outside the nine-dash line claim, but others appeared to straddle it or lie entirely inside it.[176] Chinese survey vessels began extensive exploration in the areas south of the Paracels in 2007. That same year, PRC maritime law enforcement vessels began to actively interfere with the survey operations of foreign firms in disputed oil and gas blocks, conducting "special operations" like ramming a Vietnamese oil supply ship.[177] Chinese law enforcement vessels detained and "expelled" a Philippine seismic survey vessel operating at Reed Bank in March 2011, and, in May of that year, severed the towed seismic array of a Vietnamese survey ship.[178] Chinese diplomats protested in 2010 against the Philippines gas blocks SC54, SC14, SC58, SC63, "and other nearby service contracts as located deep within China's nine-dash line."[179] Yet none of these blocks lies wholly within the claim lines, and several appear to lie entirely outside of the dashes.

In June 2012, CNOOC complemented the government's assertion of PRC rights in these disputed parts of the SCS by tendering foreign bids for nine large oil blocks stacked along the western edge of the nine-dash line (see Figure 3).[180] These lie southwest of the Spratlys, and they were the site of the first PRC efforts to develop hydrocarbons in the SCS beyond the Paracel area. Although the PRC nominally claimed these areas under sovereign rights from its EEZ, at least one of the blocks (BS16) lies partially beyond 200 nautical miles from any SCS feature. Except for one area in the center of these blocks, they overlap entirely with blocks also tendered by Vietnam, a number of which have been contracted by foreign firms from Canada, India, Japan, Russia, Spain, and the United States.[181] No foreign firm has yet contracted with China to develop any of these nine disputed blocks.

In several subsequent tenders to foreign firms (2012, 2017, 2019), CNOOC has not offered blocks in the southern or eastern parts of the nine-dash line despite the existence of several past and current oil and gas projects in those sectors that currently or formerly produced oil or gas for other claimant states.[182] The absence of such activity beyond the western sector of the SCS is a non-uniform practice. The intensity of PRC claims to areas claimed by Vietnam, both from the Spratlys and the Paracels in the western part of the SCS, is not matched in other sectors, which also have active hydrocarbon reservoirs. A signal event in 2014 sheds light on this non-uniformity and its implications for the hydrocarbon rules that the PRC seeks to advance.

The Case of HYSY-981

The sole case of active PRC drilling within the EEZ or continental shelf entitlement of another state beyond any provisional median line is that of CNOOC's HYSY-981 (海洋石油-981) deep-sea drilling rig. On 2 May 2014, the PRC Marine Safety Administration announced that the HYSY-981 would conduct exploratory drilling at a site 17 nautical miles southwest of Triton (Zhongjian) Island in the Paracels, declaring a 1nm "alert zone" (警戒区) around the rig.[183] Vietnamese fishing, militia, and law enforcement vessels quickly swarmed the area to evict the PRC from the site, but they encountered a well-coordinated cordon of PRC fishing, militia, and law enforcement vessels that frustrated their efforts and sank a Vietnamese fishing boat.[184]

The PRC's response sheds light on the nature of China's claimed rule for the resources of this area. First, Chinese diplomats responded to

Vietnam's objection by asserting that the oil rig was "within the territorial waters and contiguous zone of Xisha Islands and the operation is a normal oil and gas exploration activity carried out within the undisputed waters under the management of China."[185] Refusal to acknowledge that these are indeed disputed waters is a facet of China's practice only in the Paracels area. Second, the rig was moved by 27 May 2014 to an area east of the median line.[186] The location was still 17 nautical miles from the Triton Island basepoint and still in waters where Vietnam claims an EEZ entitlement, but the rig's new placement reverted to the prior practice of tacitly respecting the provisional boundary established under the 2004 agreement.[187] The operation was then cut short on 15 July 2014, a month ahead of the announced schedule.[188] These two practices demonstrate a lack of uniformity in China's claim across the nine-dash line area, showing first defiance then deference to the norm of a median line, and also treating the Paracels as distinct from other island groups.

In contrast to the muddled legal rule advanced by this short-lived drilling gambit, the PRC's on-water operation was well-executed. China's MFA alleged that some 63 Vietnamese vessels were on site at the peak of the confrontation, and it counted 1,416 instances of Vietnamese vessels "ramming" PRC government ships.[189] The PRC's response employed fishing vessels as an outer periphery, supported by MLE vessels, with PLAN hovering over the horizon.[190] This "echelon defense" demonstrated growing sophistication in preventing other claimants from interfering with the PRC's claimed resource rights.[191] Nonetheless, the rig did not ultimately return to produce from that site, and China has not subsequently conducted any drilling on the Vietnamese side of the median line, a notable inconsistency.

In summary, the PRC has achieved hydrocarbon production only in de facto undisputed zones. Foreign production, meanwhile, has proceeded unmolested in areas on China's side of provisional median lines of overlapping jurisdiction in the ECS and in the SCS. Such PRC acquiescence amounts to tacit recognition of opposable claims to hydrocarbon rights based on other states' EEZ and continental shelf claims. The more recent rounds of overt PRC protest against foreign hydrocarbon production mark an important move toward uniformity, but, by the same token, they reveal inconsistency over time. Finally, the HYSY-981 incident shows that this tacit recognition is non-uniform in the SCS, evidently

TABLE 12

PRC PRACTICE OF HYDROCARBON RULES

PRC-preferred rule	Uniformity (geographic)	Consistency (over time)	Detail
Natural prolongation of continental shelf rights supersede EEZ	No	Yes	Recognition of median lines in ECS and near Paracels (except HYSY-981)
Exclusive PRC hydrocarbon rights within all "sea areas under PRC jurisdiction"	No[a]	Yes	No disputed blocks tendered except in western SCS

[a]Growing MLE and survey vessel presence in the southern SCS since 2019 marks a notable recent change toward a more uniform practice in all "sea areas under PRC jurisdiction."

applying only to the Spratlys but not the Paracels, where China refuses to recognize Vietnam's claims.

However inconsistent its operational practice, the PRC has issued consistent (if vague) diplomatic claims to hydrocarbons throughout its claimed entitlements in the ECS and within the nine-dash line in the SCS. Lacking a historic rights justification for the former, China's assertion of hydrocarbon rights beyond 200 nautical miles from any features exceeds any declared Chinese claims. There is no authoritative account of the frequency and location of each action to enforce China's domestic rules granting them exclusive resource rights in these disputed areas, but such countermeasures have been reported since early 2007 and have not subsisted to the present.[192] The extent to which these MLE actions have successfully established China's rights can be observed in the responses of specially affected states (Table 12).

Specially Affected State Responses to China's Hydrocarbon Practice
Japan, the Koreas, the Philippines, Malaysia, Brunei, Indonesia, and Vietnam each claim EEZ and continental shelf entitlements overlapping China's claims. With the exception of the Koreas, each state has observably pursued development of hydrocarbon resources in some areas of

overlap. They each lodged objections on the same legal basis used in their opposition to China's claimed fishing rights (that is, UNCLOS zones), which need not be retread. The key difference between the fisheries and the hydrocarbon sector is the absence of a recognizable Chinese historic rights claim to the latter. Specially affected states' practice of exploiting those claimed resources and their reactions to PRC efforts to prevent them from doing so are the key observations. Additionally, some of these states' efforts to reach joint development agreements with China provide further evidence of the extent to which they have adopted, acquiesced to, or rejected China's hydrocarbon rules.

Unilateral Development of Disputed Hydrocarbons in the SCS

In defiance of Chinese claims, several states in the South China Sea have proceeded with oil and gas development within their own claimed UNCLOS entitlements, largely along the southern tier of the SCS.[193] In 2009, a leading Chinese maritime analyst claimed that SCS littoral countries had "seized huge profits from the 19 oil fields and 44 gas fields within China's traditional boundary."[194] Until late 2021, Chinese officials avoided formally acknowledging these putative breaches of its claimed hydrocarbon rights, issuing only private diplomatic protests. However China's practice proceeds, claimant states' long-standing production from certain areas in the SCS presents a formidable practical and legal obstacle to the establishment of any rules concerning the disposition of resource rights.[195]

Indeed, industry reporting confirms that Indonesia, Malaysia, and Vietnam have each produced oil or gas in wells that lie within or straddle the PRC's nine-dash line claim, including from wells that remain active today.[196] Malaysia, in particular, is presently exploiting natural gas from at least seven wells that lie within the Chinese claim line near the Luconia Shoals.[197] China's augmented law enforcement presence and efforts to interfere in these areas have not (yet) led to acquiescence or termination of Malaysian projects.[198] Despite the PRC's operational contestation, Malaysia's projects have generally proceeded without formal objection from the PRC and without diplomatic comment from Malaysia.[199]

In 2020, during a confrontation between Chinese survey and law enforcement vessels and a Malaysian survey vessel, Malaysia's foreign minister resisted criticizing China overtly and instead called for "disputes to be resolved amicably."[200] Malaysian maritime law enforcement "monitored" the situation, with one official pinpointing the Chinese vessel "in Malaysian waters" but describing its presence in benign terms: "I do not know of its purpose but it has not done any activities that break the law."[201] Malaysia's low profile in exploiting these resources and its generally positive relations with China have not prevented the dramatic increase in PRC survey activity and law enforcement presence in the Luconia Shoals area since 2019.[202]

Indonesia likewise continues to successfully develop offshore blocks within the PRC claim, but it has faced mounting Chinese objection. In the first few months of 2021 alone, Indonesia licensed several blocks straddling the nine-dash line—including one to the Russian firm Zarubezhneft at a natural gas project at the "Tuna Block."[203] Unlike several other blocks in the area that appear to intersect only partially with the ambiguous nine-dash line, this block is clearly within the Natuna "Carve-out" (see Figure 3) and yet has drawn no formal protest from the PRC. President Joko Widodo has affirmed Indonesia's sovereign rights in the area, and in 2016 he publicly encouraged increased development: "Out of 16 blocks around Natuna, only five are producing. . . . We want to push so that they enter production stage sooner."[204] Indonesia has proceeded with these seemingly controversial oil and gas projects while continuing energy cooperation with China in other fields.[205]

Indonesia began to encounter PRC obstruction in this area beginning in July 2021, when a Chinese MLE vessel began to shadow an Indonesian drilling rig in the Tuna Block. By August, a PRC survey vessel (*Haiyang Dizhi*-10) began to operate in the vicinity of the Indonesian project, accompanied by a rotating cast of CCG vessels that operated nearby Indonesian drilling.[206] Indonesia dispatched MLE vessels of its own to protect the rig, as well as at least one naval vessel (a tanker) to shadow the *Haiyang Dizhi*-10; it also stationed as many as five more warships in the vicinity.[207] By November, the appraisal drilling campaign was completed successfully. Indonesian national security officials later publicly commented for the first time on PRC protests, noting that their "reply was very firm, that we are not going to stop the drilling because it is our sovereign right."[208] The widening geographic scope and operational intensity of Chinese practices have brought about an increasingly clear and meaningful Indonesian objection.

Vietnam has long lodged firm objections to Chinese hydrocarbon claims while steadily pursuing its own in disputed waters. Recent PRC actions have jeopardized this production. The Spanish firm Repsol began drilling in June 2017 as part of a joint venture at Vietnam's Block 136/3. Later that month, the vice-chairman of the PLA's Central Military Commission, Fan Changlong, appeared in Madrid where he reportedly warned Repsol and Spanish officials against pursuing the development. He then traveled to Hanoi for a meeting with Vietnamese leadership, during which Vietnamese sources report that he raised Block 136/03 (and Block 118, leased to Exxon further north), demanding that drilling operations cease and issuing an explicit military threat; the incident prompted Vietnam's government to order Repsol to cease its activities at that block. The following year, a forty-ship PLAN flotilla began to exercise near an adjacent Repsol block (07–03) just beginning production, eliciting a second cancellation order from Vietnam.[209] Repsol subsequently terminated its leases in Vietnam in July 2020, as did the Russian firm Rosneft, which had been producing gas at nearby Block 06–01 since 2002 but had also faced episodic challenges from Chinese law enforcement.[210]

The Philippines has faced similarly concerted Chinese interference with its efforts to exploit oil and gas blocks, largely in the Reed Bank area off the northwest coast of Palawan on the west edge of the SCS. In 2002 the Philippines awarded a contract to a firm from the United Kingdom (UK) to explore a gas block in Reed (Recto) Bank near the Malampaya gas fields, which includes some undisputed Philippine blocks under production since the 1970s. By 2010, successful preliminary exploration led to a service contract within that block (SC72) to another UK firm, Forum Energy.[211] Forum began operating survey and other service vessels in the area, but in March 2011 its vessels were confronted by two PRC law enforcement vessels. Objecting to "illegal" Chinese activities in its EEZ, the Philippines dispatched law enforcement vessels and aircraft, which secured the completion of the survey.[212] However, by December 2014 the PRC's persistent operational and diplomatic interventions brought the Philippines Department of Energy to suspend all drilling and exploration in the SCS, invoking "force majeure" on the SC72 contract.[213] This decision does not amount to acquiescence to China's claim, as the Philippines did not renounce its resource rights nor are PRC firms currently exploring or exploiting those resources. Nevertheless, it marks a significant discontinuity in the Philippines' assertion of its resource rights claims. The resumption of the Philippines' activities in the area in late 2020 came only in the context of negotiating bilateral development arrangements with China (examined below).

Overall, the observed unilateral development of hydrocarbon resources within the nine-dash line by Indonesia, Malaysia, Vietnam, and the Philippines demonstrates a lack of consistency and uniformity in China's practice of enforcing its rules on resource rights, even though the claims themselves have been consistent. In particular, Indonesia and Malaysia continue to actively produce oil and gas within areas of the southern SCS claimed by the PRC, while Vietnam and the Philippines have repeatedly faced operational and diplomatic challenges that have effectively halted production—including in zones that appear to lie beyond the nine-dash line. China's growing law enforcement, fishing, and survey vessel presence in the Luconia Shoals has yet to halt Malaysian or Indonesian operations.

Attempted Joint Development of Disputed Hydrocarbons

Specially affected states have encountered persistent Chinese protests and interference over disputed hydrocarbons, but they have also heard faint overtures of cooperation from Beijing. Since the 1970s, PRC diplomats have publicly rehearsed the long-standing PRC policy line on maritime disputes—namely, "Sovereignty is ours, shelve the disputes, and pursue joint development" (albeit omitting the first clause on sovereignty, which is for domestic consumption).[214] Yet in over forty years of espousing this policy, the PRC has not achieved any actual joint development of hydrocarbons.[215] Meanwhile Japan, South Korea, Malaysia, Vietnam, and Indonesia have each successfully reached joint development agreements (JDAs) with one or more of their maritime neighbors to cooperatively develop hydrocarbon resources in disputed zones.[216] China's unsuccessful efforts to conclude agreements with these states provide important illustrations of how specially affected states have responded to China's proposed resource rules in practice.

The first meaningful steps toward a hydrocarbon JDA involving China came in the form of a "Joint Marine Seismic Undertaking" (JMSU) agreement among the national oil companies of China, the Philippines, and Vietnam in 2005.[217] Without prejudice to any maritime or territorial claims, the agreement designated a 142,886-square-kilometer area west of Palawan (covering the Reed Bank) for joint seismic surveys and scientific research. The agreement was effective for three years, and it made no provisions for commercial exploitation of resources.[218] No surveys were jointly conducted, in large part because of domestic opposition in the Philippines, where a constitutional provision ruled out the JMSU's designation of China National Offshore Oil Corporation as the lead survey entity.[219] In effect, the agreement failed because of the Philippines' objection to China's claim to resource rights throughout the scope of the nine-dash line.

The Philippines' constitutional requirement to control any exploration or development of resources under its jurisdiction continues to affect prospects for joint development with China.[220] A 2018 bilateral memorandum of understanding is presently in effect as a framework for their potential cooperation "in relevant maritime areas." The agreement establishes a steering committee composed of representatives from the foreign and energy ministries of each state, which can designate "cooperation areas" and appoint ad hoc working groups to negotiate the specific "technical and commercial arrangements that will apply in the relevant working area.[221] No cooperation areas or working groups have yet been reported, but beginning in late 2020, the Philippines reopened exploration and drilling activities that had been suspended due to tensions with China in 2014.[222] Notably, the Philippines has continued to invest in the promising SC72 find with a Canadian-UK partner, but that block's clear status inside the nine-dash line makes it a likely candidate for a PRC challenge and a long shot for joint development.[223] A PRC agreement to jointly develop that block as it is designated under Philippine law would be, in effect, a recognition of the Philippines' sovereign rights over those disputed resources and an inconsistency in China's claim to those resources. Whether China and the Philippines ultimately agree on a joint development (and, if so, which blocks they agree to develop) will be consequential for the status of China's proposed rule that the Spratlys entitle the PRC to exclusive rights to those resources.

China's second significant effort to develop a JDA began with Sino-Japanese negotiations in 2004, after Japan discovered the Chinese exploring for gas at Chunxiao. After several contentious rounds of negotiation, Japan and China reached an informal accord in December 2007 to establish a joint development zone in a 2,700-square-kilometer section of the northern East China Sea.[224] The small zone is nested within the much larger fisheries Provisional Measures Zone and is "just a little larger than Kanagawa Prefecture" according to Japan's foreign minister, Masahiko Koumura.[225] In June 2008, the two states' foreign ministries announced a "principled consensus" (原则共识) "to cooperate without prejudice to the legal positions of both parties during the transition period before the demarcation is realized." They stipulated to "select sites agreed by both parties for joint development" and "work hard to fulfill their respective domestic procedures for the implementation" of the project. The joint statement also allowed Japanese corporations to "participate, *in accordance with Chinese laws*" in the existing development at Chunxiao (Shirikaba) in the Xihu gas fields south of the joint development zone.[226] The parties agreed to make efforts to conclude a formal accord on the matter.[227]

The prospects for implementing the "principled consensus" were dashed immediately on the basis of mutual concerns about different elements of the deal. Speaking with the press the evening of the announcement, Foreign Minister Koumura was immediately confronted with the question whether Japan's investment in Chunxiao/Shirikaba under Chinese law would effectively cede that area to the PRC. Koumura explained the arrangement as allowing "Japanese corporations to invest in the location where China has already undertaken development on the Chinese side of the median line that Japan draws."[228] Japan had actively contested China's development of Chunxiao since its discovery in May 2004, awarding rival concessions to the block to Teikoku Oil and conducting naval surveillance overflights while PLAN submarines and destroyers monitored Japanese survey activities.[229] Acknowledging the legitimacy of China's operation there by investing in it under PRC law was not a welcome prospect for Japan.

Koumura faced additional pushback on whether the small northern area designated for joint exploration was equitably determined. He responded that Japan and China could not agree on where the median line was to begin with and that the "respective volumes of the area that has been assigned on either side of the median line drawn by Japan" do not "have a whole lot of meaning."[230] No median line appears in the maps published by either foreign ministry in the joint statement. Nonetheless, the perception remained that Japan had not secured an equitable split of the northern zone and, further, that the implied acquiescence to China's ownership over the Chunxiao/Shirikaba field made the agreement unbalanced from the outset.

For Beijing, the deal was unpalatable due to its implication that a median line—whether Japan's or China's projection—had been determinative. Yang Jiechi spoke to the press on the issue, emphasizing that the agreement "fully embodies that China has the sovereign rights over Chunxiao oil and gas field." Asked for further comment on whether the deal was "based on the 'median line,'" Yang stated that "China has never and will not recognize the so-called 'median line' as advocated by Japan," stressing China's claim to natural prolongation of its continental shelf.[231] Meanwhile, Japanese media and politicians described an agreement on "the development of a gas field that straddles the median line, [which] can be interpreted that China accepted Japan's proposals based on its median line claim, even if it was in a limited manner."[232] Despite Yang's protestation that the deal "will not affect China's sovereign rights and jurisdiction over the East China Sea," the perception that it had acknowledged the legitimacy of a Japanese median line rendered the deal still-born.[233]

No joint exploration or investment in either area has occurred to date, but the agreement may still be interpreted as reinforcing the role of a China-Japan median line in delimitation and disposition of seabed resources, thus weakening the consistency of the PRC claim. China has subsequently built as many as a dozen new drilling platforms in Xihu gas fields adjacent to Chunxiao on the west (PRC) side of the putative median line (including at Tianwaitian, Canxue, and Duanqiao, which Japan contends siphon off resources from the Japanese side).[234] These actions drew Japanese protests and Chinese counter-protests that these areas "lie completely within China's rights and jurisdiction."[235] This assertion effectively reinforces the median line equidistance rule that China rejects.

In sum, the specially affected states have lodged consistent objections to Chinese resource rights in disputed areas, with the particular effect of forcing recognition of the equidistance or median line principle as a qualifier for China's exercise of those rights. This manifests both near the Paracels, where China withdrew its rig, and in the ECS, where Japan negotiated an agreement that tacitly incorporates a median line. Meanwhile, in the southern reaches of the SCS, Malaysia and Indonesia have continuously produced natural gas without drawing any pointed objections from the PRC, an omission that calls into question the uniformity of its claim in that sector. Vietnam and the Philippines also engaged in some unilateral development, but persistent Chinese countermeasures since 2011 have gradually brought them to heel. Several foreign firms have abandoned contracted projects with Vietnam and the Philippines as a result of Chinese pressure (at least in substantial part), potentially reinforcing the validity of the Chinese-preferred rule. The Philippines is now furthest along in joint development talks, but these pose an acute challenge to China's rights claims if they permit development of blocks registered and operated under Philippine law (Table 13). That China has not been able to develop disputed resources itself while specially affected

TABLE 13

SPECIALLY AFFECTED STATE RESPONSES TO PRC
HYDROCARBON PRACTICE

	Extended continental shelf supersedes EEZ	Exclusive PRC rights throughout EEZ/continental shelf
Brunei	Acquiesce	Acquiesce
Indonesia	Object	Object
Japan	Object	Object
Malaysia	Object	Object
Philippines	Object	Acquiesce[a]
Vietnam	Object	Acquiesce[b]

[a]The Philippines government would surely object to this coding. However, several Philippine contracts terminated operations in response to PRC objections and interference; further, the Philippines has negotiated with the PRC for joint development in zones that are in the Philippines' EEZ and continental shelf beyond the median line between Spratly features and the Philippine mainland.

[b]Similarly, the Vietnamese government would object to this coding, but its practice provides clear evidence that Vietnam has acquiesced to certain Chinese assertions of PRC hydrocarbon rights in disputed zones.

states have done so weakens the potential impact of its preferred rules for hydrocarbons.

Synthesizing China's varying assertions of rights and jurisdiction over resources, we find that they generally do not advance consistent and uniform rules that might apply in other circumstances. However, we can conclude that they amount to an assertion of special kind of non-exclusive or preferential right. These PRC claims proceed on the basis of what might be called PRC "veto jurisdiction." That is, the PRC is sometimes indifferent to the exploitation of its claimed resources, but it evidently reserves the right to veto or block the execution of development projects. This veto jurisdiction is in large part a function of the PRC's massively upgraded and increasingly assertive maritime law enforcement fleet. PRC enforcement actions in disputed areas are not one-off events, but the product of steadily accumulating capacity and increasing precision in domestic law about the resources China claims.[236]

Enhanced MLE capacity materially advances China's practice of claiming historic rights, traditional fishing grounds, and hydrocarbon rights across its near seas. PRC leaders' prioritization of MLE forces reflects the long-standing perception that China's resources are "under threat" and that leaders must "pay attention to the seriousness of the situation, be farsighted, and actively strive for China's rights over maritime zones" lest it receive rights only in one million square kilometers rather than three million square kilometers of maritime space, according to a SOA researcher in 1988.[237] The perception that China's economic development is threatened by foreign states attempting to expropriate long-held Chinese resources is a powerful domestic stimulus for relentless assertion of the PRC's preferred resource rules.[238] This practice is thus quite distinctive to China and the acute challenges of its maritime geography, which sharply limits the likelihood that a more widely applicable rule will form.

UNCLOS is the essential problem for China, creating geographically defined zones that constrict the breadth of Chinese resource claims due to the nearby coastlines of littoral states. Officials lament that "the EEZ system and island system established by UNCLOS give other countries . . . a new basis for maritime rights, and this has led to contention."[239] This contention spills out well beyond the rights for resources among regional states, further implicating some of the international law of the sea's most basic rules concerning navigation.

CHAPTER FIVE

Navigation Rules

I don't give a damn about the fisheries anyway. Let everybody
have 200 miles to fish. They're all poverty-stricken down there
anyway. . . . Navigation we want. Let them fish if they want.
—*Richard Nixon, President of the United States*[1]

[The United States] adheres to the old maritime legal regime. . . .
[I]t equates the freedom of navigation with the absolute freedom
without any restrictions. It is contrary to the stipulations in the
UNCLOS and customary international law on the restrictions of
the freedom of navigation. It is also not in line with the principles of peaceful use of the sea, cooperation, and due regard to
other States' rights.
—*Xu Hong, Director-General of the Ministry of Foreign Affairs
Department of Treaty and Law*[2]

There has never been any problem with the freedom of navigation and overflight; nor will there ever be any in the future, for
China needs unimpeded commerce through these waters more
than anyone else.
—*Xi Jinping, General Secretary of the CCP*[3]

THE RULES FOR NAVIGATION on the world's oceans are among the
oldest customary international laws. They are also among the rules most
intimately linked to geopolitical competition among great powers since
the age of sail.[4] As it was for the English and the Dutch in the early seventeenth century, so it is with China and the United States today. The controversy, as ever, revolves around the tenuous balance between coastal
state control and flag state freedoms. The fundamental disagreements
concern the limits of a coastal state's jurisdiction to regulate the uses
of the waters under its jurisdiction. More specifically, China primarily

contests the *military* use of that space, claiming various authorities under UNCLOS and customary international law to apply its domestic law to a range of navigational activities.

What are "the rules" governing a coastal state's authority over military vessels and aircraft operating in and above its territorial sea and EEZ? This was among the central axes of debate during the Law of the Sea Conference (1973–1982). The US and the USSR found rare accord on this question, joining also with Japan and the traditional European maritime powers in favor of sustaining high seas freedoms and a liberal navigational regime.[5] China made common cause with the developing world in challenging this "worn-out doctrine of the freedom of the high seas, which was the core of the old law of the sea, and that was a clear manifestation of [the American and Soviet] desire for maritime hegemony," in the words of a PRC delegate to the Conference.[6]

By the conclusion of UNCLOS negotiations, the "worn-out doctrine" of free seas had not been discarded, but modified. A delicate balance was struck to preserve navigational freedoms for flag states while granting coastal states revolutionary new authorities over economic uses of the oceans. Coastal states gained new rights and jurisdiction over huge tracts of ocean space that were previously high seas (that is, the broadened 12nm territorial sea and the 200nm EEZ), while flag states secured the right of innocent passage through the territorial sea, the right of transit passage through international straits, and high seas freedoms of navigation and overflight in the EEZ "subject to the relevant provisions of this convention" (Art. 58).[7]

Interpretations of the compromise between flag state navigation and coastal state jurisdiction struck in UNCLOS vary widely.[8] The PRC reads UNCLOS and customary international law as preserving only a limited set of freedoms for flag states in the exclusive economic zone and granting an implicit coastal state authority to regulate innocent passage. PRC officials argue that on these matters, "China's practices conform with the Convention and the contemporary international practice," thus appealing to selected customs to fill interpretive gaps in UNCLOS.[9]

That Chinese view is counterposed against an interpretation of international law that does not permit states to exercise jurisdiction beyond positive rules defined in international law.[10] Applied to UNCLOS, this essentially liberal doctrine regards the silence of the treaty on military

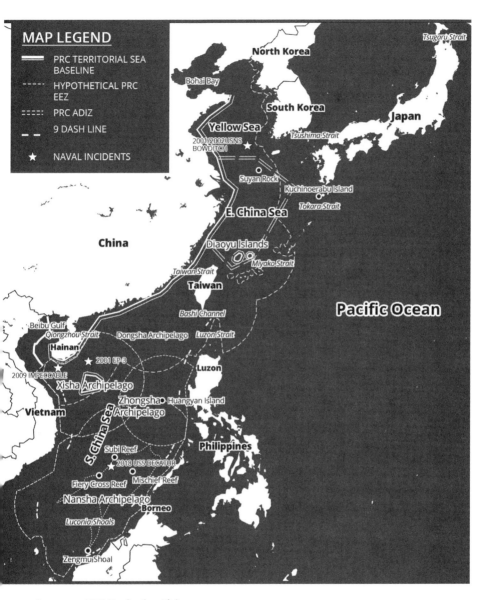

FIGURE 4. **PRC Navigation Claims**

The EEZ claims and Nansha/Spratly territorial sea baseline claims depicted here are hypothetical because the PRC has yet to issue a formal claim. They derive from the strict reading of PRC rules claiming straight baselines around offshore archipelagos and full 200nm EEZ projections from all baselines. (Data from PRC MFA, "Declaration on the Baselines of the Territorial Sea"; Asia Maritime Transparency Initiative, "Reading Between the Lines"; CLCS, "Submission by the PRC Concerning the Outer Limits of the Continental Shelf"; Congressional Research Service, "China's Actions in South and East China Seas." Map design by Paul Franz | Data: Mapcreator and openstreetmap.org.)

activities as permissive for flag states that seek to exercise freedoms that have not been expressly abridged. This view is necessarily restrictive for coastal states seeking to read in new sovereign authority. However, just such an expansive reading of sovereignty is the basic principle on which China's preferred navigational rules rest. The delicate balance between coastal and user state rights to sail the world's oceans hinges on how these rules for navigation are interpreted and applied (Figure 4).

RULES ON INNOCENT PASSAGE

UNCLOS Section 3 affirms a "right of innocent passage" for "ships of all States," defining it to mean "navigation through the territorial sea" in "continuous and expeditious" fashion (Art. 17). This right includes warships and other government vessels, which are elsewhere specified in the Convention. Simultaneously, "the coastal State may adopt laws and regulations, in conformity with the provisions of this Convention and other rules of international law, relating to innocent passage through the territorial sea"; the Convention provides a list of specified jurisdictional competencies pertaining largely to the maintenance of "safety of navigation" (Art. 21).[11]

The UNCLOS rules on innocent passage also assign duties to the coastal state, which "shall not impose requirements on foreign ships which have the practical effect of denying or impairing the right of innocent passage" (Art. 24). Separately, the Convention states that "if any warship does not comply with the laws and regulations of the coastal State concerning passage through the territorial sea and disregards any request for compliance therewith which is made to it, the coastal State may require it to leave the territorial sea immediately" (Art. 30). Thus, the coastal state may regulate defined activities of military vessels but cannot deny the right of innocent passage; it may only exercise its domestic law "in conformity" with UNCLOS. China, along with as many as 50 of the 150 coastal states, interprets this to allow it to require some form of permission or notification from warships seeking to exercise their right of innocent passage through its territorial sea.[12] The basic questions at hand are how China has put this rule into practice and how specially affected states have responded.

PRC Practice on Innocent Passage

The PRC has adopted a specific and long-standing position on the question of foreign warships' exercise of innocent passage in the territorial sea: the coastal state may enact laws and regulations requiring prior permission or notification for such activities. This has manifested in practice largely as a requirement for prior authorization on innocent passage for military vessels.

China first formally adopted this position in the 1958 "Declaration on the Territorial Sea," which states: "No foreign vessels for military use and no foreign aircraft may enter China's territorial sea and the air space above it without the permission of the Government of the PRC. While navigating in the Chinese territorial sea, every foreign vessel must observe the relevant laws and regulations laid down by the Government of the PRC" (Sec. 3). The Declaration makes no mention of the "innocent passage" rule, which had been codified several months prior with the 1958 Convention on the Territorial Sea.[13] PRC authorities and legal scholars were aware of this rule at the time but chose to shun this product of the "illegitimate" UNCLOS I negotiations in Geneva from which the PRC government was excluded.[14]

During the third UNCLOS Conference (1973–1982), however, Chinese delegates were highly attentive to the question of innocent passage for warships. They unsuccessfully advocated for greater coastal state authority over foreign warships' innocent passage, and then they rejected the terms that prevailed in the agreed treaty.[15] Even in signing and ultimately ratifying it, PRC officials expressed the view that "the Convention is not entirely satisfactory to us" on that count in particular.[16]

The treaty's failure to adopt China's proposed amendments on innocent passage for warships was the most specific of the "imperfections and even serious defects" Chinese officials found in the final text.[17] PRC delegates to the Conference often "reiterated that the provisions governing innocent passage through the territorial sea did not prejudice the right of the coastal State to require prior authorization or notification for the passage of foreign warships through the territorial sea in accordance with its laws and regulations." As it became clear that no such authority would be granted, the PRC delegation professed to be "puzzled by the opposition of a small number of delegations to so modest a proposal;

their attitude appeared to imply that they were not willing to respect the security of a coastal State."[18] The PRC delegation lamented that "there were no clear provisions regarding the regime of the passage of foreign warships through the territorial sea," and they resolved to fix this defect in subsequent practice.[19]

As the UNCLOS text drifted away from Beijing's preferred restrictions on warships, the PRC State Council began enacting domestic rules on innocent passage. First came the 1979 Regulations Governing Supervision and Control of Foreign Vessels that applied to "all foreign vessels," foreign warships among them.[20] The regulations were designed to "safeguard the sovereignty of the PRC, to maintain traffic order in port areas and coastal waters [defined as territorial seas and internal waters], to ensure safety of navigation, and to prevent pollution of waters" (Art. 1). Shortly after the unsatisfactory conclusion of the Conference, the PRC enacted a 1983 Maritime Traffic Safety Law that refined this rule: "Military vessels of foreign nationality may not enter the territorial waters of the PRC without the approval of the PRC Government."[21]

The banner PRC legislation on this issue is the 1992 Territorial Sea Law, which states that "[f]oreign ships entering the territorial sea of the PRC shall be subject to approval by the Government of the PRC" (Art. 6). This requirement of prior approval is the most restrictive of several positions Chinese officials considered. Then-director of the State Oceanic Administration, Yan Hangmo, explained the decision in his official remarks on the draft of that legislation: "The passage of foreign military ships through the territorial sea involves national security. The opinions and practices of different countries on this matter are different. There are basically three systems: one is the innocent passage regime, the second is the notification regime, and the third is the approval system. In view of the reality of our country, the 'Draft' adopts the approval system for foreign military ships to pass through our territorial waters . . . [which is] conducive to maintaining China's security and consolidating coastal defense."[22]

Despite that explicit decision to opt for prior authorization as the rule, China soon introduced a notable inconsistency into that requirement. In announcing its ratification of the treaty in 1996, the PRC government stated: "The PRC reaffirms that the provisions of the UNCLOS concerning innocent passage through the territorial sea *shall not preju-*

dice the right of a coastal State to request, in accordance with its laws and regulations, a foreign State to obtain *advance approval from or give prior notification to* the coastal State for the passage of its warships through the territorial sea of the coastal State."[23]

Two elements of this declaration stand out. The first is its inclusion of prior *notification,* an inconsistency with China's prior authorization rule. This distinct change in position appears to be a product of China's desire to make its proposed rule more widely palatable to the group of states whose legislation called only for that less demanding alternative. The second is the determination to exempt the PRC from the UNCLOS rule conferring a definite right of innocent passage for "all ships" military and civilian (Art. 17). The UNCLOS provisions on innocent passage that the PRC could not eliminate at the Conference "shall not prejudice" China's right to practice according to its preferred innocent passage rule. Recalling the UNCLOS prohibition on any acts that "purport to exclude or to modify the legal effect of the provisions of this Convention in their application to that state" (Art. 310), Beijing's decision to exclude itself on innocent passage produces a distinct "inconsistency [that] might be contested by other states in the exercise of their rights under the Convention."[24]

This discrepancy between the 1992 Territorial Sea Law and China's 1996 signing declaration has not been resolved. There are no further PRC legal instruments specifying the procedure to be adopted, by which agency, and which actions will constitute non-innocent passage for military vessels. The Supreme People's Court instructed judges to recognize that "innocent passage has a strict definition. Fishing, conducting research, or survey activities (测量活动) are all explicitly excluded from the innocent passage regime in the Convention."[25] This court explanation does not note military vessels, per se, but its specification of "survey activities" implicates certain military operations.

Despite the lack of specificity and the minor inconsistency on permission versus notification, the PRC rule is generally consistent and uniform on its underlying principle: the right of the coastal state to regulate its territorial sea is superior to the right of foreign warships to conduct innocent passage. In effect, China's sovereign discretion outweighs the black letters of the treaty—notably, specifically those black letters for which Chinese delegates failed to secure their desired rule during

UNCLOS negotiations. China's requirement for prior permission also lacks specified legal criteria for permitting a foreign warship innocent passage. The actual circumstances under which such authorization has been granted or denied are therefore relevant for evaluating the practice.

PRC Enforcement of Rules on Military Innocent Passage

To date, there are no public instances of the PRC granting permission to a foreign military vessel's innocent passage.[26] The main instruments of the PRC rule (the 1983 Maritime Traffic Safety Law and 1992 Territorial Sea Law) do not even designate the responsible agency, stipulating only that any foreign military vessel "must be approved by the Government of the PRC." There is likewise no documented evidence of any state requesting such permission. The PRC practices that are relevant here are thus official responses to foreign military vessels exercising innocent passage in its claimed territorial seas, a practice only observable to date in the operations of the US Navy (USN).

Indeed, the US is the only state that has publicized its assertions of the right of innocent passage in the PRC's claimed territorial sea. From the "Second Taiwan Strait Crisis" in September 1958 to April 1962, the PRC issued some two hundred "serious warnings" to USN vessels patrolling waters that China regarded as territorial seas.[27] The USN vessels, meanwhile, regarded the waters in question as high seas because China had not yet drawn any territorial sea baselines (and would not do so until 1996).[28] By 1964, the PRC sought to further restrict this routine presence and passed a regulation declaring the Qiongzhou Strait between Hainan and the mainland as an inland waterway through which no right of innocent passage could be exercised and through which "all military vessels of foreign nationality are not allowed to pass."[29] This regulation remains in effect and represents the PRC's most extreme restriction on innocent passage—though accomplished through the application of a separate PRC rule on straight baselines such that the waters in question were designated internal waters, not territorial sea.[30]

During US combat operations in Vietnam in 1965, China began to protest USN activity in its claimed territorial sea surrounding Triton Island, and it further challenged reciprocal South Vietnamese efforts to impose its own 12nm territorial sea as "infringing on the PRC's territorial sovereignty and freedom of navigation of the seas."[31] At the time, however, there were still no declared Chinese baselines, and the USN was operating on the basis of "hypothetical straight baselines" drawn by the State Department Office of the Geographer.[32] The US charts used low-water lines and fringing islands to project normal baselines around parts of the PRC. Notably, those baselines do not enclose some of the outlying Paracel features (for example, Triton Island), which were evidently not recognized as islands.[33] The USN therefore regarded waters beyond 12 nautical miles of these hypothetical baselines as high seas and did not accept China's protests that the waters were territorial sea.

After a period of rapprochement following the Vietnam War that disinclined either side from publicizing any strife in PRC territorial seas, 1986 marked the first formal American challenge to the PRC's innocent passage rule. It came in the form of a diplomatic démarche from the US State Department and an operational assertion by the US Navy—that is, an unnotified innocent passage through an undisclosed PRC territorial sea. No public PRC protest against this action was reported, although a private démarche was likely issued.[34]

After the 1992 enactment of the PRC Territorial Sea Law, USN exercises of innocent passage became more frequent, with at least four in the period 1992 to 1996.[35] Yet public protests from PRC officials to these operations began only in 2011. Xu Hong, director-general of the MFA Treaty and Law Department, delivered a detailed response to one such operation in May 2016:

> As a matter of fact, under UNCLOS "innocent passage" has its special meanings. By definition it must be innocent and it must be just passage. According to the definition of "innocent" in the UNCLOS, when a foreign ship passes through the territorial sea of a coastal State, it shall not be prejudicial to the peace, good order or security of the coastal State. [Xu then cites verbatim the restrictions specified in UNCLOS Art. 19] . . . In the UNCLOS, there is no clear provision on whether foreign military ships enjoy the right of innocent passage in other States' territorial sea. Many States in the world require the foreign military ship to obtain prior approval or give prior notification before it enters their territorial sea. The purpose is to safeguard the peace and security of the coastal State. Such stipulations are not intended to limit the right of innocent

passage, but rather to ensure that it could be safeguarded under the purposes and principles of the UNCLOS. There are vast waters for the US naval ships to navigate. But it deliberately has them go through the narrow sea belts in proximity to China's maritime features. It is apparently neither "innocent," nor "passage."[36]

This lengthy official statement crystallized the PRC's interpretation of this rule—that is, that UNCLOS allows coastal states to restrict innocent passage of foreign warships. The statement also highlights the reasoning behind the rule, which rests on a customary international law validation of such restrictions, observed in the practice of other states.

Official PRC readouts on these episodes from the MFA, from the Ministry of National Defense (MND), and increasingly from the PLA's Southern Theater Command consistently claim that the USN "illegally entered" or "trespassed" in violation of China's sovereignty. From 2015 to 2020, just over half of these protests (16 of 29) further charge that the US "violated" either PRC law or international law, but they do not specify the violation beyond invoking China's sovereignty. PRC officials also typically claim that the PLA "expelled" or "warned away" the USN vessels. An element of non-uniformity is evident in these statements: 71 percent of the statements have come in response to operations off the Paracels, despite equal numbers of USN innocent passage transits in the Spratlys.[37] In rare instances, official spokespeople cite China's 1992 Territorial Sea Law, its baselines, and/or the requirement for prior authorization for warships.[38]

PLAN intercepts of USN innocent passages have seldom been confrontational, and they need not be to sustain the PRC claim that the operations are unlawful. However, at least one intercept nearly led to a collision between the USN destroyer USS *Decatur* (DDG-73) and the PLAN destroyer *Lanzhou* (170) in September 2018 near the submerged Gaven (Nanxun) Reef in the Spratlys.[39] Video of the incident shows PLAN sailors placing buoys along the side of the *Lanzhou* to dampen a potential impact as it maneuvered within forty meters of the US vessel, which took evasive action to avoid a collision.[40] The MFA spokesperson described the incident in detail, stating that the "PLAN conducted identification and verification of the US ship in accordance with the law, and issued a warning to expel it."[41] Subsequent encounters have occurred at a range of one hundred meters, with PLAN vessels tacking into the "continuous and expeditious" path of their USN counterparts and risking collision.⁴² Such dangerous intercepts do not strengthen the legal status of China's proposed rule; they appear intended mainly to disincentivize unauthorized innocent passage. The PRC practice of objecting to serial challenges to its innocent passage rule in these cases is consistent but only partly uniform, with greater enforcement in the Paracels.

PLAN Exercise of Innocent Passage

The PRC's practice of this rule may also be observed in the People's Liberation Army Navy's operations in foreign territorial seas. Prior to the 2000s, PLAN vessels made periodic port calls and conducted joint exercises beyond "the first island chain" (that is, the islands of Japan, Taiwan, the Philippines, and Malaysia that create the semi-enclosed seas surrounding China). But it was not until the December 2008 establishment of an ongoing counterpiracy mission in the Gulf of Aden that the PLAN began operational deployments outside of the Asia-Pacific.⁴³ Since that time, the PLAN has expanded the scope and sophistication of its operations beyond that geographic boundary. PLAN vessels thus routinely find themselves in foreign waters, where we can observe whether and when they adhere to the rules promoted by the PRC at home.

There are only four reported instances in which PLAN vessels have operated within foreign territorial seas, though (as with all naval operations) there may be unobserved cases due to operational secrecy. The first came in September 2015, when a five-ship PLAN task force sailed through the 12nm territorial sea of the Aleutian Islands off the coast of Alaska. Beijing did not notify or seek prior permission from the US, and the US made no objection to the operation. A spokesperson from the US Northern Command noted that the ships "transited expeditiously and continuously through the Aleutian Island chain in a manner consistent with international law."⁴⁴ The second such instance came in July 2017, when three PLAN vessels passed through the English Channel in either French or British territorial seas en route to joint exercises with the Russian navy in the Baltic Sea. This action drew no protest from either Britain or France, neither of which require such transits to be notified or approved.⁴⁵ These unnotified, unauthorized innocent passages contravene the PRC rule, on its face. However, they do not violate US or UK law, and they can be interpreted as consistent and uniform practical expressions of the PRC principle that coastal states may determine the rule for innocent passage in their territorial seas.

The other two cases involve Japan, and they entail violations of China's own principle for determining innocent passage rules. The first occurred in 2004, when a submerged PLAN Han-class nuclear attack submarine entered the Japanese territorial sea near Ishigaki and Miyako islands and lingered in the area. UNCLOS expressly prohibits submarines from entering foreign territorial seas submerged (Art. 20); the PRC's 1992 Territorial Sea Law restricting all foreign military innocent passage also affirms this rule. In response to Japan's objection, the PRC expressed "regret" at this incident, inadvertently reinforcing the innocent passage rules that China's practice usually contests.[46] This instance may well have been a mistake.

A second incident involving Japan occurred in June 2016, when a PLAN Dongdiao-class vessel entered the territorial sea of Kuchinoerabu Island and conducted intelligence-gathering operations.[47] In this instance, the PRC's response to Japan's objection was to argue that the action was lawful because the waters in question were part of Tokara Strait: "Chinese warships passing through the strait are exercising the right of transit passage in accordance with the Convention," rather than innocent passage.[48] However, the PLAN vessel operated inside the claimed Japanese territorial sea rather than in the corridor designated by Japan.[49] These instances of PLAN operations in Japanese waters run counter to the PRC's professed rule, and they further disregard its principle that the coastal state should determine its own innocent passage rule. They thus represent non-uniformity in its application to different countries' territorial seas.

Weighing each of these elements, we can conclude that the PRC rule as practiced does not promote a definite rule that other states might adopt. China's inconsistent position on prior notification versus prior approval has led some Chinese legal scholars to propose reforms to China's domestic law on the matter, a rare direct criticism of PRC conduct on maritime affairs.[50] Furthermore, in conducting its own unnotified and unauthorized innocent passage, the PLAN has practiced in non-uniform fashion.

TABLE 14

PRC PRACTICE OF INNOCENT PASSAGE RULES

PRC-preferred rule	Uniformity (geographic)	Consistency (over time)	Detail
Prior authorization for innocent passage of foreign warships in PRC territorial seas	Yes	Yes	PRC's UNCLOS signing statement includes "prior notification" rule but remains consistent with general principle that coastal state determines local rule
Innocent passage for PLAN vessels in foreign territorial seas	No	Yes	China generally defers to coastal state rule on innocent passage, except in Japan's territorial seas

Yet PRC practice also reveals that the coastal state's sovereign dis-cretion is the operative element. China's preferred rule is to honor the principle that a coastal state should have the authority to restrict the in-nocent passage of foreign warships; if its domestic law does not do so, China will avail itself of the right of innocent passage. This practice none-theless demonstrates that the PRC accepts that a right of innocent pas-sage exists for warships, subject to the conditional authority of the coastal state. Finally, the pattern of practice within China's own claimed territo-rial sea may be isolated as a consistent and uniform rule that may have wider influence—if only through the more general proposed principle that the coastal state may determine its innocent passage rule as an act of sovereign discretion. That possibility is conditioned on how specially affected states have responded to China's rules in practice (Table 14).

Specially Affected State Responses to the PRC Innocent Passage Practice
The states specially affected by the PRC application of this rule are those whose warships seek to enter China's claimed territorial waters. This necessarily includes the states that also claim sovereignty over the

various disputed islands from which China projects a territorial sea—including the undelimited territorial sea around the whole Spratly group. This group thus consists of Japan, the Philippines, Vietnam, and Malaysia, who have in varying degrees been obstructed in their navigation to and around claimed territory in the ECS and SCS. Additionally, the US is part of this group by virtue of its special interest in preserving the right of innocent passage.

For Japan, its response to China's innocent passage rules is complicated by the fact that Japan administers the disputed Diaoyu/Senkakus alongside a parallel attempt by the PRC to do the same. Pressing the Chinese claim, PRC maritime law enforcement has operated regularly in the territorial waters of the Diaoyu/Senkaku group since 2012, challenging Japan's claim to sovereignty over the features and its continuous administration of the waters since the 1970s.[51] Japan also operates its coast guard and fisheries law enforcement in the area. Neither side routinely operates military forces in the territorial sea surrounding the Diaoyu/Senkaku, rendering the innocent passage question moot in this limited geographic area. Japan reportedly contemplated but did not execute an innocent passage challenge to one of China's claims in the South China Sea, limiting its actions to exclusive economic zones and high seas.[52] Japan's reluctance to challenge China's innocent passage restriction even when operating its military in the vicinity of PRC territorial seas can be regarded as acquiescence to the rule.

Among the three territorial claimants in the SCS, none has overtly challenged China's innocent passage rule. The reasons for this omission are likely due primarily to the desire to avoid confrontation with the militarily superior PLA or provoke needless political conflict, but there is an additional legal element in play. In the case of Vietnam, its own domestic law requires prior notification of foreign military vessels seeking to exercise the right of innocent passage.[53] Malaysia imposes a narrower restriction on innocent passage, requiring "nuclear-powered or vessels carrying nuclear material or material of a similar nature" to receive prior authorization.[54] Malaysia's interpretation of the rule thus permits coastal states to limit the right of innocent passage for warships on the basis of their domestic law. Finally, the Philippines' constitution does not recognize any right of innocent passage through its archipelagic waters.[55]

Each of these SCS states has effectively acquiesced to China's innocent passage rule, both by virtue of their own laws and by failure to object to or challenge China's prior permission requirement. Notably, however, each of them has contested China's right to deny their own warships entry into waters surrounding SCS features that they claim. The Philippines challenged China's right to limit its resupply of a marine unit on Second Thomas Shoal in 2014, arguing in their memorial to the SCS Arbitration that China's unsafe conduct "violate[d] its duty under UNCLOS Art. 24 not to hamper innocent passage."[56] Similarly, in 2015 the Vietnamese reported encounters with Chinese maritime law enforcement that tried to deny access to Vietnamese vessels entering territorial seas surrounding Vietnamese-occupied Spratly features.[57] Malaysia has not defined the territorial seas around its claimed Spratly features but has since 2016 publicized its navy's efforts to warn off PRC vessels while operating in "Malaysian waters" off the Luconia Shoals.[58]

None of these episodes, however, amounts to a uniform objection to China's rules on innocent passage. Because each of these states' own domestic law purports to restrict foreign warships' right of innocent passage in some fashion, and none has challenged China's somewhat stricter requirements, they may each be considered to have at least partially adopted China's preferred rule. Yet Vietnam, Malaysia, and the Philippines each object to the PRC's efforts to enforce its innocent passage rules in territorial seas they claim themselves. This contentious circumstance makes the formation of a rule somewhat less likely, despite a pattern of regional acquiescence.

In contrast to the muted responses of regional states, the United States has serially challenged the PRC's restrictions on innocent passage. These challenges are one manifestation of a significantly wider "Freedom of Navigation Program" that the US has implemented since 1979 to challenge "excessive maritime claims" around the globe. The program is run jointly through the Department of State, which issues démarches to foreign states regarding their excessive claims, and the Department of Defense, which conducts operational assertions to demonstrate US claims.[59] The US began issuing annual reports on these actions in 1991, challenging China's innocent passage restrictions at least once per year since 2011 (with the exception of 2014). Since 2017, the Department of

TABLE 15

**SPECIALLY AFFECTED STATE RESPONSES ON INNOCENT
PASSAGE PRACTICE**

	Innocent passage prior notice/authorization for warships
Japan	Acquiesce
Malaysia	Acquiesce (partial adoption: requires prior authorization for nuclear power/materials)
Philippines	Acquiesce (partial adoption: requires prior authorization for archipelagic waters)
USA	Object
Vietnam	Acquiesce (partial adoption: requires prior notice)

Defense has also listed the general locations of these challenges, which have targeted the Paracels in each year and the Spratlys since 2018.[60]

The US Navy's practice of exercising its right of innocent passage in China's territorial seas is unique. Even as US allies begin to conduct exercises of their freedom of navigation, only the USN asserts innocent passage in foreign territorial seas. Meanwhile, Vietnam, Malaysia, and the Philippines each adopt some form of coastal state restriction on innocent passage that the USN challenges. There is thus regional support for the PRC principle that coastal states may restrict innocent passage at their discretion. Nonetheless, the PRC's more restrictive variant of the rule requiring prior authorization for warships is not widely shared in the region. The evidence supports a conclusion that a regional custom permitting coastal states to restrict innocent passage of warships may indeed exist in East Asia, even if the US has established itself as a persistent objector (Table 15).

RULES FOR NAVIGATION IN THE EEZ

The EEZ regime in UNCLOS codified a unique compromise between coastal state jurisdiction and flag state navigational freedoms. It is a "carefully constructed balance which reflects both legal doctrine and political realities" and thereby leaves room for states with conflicting interests to advocate for their preferred interpretations.[61] As Nixon inelegantly described the bargain: "Navigation we want. Let them fish if they want."[62] However, beyond the fishing rights that spurred the formation of the EEZ, coastal states now enjoy a range of authorities that have ushered in creeping jurisdictional claims. In China's case, these have manifested as claims to "security" jurisdiction over the EEZ.

The basic interpretative differences are clear: maritime powers prize the high seas freedoms preserved in UNCLOS and customary international law, while states that perceive themselves as vulnerable to the maritime powers prize the application of coastal state jurisdiction over an expanding set of activities in the EEZ, which they likewise see as validated by UNCLOS and custom. On the one hand, the EEZ recognizes the sovereign rights of the coastal state over the resources in that zone and vests the coastal state with specific jurisdiction over artificial structures, in order to protect the marine environment and manage marine scientific research (UNCLOS, Art. 56). On the other hand, it assigns "duties" to the coastal state, which "shall have due regard to the rights and duties of other States": these are enumerated as freedoms of the high seas for "navigation and overflight and . . . the laying of submarine cables and pipelines, and other internationally lawful uses of the sea related to these freedoms, such as those associated with the operation of ships, aircraft and submarine cables and pipelines, and compatible with the other provisions of this Convention" (Art. 58).

While both flag states and coastal states are enjoined to exercise "due regard" for the rights and duties of the other, the Convention does not define how this is to be implemented where the content of those rights and duties are not mutually agreed (Art. 59). It only gestures vaguely to "equity," "relevant circumstances," and the "respective importance of the interests involved," leaving significant indeterminacy in the regime when conflicts arise in practice.[63] The EEZ regime also depends upon all parties conforming their practice to the other "relevant provisions" of UNCLOS (Art. 55). These include Part V on the EEZ, Part VI on the Continental Shelf, Part XII on Protection and Preservation of the Marine Environment, and Part XIII on Marine Scientific Research. For Beckman and Davenport, "[t]he key point is that the coastal State has no residual jurisdiction to regulate matters in its EEZ. Since the EEZ is not subject to its sovereignty, its jurisdiction is limited to that set out in the provisions in UNCLOS."[64] Yet in practice, some coastal states have appealed to precisely such residual jurisdiction or have otherwise read into the EEZ regime certain forms of jurisdiction by which they may regulate navigational activities unconnected to the economic use of the zone.

The regime of the EEZ laid out in Part V of the Convention codifies a sui generis regime, a non-sovereign zone that is also not entirely international. It is defined by overlapping rights for coastal states and flag states alike. O'Connell observes that "[t]he doctrine of the EEZ has no theoretical antecedents, and thus depends for its viability and its content upon changes in customary law brought about as a result of State practice."[65] The importance of state practice in preserving navigational freedoms or eroding them is almost universally acknowledged. James Kraska, a former US Navy judge advocate and oceans policy adviser to the Joint Chiefs of Staff, observes that "the 1982 Convention codified those [high seas] rights and freedoms [in the EEZ], preserving them in a widely accepted global treaty. But evolving state practice is weakening freedom of navigation in the EEZ. Reinterpretation of customary international law and the provisions of UNCLOS, combined with an active campaign by some nations and non-state groups to transform the rules of the EEZ, are weakening the rights of the international community inside the zone."[66]

The zone and its juridical underpinnings have thus foreseeably brought about contests in practice, most acutely between China and the United States. The creeping "territorialization of the EEZ" has particular salience in the conflict between China and the United States.[67] As China's military and economic capabilities have come into contact with America and its allies in the waters of the East Asian littoral, specific disputes over its jurisdictional authority have surfaced over (1) military activities in the EEZ (to include its airspace) and (2) the regulation of marine scientific research. China's proposed rules on each of these may be observed in its practice and then evaluated in light of specially affected state responses.

PRC Practice on EEZ Jurisdiction

The most striking element of China's practice regarding its jurisdiction in the EEZ is that there is no delimited PRC EEZ. None of China's boundaries have been settled, so the most that can be said is that China claims 200nm EEZs from all of its land territory, including the disputed islands in the SCS and ECS (see Figure 4 for these projections). A second major characteristic is the vagueness by which PRC formal domestic law and regulation create restrictions on navigation. Although PRC law is expansive and detailed on its jurisdiction to prescribe and enforce rules on navigation within its territorial sea and internal waters, it is nearly silent on such authorities within the EEZ.[68] Those few laws and regulations that do purport to regulate EEZ navigation do so with unspecified references to "national defense" or "national security" interests. PRC officials and experts derive those authorities from particular interpretations of UNCLOS and custom in ways that have differed substantively over time.

Claims to EEZ Security Jurisdiction

The PRC's first formal statements on navigation in the EEZ came in a working paper to the UN Seabed Committee in 1973. The relevant part of that paper reads: "The normal navigation and overflight on the water surface of and in the airspace above the economic zone by ships and aircraft of all States shall not be prejudiced. . . . A coastal state may enact necessary laws and regulations for the effective regulation of its economic zone. Other States, in carrying out any activities in the economic zone of a coastal state, are required to observe the relevant laws and regulations of the coastal State."[69] This statement of the PRC's position does not propose any substantive content to those coastal state laws and regulations, but it lays out the basic principle in play: sovereign states should enjoy considerable discretion to decide when, where, and how to apply domestic law and regulation in their jurisdictional waters.

The Convention as agreed does not reflect this PRC preference. Yet, in its declaration on ratification in 1996, the PRC did not seek to exempt itself from the treaty regarding EEZ jurisdiction as it did for innocent passage. Instead, EEZ restrictions have appeared in ambiguous terms in a small number of domestic legal instruments. The first of these is the 1992 Law on the Territorial Sea and Contiguous Zone, which states that

"China has the right to exercise control in the contiguous zone to prevent and impose penalties for activities infringing laws or regulations concerning security, the customs, finance, sanitation or entry and exit control within its land territory, internal waters or territorial sea" (Art. 13). This list is identical to that provided in UNCLOS Article 33—except for the addition of "regulations concerning security," which are nowhere prescribed in the Convention. The contiguous zone is effectively a special component of the EEZ, which also begins seaward of the territorial sea limits and thus completely overlaps it. As regards matters of navigation and resources, the EEZ is the only set of rules that provides the coastal state with any rights and jurisdiction.[70]

The 1998 Exclusive Economic Zone and Continental Shelf Law establishes a 200nm zone in terms nearly identical to those of the Convention—with the critical addendum of "historic rights." The legislation provides that "any State, provided that it observes international law and the laws and regulations of the PRC, shall enjoy in the EEZ and continental shelf of the PRC freedom of navigation and overflight and of laying submarine cables and pipelines" (Art. 11). This reference to the laws and regulations of the PRC performs the same function here as elsewhere, reserving undefined authorities for coastal state jurisdiction. While the laying of submarine cables and pipelines is expressly reserved as requiring "authorization by the competent authorities," there is no such restriction on navigation and overflight. Yet an apparent PRC rule to restrict both—at least within China's claimed EEZ—is evident in practice.

One clause in particular demonstrates the potential for "jurisdictional creep" drafted into China's EEZ law. It refers to artificial islands, installations, and structures, over which the state "shall have exclusive jurisdiction . . . with regard to customs, fiscal, health, security, and immigration laws and regulations" (Art. 8). These jurisdictional competencies, security most notable among them, are the same as those China claims in the contiguous zone. Without specification in the legislation as to where the additional "security" jurisdiction applies, it may be interpreted to apply not only in the waters immediately surrounding artificial islands (like those in the Spratlys) but also across the EEZ in areas determined by the PRC to have some connection to those man-made features.

The content of this claimed security jurisdiction requires fuller inquiry into PRC efforts to regulate its EEZ.

Claims to Regulate Marine Scientific Research

A second area of PRC law that challenges navigation rules concerns marine scientific research (MSR). Since 1973, when the PRC submitted a working paper to the UN Seabed Committee on the subject, officials have invoked the primacy of the coastal state's domestic law over the conduct of MSR by construing the latter in broad and indeterminate fashion.[71] Without formally defining the term, the PRC retains significant discretion to designate a wide range of activities as MSR falling under its jurisdiction.

A 1992 Survey and Mapping Law established a domestic regime for all survey and mapping in "sea areas under the jurisdiction of the PRC" and premised these activities on "national defense construction."[72] A 2002 revision stipulated that "foreign organizations and individuals engaged in surveying and mapping activities in the territory of the PRC and other sea areas under its jurisdiction must be approved [by the State Council] . . . and abide by the relevant laws and administrative regulations of the PRC"; it further requires that such activities be undertaken in joint ventures or in cooperation with the "relevant departments or units of the PRC . . . and must not involve state secrets or endanger national security" (Art. 7).[73]

An additional set of regulations pertains specifically to MSR, the 1996 Regulations on Foreign-Related Marine Scientific Research. Such activities require State Council approval and must not "violate the relevant laws, regulations, and rules of the PRC" (Art. 10). Subsequent instruments to implement this regulation—issued by the PLA General Staff, the Ministry of Foreign Affairs, State Oceanic Administration, Ministry of State Security, and other organizations—provide detailed guidance to law enforcement agencies for enforcing and supervising China's MSR regime for foreign vessels.[74]

MSR is among the jurisdictional authorities in the EEZ provided by UNCLOS (Art. 56), on the basis of its connection to economic uses of the resources in that zone. The "right to conduct marine scientific research" is articulated in Article 238, but the substantive content of MSR is not defined in UNCLOS. In PRC law MSR has manifested as a blanket authority to regulate a wide range of activities, which in practice have included non-economic military hydrographic and oceanographic surveys. China's broad and sustained interpretation of this rule reflects a view expressed by Chinese delegates from the outset of the UNCLOS Conference, where Ling Ching argued for an intrinsic connection between the coastal state's sovereign rights to resources and the requirement for its jurisdiction over all activities in the EEZ, not just economic ones:

> The theoretical basis for the denial of coastal States' exclusive
> jurisdiction over the economic zone, as set forth in the draft
> articles, was the assertion that the economic zone which fell
> within the scope of national jurisdiction should be treated as part
> of the high seas. If the economic zone were truly part of the high
> seas, there would be no point in discussing the establishment
> of such a zone and the coastal States would then have to submit
> to the will of the super-Powers which monopolized the high
> seas. Furthermore, the document provided that each State might
> freely carry out fundamental scientific research unrelated to the
> exploration and exploitation of the living or mineral resources of
> the economic zone. [The PRC] delegation wondered whether there
> could be any fundamental scientific research in today's world
> that was not related, directly or indirectly, to specific military or
> economic purposes. It might also be asked what were the criteria
> for determining what kind of scientific research was related
> to the exploration and exploitation of resources and what was
> unrelated.[75]

This assertion of a broad and indeterminate scope for MSR remains consistent. Chinese law of the sea experts suggest that military surveys are regulated under Chinese law because they are intrinsically threatening to the coastal state. Some point to UNCLOS terms that reserve uses of the EEZ "for peaceful purposes" (Arts. 58 and 246) and specify that MSR must likewise be "conducted exclusively for peaceful purposes" (Art. 240). They cite the treaty's general emphasis on "peaceful use" of the oceans (Preamble, Art. 301, and Annex VI) as well as the UN Charter's proscription on "threat or use of force" (Art. 2.4).[76] The

Supreme People's Court has offered at least partial specification of the rule in opining that "in recent years, foreigners have illegally entered the waters under our jurisdiction to carry out illegal activities such as fishing and oceanographic surveys. This judicial interpretation upholds administrative organs' authority to impose corresponding compulsory measures and administrative penalties against foreign ships and personnel illegally entering our jurisdictional waters."[77] The salient component of these interpretations concerns oceanographic survey activities, which the SPC implied have bearing on China's "sovereign rights and jurisdiction," including those related to the EEZ.

Given the uncontroversial right for coastal states to regulate MSR in their jurisdictional zones, China's domestic law leaves the substance of such activities undefined. This allows significant discretion for the "relevant agencies" (among them maritime law enforcement and the PLA) to regulate activities judged to be MSR on the basis of perceived threats to "maritime rights and interests" and the needs of national defense.

PRC Implementation of Navigational Rules in Its Claimed EEZ

As represented in PRC law and regulation of the EEZ, China's rules for navigation of military vessels and aircraft are generally consistent over time and uniform across the zone. This practice is best observed in major episodes in which the PRC has attempted to enforce its domestic law on foreign warships and military aircraft, including restrictions on military survey as a form of MSR. The episodes themselves tend to involve one or more elements of the PRC's navigational rules.

The principal objects of PRC enforcement of its navigational rules have been US Navy vessels and aircraft. While American military assets have continuously operated in the East Asian littoral since entering the Pacific theater in World War II, practical Chinese efforts to enforce its navigational rules began after the promulgation of the 1992 Survey and Mapping Law, the first PRC legal instrument to regulate EEZ activities. Since then, the PRC and the US have established a pattern of encounters in China's claimed EEZs. These have elicited a changing set of responses from PRC officials, ranging from indifference to diplomatic complaint, operational interference, and collisions. Analysis of these provides a critical test of the nature of the proposed PRC rules in this domain.

The first notable military encounter in China's claimed EEZ came in October 1994. The USN aircraft carrier USS *Kitty Hawk* (CV-63) and its battle group were operating in the Yellow Sea when they detected a nearby PLAN Han-class nuclear attack submarine.[78] The carrier began to track the submarine, launching anti-submarine aircraft and dropping sonobuoys to locate it. In response, the PLA scrambled fighter jets and later issued warnings that "another such incident could lead to a military clash."[79] No formal statement on the tense incident was publicized, but the US defense attaché in Beijing reported that the PLA issued a verbal threat to employ force if the incident were to be repeated. The MFA dismissed the entire event as "rumors . . . nothing happened."[80] No assertion of Beijing's navigational rules was yet in evidence, but the demonstrated intent to complicate or deny American military navigation in China's claimed waters would soon manifest in more assertive action.

On 1 April 2001, a USN EP-3 electronic surveillance aircraft was operating 70 nautical miles south of Hainan Island in the SCS when it was intercepted by a pair of Chinese J-8 fighter aircraft, one of which veered into the path of the much larger and slower USN aircraft. The collision led to the death of a Chinese pilot and the emergency landing of the EP-3 at the PLAN's Lingshui airfield.[81] In the midst of the diplomatic crisis that ensued, the PRC MFA spokesperson argued that the US had violated domestic and international law by conducting "reconnaissance . . . which overran the scope of 'free overflight' according to international law. The move also violated the UNCLOS, which stipulates that any flight in airspace above another nation's EEZ should respect the rights of the country concerned. . . . [A]ccording to international law or Chinese domestic laws, China has the right to investigate the plane which caused all this trouble." This lengthy statement was published in English to give publicity to the first clear articulation of China's claims to restrict EEZ navigation. It included details relevant to the law of the sea, including the distance from China's baselines (104 kilometers), characterized as the "airspace over Chinese exclusive economic waters [sic]."[82]

China further refined the claim in September 2002, issuing a statement in response to the military hydrographic survey activity of an unarmed USN research vessel, the USNS *Bowditch* (T-AGS-62), which was conducting a military oceanographic survey in the Yellow Sea. This same vessel had been warned off the prior year, but PRC officials had not invoked any domestic law or defined jurisdiction. In the diplomatic démarches shared between the two sides after that incident, the US communicated that such military surveys did not qualify as MSR and therefore could not be regulated under UNCLOS.[83] This crystallized the differences in the Chinese and American positions on the rule and led to a significant amendment of China's domestic law to assert its jurisdiction over military surveys.

New Rules on Military Surveys

In August 2002, the PRC amended its 1992 Survey and Mapping Law to require that all foreign activity of this type must be authorized by "the competent department of military survey and mapping, and [must] abide by the relevant laws and administrative regulations of the PRC."[84] The MFA spokeswoman, Zhang Qiyue, was evidently aware of this change in the PRC's rule; she stated that "without China's permission, the US naval ship *Bowditch* conducted activities in China's EEZ in violation of the international law of the sea. This also violates China's relevant rights, interests, and jurisdiction over its EEZ. We demand the US side abide by international laws and hope the USN ship will stop activity in China's EEZ." Pressed to clarify, she stated that "actually, details are not that important. . . . The UNCLOS has clear provisions for the EEZ and today's press conference is not devoted to the discussion about it. I suggest you look it up in the UNCLOS, which has made very clear that one country is entitled to relevant rights, interests, [and] jurisdiction over its EEZ."[85]

With the initiation of regularized "rights-protection" patrols beginning in 2007, Chinese maritime law enforcement began to operationally enforce these MSR prohibitions across its claimed EEZs. One report details such actions in the period 2007 to 2010, citing 100 instances of Chinese MLE forces "shadowing and surveilling US military survey activities in areas under our jurisdiction," "discovery" of approximately 350 ships and 400 foreign aircraft (some of them military survey vessels) in the East China Sea, and over 200 "tracking and surveillance actions on rights-protection targets such as foreign maritime surveillance ships, missile survey ships, electronic reconnaissance ships, coast guard ships, and military vessels and aircraft, thus maximally asserting our country's areas of jurisdiction in the Yellow Sea."[86] These operations have become routine, as have the bridge-to-bridge communications between ship captains from the US and China. Incidents are rare, but the few that have been publicized reveal important details about the PRC's military survey rule and its inconsistent application.

The most well-documented confrontation arising from China's enforcement against military surveys occurred in March 2009, showcasing the PRC's multifaceted legal and operational efforts to deny USN activity in its claimed EEZ. The USNS *Impeccable* (T-AGOS-23) is a surveillance ship crewed by civilian and naval personnel. The unarmed vessel employs a large towed sonar array used to gather underwater acoustical data and detect submarine activities, and it was operating in the PRC EEZ south of Hainan Island, the location of the PLAN South Sea Fleet's main nuclear submarine base.[87] Beginning on 4 March 2009, Chinese maritime law enforcement vessels and aircraft harassed the *Impeccable* and another nearby surveillance vessel, the USNS *Victorious* (T-AGOS-19), employing high-intensity spotlights, unnotified close approaches at high speed, and low-altitude fly-bys. The PLAN intelligence vessel communicated bridge-to-bridge to *Impeccable* that her operations were unlawful and directed the ship to leave immediately or "suffer the consequences."[88]

Severe consequences were narrowly averted on 8 March 2009, when the PLAN intelligence vessel, two maritime law enforcement cutters, and two fishing trawlers closed within fifty feet of the *Impeccable* and forced it to conduct an emergency "all stop" to avoid collision. During the ensuing standoff, the *Impeccable* sprayed its fire hose at one of the fishing trawlers, the other Chinese trawler tried to snag the *Impeccable's* towed sonar array with a long pole, and a PRC law enforcement vessel attempted to drive over that delicate instrument as the *Impeccable* navigated away from the confrontation.[89]

A sharp diplomatic debate followed, with the PRC disputing the statements and video evidence publicized by the US Department of Defense as "sheer lies."[90] An MFA spokesperson did not present an alternative account but instead stated the specific rules that the USN vessel had allegedly violated:

> The claims by the US are flatly inaccurate and unacceptable to
> China. On the issue of foreign ships engaging in activities in
> China's exclusive economic zone, the UNCLOS, Law of the PRC
> on the EEZ and the Continental Shelf, and Regulations of the PRC

on the Management of Foreign-Related Marine Scientific Research all have clear stipulations. The Chinese Government has *always handled such activities in strict accordance with the above regulations.* Engaging in activities in China's EEZ in the South China Sea without China's permission, US navy surveillance ship *Impeccable* broke relevant international law as well as Chinese laws and regulations. China has lodged solemn representations to the US. We urge the US to take effective measures to prevent similar incidents occurring in the future.[91]

This statement remains the most detailed official articulation of the PRC position on domestic and international law applicable to military surveys in the EEZ. Subsequent encounters have also involved civilian, law enforcement, and naval vessels in close proximity, which have variously shadowed USN surveillance and other surface vessels and engaged in aggressive intercepts. The drivers for this inconsistent pattern of enforcement may be variation in the specific operations of the foreign vessels in question. The *Impeccable*'s proximity to Chinese submarines and possible use of active sonar may have violated a tacit understanding or, alternatively, simply caused greater security concern than normal surveillance.

Taiwan Strait Transits

The pattern of PRC enforcement of its EEZ navigation rules is especially notable with regard to Taiwan Strait transits (TSTs). China claims these waters within its 200nm EEZ, but they appear to have a non-uniform legal status compared to its other EEZs, as well as an inconsistent and selective pattern of enforcement. This issue first surfaced with the December 1995 TST of the US aircraft carrier USS *Nimitz* (CVN-68) after a series of PLA ballistic missile tests and amphibious exercises intended to chill the growing independence movement on Taiwan. This was the first TST conducted by the USN since the normalization of ties with the PRC in 1979, and it elicited a strong warning from Beijing. In this first instance, the PRC's warning was not issued on the basis of a legal argument concerning military operations in its EEZ.[92]

Indeed, Beijing did not declare its 200nm EEZ until May of the following year in advance of ratifying UNCLOS. This "Third Taiwan Straits Crisis," however, set in motion a series of encounters that help clarify China's preferred rule. The US did not attempt another TST until December 2007, again conducted by the *Nimitz* and her battle group. On this occasion, the MFA "expressed grave concern to the US and requested it to take prudent actions in this sensitive area."[93] This expressed desire for prudential decisions on the part of foreign navies is part of an observable pattern of selective application of the PRC's EEZ navigational rules in the Taiwan Strait.

This inconsistency became stark in April 2019, when the French naval frigate *Vendémiaire* (F-734) sailed through the strait en route to a naval parade in Qingdao, where the PRC was celebrating the 70th anniversary of the PLAN. In response, the PRC Ministry of National Defense charged the French vessel with "illegally entering Chinese waters" and "sent navy ships in accordance with the law and the rules to identify the French ship and warn it to leave," rescinding its invitation to the parade.[94] That same week, however, an Indian Navy destroyer INS *Kolkata* (D63) along with a supply ship INS *Shakti* (A57) conducted a TST. The captain of the Indian destroyer reported that "we are very happy that we were facilitated by the PLA Navy and they ensured that we had a safe passage to Qingdao."[95] Both nations conducted what appear to be identical transits through China's claimed EEZ, but the rule was enforced only against the French.

Later that same month, a TST by the USN destroyer USS *Curtis Wilbur* (DDG-54) and a US Coast Guard cutter USCG *Bertholf* (WMSL-750) drew a mild response from the PRC, with the Ministry of National Defense spokesperson noting only that "we are clear about the situation of the US ships passing through the Taiwan Strait. The relevant movements are under our control throughout the entire process. China has expressed concern to the US."[96] Then in June 2019, the Canadian frigate HCMS *Regina* (FFH 334) and her Naval Replenishment Unit *Asterix* conducted a TST en route from a port call in Vietnam, which the PRC Ministry of National Defense interpreted as an "unfriendly gesture" and "lodged solemn representations" urging a "responsible attitude."[97] The same MND spokesperson, Ren Guoqiang, noted that "we were clear about the transit of Canadian vessels through the Taiwan Strait and monitored the vessels for the whole process."[98]

The USN has since conducted regular TSTs on a monthly basis, but without drawing specific legal complaints from Beijing. Instead, the conduct has been condemned for its "signaling to Taiwan independence forces," with China vowing to "maintain a high level of alert at all times, respond to all threats and provocations at any time, and resolutely defend national sovereignty and territorial integrity."[99] PLAN spokespeople have stated that "the move artificially creates risk factors in the Taiwan Strait, deliberately undermines regional peace and stability, and we are firmly opposed to this."[100] The political salience of the Taiwan issue has evidently displaced the undefined legal rule for Beijing, which now urges prudential action instead of legal compliance. The inconsistency of legal argumentation in the case of TSTs and non-uniformity of application to different states are not practices that suggest a new rule.

Refining Rationales for EEZ Restrictions

As its capacity and capability to monitor and patrol its claimed EEZs has improved, the PRC's operational and diplomatic responses have become more consistent—and sometimes confrontational. In the period from 2002 to 2018, Chinese military, MLE, and/or civilian assets were involved in at least twenty incidents of dangerous air intercepts or near-collisions at sea with foreign military vessels and aircraft operating in and above PRC-claimed EEZs (twice with Indian naval vessels).[101] During this period, PRC officials routinized their complaints, the PLA steadily built capacity to conduct operational intercepts (or at a minimum monitor USN activities), and the PRC international law community (guided by the Ministry of Foreign Affairs) steadily refined the legal arguments meant to counteract the growing frequency and intensity of US military operations in the SCS and ECS.

These legal arguments all reflect the basic principle that China, as the coastal state, is permitted to regulate foreign military activities in its EEZ under the law of the sea. Typically, both international law and UNCLOS are cited as the basis for these claims, but the specific rules invoked include: (1) potential harm to marine mammals from sonar acoustics, (2) the potential for military hydrographic data to be used commercially, (3) the intrinsic threat to "peace and good order" entailed by the presence of military aircraft and vessels, (4) that freedom of navigation is not "freedom of military operations," (5) that military survey is "MSR," and many variations on these themes.[102] The PRC ambassador to the Philippines offered the most succinct and extreme version of the rule: "No freedom of navigation for warships and airplanes."[103]

While the repertoire of legal arguments has thus varied considerably, the interest underlying them has been constant. A 2015 PRC Defense White Paper, *China's Military Strategy*, articulates the main strategic concern: "Some external countries are also busy meddling in South China Sea affairs; a tiny few maintain a constant close-in air and sea surveillance and reconnaissance against China. It is thus a long-standing task for China to safeguard its maritime rights and interests." Since 2018, in military-to-military dialogues and Track 1.5 and Track 2 dialogue settings, complaints over the "frequency and intensity of close-in surveillance and reconnaissance" have largely displaced the earlier emphasis on legal restrictions on military activities in EEZs. This shift has occurred in the context of a growing number of voices in the PRC law of the sea and naval communities emphasizing the importance of EEZ navigation for the PLA as it steadily expands its operational footprint across the globe.

PLA Activities in Foreign EEZs

The PLAN turned its gaze from the "near seas" of the SCS, ECS, and Yellow Sea to the "far seas" only in the mid-1980s. By 1985, a "strategic transition" was underway with the first sustained PLAN operations beyond the "first island chain" in the Indian Ocean.[104] These deployments have only grown in scale and complexity since then, bringing PLAN warships routinely into the EEZs of foreign states as out of area deployments began in the late 2000s.[105]

Since 2012, the PLAN has operated within the EEZs surrounding the US territory of Guam and the state of Hawaii. From 2014, PLAN air and naval operations have been reported in undisputed EEZs surrounding Japan, Alaska, Australia, the Philippines, Australia, India, Sri Lanka, Malaysia, Indonesia, and Pakistan.[106] None of these operations has been publicly notified or approved. MND spokespeople argue that there is no general rule prohibiting such actions: "In non-territorial waters, China, like other countries, enjoys the right to freedom of navigation on the high seas."[107] This invocation of "high seas" freedoms in foreign EEZs is distinctly non-uniform, a marked departure from Beijing's jurisdictionalized view of its own EEZ.

A noteworthy instance of this in practice came in 2014, when the PLAN was invited for the first time to the US Navy's Rim of the Pacific Exercise (RIMPAC) in Hawaii. While PLAN vessels exercised with foreign counterparts from twenty-three other nations, an uninvited PLAN Type-815 *Dongdiao*-class Auxiliary General Intelligence (AGI) ship loitered in the EEZ near Oahu conducting electronic surveillance on the exercise. China made no comment on the matter, while the USN Pacific Fleet spokesman noted that "we continue to uphold the principle of freedom of navigation and overflight in accordance with international law," welcoming the ship so long as it remained outside the territorial sea and did not disrupt the exercise. Subsequent similar PLAN operations in US EEZs have been similarly uncontested.[108]

Frequently, these activities involve AGIs and other surveillance and intelligence vessels conducting "military surveys," which China forbids in its own jurisdictional waters as MSR. The rule as applied appears to recognize the coastal state's domestic rules on military activities in EEZs. The Chinese MSR fleet is state-owned and explicitly conducts research for military as well as scientific purposes in numerous foreign EEZs. These vessels sometimes do so as part of joint surveys with the coastal state, as has occurred by agreement with Nigeria, Pakistan, and Portugal.[109] By contrast, Chinese MSR vessels have conducted surveys in the Philippines' undisputed EEZ east of Luzon even after authorization was denied by Philippine authorities.[110] These are non-uniform practices, with the PRC asserting a right to military survey in some waters but accepting coastal state authority to regulate it elsewhere.

While there is indeed a scientific component to such research, the organizations conducting the research gather data about ocean salinity, currents, bathymetry, and waves, and they share the data with the PLAN.[111] Such activities are forbidden in China's own EEZ, where the PLA, MFA, and Ministry of State Security, among other leading PRC security agencies, have urged Chinese officials to deny other states reciprocal agreements for conducting MSR. One set of administrative provisions advises Chinese officials that foreign MSR in China's jurisdictional zones should be undertaken with extreme caution: "cooperation with maritime powers such as the US and Japan should not proceed without being fully aware of foreign parties' attempts to collect China's sensitive marine information or unlawfully classified information."[112]

Synthesizing the PRC's practice within its jurisdictional waters and in those of other states, the rule as applied is inconsistent and non-uniform. PRC officials invoke varied legal arguments—and sometimes

TABLE 16

PRC PRACTICE OF EEZ RULES

PRC-preferred rule	Uniformity (geographic)	Consistency (over time)	Detail
Restricted EEZ military exercises	No	Yes	Unauthorized PLAN navigation and exercises in foreign EEZs
EEZ military survey regulated as MSR	No	No	Unauthorized military surveys in foreign EEZs; intermittent enforcement in PRC EEZ
Restricted overflight	No	No	Unauthorized PLAN flights in foreign EEZs; intermittent enforcement over PRC EEZ
Restricted Taiwan Strait transit	No	No	Application varies by state and over time (not a rule-like policy)

no legal argument at all—in different parts of the Chinese-claimed EEZ. Meanwhile, in foreign EEZs, the PLAN has conducted operations (including surveillance), carried out military surveys, and collected intelligence without requesting coastal state permission, as would be required in its own EEZ. The fundamental PRC rule is evidently that the coastal state as sovereign may decide on its domestic rules—in the EEZ as in the territorial sea. However, the rules applied in the PRC's own EEZ appear to vary considerably depending on the state conducting the action and the body of water in question. Such inconsistent and non-uniform practice does not conduce to projecting a rule that others may adopt. Foreign responses to this PRC practice will further illuminate the degree to which coastal state restrictions on military navigation in EEZs may nevertheless have some wider influence (Table 16).

Specially Affected State Responses to China's EEZ Practice

The states specially affected by the PRC application of its EEZ navigation rules are (1) those whose warships, military aircraft, or military survey vessels seek to operate in China's claimed EEZ and the airspace above it and (2) those countries in whose EEZ the People's Liberation Army seeks to exercise freedom of navigation and overflight or conduct military surveys. The first category inevitably includes those countries whose EEZs overlap with China's, thus rendering their operations within their own claimed waters potentially subject to PRC restriction—namely, the Yellow Sea, SCS, and ECS littoral states. Additionally, the group of states whose navies routinely operate in EEZs across the globe are specially affected by restrictive rules. These include the US most prominently but also several other states with navies supporting their national interests in maintaining access to the economically and strategically vital waters of East Asia: Australia, India, France, the United Kingdom, and Germany have been notably active in this regard.

East Asian Littoral States

Among the SCS littoral states, both Vietnam and Malaysia have domestic laws restricting military activities in their EEZs. Malaysia's is a blanket prohibition on military exercises within its EEZ.[113] China has disregarded this rule, despite its similarity to its own rule, exercising and conducting surveys regularly in the area surrounding Luconia Shoals and James Shoal, but Malaysia has not formally objected to these practices. However, PRC practice in Malaysia's claimed EEZ is, in effect, a disconfirmation of the PRC's preferred rule: by disregarding Malaysia's domestic law and regulation, China undermines its own claim to impose similar restrictions.

Vietnam adopts restrictions on EEZ navigation that are nearly identical to the PRC's. It claims "security jurisdiction" in its contiguous zone as well as a blanket coastal state discretion to set limits on EEZ freedom of navigation: "[w]hen exercising the freedoms of navigation and overflight in the exclusive economic zone and continental shelf of Viet Nam, organizations or individuals are not permitted to . . . [c]onduct any act against the sovereignty, defense and security of Viet Nam."[114] China has disregarded these restrictions as well, conducting military surveys and exercises and interfering with the navigation of Vietnamese vessels in their overlapping EEZs.[115] While Vietnam has not succeeded in regulating the operations of the PLAN (or PRC armed law enforcement vessels) in its claimed EEZ, this seeming acquiescence resembles Malaysia's in that it effectively undermines China's own preferred rule of coastal state jurisdiction over such activities.

Indonesia and the Philippines adopt no navigational restrictions in their claimed EEZs. PLAN activities—even those in disputed or overlapping zones—therefore have indeterminate effect. China's rule permits those states to restrict military navigation in their jurisdictional zones, yet those states decline to do so and thus effectively permit the PLAN actions in question. This permissive attitude also reflects the limitations of these smaller states' capacity to monitor the waters under their jurisdiction. Analyzing their remote sensing capabilities, Greg Poling observes that "in Malaysia, the Philippines, and Vietnam, sea blindness is the rule, not the exception"—thus PLA activities in their claimed zones likely go unobserved in many or most cases.[116] The persistence of jurisdictional disputes over SCS waters, however, confounds any determinate conclusion about the impact of PLA practice in EEZ areas claimed by the PRC.

Several other East Asian states have adopted some form of restrictions on military activities in EEZs, including Cambodia, Myanmar, Thailand, and North Korea.[117] As in the case of innocent passage, the widespread adoption of coastal state restrictions on military activities in EEZs within the region raises the possibility that a regional customary norm may exist—though China's defiance of these other coastal states' restrictions should be regarded as a significant obstacle to its crystallization as a recognized rule.

In the ECS and Yellow Sea, PLA operations in Japanese- and Korean-claimed EEZs have drawn significant attention but no protests because neither state recognizes a coastal state authority to restrict such activities. South Korea has nonetheless expressed concern about the growing frequency of such activities, citing some 602 instances of PLAN vessels operating in its claimed waters in the years from 2016 to 2019.[118] Some of these actions have been military survey and intelligence collection—though again, because China also claims the area as its own EEZ, inferences about the intended rule are confounded.[119] A similar ambiguity is present in the case of Japan's response to PLAN activities in its claimed EEZ surrounding the disputed Diaoyu/Senkaku Islands.[120]

However, PLAN vessels and aircraft have also operated routinely in Japan's undisputed EEZs.[121] While Japanese law recognizes this right, its officials have taken exception to regular PLAN activity in and around the several narrow straits between Japanese islands that have not been designated as "straits used for international navigation" and that are completely or partially within its territorial seas.[122] The presence, in particular, of submerged PLAN submarines that likely collect hydrographic and intelligence data (that is, conduct military surveys) is another example of engaging in "activities that by its own interpretation of international law China does not countenance even in the non-sovereign waters of its EEZ."[123] For example, China's Ministry of National Defense has described transits of its warships through the Miyako Strait as being "in full compliance with international law and international practice" despite clear prohibitions on such activity in Chinese waters.[124] Again, this PRC interpretation is consistent at least on the basic principle that the coastal state has the right to regulate military activities in its EEZ—but if the state does not choose to regulate, such practices are not categorically prohibited.

Since at least 2016, the Japan Maritime Self-Defense Force (JMSDF) has exercised with its US Navy allies in the South China Sea, conducting intelligence, surveillance, and reconnaissance activities and drills.[125] Despite some discussion of also challenging PRC innocent passage restrictions, Japan has so far avoided inflaming PRC sensitivity to JMSDF presence in those waters.[126]

The Special Case of East China Sea Airspace

The PRC's declaration of an "Air Defense Identification Zone" (ADIZ) over parts of the East China Sea in November 2013 is a special case implicating EEZ overflight.[127] This zone does not purport to confer any jurisdictional authority, but the PRC nonetheless requires identification for all aircraft, commercial and civilian, transiting the zone. Although the ADIZ is not strictly related to the law of the sea, nor even international law, it bears on the question of military overflight in EEZs.[128] The announcement of the ADIZ did not invoke the EEZ, nor any law of the sea rules in China's domestic law, but the zone described is 200 nautical miles in breadth and thus coextensive with part of China's EEZ claim and its limited authority in the airspace above it.[129] It also overlaps with the ADIZs declared by Japan, Korea, and Taiwan, posing issues for de-conflicting airspace in the region.

A distinctive element of China's rule is its requirement that aircraft "shall obey the instructions of the ECS ADIZ management agency or its authorized units. The Chinese armed forces will take emergency defensive measures for aircraft that do not cooperate with identification or refuse to obey instructions." The PRC applies this standard to all air-craft in the ADIZ, including those that do not intend to enter the state's territorial airspace (that is, within 12 nautical miles).[130] The combination of these rules distinguishes China's declared ADIZ from those in the US, Canada, Japan, and other nations. Notably, however, South Korea also requires all ADIZ transits to file flight plans regardless of destination.[131]

In response to this restriction, the US promptly exercised its claimed freedom of overflight by sending two Air Force B-52 bomber aircraft un-notified through the zone within two days of the announcement; it has further challenged the restriction with "freedom of navigation opera-tions" each year since 2014.[132] Japan and Korea both conducted similar activities with military aircraft within the week. These overflights did not draw a PRC operational response, as promised in China's statement, but evoked instead only a belated acknowledgment that the PLA Air Force had detected the aircraft. After China had rejected a request to remove the area of overlap, Korea further extended its ADIZ to cover the area of the East China Sea above Ieodo/Suyan Rock. Japan protested China's re-striction as "dangerous" and has repeatedly defied the injunction to iden-tify its aircraft in the zone; it has further instructed Japanese civilian car-riers to disregard that requirement.[133] Japanese Prime Minister Shinzo Abe demanded that the measure be rescinded, describing it as "unjustly violating the freedom of overflight over the high seas," to which the PRC responded that the ADIZ "conforms to international laws and conven-tions and does not affect the freedom of overflight."[134]

The PRC has largely declined to enforce its ADIZ requirements in the face of concerted opposition to the proposed rule from Japan, Korea, and the United States. MFA spokespeople have instead reassured for-eign observers that "the legal status of the related airspace remains unchanged. . . . [T]he freedom and order of overflight above the ECS has not been affected at all and have been as secure and free as ever." Periodically, PRC officials and analysts float the possibility of instituting an ADIZ in the SCS "if the level and intensity of foreign military aviation activities continues to elevate in the future."[135] However, the PRC's experience with the ECS ADIZ and its practical inefficacy for restricting military overflight make such an eventuality less consequential for the status of EEZ airspace.

Objections from Non–East Asian Specially Affected States

The most consistent objections to China's EEZ navigational rules by states outside of the region have come from the United States, many through the instrumentality of its Freedom of Navigation Operation (FONOP) program. Other states have largely expressed their protests in diplomatic notes, but a growing number of them have begun to exercise their military navigational rights in and above Chinese waters, including Australia, France, Germany, Japan, and the United Kingdom.[136]

The US FONOP program has formally demonstrated America's objections to excessive maritime claims by coastal states all around the world, with particular attention to China over the last decade. Although its application to China has focused on straight baseline and innocent passage claims, a growing proportion of its FONOPs have challenged China's putative restrictions on EEZ airspace and military survey. Since 2007, at least one FONOP per year has specifically targeted one or more elements of China's EEZ restrictions. Additional FONOPs have targeted other rules that bear on EEZ waters and airspace, challenging the ADIZ in the East China Sea (since 2014) and the projection of territorial airspace from low-tide elevations in the South China Sea (since 2018).[137]

A significant number of the FONOPs have also challenged the validity of PRC straight baselines enclosing outlying archipelagos at the Paracels and the Spratlys. Although they are ostensibly challenges to baselines, these actions also contest the PRC's claimed right to exercise jurisdiction over EEZ military activities. Sailing through these baselines (or hypothetical baselines in the Spratlys) at a distance of greater than 12 nautical miles from rocks and islands, the US Navy vessels effectively assert the right to freedom of navigation for warships in EEZs. Such challenges have occurred every year since 2013.[138] These efforts demonstrate at least one consistent and uniform state practice of operating in China's restricted zones.

As the PRC's reaction to US navigation in its jurisdictional waters has intensified, several NATO allies have conducted (or announced intention to conduct) "freedom of navigation" patrols of their own. Since April 2018, the United Kingdom's Royal Navy has transited at least five vessels through EEZs in the South China Sea and declared that "all Government ships, including naval ships, enjoy the right of innocent passage in the territorial sea and freedom of navigation in the contiguous zone and EEZ under UNCLOS."[139] According to the PLAN Commander Sun Jianguo, France has periodically transited the SCS en route to its territories in the South Pacific since at least 2015.[140] A French naval frigate conducted a Taiwan Strait transit in 2019, and in 2021 the French operated a nuclear submarine on patrols in the EEZs of the South China Sea.[141] The German navy announced in March 2021 that a frigate will conduct patrols in the SCS, its first entrance into those waters since 2001.[142]

Australia has also begun to publicize its naval presence in the SCS, since 2017 conducting annual "Indo-Pacific Endeavor" deployments that transit claimed PRC EEZs in the South China Sea. Through its consistent military diplomacy with Malaysia, Indonesia, and Singapore, Australia has reportedly operated naval vessels in areas of the SCS (though not necessarily within the PRC's claimed EEZ) for decades.[143] In 2020, the Australian naval frigate *HMAS Arunta II* (FFH 151) conducted surface, subsurface, and air defense exercises in the SCS alongside vessels from the US Navy and the Japan Maritime Self-Defense Force.

Among the specially affected states, the United States has been the most persistent in its objections to PRC navigational restrictions in the EEZ. The US Navy's particular interest in military navigation in the East Asian littoral has brought to the fore several elements of China's proposed rules, with the effect of inviting further protest—including operational assertions—from several other navies that seek to exercise their freedoms of navigation and overflight in Chinese-claimed waters. Littoral claimant states have been more circumspect about confronting the PRC on this count, some of them (Vietnam and Malaysia) due to comparable restrictions in their own domestic law. However, routine military navigation and overflight by the SCS littoral states is likely to occur regularly in disputed EEZs, which often cannot be avoided en route to high

TABLE 17

SPECIALLY AFFECTED STATE RESPONSES TO PRC EEZ PRACTICE

	Restrictions on military survey	Restrictions on EEZ airspace	Restrictions on EEZ military exercises	Taiwan Strait transit
Japan	Object	Object	Object	Acquiesce
Korea	N/A	Object	N/A	N/A
Malaysia	Adopt	Acquiesce	Adopt[a]	N/A
Philippines	Acquiesce	Acquiesce	Acquiesce	N/A
USA	Object	Object	Object	Object
Vietnam	Adopt	Acquiesce	Adopt	N/A
Australia, France, Germany, and UK	Object	Acquiesce	Object	Object

[a]Malaysia does not observably enforce its domestic law against PLA operations in its claimed EEZ.

seas. Because public reporting on military activities is unsystematic, the likely phenomenon of unobserved exercise of freedom of navigation and overflight in the region poses a challenge to conclusive analysis. Nevertheless, the inconsistency of the PRC rule over time shows in the varied manner and intensity of its official responses to increased foreign military activities. Moreover, the non-uniformity of its application to different claimed EEZs—treating the Taiwan Strait, the ECS, and SCS according to different rules in practice—further works against the emergence of a regional custom or a wider rule (Table 17).

On their face, China's navigation rules are incoherent. They appear to apply only under certain circumstances, in certain waters, and they seem to not apply to China's own navigation in other coastal states' jurisdictional zones. Yet there is no necessary contradiction between China's own military activities within the jurisdictional zones of other states and its practice of advocating and enforcing rules against other nations' military navigation and overflight in its territorial seas and EEZs. Underlying these superficially incompatible practices is a unifying rule: the sovereign coastal state decides who may enter its claimed waters and what they are permitted to do there. If foreign states adopt a more permissive attitude, there is no lack of coherence in the PLAN exercising the full extent of its freedoms under a particular coastal state's regime.

This seeming contradiction confounds many US observers, who expect China will (or should) promote freedom of military navigation as the PLAN operates more extensively out of area. "As the world's foremost maritime power," explained US Department of State Legal Adviser John Bellinger in Senate testimony, "our security interests are intrinsically linked to freedom of navigation. We have more to gain from legal certainty and public order in the world's oceans than any other country."[144] Securing legal, normalized access to the world's oceans has been sacrosanct in American policy and practice of naval navigation and strategic mobility for generations.[145] But China regards its naval navigational ambitions as qualitatively different from those of the United States. As one PLAN analyst explains it:

> We fail to see that the needs and approaches of the Chinese navy going out are different from those of the United States. When China's navy goes out, it definitely needs a broader space for freedom of navigation and will certainly enter foreign territorial waters, but this does not mean that it should ignore the laws of other countries or even invade their territorial waters at will, as the United States does. Many people follow the logic [of reciprocity] "if you want to take something, you must first give it to someone else" and believe that PRC domestic laws should be amended to gain more freedom of navigation for the Chinese Navy to go out. While this logic may seem reasonable, it actually ignores the difference between the freedom needed by the Chinese navy to go out and the US-style freedom of navigation.[146]

Chinese leaders and strategists, while prizing their own freedom of navigation, do not share the American interest in upholding and enforcing the rules that make a relatively open maritime order possible. The extant navigational regime on the world's oceans is permissive of China's activities precisely because the US Navy has expended so much blood, treasure, and manpower to keep it that way. China does not perceive a need to make a comparable and redundant investment in free navigation. It is therefore free to pursue restrictive rules that accrue only to its own benefit, without any expectation that other states will adopt like practices in their home waters. In fact, as the PLAN becomes a global force, it is advantageous for other states *not* to adopt the rules that China applies to them.

China's practice of restricting military access in the "sea areas under PRC jurisdiction" (and associated airspace) lends a distinctly regionalized character to the observed patterns of navigation in East Asia. Within its "near seas," China's extraordinary build-up of military capability and law enforcement capacity allows for effective, practical denial—or at least coercion—of all but the strongest maritime powers. The local, specially affected states themselves are somewhat supportive overall of a variety of navigational restrictions—and especially on innocent passage. In EEZs, these states largely lack the capability and tolerance for risk against a superior Chinese force whose assertiveness has made credible the threat that worse consequences are possible. Japan and South Korea, meanwhile, as strong powers with a still stronger ally in the United States, have largely eschewed naval operations in the South China Sea and have made a separate and tenuous peace in the northern littoral area of East Asia.

The "range rings" view of China's impressive military capability to prevent access and deny operations in the western Pacific misses the basic premise of the "open" order that the US seeks to uphold.[147] Overlapping strategic power projection is one necessary consequence of a set of rules that permits modern warships and submarines to operate across the globe. The US and other maritime powers are reconciled to this reality and taking efforts to secure their access at acceptable levels of risk. Foreign military navigation therefore persists in PRC-claimed waters as elsewhere. If anything, its operational tempo is increasing as the US and its allies seek to focus geostrategic attention on the East Asian littoral.

Commercial navigation, meanwhile, remains essentially unhindered.[148] Xi Jinping is half-correct, then, when he asserts that "[t]here has never been any problem with the freedom of navigation and overflight; nor will there ever be any in the future, for China needs unimpeded commerce through these waters more than anyone else."[149] Military freedom of navigation does face a problem, but one that is manageable within the tenuous balance of the existing maritime order.

That balance is subject to change if China consistently and uniformly employs the "weapon of international law" in tandem with its steady build-up of a naval, constabulary, and other operational means of excluding undesirable vessels from maritime space. China's practices cannot change the regional rules without such coordination. But Beijing's boat may be lifted by wider trends in creeping "security" jurisdiction in territorial seas and EEZs across the globe.[150]

CHAPTER SIX

Dispute Resolution Rules

[T]here is the issue of what are called in China the Diaoyu Islands and in Japan the Senkaku Islands. This sort of thing is an
issue that we need not bring out in a meeting like this one. . . .
Our generation may not have enough wisdom to resolve it, but
the next generation will probably have more wisdom than we do
and be able to resolve this issue.
—*Deng Xiaoping, Vice Premier of the People's Republic of China*[1]

China insists on resolving the disputes with the countries directly
affected through negotiations and consultations on the basis of
respect for historical facts and in accordance with international
law. We are fully capable and confident of working with ASEAN
countries to maintain peace and stability in the South China Sea.
—*Xi Jinping, General Secretary of the Chinese Communist Party*[2]

China did not accept or participate in the [South China Sea] arbitration so as to safeguard its own lawful rights and interests, as
well as the authority and integrity of the UNCLOS.
—*Ma Xinmin, Deputy-Director of the Ministry of Foreign Affairs
Department of Treaty and Law*[3]

CHINA'S DISPUTES OVER NAVIGATION, resource, and geographic
rules necessarily engage another critical element of international law of
the sea: dispute resolution rules. The Convention's formal provisions for
the settlement of disputes are, in principle, applicable to virtually any
dispute over the interpretation and application of law of the sea rules—
to include all of China's maritime disputes, but not its territorial sovereignty disputes. In practice, states only rarely avail themselves of these
formal dispute resolution mechanisms (DRM), which are themselves
the objects of dispute over their proper interpretation and application.

The *Philippines v. China* arbitration ("SCS Arbitration") continues to stimulate new developments in China's practice on these questions, as well as that of specially affected states. As in all of China's maritime disputes, sovereignty holds special importance in this unfolding process. Fundamentally, the question is whether "the rules" are susceptible to any authoritative interpretation beyond that of the individual and autonomous sovereign. The question of consent, so central to positive theories of international law, also looms large in this arena.[4] In general, states jealously guard their sovereignty and find ample justification under international law to do so. No international court or tribunal has jurisdiction over a dispute without some form of consent of the parties. Analysis of the conditions and contingencies under which China has sought resolution to its maritime disputes yields particular insights into the rules China seeks to apply for resolving disputes concerning the law of the sea.

State practice of these dispute resolution rules is a source of considerable disagreement and contention, not least in China's maritime disputes. PRC practice manifests three non-exclusive modes of approaching such disputes: (1) narrowing the scope of UNCLOS compulsory dispute settlement; (2) advancing alternative methods for resolving disputes through diplomacy; and (3) withholding acknowledgment of the very existence of a dispute to be settled. This chapter addresses how each of these manifests China's practice and how it is met by the counterparties to its maritime disputes.

UNCLOS DISPUTE RESOLUTION RULES

States are not subject to the jurisdiction of international tribunals absent their express consent.[5] UNCLOS parties have expressly consented to certain types of compulsory dispute resolution. UNCLOS Part XV obliges states that ratify the treaty to accept one of several choices of forum to resolve "any dispute concerning the interpretation or application of this Convention" (UNCLOS, Art. 286). Among major multilateral treaties, only the World Trade Organization similarly prescribes such compulsory jurisdiction, requiring state consent to third-party settlement of certain classes of dispute as a condition of ratification.[6]

This "compromissory clause" of UNCLOS means that China, like all other states that have ratified the treaty, has rendered its prior consent to accept the jurisdiction of a court or tribunal under certain circumstances. Those circumstances are defined in UNCLOS Article 279, which recognizes the UN Charter's Article 2(3) provision that "All Members shall settle their international disputes by peaceful means" and "shall seek a solution by the means indicated in [UN Charter] Article 33": namely, "by negotiation, enquiry, mediation, conciliation, arbitration, judicial settlement, resort to regional agencies or arrangements, or other peaceful means of their own choice." If the parties have failed to reach a settlement by these general means, then any of them may submit the dispute to one of the various compulsory procedures for resolving disputes—including the Annex VI International Tribunal for the Law of the Sea (ITLOS), the International Court of Justice (ICJ), or one of two types of ad hoc arbitral tribunal (Annexes VII and VIII). These arbitral bodies must determine their own jurisdiction in preliminary hearings (Art. 288.4).

It takes only one party to initiate a dispute resolution procedure that is final and binding on all parties (UNCLOS, Art. 296). However, there are defined limits on this unilateral recourse to arbitration. A state may decline to accept DRM for certain classes of dispute if it has formally exercised the "optional exceptions" listed in Article 298.[7] By invoking this provision, states may exclude all or some of the following issues from compulsory procedures: sea boundary delimitations, historic bays or titles, military activities, and matters that fall under the purview of the UN Security Council in exercise of its functions under the UN Charter (Art. 298.1.a-c). This DRM system is available only to parties to the Convention (and thus excludes the United States).

The contentious SCS Arbitration case between China and the Philippines provides an especially salient test of these UNCLOS rules. To date, China has taken the position that its maritime disputes are not subject to those formal mechanisms under UNCLOS. The PRC instead advocates "resolving the disputes *with countries directly affected through negotiations and consultations* on the basis of respect for historical facts and in accordance with international law," as Xi told southeast Asian leaders in 2015.[8] Considered alongside other PRC practice on dispute resolution rules, this seminal case affords insights into China's actions to shape and change the dispute resolution rules in the law of the sea.

PRC Practice in UNCLOS Dispute Resolution

Well before the initiation of the SCS Arbitration in 2013, the PRC established a principled opposition to mandatory dispute resolution procedures on any matter that might be construed as touching on its sovereignty. PRC legal scholars have been asserting as much since at least the early 1960s, arguing that "on sovereignty questions . . . it is never possible to seek a settlement from any form of international arbitration."[9] Taken to a logical extreme, this sovereigntist stance excludes third-party resolution of any law of the sea disputes because all maritime rights and jurisdiction must begin with sovereign title. This sovereign sensibility has informed the PRC's practice in other treaties, where it has generally avoided consenting to compulsory dispute resolution.[10]

PRC Reservations About Compulsory Procedures

China made known its views on law of the sea dispute resolution during the negotiations of the UNCLOS Conference. The PRC delegation anticipated additional legal disputes about its maritime claims, which compounded existing sovereignty disputes over islands in the South and East China Seas. In light of certain provisions in the evolving Convention's text, China's head of delegation assessed the treaty's emerging regimes as "increasing the contradictions with their neighbors and making it more difficult to solve disputes."[11] The PRC's most eminent international legal scholar, Wang Tieya, joined the Chinese delegation and made his only official comment to the plenary group on the subject of dispute resolution for maritime boundaries. These were guaranteed to be problematic because China is enveloped by semi-enclosed seas, all less than 400 nautical miles in breadth.[12] He referred to the previous comments of PRC delegates on the matter as "quite unambiguous" and reiterated that "*any* compulsory and binding third-party settlement of a dispute concerning sea boundary delimitations must have the consent of all parties to the dispute. Otherwise, such a form of settlement would not be acceptable to the Chinese delegation."[13]

China's vocal and consistent opposition to compulsory DRM provisions at the Conference did not win out in the agreed articles. In consequence, the PRC sought to exempt itself from this aspect of the "package deal" of UNCLOS when it ratified the treaty in 1996, despite the explicit prohibition on such "reservations and exceptions" in Article 309.[14] In a statement issued in May 1996, prior to submitting its ratification instrument, China announced that "the PRC will effect, *through consultations,* the delimitation of boundaries of maritime jurisdiction with the states with coasts opposite or adjacent of China respectively on the basis of international law and in accordance with the equitable principle."[15] In proclaiming that "consultations" were the sole procedure by which it would address disputes on maritime boundaries, China aimed to exclude itself altogether from any third-party mechanisms.

Curiously, the PRC did not at that time exercise its right under Article 298 to formally exclude itself from mandatory settlements. Only in August 2006, a decade later, did the PRC issue a declaration under Article 298 stating that it "does not accept any of the procedures provided for in Section 2 of Part XV of the Convention" concerning historic bays and titles, maritime boundary delimitation, and military and law enforcement activities.[16] Given China's overriding concern for its sovereignty and general wariness of third-party dispute resolution, this exclusion is consistent with its overall practice in international law and its stance in the UNCLOS arbitral suit launched by the Philippines not seven years later.[17]

The SCS Arbitral Process

In January 2013, the Republic of the Philippines Ministry of Foreign Affairs filed a Statement and Notification of Claim under Article 287 and Annex VII of UNCLOS III.[18] The Philippines sought relief from fifteen alleged Chinese violations of UNCLOS, presented in a wide-ranging litany of wrongs including the PRC "historic rights" claim, professed entitlements from submerged and artificial features in the South China Sea, dangerous seamanship, and poor environmental stewardship.[19] Within days of the Philippines' claim, the PRC officially rejected the entire procedure, declined to participate, and instead launched a concerted and ongoing campaign in the court of public opinion to vindicate its position on the matter.

In a series of official statements, including two official position papers on the arbitration and a semi-official "critical study" on the awards, the PRC laid out both its SCS claims and its stance on third-party dispute settlement in much greater detail and precision than at any time prior.[20] The first Chinese riposte came on the day of the Philippines notification;

it emphasized the PRC's position that "[t]he key and root of the dispute between China and the Philippines over the South China Sea is territorial [sovereignty] disputes caused by the illegal occupation of some islands and reefs of China's Nansha Islands."[21] Within a month, the MFA issued China's formal position on the matter in a diplomatic rejoinder to the Philippines, articulating "Four Nos": (1) no acceptance, (2) no participation, (3) no recognition, and (4) no implementation.[22] China urged the Philippines to "return to the correct path of bilateral negotiations to resolve disputes" and committed from the outset that it would not officially appear, submit claims, nor consider any arbitral award "final and binding" as provided in UNCLOS Article 296.[23]

The MFA published a "Position Paper" in December 2014 that elaborated the legal reasoning behind China's categorical rejection of the procedure.[24] While the document was not submitted formally to the tribunal, the PRC released it the week before the deadline to officially submit materials in response to the Philippines' claim, and the PRC ambassador to the Netherlands hand-delivered two letters to the Permanent Court of Arbitration (PCA) in the Hague notifying the court of the position paper and stating that it "comprehensively explain[s] why the Arbitral Tribunal . . . manifestly has no jurisdiction over the case."[25] The letter asserted that China's lack of response to any issues raised by the tribunal "shall not be understood or interpreted by anyone in any sense as China's acquiescence in or non-objection to any and all procedural or substantive matters already or might be raised by the Arbitral Tribunal."[26]

Nonetheless, the tribunal determined that China's communications "effectively constitute a plea" and resolved to bifurcate the proceedings into separate jurisdictional and merits phases in order to consider China's preliminary objection.[27] The tribunal then extensively considered the Chinese arguments as set out in the position paper, and it frequently cites the document in the two awards it issued, the October 2015 Award on Jurisdiction and Admissibility (hereafter, Jurisdiction Award) and the July 2016 Award on the Merits (hereafter, Merits Award).

The PRC position paper's first argument is that "[t]he essence of the subject-matter of the arbitration is the territorial sovereignty over several maritime features in the South China Sea, which is beyond the scope of the Convention and does not concern the interpretation or application of the Convention."[28] The Convention authorizes an arbitral body to rule only on "interpretation and application" of the Convention, which addresses only maritime matters.

The Philippines' claim, in the Chinese rendering, was undertaken in bad faith, smuggling in a sovereignty dispute under the guise of questions of maritime entitlement. "The Philippines," the position paper alleges, "is well aware that a tribunal . . . of the Convention has no jurisdiction over territorial sovereignty disputes. In an attempt to circumvent this jurisdictional hurdle and fabricate a basis for institution of arbitral proceedings, the Philippines has cunningly packaged its case in the present form. . . . This contrived packaging, however, fails to conceal the very essence of the subject-matter of the arbitration, namely, the territorial sovereignty over certain maritime features in the SCS."[29] On this basis, the PRC concluded, the arbitration could not proceed without a determination of sovereignty that it had no authority to render.[30] This high bar for admissibility would preclude virtually all use of UNCLOS compulsory dispute resolution, an outcome consistent with China's stated preferences.

The status of low-tide elevations (LTEs) also figures into China's argument on sovereignty. The position paper notes that two of the Philippines' submissions (numbers four and six) ask the tribunal to determine whether or not a given feature is in fact a naturally formed island under UNCLOS Article 121 or an LTE, which cannot be the subject of a sovereign title. The PRC argued that ruling on this issue would potentially breach the tribunal's jurisdiction under UNCLOS: "[w]hether low-tide elevations can be appropriated as territory is in itself a question of territorial sovereignty, not a matter concerning the interpretation or application of the Convention. The Convention is silent on this issue of appropriation."[31] This is itself not a substantive position on the rules for LTEs (discussed in chapter 3), but rather an assertion that those UNCLOS rules on LTEs have narrow applicability on a matter governed in the first instance by customary international law on sovereignty.

The second line of argument in the position paper faults the Philippines for breaching "a long-standing agreement between China and the Philippines on resolving their disputes in the SCS through friendly consultations and negotiations."[32] The PRC locates the substance of that agreement in a series of joint statements by the parties beginning in 1995 wherein they "agree to promote a peaceful settlement of disputes through bilateral friendly consultations and negotiations in accordance with universally-recognized principles of international law, *including* the 1982 UNCLOS."[33] They cite additionally the multilateral Association of Southeast Asian Nations (ASEAN) "Declaration on the Conduct of Parties in the South China Sea" (DOC) of 2002, in which China and the Philippines resolved to undertake "friendly consultations and negotiations by sovereign states directly concerned."[34] The crux of this claim is that UNCLOS is not the appropriate body of rules governing the dispute. Instead, the treaty is superseded by non-binding diplomatic statements issued in the course of China-Philippines diplomacy that "establish an obligation between the two countries" to forego third-party dispute resolution.[35]

China had successfully advocated for the DOC to *not* be a binding legal instrument yet cites it here as part of a diplomatic record that constitutes a binding agreement.[36] In Chinese domestic law, this is a distinction without a difference. The PRC's 1990 Law on the Procedure of the Conclusion of Treaties does not distinguish between "treaties" and "important agreements" nor provide a standard for "important."[37] The determination of which agreements will count as "important" (and thus entail legal obligations on par with formal treaties) is left to the State Council, which is authorized to decide which agreements will count as legally binding.[38]

The third and final argument of the position paper asserts that even if the prior two arguments are dismissed, the "subject-matter would still be an integral part of maritime delimitation and, having been excluded by the 2006 Declaration filed by China [under UNCLOS Art. 298], could not be submitted for arbitration."[39] In arguing against the tribunal's jurisdiction on this count, the PRC again alleges that the Philippines acted with bad-faith political motives "[t]o cover up the maritime delimitation nature of the China-Philippines dispute and to sidestep China's 2006 declaration."[40] The alleged "cover up" is the act of presenting the tribunal with claims about entitlements in such a way that "a so-called 'legal interpretation' on each of them . . . would amount to a de facto maritime delimitation."[41] The Philippines' submissions include issues that have been considered in previous, successful maritime boundary delimitations; ergo, the position paper reasons, the Philippines was simply seeking a backdoor to effect a maritime delimitation. The PRC positions itself as the defender of the Convention against alleged abuses that, taken to their logical extreme, would undermine the function of the treaty.

China's mode of championing UNCLOS is to exclude the treaty's application to its maritime disputes. The position paper concludes that the South China Sea issue "is compounded by complex historical background and sensitive political factors. . . . China always maintains that the parties concerned shall seek proper ways and means of settlement through consultations and negotiations on the basis of respect for historical facts and international law."[42] If historically complex and politically sensitive matters are always to be excluded, the scope of jurisdiction for dispute resolution under UNCLOS is far narrower than the treaty's black letters denote.

Finally, the position paper enjoins the tribunal to consider that it is not China but rather "the Philippines [that] contravenes the general principles of international law and international jurisprudence on the settlement of international maritime disputes."[43]

This argumentation goes well beyond what would be necessary to establish a jurisdictional exception. It is instead a principled statement of China's desired rule about the supremacy of sovereign will over undesired legal obligation. This universal exception may be intended only to "exempt" China from this particular suit.[44] Inquiry into China's subsequent practice on this and other mandatory dispute resolution under UNCLOS will shed further light on this basic question of uniformity.

The SCS Jurisdiction Award

The tribunal delivered a preliminary Award on Jurisdiction and Admissibility on 29 October 2015, in which it found jurisdiction on seven of the fifteen claims submitted by the Philippines and left seven others for consideration on the merits because they raised factual questions about the status of features as islands, rocks, or LTEs and the locations of specific activities. (The fifteenth claim was returned to the Philippines for further clarification.)[45] While preliminary and partial, this award substantially dismissed the Chinese plea—in particular the bid for PRC sovereignty to override the tribunal's writ to arbitrate issues of interpretation and application of the Convention.

The PRC Ministry of Foreign Affairs preempted the Jurisdiction Award with a statement the week prior to its release: "As a sovereign state and a signatory to the UNCLOS, China enjoys the right to independently choose methods and procedures for dispute settlement. China has always insisted on resolving territorial disputes and maritime jurisdiction disputes with neighboring countries through negotiations and consultations."[46] The statement reinforces China's position that whatever the content of the pending award, it "will not have any effect." It goes beyond claiming a specific exemption for the PRC, suggesting a general position of principle: against the Philippines' "abuse of the Convention's mandatory dispute settlement mechanism . . . [China] maintain[s] the integrity and authority of the Convention."[47] An MFA spokesperson further invited the Philippines to return to "Yangguan Avenue" (阳关大道)—that is, the wide and correct path toward bilateral negotiations with the PRC.[48]

Over the ensuing months, the PRC launched an intensive public relations campaign against the tribunal that consistently reiterated its various complaints on jurisdiction, despite the procedure's continuation to the merits phase. The effects of this campaign are analyzed below with regard to specially affected states, but it bears noting in the context of PRC practice that the refusal to acknowledge the tribunal's authority even after it had found jurisdiction (pursuant to UNCLOS, Art. 288.4) established a further position on the appropriate rules. The MFA's director-general of the Treaty and Law Department, Xu Hong, framed this as a *universal* objection:

> The Arbitration brings our attention to the question that the international community should be concerned of, i.e., how to interpret and apply the compulsory arbitration procedures under the UNCLOS comprehensively, accurately and in good faith. If other States follow the Philippines to abuse the compulsory arbitration procedures . . . the consequence would be the opening of the "Pandora's Box" of lawsuit abuse, and that the declarations excluding compulsory arbitration made by over 30 States will be rendered completely meaningless. . . . [It will] sabotage the international order of the sea established by UNCLOS. . . . Dispute settlement mechanism is one of the pillars of the legal order of the sea established by the UNCLOS. . . . Under this mechanism, the means of dispute settlement chosen by the States Parties on their own should be applied as the preferred procedures, and the compulsory proce-

dures are secondary and complementary. . . . [I]n the Convention, the respect for the States' choice on their own [sovereign] will or autonomous willingness is underlined.[49]

Where prior arguments had focused on the particular facts of the case, the PRC counterclaims increasingly promote a vision for the "legal order of the sea" as a whole, of which UNCLOS is an important but non-exhaustive and subsidiary element. "The tribunal shall not decide on its jurisdiction arbitrarily, but prudently in line with international law including the UNCLOS," explained Vice-Foreign Minister Liu Zhenmin. "When we refer to international law, we need to know in the first place what international law is all about."[50] This posture marks a distinct change in the scope of PRC claims about the rules for dispute resolution and their potential bearing on maritime order.

Senior MFA officials regularly promoted this universalizing stance to foreign media, consistently portraying China as upholding the rules against foreign subversion. Liu Zhenmin took an interview with US newspapers in which he stressed that "the arbitral tribunal established at the request of the Philippines is not an international court or a permanent court of arbitration, but a temporary arbitral tribunal comprising five arbitrators designated by Mr. Shunji Yanai, former president of UNCLOS."[51] The leading PRC foreign affairs official, Yang Jiechi, further criticized Yanai as "a right-wing Japanese intent on ridding Japan of post-war arrangements";[52] the CCP organ *People's Daily* ran an English-language article "Shunji Yanai, Manipulator Behind Illegal South China Sea Arbitration."[53] PRC scholars parroted these ad hominem attacks, including at the annual meeting of the American Society of International Law, showing a new facet of China's campaign to propagate an image as the defender of UNCLOS.[54]

The SCS Merits Award

The greatly anticipated Merits Award of 12 July 2016 catalyzed another series of official pronouncements that clarified PRC positions on a range of rules.[55] Rhetorically, at least, a consistent line remained. A White Paper issued by the State Council the day after the award retread the various earlier objections: "The PRC solemnly declares that the award is null and void and has no binding force."[56] MFA Vice-Minister Liu Zhenmin pronounced the award "just a piece of waste paper."[57] Yet the practice of the PRC with regard to the substantive relief decreed in the award is inconsistent with its prior stance in at least one respect.

The tribunal found that "Scarborough Shoal has been a traditional fishing ground for fishermen of many nationalities [including China, Taiwan, the Philippines, and Vietnam], and declares that China has, through the operation of its official vessels at Scarborough Shoal from May 2012 onwards, unlawfully prevented fishermen from the Philippines from engaging in traditional fishing at Scarborough Shoal."[58] Without acknowledging the award, Chinese law enforcement began to allow Philippine-flagged fishing boats back into the territorial sea of Scarborough Shoal later in 2016.

This marks the sole act of partial PRC compliance with the award—though one that advantages China's own claims to traditional fishing rights throughout the SCS.[59] In making this limited concession to the Philippines, China affirmed its bid to continue its own traditional fishing in the territorial seas and other jurisdictional waters of neighboring states. The China Coast Guard has maintained a close cordon on the shoal and can unilaterally reverse this limited concession to the Philippines—and indeed has done so consistently during the PRC's unilateral summer fishing ban.[60]

Apart from that notable exception, no other substantive elements of the Merits Award have been honored in PRC practice, which continues in open breach of the rest of the award. One possible, additional exception noted by some authors concerns the final, generalized Philippines' claim that China "shall comply with its duties under UNCLOS," which the tribunal considered to be "beyond dispute."[61] China is practicing consistently with its general interpretation of UNCLOS, rather than in exercise of an "exemption" from this specific procedure.

PRC Practice on Other UNCLOS Dispute Resolution Mechanisms

The PRC's categorical rejection of the SCS Arbitration is only one facet of its practice on compulsory DRM under UNCLOS. Chinese judges sit on UNCLOS arbitral panels, while Chinese diplomats and maritime officials attend closely to other law of the sea cases, past and present. The MFA director-general of Treaty and Law, Xu Hong, has described PRC practice within the UNCLOS compulsory DRM system as "quite successful and highly appreciated by all parties. We have also accumulated experience from it . . . and Chinese views have been adopted by the courts."[62] Notably, four PRC judges (among them MFA and SOA officials) have served on the International Tribunal for the Law of the Sea, the standing tribunal under UNCLOS Annex VI.[63]

Among the PRC's ITLOS judges, Gao Zhiguo in particular has written several separate opinions that consistently vindicate Chinese views. One affirms the validity of natural prolongation in issues of maritime delimitation.[64] Another Judge Gao opinion advances the Chinese position on exclusions under Article 298 in regard to "military activities," offering reasoning that might be applied in a future case involving a complaint against Chinese law enforcement or naval activity in its own claimed jurisdiction zones: "Article 298 of the Convention is a carefully designed and articulated compromise between the compulsory dispute settlement procedures on the one hand and State sovereignty and jurisdiction on the other hand. It serves as a balance by permitting States to except certain disputes concerning sensitive issues of sovereignty."[65] Sovereignty is plainly the weightier side of that balance for Judge Gao and the PRC.

In light of this substantial participation by PRC judges and diplomats, Xu Hong regards "the so-called ruling in the SCS arbitration case as a counterfactual" or "negative example" that serves to reinforce the consistent PRC rule that such mechanisms are legitimate only when properly employed.[66] Ma Xinmin, another MFA official and Xu Hong's former deputy, has argued that "China is involved in constructive judicial practices under the UNCLOS system."[67] Notwithstanding the aberration of the SCS Arbitration, Ma cites China's written submissions to ITLOS and the Sub Regional Fisheries Commission, the latter contesting the exercise of "advisory jurisdiction" of the ITLOS, which may be interpreted as promoting China's stance on the limited scope of DRM.[68] There is a consistent and uniform thread in these submissions and opinions toward narrowly construing the jurisdiction of third-party arbitral bodies.

In pending cases involving other parties, China has seldom made official remarks about the procedure. However, Chinese officials have commented on aspects of other cases that bear substantive similarities to the SCS Arbitration, offering an opportunity to observe whether their position is uniform and consistent when it comes to other sovereign states. One ITLOS case in particular has garnered Chinese interest, that of the *Arctic Sunrise*. The Netherlands initiated the case in 2013 to seek "provisional measures" for the prompt release of a Dutch-flagged vessel and crew seized by the Russian Federation.[69]

The *Arctic Sunrise* procedure ran concurrently with the early phase of the SCS Arbitration, and it involved a comparable Russian refusal to appear or accept the tribunal's jurisdiction.[70] The MFA publicized favorable comparisons of China's case to Russia's, noting that "China's refusal to accept or participate in arbitration is to defend the right to independently choose the method of dispute settlement, which is in line with international practice."[71] The article further cited two other instances of states refusing to accept compulsory jurisdiction in ICJ proceedings involving law of the sea issues: Turkey in the *Aegean Sea Continental Shelf* (1978) and America in the *Case Concerning the Military and Paramilitary Activities In and Against Nicaragua* (1986).[72] These citations regard the latter cases as evidence of a representative customary practice of excluding compulsory DRM when sovereignty is allegedly at issue. The China Society of International Law's "Critical Study" also cites these (and other) cases in support of the PRC's decision to reject the procedure and its "so-called" arbitral award.[73]

Chinese scholars showed particular interest in *Arctic Sunrise*, asking "[h]ow does 'non-response' affect the dispute settlement mechanism in UNCLOS?" Russia's practice purportedly lent further legitimacy to China's non-recognition of the SCS Arbitration, which was "already even more justified." Assessing that courts remain loathe to penalize non-appearing parties, one scholar nonetheless urged China to "exercise some restraint[;] . . . otherwise it will be vulnerable to recourse under the UNCLOS dispute settlement mechanism." That the US, as a non-party to UNCLOS, is not likewise vulnerable to these compulsory mechanisms is a common grievance in Chinese law of the sea circles.[74]

Indeed, that recognized potential for further UNCLOS arbitral suits against China has generated a sustained discussion on this issue in PRC legal academia and concern among officials. Vietnam is judged the most likely antagonist, and Chinese law of the sea experts believe "it would follow what the Philippines did by packaging its disputes with China in a deliberate way for jurisdiction and admissibility."[75] Such a Vietnamese claim would presumably stand to benefit from the precedent set in the

SCS Arbitration. In that event, "China is highly likely to step up retaliatory measures outside the tribunal regardless of the uncertainty [over] whether it will present itself in the courtroom or stick to the standpoint [of non-appearance adopted in the SCS Arbitration]."[76] Many in the PRC's law of the sea community were privately displeased that China opted not to appear for the jurisdictional phase of the SCS Arbitration, which would have at least assured the chance to appoint sympathetic arbitrators, if not prevail on the merits. A PRC appearance to contest jurisdiction in a future case would nonetheless be consistent with its position on the rule that such jurisdiction must pass a very high bar of individual sovereign will.

Overall, PRC practice in this area of the law of the sea is consistent and uniform. It has only faced one adversarial case, and it stated a principled position on the rules that substantially reduces the scope of any compulsory dispute settlement under UNCLOS in deference to sovereign prerogatives. PRC judges, scholars, and diplomats have further reinforced this position, suggesting that the practice will likely continue along this course. The degree to which specially affected states have responded to China's position in the SCS Arbitration will reveal the potential for this purported rule to influence UNCLOS dispute resolution beyond that critical case (Table 18).

TABLE 18

PRC PRACTICE OF UNCLOS DISPUTE RESOLUTION RULES

PRC-preferred rule	Uniformity (geographic)	Consistency (over time)	Detail
No compulsory application of UNCLOS dispute resolution mechanisms	Yes	Yes	Claimed reservation from UNCLOS to reject all compulsory settlement; defiance of SCS Arbitration
Blanket sovereign exemption	Yes	Yes	Applicable to all PRC sovereignty disputes and their associated maritime disputes

Specially Affected State Responses to PRC UNCLOS
Dispute Resolution Practice

The SCS Arbitration awards were "the most anticipated decisions from an international tribunal in the law of the sea since the entry into force of UNCLOS in 1994."[77] They have also been highly controversial due to China's objections, with significant potential to influence future cases. Strictly as a matter of legal effect, the awards bind only the Philippines and China.[78] However, because the tribunal rendered judgments on specific entitlements from features in the Spratlys as well as on the "historic rights" claim from China's nine-dash line, those states with SCS entitlement and resource claims are also appropriately considered as "specially affected." Other UNCLOS parties may likewise be reasonably considered as specially affected states—although only to the extent that the interpretation and application of the rules of UNCLOS rendered in the awards has bearing on actual or potential cases that may involve those sovereign states. Despite its interest, the United States has no standing in this group because, as a non-party to UNCLOS, it is not subject to any compulsory law of the sea dispute resolution.

The Republic of the Philippines

As the only state other than China formally bound by the award of the SCS Arbitration, the Philippines' response is of special consequence. The administration of Philippine President Rodrigo Duterte took office on 30 June 2016, less than two weeks before the final award was rendered, and immediately adopted a deferential attitude toward Beijing's refusal to acknowledge the award. Duterte even went so far as to describe the award as just "a piece of paper," conspicuously mirroring China's Vice-Foreign Minister Liu Zhenmin's "piece of waste paper" comment.[79] Yet Duterte has also described the Philippines' constitution as no better than "toilet paper" in enforcing Philippines' maritime rights against China.[80] This extreme dismissiveness toward binding legal instruments has not been reflected in the Philippines' state practice.

In practice, the Duterte administration has not relinquished the Philippines' claim nor renounced the validity of the arbitral award. In fact, in private diplomacy the Philippines quietly rejected China's invitation after the award to negotiate the matter bilaterally and has subsequently issued several official statements affirming the award.[81] These were fairly muted until the fourth anniversary of the award in 2020, when the Philippine secretary of foreign affairs, Teodoro Locsin, publicly embraced the award "as a reaffirmation of UNCLOS" and further pronounced the Philippines' "adherence to the award and its enforcement without any possibility of compromise or change. The award is non-negotiable."[82] In more recent frictions with the PRC over waters deemed outside PRC jurisdiction by the arbitral award, the Philippines' Department of Foreign Affairs has further emphasized that "the UNCLOS—to which both the Republic of the Philippines and China are parties—and the final and binding 12 July 2016 Award in the SCS Arbitration are clearly the only norm applicable in this situation."[83]

From the Philippines' official position, the SCS Arbitration "conclusively settled the issue of historic rights and maritime entitlements in the South China Sea."[84] While it is incapable of enforcing the award against China itself, the Philippines has formally and positively affirmed the dispute resolution rules of UNCLOS and further proposed that "[t]he arbitral tribunal's award of 12 July 2016 represents a victory, not just for the Philippines, but for the entire community of consistently law-abiding nations."[85] Whether the rest of that community has similarly understood the award has significant bearing on whether that "victory" is at hand.

Other States with SCS Entitlement Claims

The SCS Arbitration bears directly on those states with claims to jurisdictional entitlement claims within the scope of China's nine-dash line. The Merits Award interpreted and applied UNCLOS Article 121 concerning entitlements due to islands and rocks, a controversial task that the ICJ had sidestepped on numerous occasions in the past.[86] According to Clive Schofield, a leading law of the sea scholar and expert witness for the arbitration, the tribunal's reasoning on entitlements "arguably represents an important clarification of one of the most ambiguous provisions of UNCLOS and is certainly the first judicial attempt to meaningfully address the central conundrum of the Regime of Islands."[87] Although the award is final and binding only on China and the Philippines, the maritime entitlements of all the littoral states are potentially affected by this authoritative interpretation of the treaty. Even in the nearly certain event that China does not revise its own claims to comply with the award, these states have a vested interest in the judgment that none of the Spratly Islands is an "island" capable of generating 200nm entitlements.[88]

Among the other littoral states, neither Brunei nor Malaysia has positively affirmed the SCS arbitral award. Vietnam, however, has done so and further expressed special interest in the case by submitting a formal note verbale requesting "the attention of the Tribunal" to "protect its rights and interests of a legal nature in the South China Sea . . . which may be affected in this arbitration."[89] The tribunal determined that Vietnam's presence was not "indispensable" to finding jurisdiction in the case, but with the Philippines' consent and China's non-objection, proceeded to "authorise the [PCA] Registry to provide Viet Nam with documents and orders issued by the court."[90] Vietnam did not seek to intervene further in the case, but it has dangled the prospect of launching a similar suit.[91] A Vietnamese spokesperson further announced that "Vietnam welcomes the arbitration court's final decision of 12 July 2016."[92]

Indonesia's maritime boundary delimitation dispute with China is specially affected by the award. In principle, the tribunal's determination that no Spratly Islands generate 200nm entitlements eliminates that dispute altogether, because Indonesia's EEZ claim is well beyond 12 nautical miles of any PRC-claimed feature.[93] The Indonesian government submitted a note verbale to the UN stating that its entitlement claims have been "confirmed by the Award of 12 July 2016." The note further addresses the effects of the award on the Chinese nine-dash line that generates their maritime boundary dispute, stating that the award "confirms" that the map "lacks international legal basis" and rejects the idea that Indonesia might be "bound by any claims made in contravention to international law, including UNCLOS 1982."[94]

Taiwan, while excluded from any official standing, rejected the SCS Arbitration in toto and further submitted an amicus curiae regarding the status of Itu Aba (Taiping) Island, the sole feature it occupies in the Spratlys and a key entitlement consideration for the tribunal.[95] Taiwan is obviously a specially affected entity, but its lack of formal standing as a sovereign state and the inseverability of its claims from the mainland's disqualify its practices on this (and other questions). Thus, among the states with entitlements in the SCS, three of the five have affirmatively pronounced the validity of the award and, in so doing, rejected China's particular and universal arguments about dispute resolution rules.

Other Specially Affected States

UNCLOS member states are specially affected by the SCS Arbitration, and several have expressed particular interest in the rules at stake in China's rejection of the UNCLOS arbitral procedure and awards. Relative to the Philippines or other Spratly claimants, the weight of their endorsement or protest against the PRC position is subject to reasonable doubt, but their practices are nonetheless consequential for the wider applicability of China's appeal to a universal sovereign exception on matters of UNCLOS compulsory dispute resolution (Table 19).

Australia, Canada, France, Germany, Japan, New Zealand, and the United Kingdom have made formal statements that classify China's historic rights claims as "invalid" or "illegal" as a result of the award.[96]

TABLE 19

SPECIALLY AFFECTED STATE RESPONSES TO PRC UNCLOS DISPUTE RESOLUTION PRACTICE

	Sovereign exception to compulsory DRM
Brunei	Acquiesce
Indonesia	Object
Malaysia	Acquiesce
Philippines	Object (SCS Arbitration)
Vietnam	Object (SCS Arbitration *amicus curiae*)
Australia, Canada, France, Germany, Japan, New Zealand, and the United Kingdom	Object (reject PRC non-acknowledgment of SCS Arbitration)
Afghanistan, Gambia, Kenya, Lesotho, Liberia, Montenegro, Niger, Pakistan, Papua New Guinea, Sudan, Togo, Vanuatu	Adopt (support PRC non-acknowledgment of SCS Arbitration)

Notably, however, most states have issued no statement on the award, while twelve states have made official statements that dismiss the tribunal as illegitimate but withhold any comment on its substantive findings. These are Afghanistan, Gambia, Kenya, Lesotho, Liberia, Montenegro, Niger, Pakistan, Papua New Guinea, Sudan, Togo, and Vanuatu.[97] China's MFA claims that sixty states joined PRC in objecting to the SCS Arbitration; however, this number includes states that merely expressed support for China's principle of resolving disputes through consultation and dialogue, rather than support for China in the specific case with the Philippines.[98] That "alternative" mode of dispute resolution without recourse to formal or compulsory third-party settlement deserves careful attention as the PRC's preferred rule for dispute resolution.

ALTERNATIVE MARITIME DISPUTE RESOLUTION RULES

UNCLOS does not automatically prescribe compulsory dispute resolution. As detailed above, the primary means for resolving disputes over the law of the sea, as in virtually any matter of international law, is through negotiations among the states involved. UNCLOS Part XV invokes the UN Charter as establishing the basic rule to settle international disputes peacefully: "The parties to any dispute, the continuance of which is likely to endanger the maintenance of international peace and security, shall, first of all, seek a solution by negotiation, enquiry, mediation, conciliation, arbitration, judicial settlement, resort to regional agencies or arrangements, or other peaceful means of their own choice" (UNC, Arts. 2.3 and 33).

These methods notably include several third-party mechanisms, but under UNCLOS Article 286, no compulsory third-party resolution is prescribed until parties have exhausted settlement efforts by those primary, mutually agreed means. The question at hand, then, is the degree to which the PRC has put in practice a rule that systematically precludes recourse to such third-party measures.

PRC Practice of Alternative Maritime Dispute Resolution Rules

China's practice in resolving its maritime disputes is remarkably different from its practice in territorial disputes. On the latter, Taylor Fravel provides strong evidence that the PRC "has been more likely to compromise over disputed territory and less likely to use force than many policy analysts assert, international relations theories might predict, or China scholars expect."[99] These boundary agreements were each effected through bilateral agreement.[100] Yet China's observed historical penchant for "compromise" on land does not extend to the maritime domain, where China has yet to compromise on any of its maritime claims. Instead it has escalated to conflict at a disproportionate rate and has settled only one minor island dispute.[101] Islands account for two of the six instances of escalation that Fravel codes but only one of the seventeen episodes of compromise. Moreover, China has not engaged in any third-party dispute resolution regarding any of its territorial or maritime claims—to include the SCS Arbitration, which China comprehensively rejected.

The PRC's resistance to any external dispute resolution has been a constant in its practice on all matters that pertain directly or indirectly to sovereignty. By contrast, the PRC's predecessor as mainland government, the Republic of China, was an enthusiastic early adopter of the League of Nations, particularly its creation of the Permanent Court of International Justice (PCIJ). "The Chinese delegation vigorously supported it and urged all states to accept the [PCIJ's] compulsory jurisdiction as prescribed in the Draft statute."[102] The ROC's ratification of that instrument represents the last Chinese government to formally accept compulsory dispute resolution on any matter implicating its sovereignty; it also falsifies the oft-heard claim that formal adjudication is stigmatized in Chinese culture.[103]

Early PRC Practice on Dispute Settlement

With the ascendance of the CCP on the mainland, China's openness to compulsory third-party DRM was promptly discontinued. Jerry Cohen and Hungdah Chiu comprehensively assessed the PRC's practice in its early decades, concluding that "[t]he PRC's attitude toward dispute resolution seems similar to that of the Soviet Union. Although both of these states and their scholars generally endorse all of the traditional means of peaceful settlement, they are suspicious of all forms of third-party assistance. . . . This attitude is, of course, not uncommon among non-Communist states and for similar reasons. Nevertheless, because of their minority position in the world and their belief that law is a tool of the ruling class, Communist states have exhibited an even more profound distrust of institutions for international adjudication."[104] This "profound distrust" of external sources of dispute resolution persists to the present and is most prevalent in any matter that may be construed to bear on PRC sovereignty.

The PRC's early practice on dispute resolution did not, however, categorically rule out all third-party dispute settlement. At Bandung in 1955, Premier Zhou Enlai addressed the Asian-African Conference and emphasized the centrality of the Five Principles of Peaceful Coexistence for successful dispute settlement, stating that "when these principles are ensured of implementation, there is no reason why international disputes cannot be settled through negotiation."[105] The Final Communiqué from the Asian-African Conference, however, resolved that all parties accepted "[s]ettlement of all international disputes by peaceful means, such as negotiation, conciliation, *arbitration or judicial settlement* as well as other peaceful means of the parties' own choice, in conformity with the Charter of the United Nations."[106]

The early PRC evidently accepted some recourse to settling international disputes in court, if only in principled solidarity with its Third World allies. In practice, however, China has excluded matters of sovereignty from any of the third-party DRM to which it has agreed. Several early PRC treaties evince the development of a consistent and uniform practice of excluding such means of dispute settlement. The still-active dispute over the Sino-Indian boundary provides some illustrative examples. In 1959, the MFA wrote to the Indian government that the "Chinese government . . . has consistently held that an overall settlement of the boundary question between the two countries should be sought by the Chinese and Indian sides, taking into account the historical background and present actual situation, in accordance with the Five Principles and through friendly consultations. . . . [A]s to some of the disputes, partial and provisional agreements could be reached through negotiations."[107] History, PRC principles, and bilateral negotiations are the operative elements of this proposal.

Following active hostilities at that border in 1962, the PRC continued to assert that "the Sino-Indian boundary dispute is an important issue involving the sovereignty of both countries. . . . It goes without saying that this issue can be settled only through direct negotiations between the two parties, and absolutely not through any form of international arbitration." The PRC deplored what it perceived as India's inconsistent stance on arbitration: "At one time the Indian government said that arbitration was not applicable to disputes over sovereignty, at another it said that it was applicable." India's proposal to arbitrate this matter was considered an effort to "make negotiations impossible by setting up an array of obstacles."[108]

Along China's northern flank, it faced similar challenges from the Soviet Union. After a Sino-Soviet border skirmish in March 1969 near Zhenbao Island, the PRC government issued a statement affirming that the "Chinese government has consistently stood and worked for the settlement of boundary questions with its neighboring countries through negotiations and for the maintenance of the status quo of the boundary pending a settlement." The statement further urged the Soviets to resume their previously expressed "willingness to resume 'consultations.'"[109] In these and many other disputes implicating PRC sovereignty, such negotiations and consultations are consistently and uniformly the preferred method of dispute settlement.

On matters in which sovereignty is not at issue, however, the PRC does not uniformly insist on foregoing all third-party dispute resolution. Even with the Soviets, China's greatest external security threat in this period, China concluded a Treaty of Commerce and Navigation that "requires enforcement of any arbitration awards that may be made in the settlement of contract disputes between juridical persons."[110] The private or commercial nature of the disputes in question made compulsory arbitration acceptable to the PRC. The PRC's later willingness to accept such mechanisms under the World Trade Organization is another illustration of this key difference.[111] While some treaties with no sovereignty implications have not similarly included arbitration clauses (for example, the 1962 PRC-Ghana Treaty of Friendship), the PRC has not concluded any treaty or agreement that permits recourse to third-party settlement involving a boundary or any another matter with a sovereignty nexus.

PRC Alternatives to UNCLOS Dispute Resolution Mechanisms

The PRC's ratification of the UNCLOS treaty is unique as the only clear case in which China has accepted compulsory dispute resolution for issues that conceivably touch on sovereignty. The decade-long delay in the PRC's exercise of its Article 298 exemption is a puzzle for which no satisfactory answer has yet been produced.[112] With certainty, UNCLOS excludes questions of sovereign title altogether from the interpretation or application of the treaty. However, as the PRC argued so persistently in the SCS Arbitration, many law of the sea issues—like entitlements, law enforcement activities, fishing activity, and many other seemingly non-sovereign elements—may touch the PRC's third rail of sovereignty.

The PRC diligently protested the application of compulsory measures to many law of the sea matters at the Conference and later rejected their inclusion within the treaty.[113] Chinese representatives and officials were unequivocal in reserving any matter relating to sovereignty from such provisions, as expressed by PRC Conference delegate Lai Yali:

> The Chinese Government had consistently held that States should settle their disputes through negotiation and consultation on an equal footing and on the basis of mutual respect for sovereignty and territorial integrity. Of course, States were free to choose other peaceful means to settle their disputes. However, *if a sovereign State were asked to accept unconditionally the compulsory jurisdiction of an international judicial organ, that would amount to placing that organ above the sovereign State, which was contrary to the principle of State sovereignty.* Moreover, problems within the scope of the State sovereignty and exclusive jurisdiction of a sovereign State should be handled in accordance with its laws and regulations. That was why [the Chinese] delegation considered that the provisions [in draft] concerning the compulsory jurisdiction of the law of the sea tribunal were inappropriate. Since the question of the settlement of disputes involved the sovereignty of all States, the procedures to be followed must be chosen by States themselves. If most States agreed to draft specific provisions on dispute settlement procedures, those provisions should not be included in the convention itself but should form a separate protocol so that countries could decide for themselves whether to accept it or not.[114]

Yet before China opted to partially exempt itself from compulsory dispute resolution under Article 298, its official statements on that UNCLOS mechanism were largely positive. Xue Hanqin, then an MFA official and later to become the PRC's current judge on the ICJ, addressed the UN in 2000, stating that "we believe that the Tribunal [on the International Law of the Sea] will play a greater role in the settlement of maritime disputes and in maintenance of international order of the sea."[115] This "greater role" for the UNCLOS arbitral organ is nonetheless confined to issues that cannot be construed to bear on sovereignty. PRC officials have consistently supported the work of ITLOS—and indeed appointed four judges to the body—but have equally consistently sought to define its jurisdiction to exclude any "maritime rights and interests."[116]

This exclusion extends to other bodies under UNCLOS, like the "Regular Process for Global Reporting and Assessment of the State of the Marine Environment," about which a Chinese representative told the UN that it is "imperative that this Process be country-led, abide by the relevant international law *including* the Convention, respect coastal States for their sovereignty, sovereign rights and jurisdiction, refrain from intervening in disputes between States over sovereignty and maritime delimitation, and focus on making recommendations on the sustainable development of the oceans."[117] With remarkable consistency, Chinese officials have minimized the scope of the UNCLOS dispute resolution mechanisms and insisted on the overriding importance of sovereign discretion.

Once the Philippines' suit was underway, PRC official statements on the issue became more pointed on the historical component of claims and in asserting the applicability of bodies of rules beyond UNCLOS: "We maintain that maritime disputes should be resolved peacefully in accordance with the purposes and principles of the UN Charter and the provisions of the Convention, and that the lawful rights of countries to independently choose means to peaceful settlement should be respected. Before the relevant issues are resolved, parties concerned should engage in dialogue and seek cooperation in order to maintain the peace and stability of the relevant parts of the oceans and seas."[118]

The sequence thus proposed by Ambassador Liu Jieyi in 2014 is broadly consistent with UNCLOS Part XV. The principal departure from the treaty is an interpretative one, hinging on how much bilateral negotiation must precede a recourse to third-party settlement. Importantly, even after the SCS arbitral award, the PRC has continued to "support the role of the ITLOS in peaceful settlement of maritime disputes. As the dispute settlement mechanism provided for in the UNCLOS is a well-designed whole that reflects the concerns of all parties in a balanced manner, the interpretation and application of the mechanism must be in good-faith

and accurate, its integrity must be maintained and its misuse avoided."[119]
This show of confidence in the mechanism as constituted is consistent
with the PRC's practice of accepting third-party dispute resolution as
long as there are no implications for sovereignty.

That stance appears to extend uniformly beyond law of the sea matters. In 2013, the PRC's UN representative addressed the General Assembly's Sixth Committee (Legal) on the sub-topic of "the rule of law
and peaceful settlement of international disputes." He stated that the
PRC "proposes to settle international disputes properly through *negotiation, dialogue and consultation*. . . . [T]he freedom of states concerned to
choose means of peaceful settlement of international disputes must be
respected according to law."[120] This is a pointed omission of "arbitration
and judicial settlement," listed in Article 33(1) of the UN Charter among
other available options for international dispute resolution. Those procedures are by no means mandatory, but it is notable that China has deliberately excluded them from consideration in dealing with international
disputes.[121]

This UN recital of PRC principles on settlement of international
disputes adds further that "[t]he Chinese delegation believes that the decision to resort to arbitrary [sic] or judicial institutions to settle international disputes should be based on the principles of international rule
of law and premised on equality and free will of states concerned. Any
action to willfully refer disputes to arbitrary [sic] or judicial institutions
in defiance of the will of the states concerned or provisions of international treaties constitutes a violation of the principles of international
rule of law and is thus unacceptable to the Chinese government."[122] The
"arbitrary" application of third-party dispute resolution is an offense to
China's belief in the sovereign's full prerogative to exempt itself from
any unwanted dispute resolution procedure.

The South China Sea Code of Conduct

PRC practice in negotiations with ASEAN over a South China Sea "Code
of Conduct" (COC) is a critical manifestation of its position on alternative
dispute resolution mechanisms. China joined this process in 1995, and
it represents the sole multilateral venue in which Beijing participates in
discussions of its maritime disputes. China fosters ongoing "dialogue
and consultation" (对话协商) with ASEAN to achieve dispute *manage-*

ment rather than settlement. The COC process has emerged as China's preferred venue to promote its dispute resolution rules, serving as an alternative to third-party DRM for its maritime disputes.

Prior to 1995, China had resisted any form of formal multilateral discussion of its maritime disputes.[123] However, beginning in 1990, Indonesia convened a series of informal dialogues among the SCS claimants that ultimately drew China into a sustained discussion on maritime disputes with its southeast Asian neighbors.[124] In July 1992, ASEAN for the first time issued a "Declaration on the South China Sea," which mildly "emphasize[d] the necessity to resolve all sovereignty and jurisdictional issues pertaining to the SCS by peaceful means."[125] By 1994, ASEAN moved to formalize its engagements with China at the First ASEAN Regional Forum (ARF) in Bangkok, Thailand, in July 1994.

The consensus-based ASEAN already adhered to norms and rules to which China could subscribe as a formal "consultative partner" with ASEAN through ARF.[126] ASEAN foreign ministers nonetheless placed the sensitive issue of the South China Sea on the ARF agenda in 1995, "express[ing] concern on overlapping sovereignty claims in the region. They encouraged all claimants to reaffirm their commitment to the principles contained in relevant international laws and conventions, and the ASEAN's 1992 Declaration on the South China Sea."[127]

With UNCLOS effective since 1994 and all claimant states' ratifications already deposited (or soon to be deposited), the fact of overlapping maritime claims had already produced significant controversy.[128] The advent of new UNCLOS entitlements is one likely driver for China's 1994–1995 seizure of a Philippine-claimed feature in the Spratlys, Mischief (Meiji) Reef. The Philippines secretary of defense, Orlando Mercado, deplored China's "creeping invasion" and extracted a bilateral joint statement from China in 1995 that committed the parties to "a gradual and progressive process of cooperation . . . with a view to eventually negotiating a settlement of the bilateral disputes."[129] The issue thus irretrievably "internationalized" against China's desires, PRC Foreign Minister Qian Qichen addressed the issue of the Spratlys at the 1995 ARF meeting, the first time Chinese representatives had ever discussed the issue in an official multilateral setting. Qian "publicly agreed at the 1995 ARF that competing claims should be resolved on the basis of UNCLOS, and he reiterated an earlier Chinese proposal that in the meantime the sovereignty question should be shelved and efforts made to begin the joint development of resources."[130]

This series of consultations and negotiations culminated in a 2002 "Declaration on the Conduct of Parties in the South China Sea" (DOC).[131] The DOC is a non-binding expression of intent among ASEAN member states and China that reiterates their commitment to "undertake to resolve their territorial and jurisdictional disputes . . . through friendly consultations and negotiations by sovereign states directly concerned."[132] This language limited dispute resolution to the territorial claimants, a minority in ASEAN, and established a multilateral commitment to engage in "cooperative activities" to build confidence while working "on the basis of consensus toward the eventual . . . adoption of a code of conduct."[133]

That Code of Conduct (COC) remains unconsummated after two decades of meetings and workshops at the official and unofficial levels. The PRC has moved this process to the center of its ASEAN diplomacy, promoting a "dual-track approach," which Foreign Minister Wang Yi explained to "mean that disputes related to the SCS should be addressed properly through negotiations and consultations among countries directly concerned, and China and the ASEAN countries should work together to safeguard peace and stability in the SCS."[134] That is, dispute *settlement* is to proceed on the track of direct bilateral negotiations with China; dispute *management* is to proceed on the other track, in the form of multilateral efforts involving less interested non-claimants to maintain stability and "pursue joint development."

No PRC joint development has come of this process, and we may reasonably question whether Beijing intends or expects to accomplish that stated objective. There is, however, little question about certain Chinese preferences for the COC instrument that is under negotiation. Chinese diplomats have recently expressed satisfaction at the UN that the COC process was "brought back to the right track of dialogues and consultations" after the rupture of the SCS Arbitration and has now "entered text consultation stage" in the form of a "Single Draft COC Negotiating Text."[135] This draft has been circulating among regional diplomats and experts since 2018, reflecting consensus on a small number of "agreed principles"—including that the COC "is not an instrument to settle territorial disputes or maritime delimitation issues"—and a large volume of disparate draft language from all of the participants reflecting varied ambitions for the code.[136]

With its preferred "dialogue and consultation" procedure firmly ensconced in ASEAN practice, China's few substantive inputs into the "Single Draft COC Negotiating Text" suggest areas of "practical maritime cooperation" and exclude recourse to any third-party dispute resolution—and, in fact, to further deny third-party involvement in SCS maritime disputes altogether.[137] One PRC "Option" proposed in the draft reads, "The Parties shall not hold joint military exercises with countries from outside the region, unless the parties concerned are notified beforehand and express no objection."[138] By inference, China's proposal to exclude external parties is directed at the United States, a treaty ally of the Philippines and Thailand and a frequent "unwelcome guest" in the SCS. The proposition is unlikely to be accepted by consensus, but it indicates China's desire to establish alternatives to UNCLOS rules. Even if the COC is not legally binding, an agreed document that establishes extra-UNCLOS restrictions on navigation would rapidly take on the character of a regional custom.

The PRC's alternative to formal third-party DRM is clear and consistent in its practice with the SCS claimants. The SCS Arbitration in particular has stimulated China to emphasize on many occasions that "on issues concerning territorial sovereignty and maritime delimitation, China does not accept any recourse to third party dispute settlement; nor does China accept any solution imposed on it."[139] Whether this practice is also uniform across all of China's maritime disputes can be determined by examining the cases of Japan and South Korea.

Dispute Resolution Alternatives in the East China and Yellow Seas

The multilateralism observed in the South China Sea is not present in the East China Sea and Yellow Sea, where China has pursued a steady diet of bilateral "dialogue and consultation" with Japan and South Korea.[140] For China's practice to be uniform, it should apply the same rule of excluding any third-party DRM from maritime disputes.

China and Korea each ratified UNCLOS in 1996, and, as in the case of the SCS, their overlapping claims to maritime entitlements catalyzed a process of negotiation over boundaries and other maritime issues. The achievement of a Fisheries Agreement in 2001 is the only concrete

outcome of these bilateral dialogues to date. Maritime boundary delimitation has been the object of a series of dialogues since 1996, with officials from both sides gathering annually without any publicly reported
discussion of dispute resolution mechanisms.[141] These talks have been
desultory, with Korean officials noting as late as 2012 that "the negotiation hasn't occurred yet."[142] Only in 2015 after a visit by Xi Jinping to
Seoul did the parties conduct their "first formal meeting on the delimitation of maritime boundaries."[143]

The issues at stake in China-Korea negotiations do not involve any
sovereignty disputes. According to the PRC's Ministry of Foreign Affairs,
they have focused solely on issues in the Yellow Sea, setting aside the
complexity of overlapping claims with Japan in the East China Sea.[144] The
sole feature that is contested between them, Ieodo (Suyan) Rock, is submerged and neither side claims sovereign title to it.[145] This circumstance
would in principle make China more receptive to the idea of employing
a formal DRM because sovereignty is not plausibly at stake, but its Article 298 exception precludes that from being imposed unilaterally by
the Koreans. The PRC's practice is thus uniform with that general rule
as practiced in the SCS.

The China-Japan pattern of dialogue on maritime issues is far more
fraught. At the working level, it is similar to the meandering process with
Korea, as a "step-by-step approach by making temporary arrangements
with a view to gradually and progressively achieving a final settlement
of the dispute."[146] But China's dispute with Japan differs fundamentally
from that with Korea in its core antagonism over Diaoyu/Senkaku sovereignty. Intense Sino-Japanese operational, diplomatic, political, and
social confrontations regarding those features have episodically desta-
bilized the broader Sino-Japanese relationship.[147] Conforming with its
practice on sovereignty disputes in the SCS, China does not propose to
resolve this dispute through any third-party mechanism—and in any
event, Japan does not formally recognize the existence of that dispute.

Across the board, China has proposed a consistent and uniform
rule for settling its maritime disputes: bilateral negotiation, with the categorical exclusion of any external dispute resolution procedure. Instead,
China proposes an alternative set of "rules and mechanisms" for managing, not resolving, its maritime disputes.[148] These manifest as the Code
of Conduct process in the SCS and in regular consultations in the ECS

TABLE 20

PRC PRACTICE OF ALTERNATIVE DISPUTE RESOLUTION RULES

PRC-preferred rule	Uniformity (geographic)	Consistency (over time)	Detail
Sovereignty nexus precludes all DRM	Yes	Yes	Rejects sole suit brought against it; excludes "maritime rights and interests" and other sovereignty-adjacent LOS matters from compulsory measures
Bilateral "dialogue and consultation"	Yes	Yes	Normal practice; multilateral negotiations only with ASEAN, and these still exclude DRM

and Yellow Sea, each "shelving" sovereignty and "maritime rights and interests" entirely. The responses of specially affected states to this practice will indicate the extent to which the region is receptive to this Chinese-preferred dispute resolution rule (Table 20).

Specially Affected State Responses to China's Alternative DRM Practice
In principle, any state that has ratified UNCLOS may have a cause of action against China on the question of interpretation or application of the Convention. This low threshold would include the several states that object to China's navigational rules, to include the regional as well as extra-regional states that have sought to exercise their rights of innocent passage and EEZ navigation and overflight. These states could conceivably pursue dispute resolution through the Convention's DRM provisions as a recourse to failed bilateral negotiations (UNCLOS, Arts. 279, 286). The US, as a non-party to UNCLOS, is again excluded from this process. America could only pursue third-party dispute resolution with China by mutual consent, a highly unlikely prospect.

The states specially affected by China's exclusive "dialogue and consultation" rule are only those who have already engaged in the requisite bilateral negotiations and might reasonably bring a suit. By virtue of their participation in the DOC and COC processes, all ASEAN claimants have effectively (if in non-binding fashion) agreed that bilateral consultation and negotiation is the principal mode for resolving their disputes. Among them, only the Philippines and Vietnam have even dangled the prospect of initiating another UNCLOS arbitral suit, but each is entitled to do so after at least two decades of fruitless bilateral and multilateral negotiations over disputes with China. Further north, Japan and South Korea have followed the track of bilateral consultation and negotiation on non-sovereign matters. Unlike in the SCS, however, neither of these northeast Asian states has issued public or formal affirmation of the PRC's preferred mode of dispute resolution. Both maintain the option of third-party DRM, but only Japan has given any indication that it might seek such recourse.

Japan's Quiet Appeal to Litigation

In a November 2012 *International Herald Tribune* opinion piece, the Japanese foreign minister, Genba Koichiro, affirmed that "Japan has accepted the jurisdiction of the ICJ as compulsory." He then posed to himself the rhetorical question: "Why does not Japan refer the issue [of the Diaoyu/Senkaku Islands] to the International Court of Justice?" Genba laid the onus on China to bring a suit if it believed that the current situation of Japanese administrative control of those islands was unlawful: "Since China is undertaking various campaigns to promote their assertions in international forums, it seems to make sense for China to seek a solution based on international law. Why don't they show any signs of accepting the jurisdiction of the ICJ as compulsory and taking their arguments to the ICJ?"[149] After this informal but authoritative invitation to litigate the Diaoyu Islands, no Japanese official has reiterated Genba's claim, but neither has anyone formally renounced it.[150] The quiet nature of this proposal reflects its sensitivity in Japan, which officially denies the very existence of a dispute over sovereign title.[151]

Japan has kept the door to litigation open, but only in a precise fashion that the PRC will almost certainly never take up. In October 2015 the Government of Japan formally recognized the jurisdiction of the ICJ as compulsory "*ipso facto* and without special agreement"—but only "in relation to any other State accepting the same obligation, and on the condition of reciprocity, the jurisdiction of the ICJ over all disputes arising on and after September 1958 with regard to situations or facts subsequent to the same date and being not settled by other means of peaceful settlement."[152] This cut-off date implicates the 4 September 1958 PRC "Declaration on the Territorial Sea," which the Government of Japan prefers as the "critical date" for the onset of the Diaoyu/Senkaku dispute.

China considers the critical date to be no later than 1895, so bringing Japan to the ICJ on terms that exclude the historical basis of China's claim would be a spectacular concession.[153] Initiating a procedure under the premise that the dispute arose in 1958 would place China's first objection some sixty-three years after Japan's annexation of the islands—and even then in a statement that only claimed Diaoyus by association rather than by name (the 1958 Declaration refers only to "Taiwan and its surrounding islands").[154] In any event, China's otherwise consistent practice of categorically excluding anything even remotely sovereignty-related from third-party dispute resolution makes taking a sovereignty dispute to the ICJ nearly unthinkable.

An Asian Way of International Dispute Settlement?

Several of the claimant states in China's maritime disputes have therefore objected, in principle and in practice, to the rule that such disputes may not be referred to third-party dispute settlement. Japan, the Philippines, and Vietnam have either launched such procedures or affirmed their validity. The other specially affected states, by contrast, have given no such indications in their practice and appear to acquiesce to or even support China's rule on direct, bilateral negotiations as the exclusive mode of settlement for their disputes.

Vietnam has notably been the leading proponent for the Code of Conduct to be a binding instrument. In its draft language submitted to the "Single Draft COC Negotiating Text," Vietnam has proposed that the agreement "shall be subject to ratification . . . and shall register the present COC pursuant to article 102 of the Charter of the United Nations."[155] Nonetheless, the Vietnamese proposals also include the provision that "[t]he Contracting States shall settle their disputes . . . through friendly negotiations, enquiry, mediation, conciliation and other means as may be agreed by the disputing Contracting States."[156] Failing these procedures, which pointedly exclude binding third-party measures, the Vietnamese position refers parties to the Treaty of Amity and Cooperation in Southeast Asia (TAC), which provides that states "shall at all times settle such disputes among themselves through friendly negotiations."[157] While the Vietnamese proposals and the TAC do not forbid recourse to the binding third-party measures proposed in the UN Charter Article 33, that option is available only as a last resort.[158]

The ASEAN states' circumspect attitude toward compulsory DRM, as reflected in the Code of Conduct process, is characteristic of the organization as well as the practice of states throughout the region. Simon Chesterman observes that "Asian states tend to be the wariest of international dispute settlement procedures" and show a "general wariness of delegating sovereignty."[159] He notes that only eight states in the region have accepted ICJ compulsory jurisdiction, and only 15 percent of Asia-Pacific states overall. This contrasts to 30 percent of Eastern European states, 39 percent of Latin American/Caribbean states, 41 percent of African states, and 69 percent of Western European and "Other Group" states in the UN. "Unsurprisingly," he comments, "Asian states are also less likely to have used the ICJ" to settle disputes.[160]

The partial exception to this regional practice appears to arise in matters of trade and investment. Asian states have been relatively open to joining the WTO and the International Center for Settlement of Investment Disputes (though Asian states are still the least likely regional group to do so). Moreover, Korea, India, and especially China have concluded a large number of bilateral investment treaties that include arbitration clauses. Despite this relative willingness to accept third-party DRM on non-sovereign issues, Asian states still remain hesitant to employ those mechanisms, initiating fewer disputes in the WTO than their proportion of international trade would predict.[161]

Notwithstanding Asia's proportionally low usage of compulsory DRM, Tommy Koh (the former UNCLOS conference president and a leading international law scholar) asserts that "the countries of Southeast Asia have a positive track record of referring their disputes to the international legal process."[162] To this point, Koh cites several intra-ASEAN adjudications and arbitrations—including ICJ determinations of sovereignty claims among Indonesia, Malaysia, Singapore, Thailand, and Cambodia, and ITLOS resolution of maritime boundaries between Myanmar, Bangladesh, and India. These cases do not negate the general

TABLE 21

SPECIALLY AFFECTED STATE RESPONSES TO PRC ALTERNATIVE
DISPUTE RESOLUTION PRACTICE

	Bilateral negotiation without recourse to third-party DRM
Brunei	Acquiesce
Indonesia	Acquiesce
Japan	Acquiesce[a]
Korea	Acquiesce
Malaysia	Acquiesce
Philippines	Object (SCS Arbitration)
Vietnam	Object (SCS Arbitration and "Code of Conduct" proposals)

[a]With the partial exception of Foreign Minister Genba's informal referral of Senkaku/Diaoyu dispute to ICJ.

pattern of reluctance, but they are sufficient to demonstrate that there is no uniform or consistent regional practice of completely excluding recourse to such measures. This finding diminishes the prospect that such an exclusion might be consolidated as a regional rule (Table 21).

RULES ON NON-RECOGNITION OF DISPUTES

No rule of international law, nor even any norm of international relations, precludes states from simply refusing to acknowledge the existence of a dispute. Where international courts are involved, certain general principles for recognition of disputes are frequently invoked. This was the case in the SCS Arbitration, for example, where the tribunal recognized that "the concept of a dispute is well-established in international law" and cited UNCLOS Article 288 as affirming that the tribunal may exercise its jurisdiction if it is satisfied that a dispute over the interpretation or application of the Convention exists.[163] This is to be an "objective" determination based on whether there is an observable disagreement over a "point of law or fact, a conflict of legal views or of interests between two persons"—not whether one party subjectively holds that a dispute is non-existent.[164] All that is necessary for a court's recognition is the existence of opposable claims at the time that the suit was initiated, such that the judges can interpret the nature of that dispute.[165]

Absent any state's referral of a dispute to a third-party settlement procedure, however, the non-recognition of disputes may persist indefinitely. If a state claiming that it has a dispute with another party does not persistently mount that complaint, it is reasonable to expect that the dispute may effectively cease to exist. China's practice in several of its disputes on both sides of the "non-recognition" ledger demand further analysis.

PRC Practice of Dispute Non-Recognition

China has refused to recognize aspects of at least two of its maritime disputes. One of these cases concerns the Philippines' claims in the SCS Arbitration. The second is China's blanket non-recognition of the dispute with Vietnam over the Paracel Islands. However, the PRC finds itself in the opposite position with respect to Japan and Indonesia, which both reject the existence of all or part of their maritime disputes with China. On its face, these opposite positions in different disputes seem to rule out any uniform PRC position on this matter. However, its practice in these cases reveals certain substantive differences about the relevant rules China invokes to justify its varying stance.

Non-Recognition of Philippines' Claims in the SCS Arbitration

In substance, China's rejection of the Philippines' suit in the SCS Arbitration is a practice of non-recognition. PRC official and quasi-official arguments recognized the existence of a *sovereignty* dispute but rejected the Philippines' contention that a dispute existed over the entitlements assigned to those sovereign features.[166] Because China adopts the position that the "Nansha Archipelago" is an integral whole, it has not made any specific claims to entitlements from the individual features in that island group. While the tribunal did not accept this reasoning, China's position is revealing.

PRC non-recognition of the arbitral suit was not simply a blanket rejection, but extended into the individual claims brought by the Philippines. Because China has declared no baselines around the Spratlys as a whole or individually, some advocates of the PRC position assert that there is no opposable claim that might generate a dispute with the Philippines (or any other Spratly claimant): "The Philippines did not identify a single document or statement by China that contradicts its position on the status of the individual maritime features in question."[167] In the absence of such PRC practices, claimant states are also in the uncomfortable position of objecting to unpublished Chinese claims that must be inferred (as has been done in the maps in this volume). This issue also arises in US Navy challenges to claims around features in the Spratlys that are not naturally above water at high-tide and from which China does not formally claim an individual territorial sea.[168]

Because other states have nonetheless challenged PRC claims on substantive grounds, appealing to specific rules of UNCLOS against the rules that the PRC has put into practice (as addressed in chapters 3–5), these "non-claims" are of less consequence for dispute resolution. The cases that do hold potential to advance a rule of non-recognition are those in which China categorically denies the existence of any dispute.

The Paracel Islands "Non-Dispute"

The multilateral disputes over the Spratly Islands and their associated maritime rights and jurisdiction often overshadow the bilateral dispute between China and Vietnam over the Paracel Islands in the northwest SCS. In the first instance, this dispute concerns Chinese and Vietnamese claims to sovereignty over the 130 islands, rocks, and reefs scattered across two groups, the northeast Amphitrite Group and the western Crescent Group. In consequence, there are also maritime disputes over these islands' entitlements and their bearing on potential maritime boundaries and associated resource and navigation rights. Independent of the PRC straight baselines surrounding both the Amphitrite and Crescent groups and their outlying reefs, the Paracels are substantially larger and more populous features than the Spratlys, and they may reasonably generate large maritime entitlements. The largest of the islands, Woody (Yongxing) Island, is over two square kilometers; it is the site of the prefecture-level Sansha City and populated by as many as 1,500 PRC nationals.[169]

Sovereign possession of these features has changed hands several times in the course of the twentieth century, from French, to Japanese, to Franco-Vietnamese and Japanese, to Vietnamese and Chinese, and

finally to sole PRC control.[170] But having evicted Vietnamese forces altogether in a pitched battle in 1974, the PRC has subsequently refused
to recognize Vietnam's claim to sovereignty over the archipelago.[171] The
historical occupation and use of these islands is the object of a huge
volume of nationalist historiography on both sides, but the "correct" disposition of sovereign title is not of analytical concern.[172] The question
at hand concerns how China has sought to eliminate the possibility of
any settlement of the dispute by rejecting outright the legitimacy of Vietnam's claim.

PRC practice in sustaining this non-recognition relies in the first
instance on its "actual control" (实际控制) of the features, which Vietnam lacks capability to meaningfully contest. From a legal standpoint,
China argues that "historical facts cannot be forged" and cites former
Democratic Republic of Vietnam (North Vietnam) officials' diplomatic
recognition of PRC sovereignty as a basis for "estoppel," precluding the
contemporary Socialist Republic of Vietnam from mounting another
claim.[173] These and similar statements have been common since 1974,
as the PRC has sought to sever the issue of the Xisha/Paracels from that
of the Nansha/Spratlys. In a letter to the UN secretary-general in 2014,
China made its clearest formal statement on the matter: "The Xisha Islands are an integral part of China's territory, over which there is not the
slightest dispute. There are overlapping claims to the waters between
China's Xisha Islands and the coast of the Vietnamese mainland, and the
two sides have not yet conducted delimitation of the EEZ and continental
shelf in these waters."[174]

This categorical rejection of Vietnamese claims, however, is not altogether consistent. In 1975 Deng Xiaoping suggested to his Vietnamese counterpart Le Duan that "negotiations can be undertaken in the
future," implying that the PRC's non-recognition of Vietnam's claims is
not absolute.[175] Through the DOC and the ongoing COC process, China
has further consented to treat the "South China Sea" as the relevant area,
rather than maintaining its preference to specifically limit the engagement to the Spratly group and its surrounding waters.[176]

Nonetheless, in its negotiations with Vietnam, Beijing has not proceeded from the premise of "shelving the dispute" over the Paracels as
it has with respect to the Spratlys. Instead, China practiced as though
its sovereignty over the Paracels was undisputed and sought to make

the overlap between the putative Xisha Archipelago EEZ and that of the Vietnamese mainland the principal object of disagreement. The status of the median line in the parties' resource exploitation and law enforcement practices reinforces this Chinese preference, though Vietnam has protested this arrangement.

If there is a consistent PRC rule to be inferred from this practice, it is that actual control of features and their surrounding waters is sufficient to displace normal modes of dispute resolution. China's responses to other states' non-recognition of its claims, however, will demonstrate the extent to which this practice is also uniform across other cases.

Disputing the Diaoyu/Senkaku Islands Non-Dispute

A comparable phenomenon appears in the East China Sea, where Japan maintains administrative control over the uninhabited Diaoyu/Senkaku Islands and insists that no sovereignty dispute exists by virtue of China's non-contestation of Japan's annexation of the islands in 1895. China has lobbied consistently for Japan to recognize the dispute since the US agreed in 1971 to revert the islands' "administrative rights" to the Government of Japan after post-war occupation.[177] The PRC protested this transfer and (decades later) published a 2012 White Paper on the subject, stating that "Diaoyu Dao and its affiliated islands are an inseparable part of the Chinese territory. Diaoyu Dao is China's inherent territory in all historical, geographical and legal terms, and China enjoys indisputable sovereignty over Diaoyu Dao."[178]

There have been several distinct phases in the PRC's practice on this issue. In the 1958 "Declaration on the Territorial Sea," the Diaoyu Islands were notably not among the other islands named as "territories of the PRC," which included all of the SCS islands, the Penghu Islands in the Taiwan Strait, "as well as Taiwan and its surrounding islands."[179] China explains this omission as a function of its belief that the Diaoyu/Senkaku "appertain" to Taiwan and are thus included in that latter phrase.[180]

The US reversion of occupied islands to Japanese control in 1971–1972 occasioned substantial new PRC attention to the status of these features.[181] Hydrocarbon potential had been only recently discovered in the area, stimulating Chinese interest in this purported "second Persian Gulf."[182] Simultaneously, China and Japan were negotiating the normalization of their relationship, during which PRC Premier Zhou Enlai stated, "I do not want to discuss the Senkakus at this time. It is not right to discuss this matter now. Because there is oil, it is a problem. If there was no oil, neither Taiwan nor the US would be an issue."[183] China had indicated its claim but did not allow that inchoate dispute to derail the broader aim of Sino-Japanese normalization. Deng Xiaoping continued to follow this "shelve the disputes" line in concluding a bilateral treaty in 1978.[184]

This tacit agreement to avoid controversy was disrupted repeatedly over the ensuing decades by nationalist demonstrations by citizens of both countries (as well as from Taiwan and Hong Kong). Chinese and Japanese activists clashed over the establishment and maintenance of lighthouses on the features, fishermen vied for access to the resources, and flags were raised and lowered on various Diaoyu/Senkaku features as citizens from both countries mobilized around the issue. PRC officials began to publicly condemn Japanese actions as violations of its "inherent" sovereignty and codified China's sovereignty claim to the islands in its 1992 Territorial Sea Law.[185]

December 2008 marked the start of a decisive change of tack for the PRC against Japan's non-recognition of the dispute. Chinese law enforcement vessels began to contest operationally Japan's administrative control of the islands by navigating within the islands' territorial seas (and contiguous zone), challenging the premise that the waters were under Japan's jurisdiction.[186] In the words of one PRC analyst, this first patrol "broke the situation of Japan's actual control in one fell swoop."[187] These actions garnered substantial opposition in Japan, likewise increasingly attentive to the issue. By 2012, the nationalist governor of Tokyo, a long-time Senkaku activist, began to publicly organize and fund-raise to purchase (and then develop) three of the islands from their private owner when the lease expired in March 2013. Chinese officials and activists began a counter-mobilization, with State Oceanic Administration officials announcing a plan to designate the islands for marine environmental protection and diplomats deploring Japan's action as a violation of China's sovereignty.[188]

The Japanese government opted to head off the private bid by purchasing the islands outright. This "so-called nationalization" (所谓的国有化) further inflamed PRC passions and led to a diplomatic statement condemning this "serious violation of China's territorial sovereignty, a serious injury to the feelings of the 1.3 billion Chinese people, and a serious violation of historical facts and international legal principles."[189] Simultaneously, the PRC declared straight baselines around the islands and augmented its law enforcement presence in the territorial seas surrounding the features.[190] Since these statements issued in September 2012, an average of 9.5 PRC vessels have entered the territorial waters surrounding the islands each month.[191] These operational contestations have placed continuous pressure on Japanese surveillance and law enforcement to demonstrate constantly their effective administration of the area.[192]

China's sustained on-water actions challenge the facts of Japanese jurisdiction over the Diaoyu/Senkaku and, by extension, force Japan to recognize the existence of a sovereignty dispute. PLAN vessels have reportedly entered the contiguous zone but not the territorial seas of the Diaoyu, thus honoring to some degree the Japanese control over the features, if only for prudential reasons. The PRC Ministry of National Defense publicized remarks describing these "maritime security operations" as an illustration of a "de facto 'cross-control' between the CCG and the Japan Coast Guard, breaking the previous, illusory 'unilateral control' of Japan. . . . No matter what happens, China will not allow anyone to bargain over the issue of safeguarding the sovereignty of the Diaoyu Islands. The only thing that can be discussed is how to maintain the peace and stability of the Diaoyu Islands, avoid the escalation of tension in the East China Sea, and create conditions for the improvement and development of Sino-Japanese relations."[193]

This "cross-control" is expressly designed to erode the premise that Japan "effectively administers" or controls the Diaoyu Islands themselves.[194] The PRC presence has produced significant tensions and further entrenched each side's adherence to incompatible views of the dispute itself. This is clear in a 7 November 2014 "joint statement" that was actually two separate statements by the parties expressing their incompatible positions on the Diaoyu/Senkaku question. The Chinese version, unlike the Japanese (examined below), referred to a "four-point principled agreement" reached by the two sides, which included the claim that "the two sides have acknowledged that different positions exist between them regarding the tensions which have emerged in recent years over the Diaoyu Islands and some waters in the East China Sea, and agreed to prevent the situation from aggravating through dialogue and consultation and establish crisis management mechanisms to avoid contingencies."[195] This process of dialogue and consultation is ongoing, but it appears to exclude all mention of sovereignty in lieu of addressing technical and governance issues.

The PRC's strong operational and legal reaction to the "nationalization" crisis is a clear affirmation of its sovereignty claim—but also a point of inconsistency in this practice. By 2012, the Japanese government had already declared its public ownership of several of the islands and had previously leased three of them, Uotsuri, Kita-kojima, and Minami-kojima, to private citizens in 2002 without public protest from the PRC.[196] The PRC sovereignty claim was clearly established by then, but the Chinese government did not mount a consistent protest to a near-identical practice on the part of the Japanese. Notwithstanding this omission, the underlying PRC-preferred rule is substantively the same: the state with effective control over the entirety of a given feature may deny the existence of a dispute. China's steady efforts to erode Japan's effective control of the Diaoyu/Senkaku group—and thus the premise of "no dispute"—is easily understood as an application of that rule.

Other PRC Non-Disputes

Two final non-recognition cases warrant mention. First is China's assertion that there is a dispute over maritime delimitation with Indonesia despite Indonesia's resistance to acknowledging it. In 1995, China's MFA spokesman Chen Jian pronounced China's willingness to "hold talks with Indonesia on the demarcation of their common sea border"— despite Indonesia's refusal to acknowledge the existence of any overlapping PRC maritime boundary in the southwest SCS.[197] Even as PRC fishing and law enforcement vessels have repeatedly asserted themselves in Indonesia's claimed EEZ, Indonesia has formally "reaffirmed that Indonesia does not have overlapping jurisdiction with China," rejecting outright the nine-dash line as a basis for any Chinese entitlements.[198] The PRC has nonetheless consistently asserted that "China and Indonesia have overlapping claims over maritime rights and interests in some parts of the South China Sea."[199] Lacking control over the area, the PRC is consistent and uniform in its practice here compared with that observed elsewhere.

The second and more problematic case is Scarborough (Huangyan) Shoal. It is disputed only between the PRC and the Philippines, but the PRC has held effective control over the feature since 2012. Despite this circumstance, which elsewhere has warranted non-recognition, the PRC recognizes the dispute and even affords the Philippines some degree of access to the fisheries resources of the Scarborough territorial sea. This concession may be withdrawn at any time—and indeed has been withdrawn during the PRC's summer fishing bans—so the PRC may ultimately move to physically occupy the feature and deny the existence of a dispute altogether. Elsewhere in the SCS, the features in the Spratlys are occupied and effectively controlled by four states (and Taiwan), so there is no possible application of the non-recognition rule. However, China's practice implies that non-recognition would extend to the Spratlys in the event the PRC evicts those other states and secures effective control over the area.

Altogether, then, the PRC practice on this count is virtually uniform and consistent in treating effective control of islands as a basis for denying the existence of a dispute. The practice would be reinforced if the PRC were to physically occupy Scarborough Shoal and adopt a non-recognition posture. Yet, as demonstrated by China's continuing efforts to force Japan's recognition of a Diaoyu/Senkaku dispute, the practice of the counter-parties to non-disputes may be consequential (Table 22).

TABLE 22

PRC PRACTICE OF NON-RECOGNITION OF MARITIME DISPUTES

PRC-preferred rule	Uniformity (geographic)	Consistency (over time)	Detail
No dispute recognition with effective control of disputed territory	Yes	Yes	PRC seeks to control maritime space as means of forcing dispute recognition

Specially Affected State Responses to China's Dispute
Non-Recognition Practice

Each of China's cases of unilateral non-recognition of a dispute specially affects the other state party to the (non)dispute. Those states' responses to Chinese practice bear attention as indications of whether the rule is locally or regionally effective.

In the case of Vietnam and the Paracels, the post-1975 Socialist Republic of Vietnam has continuously maintained its sovereignty claim to the "Hoàng Sa" islands. It has officially declared that claim with repeated diplomatic notes to the UN and the PRC. Since the 1974 Battle of the Paracels, however, Vietnam has had no physical presence on the islands and has been prevented from utilizing or administering the waters in their vicinity. The hypothetical median line between the Paracels and the Vietnamese coastline has served as a de facto boundary between the two states' resource exploitation and law enforcement activities, with the notable exception of the sole PRC effort to drill for hydrocarbon resources on the Vietnamese side of the line in 2014. This pattern is a tacit Vietnamese recognition of the PRC's effective control over the features. Yet periodic formal communications stating that "Viet Nam has never recognized China's sovereignty over the Hoàng Sa Archipelago" are sufficient to sustain the dispute, and, to a lesser degree, so is the implicit inclusion of the Paracels among the "South China Sea" issues addressed in the Code of Conduct process.[200]

On the other side of the non-dispute ledger, Indonesia has consistently rejected the PRC's claim to have a boundary or jurisdictional dispute in the Natuna area. In continuing to exploit the natural resources of this sea area, operationally contesting Chinese law enforcement, and sustaining non-recognition in diplomatic relations, Indonesian practice appears to confirm the rule that the state with sole effective control over the territory or maritime space in question will not recognize disputes.[201] Nonetheless, China's steady efforts to erode that effective control through regular law enforcement presence in support of PRC nationals' resource exploitation in the area may ultimately force Indonesian recognition of their maritime dispute.

The Diaoyu/Senkaku case presents the most complex test of this rule because the PRC has been intensifying its contestation of Japan's administration over the waters surrounding the features. Despite nearly a decade of continuous PRC challenge to Japan's effective control, Japan has maintained a formal position of non-recognition: "There is no doubt that the Senkaku Islands are clearly an inherent part of the territory of Japan, in light of historical facts and based upon international law. Indeed, the Senkaku Islands are under the valid control of Japan. *There exists no issue of territorial sovereignty to be resolved concerning the Senkaku Islands.*"[202] Japan has consistently protested the various PRC efforts to force its recognition of the dispute. For example, the PRC's demarcation of baselines around the Diaoyu Islands in 2012 was met with a note verbale to the UN secretary-general denouncing that "unilateral action [which] has no ground under international law including within the UNCLOS."[203]

Operationally, the Japanese Coast Guard (JCG) has sought to "continuously exercise enforcement jurisdiction around the Senkaku Islands" and established new regulations that allow the force to take more decisive actions against vessels operating within their claimed jurisdictional waters.[204] Since the early 2000s, the JCG has been building capacity specifically aimed at surveilling PRC vessels and denying them access to the disputed islands. Progressive revisions of domestic law have gradually loosened restrictions on the JCG's use of force.[205] It has established a routine of shadowing CCG vessels in the territorial sea, avoiding direct confrontations but sustaining the premise that it exercises uncontested jurisdiction in those waters.[206] Japan's other island sovereignty disputes provide further evidence of the non-recognition rule in effect in the region. With respect to the disputed Dokdo/Takeshima Islands, South Korea's effective control has also led it to adopt a "non-recognition" posture that Japan rejects.[207]

Altogether, the specially affected states mirror China's practice of non-recognition. This position effectively neutralizes any operative dispute resolution rules under UNCLOS or any other body of international law. Even if the unrequited party steadily contests the other party's refusal to admit the existence of a dispute, the continued non-recognition withholds consent to settle the matter by any means and presents a decisive obstacle to the application of international law (Table 23).

China's approach to maritime dispute resolution is the only body of rules in which its practice is virtually uniform and consistent across the board. While the responses of specially affected states have varied—

TABLE 23

SPECIALLY AFFECTED STATE RESPONSES TO PRC
NON-RECOGNITION PRACTICE

	Deny existence of disputes in areas under effective control
Indonesia	Adopt
Japan	Adopt
Vietnam	Object

particularly in objecting to China's refusal to accept the SCS Arbitration—the overall practice of the region in dispute resolution is not so dissimilar to China's. Even Japan's outwardly direct protests to China's practices are, in effect, a confirmation of the apparent regional norm of excluding sovereignty issues from legal adjudication. Especially in southeast Asia, the firm and nearly region-wide avoidance of formal third-party dispute resolution is recognizable as a potential customary rule—and especially so on issues of sovereignty. These largely post-colonial states share a basic "Eastphalian" sensibility in eschewing legal DRM for diplomatic, consensus-based "dialogue and negotiation."[208] These various parties to maritime disputes with China naturally resent Beijing's bullying, but they also share its basic regard for the inviolability of sovereignty.

However bitter the specially affected states' objections to China's application of its preferred rules on geography, resources, and navigation, their recourse to resolving their maritime disputes with China through the law of the sea's rules on dispute settlement is severely constrained. This circumstance has allowed gradual development of regional norms surrounding maritime disputes that have hindered any formal legal resolution to any of the disputed rules. This pattern may crystallize into rules of regional customary international law, a distinct possibility taken up in the conclusion.

Toward an East Asian Maritime Order

THIS STUDY HAS ANALYZED CHINA'S practice in the law of the sea in service of a simple question: is China changing the rules? By surveying specific rules whose meaning and application are contested in PRC maritime disputes (rather than the wider body of the international law of the sea), the analysis targeted cases that are also likely to reveal whether China is effectively challenging maritime order. This narrowed scope allowed for focused observation of the extent to which China's practice of the law of the sea has affected local, regional, or global rules. The dynamics of these rule changes also offer meaningful but limited insights into wider potential changes to international order.

This chapter seeks to draw together some of the key rules contested through PRC practice. Summarizing this empirical pattern, it further characterizes the overall direction of those changes in each of the four rule-sets examined (that is, geography, resources, navigation, dispute resolution) and offers some provisional conclusions about how this affects contemporary maritime order. The evidence supports the conclusion that there is no viable pathway for China to produce wholesale change to the legal rules of maritime order—but there are distinct signs of extra-legal change to maritime order in East Asia that bear further examination. In short, China is not so much changing the rules as it is reducing their importance.

SUMMARY OF CHINA'S LAW OF THE SEA

To determine whether there is presently a distinct, inchoate East Asian maritime order, it will be helpful to review the findings from the previous chapters on disputed law of the sea rules on geography, resources, navigation, and dispute resolution. In each of those interlocking fields of maritime practice, China has persistently advanced a set of preferred rules. In most cases, PRC practices have not been uniform or consistent, a pattern which limits their formal rule-generating potential. However, they are generally becoming more so through the PRC's increasingly sophisticated and capable domestic apparatus for articulating its preferred rules in the diplomatic arena and operationalizing them in ocean space. Applied in competition with persistent rival claims, these domestic laws, regulations, administrative and law enforcement agencies, and standard operating procedures are institutional expressions of PRC maritime ambitions, providing a clear window into certain desired changes to law of the sea rules.

The "weapon of international law" is only one instrument among many in Beijing's statecraft, but it is significant in the comprehensive drive to "build maritime power" and redeem "lost" sovereignty over the islands of the South and East China Seas. This irredentist territorial goal has become inextricable from China's related struggle to "safeguard maritime rights and interests" in maritime disputes, made more salient by the progressive development of the law of the sea itself. The vast expansion of coastal state maritime rights and jurisdiction in the twentieth century positioned China to ride this wave of enclosure still further toward a law of the sea that elevates sovereign autonomy and discretion above the interpretive confines of the black letters of UNCLOS. Resting on customary international law where possible and on stark exceptionalism where necessary, China's law of the sea has taken a distinctive form.

On rules concerning maritime entitlements, baselines, and boundaries, China's practice pushes the limits of geographic space. Enclosing large groups of tiny maritime features with territorial baselines, the PRC has asserted the full panoply of maritime zones from every feature, even those naturally under water. Layered on top of this UNCLOS-derived position is the extraordinary nine-dash line. This still-undefined zone presses China's claimed spatial monopoly even further seaward—or, depending on your perspective, presses landward into the coastlines of

China's southeast Asian neighbors. Widespread and uniform international rejection of the map as a basis for any valid law of the sea claim is likely to persist, but, in consequence, so too will the undetermined status of most of the South China Sea.[1]

In northeast Asia, China has not appealed to an extraordinary map that invokes extra-UNCLOS rules. Instead, in this sub-region the PRC has deployed an advantageous reading of UNCLOS rules against the known disadvantages of its semi-enclosed littoral. Beijing has pressed the superiority of the natural prolongation of territory in the form of an extended continental shelf; this stance represents the only virtually uniform and consistent element of its claims in this geographic rule-set. Set against the opposable EEZ and continental shelf claims of Japan and South Korea and taking into consideration the lack of other examples in which an extended continental shelf trumps an EEZ, this PRC-preferred rule also seems destined to remain unrealized. The concerted opposition to China's geographic rules by those states whose own maritime zones are denied has left a stalemate in East Asia. The current patchwork of overlapping presumed entitlements is likely to persist.

These spatial disagreements spill out into the disputed waters and seabed, where China's maximal entitlement claims bring about maximal contention over scarce marine resources. Here, too, the specially affected states have largely not acquiesced to the imposition of China's sovereign will on the question of sovereign rights and jurisdiction. China's appeals to at least preferential if not exclusive control over these resources based on historical usages run into the firm objection from claimants that China's purported "historic rights" and "traditional fisheries" generally do not survive the Convention. Yet by seizing these rights in fisheries with an overwhelming fishing fleet and coercive maritime law enforcement apparatus, China has in effect realized some part of its historic claims. Without the acquiescence of the other fishing nations, this practice, too, is ill-positioned to generate a rule of law or even a stable pattern of regional fisheries management.

Resources, however, can be exploited in day-to-day practice and therefore differ fundamentally from the legal abstractions of boundaries, baselines, or entitlements. In denying its nearby neighbors their UNCLOS-based sovereign rights over offshore hydrocarbons, China has exercised what amounts to "veto jurisdiction" over the exploitation of oil and gas in disputed zones. Meanwhile, China's efforts to reap the wealth of the region's seas meet the consistent opposition of littoral states that likewise cherish their marine resources. While China has not succeeded in exclusively exploiting the living and non-living resources of the disputed areas, it has diminished the effectiveness of other claimants' sovereign rights to those resources. Thus, even lacking the measure of uniformity and consistency that would allow for rule formation, China's practice is diminishing the power of UNCLOS rules to govern the allocation of resources in the SCS and ECS, at a minimum. The EEZs and continental shelves of rival claimants may exist purely in theory. The maximal hypothetical claims depicted in Figures 2 through 4 illustrate the fullest possible denial of other states' resource rights implied by PRC's proposed rules. Even if these claims are not fully implemented or realized, the effectiveness of UNCLOS resource rules is damaged when the rights they prescribe cannot be exercised in actuality.

Navigation raises a different set of possibilities. Compared to the PRC practices observed in the geographic and resource rule-sets, China's practice of its preferred navigational rules has been relatively consistent and uniform. The dominant characteristic of China's navigation practice is a blanket claim that coastal states have nearly total sovereign discretion to regulate activity in their jurisdictional zones. This broad rule has been applied most pointedly on the question of military access and activities, where it has met little objection from specially affected states. Indeed, China adopts the prevailing practice among specially affected states by imposing some restrictions on military navigation. Many regional states adopt a comparable set of restrictions; meanwhile, those that do not have been unable to challenge the steadily improving and already overwhelming capacity of China's naval and law enforcement forces across the East Asian littoral.

Especially on the rules governing innocent passage of military vessels, China's practice is poised to generate changes to the rules as applied in the region and perhaps beyond. The PRC has uniformly sought to regulate the innocent passage rights of foreign warships, a practice that is shared by many of its neighbors—and by some forty states worldwide, according to multiple independent assessments.[2] While there is no quantitative threshold for identifying a widespread and representative practice, the concentration of these navigationally restrictive states in East Asia strongly suggests the potential establishment of a customary rule. Only the US Navy directly contests this restriction in East Asia (as it does across the globe). USN practice of free navigation may be sufficient to uphold a persistent objection to the rule for the US and perhaps for its allies and partners, but the evidence supports the argument that innocent passage for warships is itself becoming a rule of special customary international law, inhering only to those states that can securely exercise it.

Further seaward, in the EEZ, the basic non-uniformity of China's practices and its navy's rapid flow into strategic maritime space around the globe leave this zone unlikely to form any clear rules—whether those preferred by China or otherwise. As has been the case since UNCLOS emerged, the EEZ seems destined to remain sui generis. However, the sheer variety of practices and restrictions adopted by coastal states across global EEZs lends credence to the expectation in some quarters that "creeping jurisdiction" that erodes navigational freedoms is the basic trend in this zone.[3] In this respect, China's preferred general rule of sovereign discretion for the coastal state over navigation in its jurisdictional zones has a certain momentum.

The final set of rules under dispute concerns how to resolve disputes about all of the other rules. These, too, bear the distinct imprint of China's regional weight. No combination of legal briefs, diplomatic harangues, or even "freedom of navigation operations" could effectively enforce the SCS Arbitration's judgment against China's practices. Yet in defying that ruling, China enacted a familiar great power exception to unwanted litigation, reinforcing a norm that is hardly novel. Similarly, the reciprocal patterns of non-recognition of disputes are familiar and perhaps even uncontroversial. At any rate, they will remain outside the scope of law of the sea rules unless and until effective control is physically wrested from an occupant of a disputed feature.[4]

More significant for the law of the sea are the alternatives to formal dispute resolution that China has pressed throughout the region. "Dialogue and consultation" are evidently the preferred methods of dispute resolution—or, more accurately, dispute management—throughout Southeast Asia. Despite the Philippines' bold arbitral gambit and the posturing of the Vietnamese to follow suit, the prospects for successful compulsory dispute resolution involving China's maritime disputes are vanishingly small.

Furthermore, the basic appeal to sovereignty that underlies China's dispute resolution practice is warmly received in East Asia, where recourse to such formal measures is already proportionally low. Such a norm does not conduce to the destruction of the UNCLOS dispute settlement system so exquisitely crafted in Part XV, but it supports the expectation that the system's application will have a regionalized character in East Asia. If states in dispute with China do not expect formal dispute resolution to produce a satisfactory result, multiple competing rules will co-exist in the region with no viable mechanism for adjudicating between them. In aggregate, this amounts to a less rule-governed maritime East Asia, and one unlikely to form agreed rules over the foreseeable future.

The patterns of practice surrounding China's maritime disputes do not admit categorical statements that one or another of its preferred rules has achieved recognizable status of international law. To some extent, such pronouncements are never possible with respect to customary international law, which is notoriously difficult to pin down. However, the method applied in this study has sought only to test whether necessary conditions have been met, not whether a new rule is definitively established. By this standard, most PRC-preferred rules are plainly ruled out by the incoherence of China's practice of them; others face lesser obstacles and must be recognized as regional behavioral regularities or even norms with the potential to crystallize into local or regional customary rules over time. Table 24 presents the four rules that have the greatest potential for wider applicability, based on the qualities of Chinese practice and the lack of uniform opposition from specially affected states.

This rule-level analysis is as far as the "bottom-up" method will take us. In sum, the Chinese practice across each of the disputed rule-sets has not observably changed the rules, and it is unlikely to do so in all but a few cases. The aggregate effect of China's law of the sea practice, however, frustrates the application of UNCLOS rules in East Asia—and perhaps beyond. As a result, certain appeals to rules of international law are becoming less meaningful because those rules do not correspond to the observed practice of the relevant states.

TABLE 24

**REGIONAL AND GLOBAL PROSPECTS FOR CHINA'S LAW
OF THE SEA RULES**

Eligible PRC rule	*Domain of potential rule change*
"Veto jurisdiction" over resource rights	Regional
Innocent passage restrictions determined by coastal state	Regional / Global
"Dialogue and consultation" dispute management	Regional
Dispute non-recognition	Global

Rather than changing the rules, China is changing the international environment in which those rules take effect. Especially within the region, the rules of the international law of the sea simply have less bearing on what states actually do in practice. Specially affected states cannot draw normal maritime boundaries; they struggle to exploit resources and navigate freely within those undelimited boundaries; they are denied legal avenues for resolving these disputes. China's practices have not altered these rules in a way that other states will accept, but rather they have undermined their application and narrowed their functional scope. Taking a holistic view and addressing these patterns from the top down will yield further insights into how these dynamic practices manifest at the abstract level of international order.

PURSUING A POST-LIBERAL INTERNATIONAL ORDER

China's leaders are pursuing certain programmatic aims in the maritime domain that reflect discernible beliefs about the proper purposes and limitations of international law itself. These are evident in several principles that lend a degree of coherence to PRC positions on the specific law of the sea rules addressed throughout this study. Most salient among these principles are (1) the UNCLOS treaty is not the only body of rules that governs maritime affairs, (2) those rules that do apply are in flux or ambiguous and thus subject to interpretation by sovereign states, and (3) legal disputes are not necessarily resolved by legal procedures.[5] The core prerogatives of sovereign autonomy underlie each of these principles. In concert, they imbue China's practices with certain general characteristics that help us understand the more systematic consequences on maritime order that may result from China's practices in the law of the sea.

One such understanding concerns the fragility of international legal order. Scholars are beginning to explore how the international legal community does not, in fact, uniformly subscribe to the universalistic and universalizing ambitions often associated with the post-war project of international law. Instead, the supposed "indivisible college of international lawyers" is demonstrably divisible, fractured across geographic and cultural lines in its conceptualizations and practices of international law.[6] The possibility of a distinctively "authoritarian" brand of international law is one relevant implication from this line of work, positing that "authoritarian use of international law will support normative development that specifically enhances authoritarianism."[7] Such normative change may be confined to the region(s) in which authoritarian norms find most purchase, though such fragmentation may have substantial consequence for the integrity of the international legal order as a whole.[8]

The more assertively and effectively authoritarian states like China and Russia put their visions of international law into practice, the more that vision may influence the norms, rules, and principles of international law as practiced by other states.[9] China and Russia have found common cause on the fundamental issue of sovereign autonomy as the *grundnorm* of the international legal system. Vowing to "uphold and promote" a hard core of inviolable sovereign autonomy, China and Russia espouse an "international order based on international law" that is substantively less universal and, perhaps most importantly, procedurally less controlled by the US and its allies.[10] Such an order can be understood as a "return to Westphalia," in which the universalizing tendencies of international law in the post–Cold War era would be rolled back to revive an earlier era in which sovereign autonomy is the controlling doctrine.[11]

Greater sovereign discretion to interpret and apply rules promotes greater indeterminacy at the level of individual rules. If every state may auto-interpret the rules to suit its interests, it is impossible for the rules themselves to provide determinate solutions. Instead, rules become more indeterminate, bearing the cumulative effects of states practicing according to their lights rather than to the black letters of the law. The evidence presented in this study suggests that the individual rules themselves are mostly resistant to China's persistent but undisciplined challenges. China's efforts to exploit the process of customary rule formation and shape rules in its favor are hardly without effect. It is just in the nature of customary international law formation that "authority in this process is diffusely held," as Monica Hakimi explains it. "Although individual actors can easily advance claims about the law, none can alone establish the law. No one entity is entitled to assess the various claims on an issue, weed out the outliers, and finally settle customary international law's normative content."[12]

However, the normative ground on which rules rest, the international legal order, is undoubtedly shifting as the tectonic plates of great power competition meet in the East Asian littoral. The normative flux brought about by China's law of the sea shows the beginning of a possible rejuvenation of a less universal type of international law. Joined by Russia and many non-Western states, this normative change may be more or less "authoritarian" but in substance it is certainly defined by sovereign supremacy. Its main dynamic is found in the increasingly powerful assertions of sovereign prerogatives over and against the post–Cold War trend toward the deeper and more transnational reach of the "zone of law" into the "zone of politics" guarded by sovereign autonomy.[13]

In the specific domain of the law of the sea, a reinforced sovereignty norm promises a maritime order marked by greater closure. In East Asia, where China directly bolsters its preferred rules with the actual or implied threat of force, there is a marked acceleration of the dominance of coastal state jurisdiction over freedom of the seas. This exceptional circumstance, however, illustrates one of the limitations of the universal application of a hyper-sovereigntist doctrine. Granting states the sole authority to auto-interpret their legal rights and responsibilities guarantees idiosyncrasy and unevenness in practice across different states and within the same states over time. An order in which sovereign supremacy is the dominant principle resists universalizing tendencies. China's practical effects on maritime order are far more significant at local and regional levels. Determining whether this promotes a separate rules-based order or merely erodes the existing order requires a final consideration of the dynamics of changing order.

CALIBRATING CHINA'S CHALLENGE

Taking a holistic, top-down view of the rules we have so far examined mostly from the bottom up, what can we say about the character of the maritime order emerging in East Asia? Has China realized its leaders' stated ambitions to "guide the direction of change in the international order" in the maritime domain?[14] In the abstract, we can envision a few basic directions of change in East Asian maritime order. It may become more globally applicable; it may grow increasingly regionalized; or it may be decaying. These are not exhaustive or entirely exclusive possibilities, but they offer a rough typology that will aid a broader set of conclusions about China's law of the sea and its implications for international order.

A global order achieves its universality through the application of general rules. These rules need not be legal or liberal or otherwise con-genial to Western preferences to warrant that designation.[15] Rather, their substance may vary but their scope of application must be universal (or near universal) for a coherent global order to exist. This ideal type is, in fact, the aspiration of proponents of UNCLOS as a "constitution for the oceans" and the "world ocean" as a single domain, physically and conceptually. But because the rules that China has put into practice in East Asia are largely not consistent or uniform, nor accepted by most specially affected states, it is relatively easy to rule out the possibility that legal characteristics of East Asian maritime order will become universal norms. The principle of sovereign supremacy has broad applicability, but because its basic implications are independence and domestically gener-ated rules, it does not conduce to a universal or global order. Although Chinese diplomats tell the UN that "the uniform application of interna-tional law should be ensured," actual PRC practice is organized around a countervailing principle.[16]

A regional order, however, is not governed by universal rules; differ-ent regions may be more or less rule-bound. The key variations lie in dis-tinct and representative patterns of state practice across regions. In this study we have observed only those patterns related to China's practice and cannot make a generalization about regional dynamics beyond East

Asia. Such a general assessment would require intensive parallel studies of other regions (for example, the Middle East, Latin America, Europe) or sub-regions like the Mediterranean, the Persian Gulf, the Caribbean, and the Baltics. However, such studies are not required to observe that China's preferred rules on coastal state authority and dispute resolution already bring about significant regional ordering effects. They need not be adopted in other regions for them to affect the overall pattern of maritime order.

It would be sufficient for other states to simply acquiesce to a regional custom (perhaps codified in an SCS Code of Conduct) to reinforce the increasingly regional character of East Asian maritime order. Such an outcome would not immediately undermine UNCLOS in the region or elsewhere, but it would meaningfully degrade its uniformity across the world's oceans. However grudging, international acceptance of a special set of Chinese claims and rules underpinning them would create a precedent for other states and regional groupings to develop non-uniform practices and idiosyncratic rules of their own. It would become more difficult for courts and arbitral panels to deny the validity of plural interpretations of important norms that hitherto prevented the fragmentation of rules as applied in different regions of the world. It may be that many law of the sea rules, but especially customary international law, necessarily have a more fragmentary, regional character.[17]

Regional orders may also be negatively defined—that is, arising not from the "positive" expression of distinctive rules in particular regions but from the disintegration or breakdown of universal rules. At a macro level, such disintegration might "yield to an international system where several leading states or centers of power—for example, China, the United States, and the European Union—establish their own economic and security spheres. The global order would become a less unified and coherent system of rules and institutions, while regional orders emerge as relatively distinct, divided, and competitive geopolitical spheres."[18] In the maritime domain, East Asia may be reasonably perceived as this sub-type of regional order. Facing persistent Chinese practices that frustrate other states' exercise of resource and navigational rights under UNCLOS, the region exhibits a set of distinct norms—perhaps not rule-like at all—that untether it in significant respects from global maritime order. China's avowed intention to remedy some of the "defects" of the

Convention are being realized, though not by substantively changing UNCLOS rules so much as narrowing the scope of their application in China's claimed waters.

Finally, a decaying order is, in a word, disorderly. Rather than exhibiting near-universal qualities or manifesting distinct regional qualities, the rules of such an order are particular and context-specific—if, indeed, they are properly considered rules at all. State practice would show no systematic pattern, and it would vary only in terms of how idiosyncratic those practices are. As in China's practice on navigational matters, rules would be applied in discriminate fashion, non-uniformly across different bodies of water and against different states and types of vessels, and inconsistently over time as exigency demands. It is beyond the scope of this study to assess whether such decay is evident in other regions, as would be necessary to make a more general assessment about the fate of global maritime order. But elements of decay are evident in East Asia, representing a countervailing trend to growing regionalization. If decay becomes the dominant trend, China's law of the sea would be sharply limited to PRC domestic law in the water space it directly controls.

Each of these ideal types tells us something different about how China's law of the sea poses a challenge to the maritime order. Judging the magnitude of that challenge and the other potential vectors of China's challenge to order, however, requires a separate optic. Doctrinally, relative power should have no bearing on whose practices matter in the formation and development of rules of international law; but it is in the nature of international politics that the most meaningful practices will be those of states with sufficient power and purpose to make their preferred rules a reality.[19] China has mobilized extraordinary resources and attention to put its vision of the law of the sea into practice, with express intent to make its practices the norm—or at least not outside the bounds of legality. Customary international law, the primary battleground for China's law of the sea in most respects, is by its nature especially susceptible to bending toward the purposes of powerful states.[20]

The contemporary maritime order is one in which the dominant states' interests are not aligned and their practices are often in direct and sustained conflict. The results of this struggle to shape and change rules in the law of the sea may serve as a proxy for their power and status overall. If this competition does not spill out into other domains, such disputes over the rules may nonetheless provide a vehicle for "incremental change" through "adjustments within the framework of the existing system."[21] This peaceful, "evolutionary" process is facilitated by the world-historically robust set of rules and institutions that characterize the contemporary international order. The PRC's rhetorical commitment to the "UN-centric" system, for example, appears calibrated to impart a sense of incremental change from within a stable, existing order.

More tragic outcomes are likely if the incremental adjustment process facilitated by international law breaks down and China chooses "exit" from the extant order.[22] China's abandonment of its Mao-era "revolutionary line" in favor of a more evolutionary "peaceful rise" within international order offers only modest reassurance that China's law of the sea will not inexorably bring about the decay of maritime order in East Asia, and perhaps beyond.[23] China's increased power and clear intent to change the rules suggest that even without revolutionary aims, it will exert ever-greater influence on individual rules and test the fabric of international order. Based on the holistic patterns observed here, China's challenge to rules is more apt to result in disintegration and decay than it is to form a coherent Chinese alternative with universal scope and applicability.

Are we witnessing a "disjuncture between the governance of the system and the underlying distribution of power" such that the maritime order must devolve?[24] Can the basic openness of the global oceans survive PRC maritime disputes? The main brake on such decay is that China's law of the sea, like the Chinese party-state system, is largely not viable for export. The new rules Beijing seeks to apply are idiosyncratic, particular to its disadvantaged geography, fueled by specific national grievances, and shaped by China's unique geopolitical position in an uncertain American hegemony. Yet China's law of the sea is already in evidence within the region, and its challenge to international order is taking shape in the littorals of East Asia.

NOTES

INTRODUCTION

1. Poling, "The Conventional Wisdom."
2. See US Dept. of State, "US Responses to Excessive National Maritime Claims."
3. United Nations Convention on the Law of the Sea, 10 December 1982, 1833 UNTS 397.
4. From Yang Jiechi, "Firmly Uphold and Practice": "积极参与现有国际规则修订和新疆域规则制定."
5. Yang Jiechi, "Conscientiously Study and Publicize."
6. That exercise is properly undertaken by a court with standing and jurisdiction to decide the matter. Discussions of compliance in international relations, meanwhile, often presume a clarity in the rules themselves such that actions may be clearly coded in or out of compliance with them. This study makes no such presumptions; it problematizes instead the process of determining what the rules are in practice.
7. Dutton, "Three Disputes and Three Objectives," 3–8.
8. On popular nationalism and China's island claims, see Chubb, "Chinese Nationalism and the 'Gray Zone'"; Downs and Saunders, "Legitimacy and the Limits of Nationalism," 116–124; Weiss, *Powerful Patriots,* 15–41.
9. The customary international law of territorial acquisition is the rule-set in play in such disputes, and there is little disagreement as to what evidence is dispositive for deciding such cases. The Eritrea/Yemen arbitration offers the following commonly cited distillation: "demonstration of use, presence, display of governmental authority and other ways of showing possession [effectivités] which may gradually consolidate into [sovereign] title." *Sovereignty*

and Maritime Delimitation in the Red Sea (Eritrea v. Yemen), 12 RIAA 211
(Perm. Ct. Arb. 1998), para. 450; see also Dutton, "Testing the Boundaries,"
6–9; Brilmayer and Klein, "Land and Sea," 703–768.

10. For an exposition on this policy line and its history, see Shi Yuanhua, "Diplomacy on Hold," 22–23.

11. Xi Jinping, "Speech on Building Maritime Power."

12. PRC Ministry of Foreign Affairs, "Shelve Disputes and Jointly Develop."

13. In terms of CCP organization, Xi is considered three generations after Deng,
who represents the second generation of PRC leadership. Mao led the first,
Jiang Zemin the third, Hu Jintao the fourth, and Xi Jinping the fifth.

14. PRC State Oceanic Administration, *China Oceans Yearbook 2000*, 10–11 (the
first instance of this "blue territory" terminology in an official publication).
The term is now used commonly in PRC official, academic, and media
reports on maritime issues, e.g., PRC Ministry of Agriculture, "Protector of
Blue Territory."

15. Xi Jinping, "Speech on Building Maritime Power." For analysis of this
desired balance in PRC maritime policy, see Hu Bo and Zhu Feng, "Future
Stability in the SCS"; Martinson, "Echelon Defense," 78.

16. Chubb, "PRC Assertiveness," 79–121. Chubb dates the increase in assertiveness to 2007, five years prior to Xi Jinping's elevation to general secretary. In
his capacity as a Politburo Standing Committee member during those years,
Xi may well have been instrumental in the earlier change in emphasis; at a
minimum, he has presided over a marked expansion of the "assertive" policy
line.

17. See Fravel, *Strong Borders, Secure Nation*, 267–299. Fravel's theory convinc-
ingly presents "delay" as the prevailing phenomenon in island disputes;
however, the focus on sovereignty alone obscures the significant escalation
of Chinese activity to assert jurisdictional and resource rights. See also
Fravel, "China's Strategy in the SCS," and Fravel, "Explaining Stability in the
Senkaku."

18. On these developments, see McDevitt, *China as a Twenty-First Century Naval
Power;* McDevitt, "Becoming a Great 'Maritime Power.'"

19. See Cable, *Gunboat Diplomacy,* 14 (defining "gunboat diplomacy" as "the use
or threat of limited naval force, otherwise than as an act of war, in order to
secure advantage or avert loss, either in the furtherance of an international
dispute or against foreign nationals within the territory or the jurisdiction of
their own state").

20. Martinson, "Echelon Defense," provides the most comprehensive available
account of the various tasks of Chinese maritime law enforcement in disputed zones.

21. China's foreign ministry announced that "[t]he main purpose of China's
construction activities is to meet various civilian demands and better per-
form China's international obligations and responsibilities in the areas such
as maritime search and rescue, disaster prevention and mitigation, marine

scientific research, meteorological observation, ecological environment conservation, navigation safety as well as fishery production service." PRC MFA spokesperson, 16 June 2015.

22. In the customary international law of territorial acquisition, a key concept is the "critical date" at which a dispute crystallizes and after which no actions should have any effect on sovereign title. Chinese officials accept and even embrace this concept, which supports their basic arguments about China's historical occupation of disputed islands. See Shu Zhenya, "Research Overview on the Study of the Critical Date," 66–77.

23. See, for example, PRC State Oceanic Administration, *China Oceans Yearbook 2010*, 127. These are regular terms in PRC official documents and policy guidance on maritime law enforcement practices.

24. Cf. prior, exclusively legal works that have catalogued China's practice in the law of the sea without analysis of political challenges to rules. See Greenfield, *China's Practice in the Law of the Sea*; Zou Keyuan, *China's Marine Legal System*.

25. Huang Huikang, "Developments in International Law."

26. White House, "Remarks by the President in Meeting on the Trans-Pacific Partnership."

27. US Dept. of State, "Secretary Antony J. Blinken."

28. US Dept. of State, "Secretary Antony J. Blinken."

29. Johnston, "Is China a Status Quo Power?" 5–56.

30. Johnston, "World of Orders," 12.

31. In Blinken's words: "China is the only country with the economic, diplomatic, military, and technological power to seriously challenge the stable and open international system—all the rules, values, and relationships that make the world work the way we want it to" (US Dept. of State, "A Foreign Policy for the American People").

32. An overview of this "compliance literature" is available in Dunoff and Pollack, *Interdisciplinary Perspectives*. See also Hafner-Burton et al., "Political Science Research on International Law." This question is typically posed as some version of "why or when do states comply with the rules?"

CHAPTER 1. ORDER, RULES, AND CHANGE IN THE LAW OF THE SEA

1. Chen Yixin, "Xi Jinping Thought on Ruling by Law Is the Latest Achievement in the Sinicization of Marxism."

2. Tommy T. B. Koh, *Building a New Legal Order*, 85–93.

3. The analysis aims to establish only a minimum, necessary threshold for a rule to change—not to confirm the sufficiency of practice for the formation of a new legal rule. Such a determination can only be made meaningful by a court or a government.

4. A secondary distinction is sometimes made between "limited-aims revisionists and unlimited-aims revisionists or revolutionary powers." See Schweller, "Managing the Rise of Great Powers," 19–21.

5. See Gilpin, *War and Change;* Carr, *Twenty Years' Crisis.*

6. Johnston, "World of Orders," 13. In presenting this common definition, Johnston cites government officials, think-tank reports, and numerous academic studies across theoretical orientations that each "overwhelmingly assume, implicitly or explicitly" the centrality of the hegemon to any conception of order.

7. Johnston, "World of Orders," 14–22.

8. Gilpin, *War and Change,* 30: dominant states "establish and enforce the basic rules and rights that influence their own behavior and that of the lesser states in the system."

9. Lasswell and Kaplan, *Power and Society,* 208.

10. Johnston, "Is China a Status Quo Power?" 11 (cautioning against assumption that "norms and rules are obvious": "in some cases, there is no plausible international community standard to follow").

11. "It is hard to deduce a coherent set of norms and institutions against which to measure the level of compliance with a liberal international order when the dominant state's own practices seem inconsistent or when it, too, opposes a wide range of extant norms and institutions." Johnston, "World of Orders," 21.

12. Johnston, "World of Orders," 22.

13. Keohane, *After Hegemony,* sets out the most influential version of this thesis, rejecting the realist axiom that order arises only from hegemonic power and proposing that institutionalized cooperative behaviors approximating order can result from individual state self-interest.

14. Ikenberry, *Liberal Leviathan,* 310.

15. Ikenberry, *Liberal Leviathan,* 36.

16. Reus-Smit, *Moral Purpose of the State,* 30.

17. Ikenberry, *Liberal Leviathan,* 12 (arguing that order is "manifest in the settled rules and arrangements between states that define and guide their interaction"); Johnston, "World of Orders," 12.

18. For a recent attempt to bridge this theoretical chasm, see Ikenberry and Nexon, "Hegemony Studies 3.0," which conceives of "orders as means, mediums, and objects of cooperation and contestation" (395).

19. Gilpin, *War and Change,* 35.

20. See Ikenberry, *Liberal Leviathan;* Franck, *The Power of Legitimacy.*

21. Gilpin, *War and Change;* Ruggie, *Multilateralism Matters.*

22. Krasner, *Organized Hypocrisy.* See also David Kennedy, "Many Legal Orders," 642 (observing that international law "is applied differently in different places. It is more dense here than there.")

23. Keohane and Nye, *Power and Interdependence.*

24. For a survey of these potential modes of regional order, see Alagappa, "The Study of International Order," in Alagappa, ed., *Asian Security Order.* See also Fairbank, *The Chinese World Order.*

25. Katzenstein, *World of Regions*. See also Mastanduno, "Partner Politics," 479–504 (depicting the Cold War American-led order as an aggregation of distinct but overlapping regional orders).

26. Johnston, "World of Orders," 22–25 (developing a conception of orders, in the plural, as emergent properties of patterned state and sub-state activities).

27. Gilpin, *War and Change*, 187.

28. The legal scholarship on what makes international law "law" (or not) is prolific and calls attention to ever more fundamental rules and norms that make any legal institutions possible. See Hart, *The Concept of Law*.

29. Gilpin, *War and Change*, 35.

30. Gilpin, *War and Change*, 35.

31. Keohane and Nye, *Power and Interdependence*, 44–46.

32. Statute of the International Court of Justice, 26 June 1945, 59 Stat. 1055, 33 UNTS 933, art. 38.

33. The third is seldom invoked and the fourth is explicitly "subsidiary." See Byers, *Custom, Power, and the Power of Rules*; Akehurst, "Custom as a Source of International Law," 1–53; Danilenko, "The Theory of International Customary Law," 9–47; Jia Bingbing, "The Relations Between Treaties and Custom," 81–109.

34. "A law is indeterminate when a question of law, or of how the law applies to facts, has no single right answer." Endicott, *Vagueness in Law*, 9.

35. Some legal scholars argue that "self-serving auto-interpretation" is constrained: "precision of individual commitments, coherence between individual commitments and broader legal principles, and accepted modes of legal discourse and argument all help limit such opportunistic behavior. Granting interpretive authority to courts or other legal institutions further constrains auto-interpretation." Abbott and Snidal, "Hard and Soft Law," 427.

36. Hart, *The Concept of Law*, 128.

37. Koskenniemi, "International Law and Hegemony," 198. See also Roberts, *Is International Law International?*; Roberts et al., *Comparative International Law*.

38. One of the most stirring critical assaults on international law argues that determinacy in international legal norms is the mark of hegemony: "Consensus is, after all, the end-point of a hegemonic process in which some agent or institution has succeeded in making its position seem the universal or 'neutral position'" (Koskenniemi, *From Apology to Utopia*, 597). For a potent critique of the "critical dogma," see Solum, "On the Indeterminacy Crisis," 462–503.

39. For the critical argument that the presumed "invisible college of international lawyers" that can resolve indeterminacy of treaty rules in a professional, consistent, unbiased way is not in evidence, see especially Koskenniemi, *From Apology to Utopia*, 35–40. See also Roberts, *Is International Law International?*

40. Buga, "Between Stability and Change," 46–68.
41. 1969 Vienna Convention on the Law of Treaties, Art. 31, para. 3.
42. Buga, "Between Stability and Change," 68.
43. International Law Commission, "Draft Conclusions on Identification of Customary International Law, with Commentaries," UN Doc. A/73/10 (2018), 12. See also the specific formula adopted in UNGA Res. 73/203, "Identification of Customary International Law" (20 December 2018).
44. There is no formal count or registry of customary international laws. Customary law has accumulated over the course of centuries of practice and is often coextensive with treaties. See Bodansky, "The Concept of Customary International Law," 667–679; Kelly, "The Twilight of Customary International Law," 450–544; Roberts, "Traditional and Modern Approaches to Customary International Law," 757–791; Guzman, "Saving Customary International Law," 115–176.
45. Roberts, "Traditional and Modern Approaches," 784.
46. See Verdier and Voeten, "Precedent, Compliance, and Change," 389–485 (pointing to the incoherent content of customary rules, which may change in response to repeated violations).
47. Finnemore and Sikkink, "International Norm Dynamics," 916 (italics in original).
48. Such attention has been rare in international relations, perhaps partly because of the methodological messiness of customary international law. See, for example, Morrow, *Order Within Anarchy*, 17: "I focus, however, on formal treaties over customary law in this project. The dual process of formal negotiation followed by ratification means that the standards of the treaty and its acceptance by states are clearer than those in customary international law. The single public treaty produced through negotiation means that all states know what the standard is even if they do not accept it."
49. UNGA Res. 73/203, Conclusion 5.
50. "Forms of State practice include, but are not limited to: diplomatic acts and correspondence; conduct in connection with resolutions adopted by an international organization or at an intergovernmental conference; conduct in connection with treaties; executive conduct, including operational conduct 'on the ground'; legislative and administrative acts; and decisions of national courts" (ILC, "Draft Conclusions," 132).
51. ILC, "Draft Conclusions," 138, 140: "State practice must be accompanied by a conviction that it is permitted, required or prohibited by customary international law. It is thus crucial to establish, in each case, that States have acted in a certain way because they felt or believed themselves legally compelled or entitled to do so by reason of a rule of customary international law: they must have pursued the practice as a matter of right, or submitted to it as a matter of obligation. . . . Forms of evidence of acceptance as law (*opinio juris*) include, but are not limited to: public statements made on behalf of States; official publications; government legal opinions; diplomatic correspondence;

decisions of national courts; treaty provisions; and conduct in connection with resolutions adopted by an international organization or at an inter-governmental conference. . . . Failure to react over time to a practice may serve as evidence of acceptance as law (*opinio juris*), provided that States were in a position to react and the circumstances called for some reaction."

52. *North Sea Continental Shelf* (F.R. Germany v. Denmark; F.R. Germany v. Netherlands), Judgment, 1969 ICJ 3 (20 February), para. 77; *Continental Shelf* (Libya v. Malta), Judgment, 1985 ICJ 13 (3 June), para. 27. According to the ILC, "Draft Conclusions," 126: "Practice without acceptance as law (*opinio juris*), even if widespread and consistent, can be no more than a non-binding usage, while a belief that something is (or ought to be) the law unsupported by practice is mere aspiration; it is the two together that establish the existence of a rule of customary international law."

53. Cassese and Weiler, eds., *Change and Stability*, 10 (comments of Georges Abi Saab).

54. ILC, "Draft Conclusions," 135.

55. ILC, "Draft Conclusions," 138.

56. ILC, "Draft Conclusions," 123.

57. Akehurst, "Custom as a Source of International Law," 17–18.

58. ILC, "Draft Conclusions," 136.

59. *North Sea Continental Shelf*, paras. 74, 77.

60. UNGA Res. 73/203, Conclusion 16: "1. A rule of particular customary international law, whether regional, local, or other, is a rule of customary international law that applies only among a limited number of states. 2. To determine the existence and content of a rule of particular customary international law, it is necessary to ascertain whether there is a general practice among the States concerned that is accepted by them as law (*opinio juris*) among themselves."

61. D'Amato, "The Concept of Special Custom," 212–213.

62. D'Amato, "The Concept of Special Custom," 213.

63. *Military and Paramilitary Activities in and Against Nicaragua* (Nicaragua v. US), Judgment, 1986 ICJ 14 (27 June), para. 199.

64. *Land, Island, and Maritime Frontier Dispute* (El Salvador v. Honduras: Nicaragua intervening), Judgment, 1990 ICJ 146 (11 September), para. 21.

65. *Asylum Case* (Colombia v. Peru), Judgment, 1950 ICJ 266 (20 November), 276.

66. *Right of Passage over Indian Territory* (Portugal v. India), Judgment, 1960 ICJ 6 (12 April), 39.

67. See International Law Association (ILA), "Statement of the Principles," 4–5; Roberts, "Traditional and Modern Approaches," 757–791.

68. ILA, "Statement of the Principles," 32–34.

69. Nicaragua v. US, para. 186.

70. UNGA Res. 73/203, Conclusion 7: "Where the practice of a particular State varies, the weight to be given to that practice may, depending on the circum-

stances, be reduced"; ILC, "Identification of Customary International Law,"
135: In "case[s] where different organs or branches within the State adopt
different courses of conduct on the same matter or where the practice of one
organ varies over time. If in such circumstances a State's practice as a whole
is found to be inconsistent, that State's contribution to 'a general practice'
may be reduced."

71. Quoted in Vagts, "Hegemonic International Law," 847. On the "state of
exception" reasoning, see deLisle, "States of Exception," 342–390; Scheppele,
"Law in a Time of Emergency," 1001–1083.

72. D'Amato, *The Concept of Custom,* 97.

73. Allott, "The Concept of International Law," 43.

74. For one prominent legal scholar, customary international law is not properly understood as forming "rules" in the first place. Many "positions have
enough support to function as [customary international law] in some settings but not enough support to manifest as rules. Their legal salience is
splintered and contingent, rather than consistent or fixed." Hakimi, "Making Sense of Customary International Law," 1511. See also Fitzmaurice, "Vae
Victus," 358–361.

75. Hakimi, "The Work of International Law," 1–46.

76. D'Amato, "Groundwork for International Law," 650, 654. For a "managerial"
view of how law facilitates negotiations and cooperation, if not necessarily
compliance, see Chayes and Chayes, "On Compliance," 175–205.

77. Hakimi, "The Work of International Law," 46.

78. An influential example is Abbott et al., "The Concept of Legalization,"
401–419. For a potent criticism of the compliance paradigm and its mistaken
explanations for the causes for high rates of compliance, see Downs, Rocke,
and Barsoom, "Is the Good News About Compliance Good News About
Cooperation?" 379–406.

79. Hurd, "The Case Against International Cooperation," 19.

80. Hurd, *How To Do Things,* 3. Hurd observes that this formulation is the
standard way to teach international relations. See Frieden, Lake, and Schultz,
World Politics, 68–74.

81. Hakimi, "Making Sense of Customary International Law," 1487–1538. In
some cases, customary international law may only "structure an argumenta-
tive practice, without authoritatively resolving what ought to be done" (1536).

82. Tommy T. B. Koh, *Building a New Legal Order,* 85–93. Koh was the president
of the UN Conference on the Law of the Sea; he delivered this speech to
delegates at the close of the conference in December 1982.

83. D. P. O'Connell, "The Influence of Law on Sea Power," 13.

84. Libya v. Malta, para. 34; *Territorial and Maritime Dispute* (Nicaragua v.
Colombia), Judgment, 2012 ICJ Rep. 624 (19 November), para. 118. See also
Bernhardt, "Custom and Treaty"; Roach, "Today's Customary International
Law of the Sea," 239–259; Churchill, "The 1982 UNCLOS," 34–38.

85. In 1989 the United States and the Soviet Union together declared that the Convention, "with respect to the traditional uses of the oceans, generally constitute[s] international law and practice." Joint Statement by the United States and Soviet Union, with Uniform Interpretation of Rules of International Law Governing Innocent Passage, 2 September 1989, *Law of the Sea Bulletin* 14, 12–13.

86. Churchill, "The 1982 UNCLOS," 37.

87. UNCLOS III, "Preamble."

88. Koh, *Building a New Legal Order,* 87.

89. *People's Daily,* "Speech by the Chairman of the Delegation"; *People's Daily,* "Chairman Mao's Theory."

90. Bull, "The Revolt Against the West," 217–223. See also Krasner, *Structural Conflict.*

91. The Conference is the subject of exhaustive commentary by participants and leading law of the sea experts, who track all of the substantive and procedural controversies at the convention. See Myron H. Nordquist et al., *Commentary on the UN Convention on the Law of the Sea,* vols. 1–2.

92. Friedheim, *Negotiating the New Ocean Regime,* 303.

93. Liang Yufan, Remarks at the 156th Plenary Meeting of the Third UN Conference on the Law of the Sea, 8 March 1982, A/CONF.62/SR.156. Complete transcripts of all open sessions of the Conference are available in the *Official Records of the Third UN Conference on the Law of the Sea,* vols. I–XVII. These records will be cited as "UNCLOS, [document number—e.g., A/CONF.62/ WS/37]."

94. Shearer, "The Limits of Maritime Jurisdiction," 52.

95. O'Connell, *The International Law of the Sea,* 1–28.

96. This liberal norm is often discussed in reference to the "Lotus principle" in international law, which holds that "all that can be required of a State is that it should not overstep the limits which international law places upon its jurisdiction." *S.S. Lotus* (France v. Turkey), 1927, Permanent Court of International Justice (ser. A) No. 10 (7 September), para. 47.

97. O'Connell, *The International Law of the Sea,* 2–9; Oxman, "Territorial Temptation," 830–851.

98. Koh, *Building a New Legal Order,* 4.

99. Beckman, "International Law, UNCLOS, and the SCS," 54.

100. Buga, "Between Stability and Change," 65–66: "[T]he ambiguous nature or formulation of many provisions can grant states considerable leeway in interpreting and implementing LOS. . . . [M]odification by subsequent practice remains a strategic tool for parties to the Law of the Sea Convention."

101. See Anand, *Origin and Development of the Law of the Sea;* O'Connell, *The International Law of the Sea.*

102. Oxman, "Territorial Temptation," 832.

103. Oxman, "Territorial Temptation," 832.

104. "Policy of the United States with Respect to the Natural Resources of the Subsoil and Sea Bed of the Continental Shelf. Presidential Proclamation, no. 2667 (28 September 1945); "Policy of the United States with Respect to Coastal Fisheries in Certain Areas of the High Seas." Presidential Proclamation, no. 2668, (28 September 1945).

105. Among the consequential efforts by these states are the "Declaration on the Maritime Zone," signed at Santiago, Chile, 18 August 1952, 1976 UNTS 326 (Chile, Ecuador, and Peru), and the "Declaration of the Organization of African Unity," signed at Addis Ababa, 19 July 1974, reproduced in UNCLOS, A/Conf.62/33.

106. Riesenfeld, "The Third UN Conference," 12.

107. Iceland's expansion of its fishing rights was the proximate cause for the series of "Cod Wars" of the 1950s and 1970s that are also generally recognized as a critical development in the formation of the EEZ regime. Also see Koh, *Building a New Legal Order,* 6 (ascribing the development of the regime almost entirely to demands for fishing rights and related jurisdiction).

108. Convention on the Territorial Sea and Contiguous Zone, 29 April 1958, 516 UNTS 206 (entered into force 10 September 1964); Convention on the High Seas, 29 April 1958, 450 UNTS 11 (entered into force 30 September 1962); Convention on Fishing and Conservation of the Living Resources of the High Seas, 29 April 1958, 559 UNTS 285 (entered into force 20 March 1966); Convention on the Continental Shelf, 29 April 1958, 499 UNTS 311 (entered into force 10 June 1964).

109. UNGA, 22nd Sess., 1515th mtg., UN Doc A/C.1/PV.1515 (1 November 1967).

110. UNGA Res. 22/2340 (XXII), UN Doc A/6716 (18 December 1967).

111. UNGA Res. 2467 A (XXIII) (21 December 1968) established a Committee on the Peaceful Uses of the Sea-Bed and the Ocean Floor Beyond the Limits of National Jurisdiction. Subsequently, the General Assembly decided to convene a third conference on the law of the sea in 1973, and it instructed the new committee to act as a preparatory body for the conference. UNGA Res. 2750 C (XXV) (17 December 1970).

112. UN Press Release, "Montevideo Declaration on the Law of the Sea," NV/185 (9 June 1970).

113. Koh, *Building a New Legal Order,* 6.

114. Keohane and Nye, *Power and Interdependence,* 110, 127.

115. Krasner, *The Third World.*

116. The Soviet Union proposed "a study of a general nature on the problem of ensuring universal application of the provisions of the Convention, including the question of the harmonization of the national legislation of States with the Convention." UN Division for Ocean Affairs and the Law of the Sea (DOALOS), "Declarations and Reservations," 29.

117. *People's Daily,* "Editorial."

118. Shan Xu, "China's Participation."

119. Shearer, "Limits of Maritime Jurisdiction," 63. The Truman Proclamations are a rare exception to this rule.

120. Leading specialists on the law of the sea argue that UNCLOS III does not prescribe specific norms and rules for most of the technical matters in the maritime domain; rather, it assigns rights and jurisdiction to coastal states that then have some discretion over how they are applied. See, for example, Churchill, "The 1982 UNCLOS," 28–30.

121. On subsequent practice, see Vienna Convention on the Law of Treaties, opened for signature 23 May 1969, 1155 UNTS 331, Art. 31(3)(b); UNGA Res. 73/202, art. 32; "Subsequent Agreements and Subsequent Practice in Relation to the Interpretation of Treaties" (20 December 2018); Buga, "Between Stability and Change," 66–68.

122. UNGA Res. 73/203, Conclusion 8.

123. While certainly not required as an analytical matter, it is noteworthy that this approach is also politically and doctrinally acceptable for the PRC. Chinese officials have affirmed that "the primacy of State practice does and should apply at all times." Report of the ILC, UN Doc A/73/100, Item 82, Statement by Mr. Xu Hong at the Sixth Committee (Legal).

124. Yee, "AALCO [Asian-African Legal Consultative Organization] Informal Expert Group," 192–194.

125. UNCLOS, A/CONF.62/SR.191.

126. UN DOALOS, "Declarations and Reservations," 11.

127. The delimitation of China's 500km maritime boundary with Vietnam in the Tonkin/Beibu Gulf is a partial exception, discussed in chapter 3.

128. See, for example, Intergovernmental Conference on Marine Biodiversity of Areas Beyond National Jurisdiction, https://www.un.org/bbnj/; International Seabed Authority, https://www.isa.org.jm/; United Nations Open-Ended Informal Consultative Process on Oceans and the Law of the Sea, https://www.un.org/depts/los/consultative_process/consultative_process.htm.

129. Dutton, "Three Disputes and Three Objectives," 3–8.

130. Brownlie, *Principles of International Law,* 203–230.

131. United Nations Treaty Collection, "Status of Treaties," Chapter XXI, Law of the Sea, https://treaties.un.org/pages/ViewDetailsIII.aspx?src=TREATY&mtdsg_no=XXI-6&chapter=21&Temp=mtdsg3&clang=_en#16.

132. See Buga, "Stability and Change," 46–68.

133. Oxman, "Territorial Temptation," 830–851.

134. See Bernhardt, "Custom and Treaty," 275–325; Churchill, "The 1982 UNCLOS," 24–45.

135. Statement on United States Oceans Policy, 1 *Pub. Papers* 378 (10 March 1983).

136. "Forms of State practice include, but are not limited to: diplomatic acts and correspondence; conduct in connection with resolutions adopted by an international organization or at an intergovernmental conference; conduct

in connection with treaties; executive conduct, including operational conduct 'on the ground'; legislative and administrative acts; and decisions of national courts." ILC, "Draft Conclusions," 133.

137. *North Sea Continental Shelf,* para. 74: "The passage of only a short period of time is not necessarily, or of itself, a bar to the formation of a new rule of customary international law." The 1945 Truman Proclamations are often regarded as a key instance of "instant custom" in the law of the sea. See Scharf, *Customary International Law,* 107–122; Cheng, "Custom: The Future of General State Practice," 513–544.

138. *The Paquete Habana,* 175 US 677, 700 (1900), para. 686; Goldsmith and Posner, *Limits of International Law,* 23.

139. "[W]hether a custom develops or changes depends not only on the actions of some states but also on the reactions of other states. This is because states are also both legislators and enforcers of international law. Thus, a breach will effectively repeal or modify an existing custom only if other states emulate the breach or acquiesce in its legality." Roberts, "Traditional and Modern Approaches," 757.

140. Many of the practices analyzed are likely to satisfy the opinio juris requirement, as they contain explicit statements of the state's belief in the legality or illegality of certain actions. Only China's opinio juris is addressed explicitly (see chapter 2).

141. For discussions of the relationship between PRC and ROC maritime claims and policies, see Song and Zou, "Maritime Legislation," 303–345; Li Lingqun, *China's Policy;* and Hayton, "The Modern Creation of China's 'Historic Rights' Claim," 370–382.

142. The standard is "near-universal" because some "modern" conceptions of customary law are explicitly deductive. They derive rules from treaties and declarations (like UNGA resolutions) rather than state practice. See Roberts, "Traditional and Modern Approaches," 758, 768–769. For a powerful argument that customary law should not be considered rule-like at all, see Hakimi, "Making Sense of Customary International Law," 1487–1538.

143. Schweller, "The Problem of International Order Revisited," 170–171.

144. Sir Arthur Watts, former UK Foreign Office chief legal adviser, argues that "it is the international legal order whose universality is important and unquestioned, rather than that of particular rules." Watts, "The International Rule of Law," 27.

CHAPTER 2. INTERNATIONAL LAW AND CHINA'S MARITIME POWER

1. CCP Central Committee, "Decision of the Central Committee on Several Major Issues Concerning the Comprehensive Promotion of Governing the Country by Law," 7(7).

2. Xu Hong, "Experiencing the Storm of International Law," 39.

3. PRC State Oceanic Administration, *China Oceans Yearbook 2002,* 40.

4. The characters may be translated more literally as "strong maritime nation," but "maritime power" is the English phrase employed in official PRC translations and thus the one used here. For a thorough study of this "maritime" agenda, see McDevitt, ed., "Becoming a Great 'Maritime Power.'"

5. Zhang Dengyi, "Properly Manage and Use the Oceans," 46. See also Chubb, "Xi Jinping," 1–10; Kardon, "China's Maritime Rights and Interests," 179–196.

6. Xi Jinping, "Speech on Building Maritime Power."

7. McDevitt, "Becoming a Great 'Maritime Power,'" v–viii.

8. Xu Hong, "Experiencing the Storm," 39.

9. Fairbank, "Chinese Diplomacy and the Treaty of Nanking, 1842," 1–30.

10. Xi Jinping, "Speech on Building Maritime Power."

11. Zhang Wenmu, *On China's Sea Power,* 174.

12. McDevitt, *China as a Twenty-First Century Naval Power.*

13. Erickson and Goldstein, "Chinese Perspectives on Maritime Transformation," xii–xxx. See also Shi Yulong, "The Strategic Role of Land and Sea Coordination."

14. Liu Cigui, "Striving to Realize the Historical Leap" (director-general of the PRC State Oceanic Administration, counting 470 invasions); Ji Guoxing, *China's Maritime Security,* chapter 1 (counting 479 invasions in the period 1840–1940, 84 of which were "large-scale" (大规模) and led to 50 unequal treaties); Jia Yu, "Reflections on Ocean Power Strategy," 4 (counting 1,860 Western ships involved in these invasions).

15. Chesterman, "Asia's Ambivalence," 17.

16. See Wang, *China's Unequal Treaties;* Chesterman, "Asia's Ambivalence," 21 (noting that the "unequal treaty" terminology was not used until the 1920s).

17. Wang, "The Discourse of Unequal Treaties," 399–425.

18. Yang Jiechi, "Deeply Understand and Make Good Use of International Law."

19. "From 1842 to before the founding of New China in 1949, China signed a total of 1,175 foreign treaties, agreements, and articles of association, most of which were unequal." Yang Jiechi, "Deeply Understand."

20. "International law is an important weapon used by developing countries to fight against imperialism and colonialism, safeguard their own interests, and promote the process of world peace and development." Yang Jiechi, "Deeply Understand."

21. Wang Tieya, "International Law in Modern China," 252; see also Wei Wenhan, "Discussing the Question of the Width of the Territorial Sea," cited in Cohen and Chiu, *People's China and International Law,* 467–468: "Vessels belonging to imperialist countries not only plied between our coastal ports to engage in trade, but even sailed freely to Chungking—a port 1350 nautical miles from the seashore—and did business all along the way. Moreover, warships also cruised up and down at will, invading and encroaching upon our rights under the excuse of protecting their merchant vessels."

22. Zhang Wei, "A General Review," 31.

23. Fairbank, *The Chinese World Order*, 262.

24. Most influential was a translation of Henry Wheaton's *Elements of International Law* undertaken by the American Presbyterian missionary W. A. P. Martin. See Cohen and Chiu, *People's China and International Law*, 8–12.

25. Wang Tieya, "International Law in Modern China," 234.

26. Fairbank, *The Chinese World Order*, 258–259, 380 fn 3 (discussing the practice of 羁縻, or using treaties in particular to manage "barbarian affairs").

27. The actual terminology used was "inner ocean" (内洋). Gao Zhiguo, "China and the Law of the Sea," 267; and Hsü, *China's Entrance into the Family of Nations*, 133. See also Wang Tieya, "International Law in Modern China," 232–234, citing the official record "The Memorial of the Tsungli Yamen to the Court" (30 August 1864), *Beginning and End of the Management of Barbarian Affairs, Tongzhi Period*, vol. 82, 30.

28. Wang Tieya, "International Law in Modern China," 233.

29. Wang Tieya, "International Law in Modern China," 234, 236, 258.

30. Commission on Extraterritoriality in China, "Summary and Recommendations," 59–60, 63. The Commission demanded completion and implementation of a legal system in China, which "should establish and maintain a uniform system for the regular enactment, promulgation, and rescission of laws, so that there may be no uncertainty as to the laws of China."

31. Treaty for the Relinquishment of Extraterritorial Rights in China and the Regulation of Related Matters. US–Republic of China. Signed 11 January 1943. VII UNTS 66. Belgium, Italy, Denmark, Portugal, and Spain had concluded treaties by the end of 1928, and the British concluded a phased agreement in September 1931 that completed in 1943. These treaties "transformed the legal-political tenet of extraterritorial jurisdiction from a permanent institution to an ad hoc arrangement, waiting to be phased out." Chen Degong, *Modern International Law*, 151.

32. By this stage, Japanese nationals and entities occupying vast swathes of Chinese territory enjoyed a great majority of the extraterritorial privileges. See Chen, *Capped Socialization*, 61.

33. This is part of standard curricula in China, e.g., Li Baojun, *Treatise on Contemporary Chinese Foreign Policy*. See also Xiao Yongping, "Revolution in Teaching and Studying Law," 153–60. For example, the US-China commercial treaty from 1946 maintained many significant aspects of extraterritoriality. Treaty of Friendship, Commerce and Navigation. US–Republic of China. Signed 4 November 1946. XXV UNTS 25, Art. II, 2–3.

34. Cohen, "Chinese Attitudes Toward International Law," 108–116. For a full treatment of the genealogy of Chinese views on sovereignty, see Carrai, *Sovereignty in China*.

35. Cassel, *Grounds of Judgment*, 3–14; Kayaoglu, *Legal Imperialism*, 149–190; Chesterman, "Asia's Ambivalence," 16–36.

36. This became a hallmark of Chinese thinking about how to manage foreigners and leverage their superior technologies and organization, reflected in the notion of 中体外用, or keeping China's core while utilizing foreign tools. The original formulation of "using the barbarian to check the barbarian" was developed by the late Qing reformer Wei Yuan, in perhaps "the first significant Chinese work on the West" (Hao and Wan, "Changing Chinese Views," 148). Yuan drew on research by an earlier Qing official, Lin Zexu, to create an "Illustrated gazetteer of the maritime kingdoms" in which he exhorted the late-Qing government to use international law (and other knowledge of the ways of foreign states) "for the purpose of using barbarians to attack the barbarians, using barbarians to negotiate with the barbarians, and learning the superior techniques of the barbarians to control the barbarians" (Alford, "Arsenic and Old Laws," 1180).

37. Wang Tieya, "International Law in Modern China," 252–253. Wang notes standard conditions in China's unequal treaties included not only the outright acquisition of Chinese territory conquered in battle, but also far-ranging provisions for consular jurisdiction over specific territory and foreign individuals, naval and commercial access to coastal ports and river systems, recognition of foreign courts and police to administer and enforce foreign law, permanent military presence in key points surrounding Beijing (and corresponding prohibitions from those zones for Chinese imperial forces and destruction of fortifications), various payments and indemnities for damages, rights to use foreign currency, rights to proselytize and educate, and fixed low-tariff rates.

38. Cohen and Chiu, *People's China*, 8.

39. Yang Jiechi, "Deeply Understand and Make Good Use of International Law."

40. Cohen and Chiu, *People's China*, 26–64.

41. See, for example, a leading Chinese international law textbook that opens with the comment: "As everyone knows, modern international law is the product of the high-level development of European politics and economics" (Jia Bingbing, *Public International Law*, 2).

42. Cited in Carr, *The Twenty Years' Crisis*, 184, 176. Virtually all of China's first generation of international law scholars were trained in the Soviet Union, and they imported the Leninist conception of law from Soviet authorities, especially A. Y. Vyshinsky, who helped reconcile the problem of using law despite its bad class origins. His theory saw Communist parties as representing the will of the proletariat, capable of revoking illegitimate laws and creating new positive law in its stead that reflects the "dictatorship of the proletariat." The influential Soviet legal theorist Marchenko argues that "[c]itizens obtain freedom, justice, and security from the state's exercise of control and power, rather than the state and its leaders deriving authority from its citizens." Cited in Howson, "Can the West Learn from the Rest?" 824. See also Cohen and Chiu, *People's China*, 26–64.

43. Cohen and Chiu, *People's China*, 32.

44. Cohen and Chiu, *People's China*, 45. This was more than an ideological position: the intervention on the Korean peninsula in 1950 was a UN action and led Chinese "volunteer" troops into combat with nominally UN forces led by the United States.

45. Xi Jinping, "Carry Forward the Five Principles of Peaceful Coexistence."

46. *People's Daily*, "The Five Principles."

47. *People's Daily* editorial, 12 December 1963, cited in Cohen and Chiu, *People's China*, 148.

48. Cohen and Chiu, *People's China*, 142–153.

49. Wallace and Weiss, "Domestic Politics, China's Rise," 2–3. Johnston, *Social States*, xxiv; Carlson, *Unifying China*, 3. See also Carrai, *Sovereignty in China*.

50. Xi Jinping, "Promote the Comprehensive Rule of Law."

51. Yang Jiechi, "Deeply Understand and Make Use of International Law."

52. PRC MFA, "Wang Yi Delivers a Speech."

53. Li Zhaojie, "China," 318. Beijing's refusal to condemn Russia's invasion of Ukraine in February 2022 stands out as a glaring exception to this principle.

54. As an example of this goal expressed in the domain of international economic law, see He Zhipeng, "International Law Debates," 553: "Due to the conditions of the formation of international society and certain political factors, the international legal system also contains unacceptable elements that need to be further improved and perfected. New and reasonable rules need to be established for new situations and problems that have arisen in the development process of international society. We must abide by and uphold the norms of international law, and work with representatives of other states to continue to work for the improvement and development of international law, and to advance international law in a direction that is conducive to the establishment of a new international political and economic order that is peaceful, stable, just, and reasonable."

55. Han and Kanter, "Legal Education in China," 550.

56. Wang Tieya, "Teaching and Research," 77; Minzner, "The Rise and Fall," 343.

57. Huang Hua related this to Jerry Cohen in 1974, who shared it with the author in February 2012.

58. Ling Qing, *From Yan'An to the UN*, chapter 7. Eventually he agreed to serve because "by then China had participated in the Seabed Committee for two years . . . and had already openly explained our positions in meetings and other fora. I just needed to do follow-up work."

59. These are "PRC Working Paper on Sea Area Within the Limits of National Jurisdiction," UN Doc. A/AC.138/SC.II/L.34, 16 July 1973; "PRC Working Paper on General Principles for the International Sea Area," UN Doc A/AC/138/SC.I/L.25/Corr.1, 6 August 1973; "PRC Working Paper on Marine Scientific Research," UN Doc. A/AC.138/SC.III/L.42, 19 July 1973.

60. PRC Permanent Mission to the UN, "Speech by An Chih-Yuan," 657–660.

61. UNCLOS, A/CONF.62/SR.25.

62. UNCLOS, A/CONF.62/SR.25.

63. UNCLOS, Art. 122: "For the purposes of this Convention, 'enclosed or semi-enclosed sea' means a gulf, basin or sea surrounded by two or more States and connected to another sea or the ocean by a narrow outlet or consisting entirely or primarily of the territorial seas and EEZs of two or more coastal States."

64. Ling Qing, *From Yan'An to the UN,* chapter 7.

65. Yu Mincai, "China and the UNCLOS," 57–58

66. Ling Qing, *From Yan'An to the UN,* chapter 7.

67. Zhang Qi, "The Contradiction Between Internationalization and Localization."

68. UNCLOS, A/CONF.62/SR.191.

69. In 2006, the PRC submitted an additional official statement opting out of compulsory jurisdiction on certain matters, including maritime boundary delimitation and military activities, in line with UNCLOS Art. 298. See discussion in chapter 6.

70. The full PRC signing statement reads: "In accordance with the decision of the Standing Committee of the Eighth National People's Congress of the People's Republic of China at its nineteenth session, the President of the People's Republic of China has hereby ratified the United Nations Convention on the Law of the Sea of 10 December 1982 and at the same time made the following statement: (1.) In accordance with the provisions of the UNCLOS, the PRC shall enjoy sovereign rights and jurisdiction over an exclusive economic zone of 200 nautical miles and the continental shelf. (2.) The PRC will effect, through consultations, the delimitation of the boundary of the maritime jurisdiction with the States with coasts opposite or adjacent to China respectively on the basis of international law and in accordance with the principle of equitability. (3.) The PRC reaffirms its sovereignty over all its archipelagos and islands as listed in article 2 of the Law of the PRC on the Territorial Sea and the Contiguous zone, which was promulgated on 25 February 1992. (4.) The PRC reaffirms that the provisions of the UNCLOS concerning innocent passage through the territorial sea shall not prejudice the right of a coastal State to request, in accordance with its laws and regulations, a foreign State to obtain advance approval from or give prior notification to the coastal State for the passage of its warships through the territorial sea of the coastal State." UN Division for Ocean Affairs and the Law of the Sea, "Declarations and Reservations," 11.

71. Zou and Song, "Maritime Legislation," 308–309.

72. Chen Degong and Gao Zhiguo, "New Development," 45.

73. Shan Xu, "China's Participation," 7; see also Chen Degong, *Modern International Law of the Sea.*

74. Zhang Haiwen, *The UNCLOS and China,* 44.

75. Ma Xinmin, "China and the UNCLOS," 10.
76. According to a leading textbook, international law "is an indispensable legal means to realize socialist modernization construction. For instance, in order to explore resources near our coast, we must study the legal status of the continental shelf, fishing zone and exclusive economic zone and international norms and customs between states in delimiting these regions. . . . We must actively join international legislative activities and strengthen the struggle within the UN so as to form the broadest international united front for anti-hegemonism." Liu Fengming, *Essentials of International Law*, 5.
77. Zhang Haiwen, *UNCLOS and China*, 21, 91.
78. The 1982 Constitution is the last of four such documents issued by the National People's Congress (NPC); it has been amended nine times since its promulgation. The establishment of a new constitution during the same year that UNCLOS was signed adds particular emphasis to the conclusion that PRC leadership has no intention to give determinate status to treaties under domestic law.
79. PRC National People's Congress, "Constitution of the People's Republic of China." Art. 67 empowers the NPC to "decide on the ratification or abrogation of treaties and important agreements concluded with foreign states"; Art. 81 establishes that the president, following the NPC decision, "ratifies or abrogates treaties and important agreements concluded with foreign states"; Art. 89 grants the State Council authority to "conclude treaties and agreements with foreign states."
80. Wang Tieya, *The Sources of International Law*, 195.
81. PRC Law on the Procedure for Conclusion of Treaties (CLI.1.4922), 28 December 1990.
82. Xue and Jin, "International Treaties," 305, 300 (italics added). The NPC evidently considered regulating this uncertain pathway during the drafting of the 2000 PRC Legislation Law, but "no specific proposal was formally tabled before the People's Congress, due to the complicated nature of implementing treaties." See also Paler, "China's Legislation Law," 301–318.
83. "China adopts an approach of 'selective adaptation' to international legal regimes in order to maximize benefits and minimize costs arising from its engagement with international legal regimes." Cai Congyan, *The Rise of China and International Law*, 152. See also Zhang Qi, "The Contradiction Between Internationalization and Localization." This "selectivity" of Chinese legal practice is also noted in several Western studies, among them Potter, *China's Legal System*.
84. See Simmons, *Mobilizing for Human Rights*, 58–59, 88–93 (on "strategic ratifiers"); Hathaway, "Between Power and Principle," 469–536; Hathaway, "Why Do Countries Commit to Human Rights Treaties?" 588–621 (identifying a range of motives and incentives that underly ratification decisions).
85. Zheng Zhihang, "A Study of the Mechanisms."
86. See Tanner, *The Politics of Lawmaking*, 12–40.

87. Jia Bingbing, "A Synthesis," 36. See also Jiang Hong, "Thoughts on the Relationship," 43–45.

88. PRC National People's Congress, "PRC Constitutional Amendment" (Art. 1, para 2).

89. Zhang and Ginsburg, "China's Turn Toward Law" (emphasizing the growing "legality" of Chinese governance); deLisle, "Law in the China Model 2.0," 68–84 (discussing law as an "organizational weapon wielded by the party-state").

90. Lenin, "A Letter to a Comrade on Our Organizational Tasks," 248. Scholars of the Soviet Union also discuss this as a "conveyer belt" model in the Russian context. See Ioffe and Maggs, *Soviet Law in Theory and Practice,* 68–81.

91. Zheng Zhihang, "A Study of the Mechanisms."

92. See Zhang and Ginsburg, "China's Turn Toward Law," 279–361; Wang Chenguang, "From Rule of Man to Rule of Law," 1–50.

93. See Cai Dingjian, *History and Reform,* 165–166; Zou Keyuan, "China's Ocean Policymaking," 150.

94. For example, internal party rules may be introduced directly into legislation. See Zou Keyuan, "China's Ocean Policymaking," 150.

95. *NPC Observer,* "Annotated Translation: 2018 Amendment to the PRC Constitution," Art. 32.

96. *People's Daily,* "The Four Comprehensives."

97. CCP Central Committee, "Decision."

98. Xinhua, "Strive to Start a New Journey."

99. Wang Chen, "Xi Jinping Thought on Rule by Law."

100. There has been a decade-long debate about what specific issues are subsumed under the category of China's "core interests"—issues of extreme sensitivity and importance on which the PRC will not negotiate. Senior leaders' statements make clear that maritime disputes implicate China's sovereignty and territorial integrity and therefore constitute "core interests." See *People's Daily,* "Why Does China Need to Declare Its Core Interests?" for an official accounting of these interests by PRC State Councilor Dai Bingguo.

101. See Wallace and Weiss, "Domestic Politics, China's Rise," 8–10 (noting "centrality" as a determinate factor in China's domestic decision-making on whether and how to contest international order with unilateral measures).

102. Both Hu Jintao and Xi Jinping called for "building maritime power" in their Work Reports to the 18th and 19th National People's Congresses in 2012 and 2017. These Congresses are held every five years and mark leadership transitions. The general secretary's report is usually regarded as the most authoritative expression of central leadership goals for the period to come. Hu Jintao, "Work Report"; Xi Jinping, "Secure a Decisive Victory."

103. Hu Jintao, "Work Report."

104. *People's Daily,* "Xi Jinping at the 8th Study Session"; Xi Jinping, "Secure a Decisive Victory" (General Secretary Work Report at 19th Party Congress). For enthusiastic accounts of Xi Jinping's many statements and actions regarding

maritime power over the course of his career, see Shen Manhong and Yu Xuan, "Research on Xi Jinping's Important Exposition on Building Maritime Power"; Deng Zhihui and Zhong Zhuo, "Feel Xi Jinping's 'Blue Faith.'"

105. PRC National People's Congress, "PRC Law on the Territorial Sea and the Contiguous Zone." Art. 1 states: "This law is formulated in order to enable the People's Republic of China (PRC) to exercise its sovereignty over its territorial sea and its rights to exercise control over its contiguous zone, and to safeguard State security as well as its maritime rights and interests."

106. Kardon, "China's Maritime Rights and Interests," 179–196.

107. Since 1984, Chinese law and politics journals have published some 3,863 articles discussing the need to "safeguard maritime rights and interests (维护海洋权益)" (author's search of full-text frequency in CNKI China Academic Journals, 21 March 2021).

108. Liu Kefu, "Push Forward the Construction."

109. For a review of the tasks and functions of the various PRC MLE agencies, see Goldstein, "Five Dragons."

110. Liu Cigui, "Some Considerations on Building a Maritime Power," 10.

111. Tobin, "Wind in the Sails." The CCG is formally a part of the People's Armed Police, the paramilitary branch of the PLA.

112. For detailed analysis of this force and its operations, see Martinson, "Echelon Defense," 11–18; Martinson, "Early Warning Brief."

113. See Sakamoto, "China's New Coast Guard Law."

114. Duan Zhaoxian, "On the Strategic Objectives."

115. Ma Kai, "Restructure the State Oceanic Administration."

116. Chang and Li, "The Disappearance of SOA."

117. A former "Central Leading Group for the Protection of Maritime Rights and Interests" has folded into the Central Foreign Affairs Work Commission, a standing body of the Central Committee "in order to better coordinate foreign affairs and maritime affairs." Xinhua, "The Central Committee."

118. Kennedy and Erickson, "China's Third Sea Force."

119. PLAN leadership is also routinely briefed by top party leadership on the importance of protecting these legal rights. Niu Tao, "Naval Organs." The imperative to "govern the military by law" (依法治军) has also been a subject of significant attention within the PLA, e.g., at a conference the author attended in 2014, "Eighth Forum on the Frontiers of the Military Legal System (第八届中国军事法制前沿论坛)," hosted by the University of Political Science and Law's School of Law.

120. Fang Xiao, "China Strengthens Coordination."

121. *People's Daily,* "To Build a Maritime Power."

122. The "maritime power" program encompasses a wide variety of economic, administrative, and environmental goals; it is by no means a predominantly naval program. See Liu Cigui, "Some Considerations on Building a Maritime Power"; McDevitt, "Becoming a Great 'Maritime Power.'"

123. The PLAN's law enforcement role includes expelling unauthorized foreign naval vessels from Chinese waters, by force if necessary. Ren Xiaofeng, *Handbook on the Law of Naval Operations,* 178.
124. Sun Yundao, "Iron Warriors," 4; Fan Xiaoting, "Analysis of the Legal Basis," 11. See also Martinson, "From Words to Actions," 10–12 (for discussion of the sequence of events leading to the implementation of regular rights patrols).
125. See, for example, PRC State Council, "National Marine Functional Zoning Plan."
126. Feng Liang and Zhang Xiaolin, "On the Navy's Strategic Use," 78.
127. The evolution of China's naval strategy is well beyond the scope of this study. For thorough discussion of this process, see McDevitt, *China as a Twenty-First Century Naval Power;* Dutton and Martinson, "Beyond the Wall."
128. Fang Xiao, "China Strengthens Coordination."
129. Zhang Zhaoyin, "Effectively Safeguard," 3. Fang Baoyu and Wang Junjie, "Navy Provides Fuel and Resource Guarantees," 1. For further analysis of MLE-navy integration, see Martinson, "Jinglue Haiyang"; Martinson, "Echelon Defense," 25–27.
130. For a table including all the various levels of legal documents produced by the party-state, see Corne, "Creation and Application," 372.
131. Xu Hong, "Experiencing the Storm," 39.
132. Xu Hong, "Experiencing the Storm," 39.
133. Chubb, "PRC Assertiveness," 79–121.
134. Liu Nanlai, "Safeguard Maritime Rights."
135. PRC SOA, "China Oceans Agenda 21," chapter 10, preamble, chapter 7(6).
136. PRC SOA, "China Oceans Agenda 21," Art.7.8.
137. PRC National Committee of the Chinese People's Political Consultative Conference, "Coordinating and Advancing." Senior leaders have been advocating for such a law since at least 2012. See Liu Cigui, "Some Considerations on Building a Maritime Power" (calling for "the promulgation of the 'Maritime Basic Law'" as soon as possible).
138. Jia Yu, "40 Years," 33.
139. Zheng Zhihang, "A Study of the Mechanisms."
140. Cai Congyan, "The Rise of China," 264. Cai argues that PRC judges' role in advancing PRC policy raises "concern about possible conflicts of interest to have courts, as adjudicators of the law, directly participate in lawmaking. This obviously is justified under the Chinese constitutional framework." For a discussion of judicial (non)independence in China, see Lubman, *Bird in a Cage,* 250–297; Zhang and Ginsburg, "China's Turn Toward Law," 295–317.
141. Zhou Qiang, "Deepen the Reform." Another senior official explains the function of PRC maritime trial courts in particular as "manifesting China's maritime judicial sovereignty, and safeguarding China's maritime rights and interests" (Jia Yu, "40 Years of Reform and Opening," 15).

142. PRC Supreme People's Court, "Provisions on Several Issues." This indeterminate definition of the scope of Chinese jurisdiction is analyzed in depth in subsequent chapters.
143. Zhou Qiang, "SPC Work Report"; Jia Yu, "40 Years of Reform and Opening," 16.
144. Li Tiansheng, "Fully Understand."
145. Zhou Qiang, "Deepen the Reform." See also SPC Vice President He Rong, who writes: "China's successful experience in building the rule of law will also contribute Chinese legal wisdom to the international rule of law. As China's economic power and political influence continue to grow globally, its voice in international governance is bound to increase. China should take this opportunity to accurately position itself and actively participate in international governance, and use the international rule of law to promote the construction of socialist rule of law with Chinese characteristics." He Rong, "China's Participation," 7.
146. PRC Supreme People's Court, "Opinion on Comprehensively Promoting the Strategy."
147. Zhou Qiang, "SPC Work Report." See also Finder, "China's Maritime Courts"; Finder, "Bulking Up the Maritime Courts."
148. Zhang Qi, "The Contradiction." SPC President Zhou Qiang makes a similar judgment, seeing mutual reinforcement between domestic and international rule-making in courts. See Sun Hang, "Zhou Qiang Puts Forward Requirements."
149. Wang Shumei, "Build an International Maritime Judicial Center."
150. He Zhipeng, "International Law Debates," 553.
151. CCP Central Committee, "Decision."
152. CCP Central Committee, "Opinions of the Central Committee on Training Programs for Excellent Legal Talents." For detailed discussion of these programs, see Roberts, *Is International Law International?* 226–229.
153. Xu Hong, "Experience the Storm," 39.
154. Zhao Jing, "Peking University Maritime Strategy Research Center." Other such institutes include the Wuhan University Institute of International Law (especially its Institute of Boundaries and Ocean Research, which has regular exchanges with the MFA), the Xiamen University Academy of International Law, the Ningbo University East China Sea Research Institute, and the Nanjing University Collaborative Innovation Center for South China Sea Studies.
155. Xi Jinping, "Speech on Building Maritime Power" (noting the presence of Gao Zhiguo, the CIMA director, at the Central Committee Political Bureau study group).
156. China Academy for Social Sciences' Institute of International Law, Wuhan University Institute of International Law, and the National Institute for South China Studies are among think tanks whose fellows the author has observed conducting research commissioned by State Council agencies.

157. Nanjing University, "Collaborative Innovation Center," Center Overview.
158. Sun Jisheng, "The Path of Shaping," 19–43; Yang Wenhua and Li Yunwei, "The Promotion of National Ideology," 1–7.
159. Wang Chen, "Actively Participate in Foreign-Related Legal Struggles."
160. This practice is also of course conducted in non-dispute settings, e.g., in multilateral forums like the UNCLOS International Seabed Authority, the Conference of State Parties to UNCLOS, and the UN's "Informal Consultative Process on Ocean Affairs and the Law of the Sea."
161. For example, the *Chinese Journal of International Law,* published by Oxford University Press, publishes annual assessments of "Chinese Practice in Public International Law" written by PRC international law scholars.
162. PRC MFA, "Yang Jiechi Attends Work Symposium."
163. Zhang and Wei, "International Law and Major Power Diplomacy," 63.
164. A thorough review of much of this discourse is found in Wang Kan, "Analysis of International Legal Research," 31–53.
165. CCP Central Committee, "Decision."
166. PRC MFA, "Yang Jiechi Gives Interview."
167. Wang Chen, "Xi Jinping Thought on Rule by Law."
168. Xi Jinping, "Secure a Decisive Victory."
169. Wang Chen, "Xi Jinping Thought on Rule by Law."
170. Huang Huikang, "Developments in International Law."

CHAPTER 3. GEOGRAPHIC RULES

1. Xi Jinping, "Speech on Building a Maritime Power," delivered to the CCP Central Committee Political Bureau.
2. Tanaka, *The SCS Arbitration,* 213: "The primary function of international law involves the spatial distribution of jurisdiction of states." Byers, *Custom, Power, and the Power of Rules,* 53: "Jurisdiction may be defined generally as the authority to engage in activities of control or regulation within a certain geographic area. In international law, jurisdiction appears always to be linked to territory in some way."
3. This rule is summarized as "the dominion of the land ends where the power of arms terminates." Bynkershoek, *De Domini Maris,* as cited in Fulton, *The Sovereignty of the Sea,* 556. See also Kent, "The Historical Origins of the Three-Mile Limit," 537–553.
4. Chinese officials and scholars routinely cite this general principle, which is uniformly applied in jurisprudence. See, for example, PRC Ministry of Foreign Affairs, "Position Paper," para. 11.
5. Jia, "The Principle of the Domination of the Land," 6.
6. Evans, "Maritime Boundary Delimitation," 261: "What is at issue [in boundary delimitation] is the generation of a line separating the overlapping entitlements of states, and so it is first necessary to establish whether the parties to a dispute do indeed have entitlements which overlap: just because a State claims that it has an entitlement does not mean that it does."

7. *Dispute Concerning Delimitation of the Maritime Boundary Between Bangladesh and Myanmar in the Bay of Bengal* (Bangladesh v. Myanmar), Judgment, 2012 ITLOS Rep. 12, para 397: "Delimitation presupposes an area of overlapping entitlements."

8. The requirement for a prior determination of sovereignty is not itself a contested norm. Though there are heated disputes over whose sovereignty should be recognized, there is little dispute over sovereignty per se as the object of those disputes. There are much wider differences in states' views of the rules that govern the scope of maritime authority assigned to the sovereign.

9. Five hundred kilometers of maritime boundary with Vietnam in the Gulf of Tonkin was delimited by agreement in 2000. Agreement Between the People's Republic of China and the Socialist Republic of Vietnam on the Delimitation of the Territorial Seas, Exclusive Economic Zones and Continental Shelves of the Two Countries in Beibu Gulf/Bac Bo Gulf, 2336 UNTS 41860 (25 December 2000): 179–206 ("China-Vietnam Maritime Delimitation Agreement"). See also Kardon, "The Other Gulf of Tonkin Incident"; Zou, "The Sino-Vietnamese Agreement," 13–24.

10. *Anglo-Norwegian Fisheries* (UK v. Norway), Order, 1951 ICJ 117 (18 January), 133.

11. *South China Sea Arbitration (SCS Arbitration),* Award, para. 156: "The Tribunal considers that a dispute concerning the existence of an entitlement to maritime zones is distinct from a dispute concerning the delimitation of those zones in an area where the entitlements of parties overlap."

12. PRC Territorial Sea and Contiguous Zone Law (CLI.1.5597), 25 February 1992. Unless otherwise cited, all named PRC legislation, regulations, rules, notices, opinions, and other official normative documents are sourced from Peking University, "PKU Law Database." Their citation consists of the issuing agency, translated instrument name (with unique PKU database citation code [法宝引证码]), date of promulgation, and any specific article/part referenced above the note. Most national-level normative documents are also accessible online at NPC, "National Law and Regulation Database," and in print, NPC, *The Effective Laws and Administrative Regulations of the PRC.*

13. Continental shelf entitlements extend "throughout the natural prolongation of its land territory to the outer edge of the continental shelf, or to a distance of 200nm from the baselines from which the breadth of the territorial sea is measured where the outer edge of the continental margin does not extend up to that distance." PRC, Law on the EEZ and Continental Shelf (CLI.1.20220), 26 June 1998, Art. 2.

14. PRC Ministry of Foreign Affairs, "Declaration on the Territorial Sea," Art. 1. That assertion that non-jurisdictional waters (high seas) lie between China and its offshore islands is no longer a component of PRC practice due to the emergence of the EEZ regime and because it contradicts China's "dashed line" claim, examined in detail in subsequent sections. A 12nm breadth is now widespread in global practice, with all but Togo and Peru formally still

adopting a broader territorial sea (author database). China was among the earlier adopters of a 12nm territorial sea standard that would later became the global norm with the 1982 UNCLOS, but China was not the first to adopt this standard, nor is it any longer a contested rule. See Noyes, "The Territorial Sea," 93; Cheng, "Communist China and the Law of the Sea," 52; Chiu, "China and the Question of the Territorial Sea," 29–78.

15. Apart from the frequently named disputed "island groups," the specific names and locations of the islands claimed by PRC is the subject of some ambiguity in PRC law. SOA Director Wang Shuguang told Japanese officials in 2005 that "China claims some 6,900 islands that are larger than 500 square meters (over 1,400 of which are either unnamed or have overlapping names). . . . It also claims nearly 10,000 other islands that are smaller than 500 square meters, most of which are unnamed and whose number, coordinates, and distribution are not fully documented. Only 433 islands are inhabited; the remaining 94% are uninhabited and are without a resident population." Sakamoto, "The Senkaku Islands," 10.

16. Jia Yu, "40 Years of Reform," 2–3.

17. State Oceanic Administration (SOA), National Island Protection Plan (CLI.4.172349), 18 April 2012, Part 1, Part 2.3 (italics added).

18. Such determinations have been the object of a long-running set of official survey, mapping, and planning efforts regarding the many small features in China's near seas. These are summarized in China Institute for Marine Affairs, *China Ocean Development Report* (2020), 75–83. See also CCP Central Committee and PRC State Council, "Several Opinions" and Ministry of Natural Resources and Ministry of Civil Affairs, Announcement on the Publication of the Standard Names of Some Islands and Reefs and Seabed Features in the South China Sea (CLI.4.341494), 19 April 2020.

19. PRC, Island Protection Law (CLI.1.125296), 26 December 2009, Art. 2.

20. SOA, Measures for the Examination and Approval of the Development and Utilization of Uninhabited Islands (CLI.4.287540), 26 December 2016, Art. 24; SOA, Measures for the Administration of Names of Uninhabited Islands (CLI.4.305920), 28 August 2017, Art. 20.

21. PRC MFA, "Position Paper," para. 25.

22. The PRC Marine Environmental Protection Law (CLI.1.304315), 5 November 2017 (amended 1999, 2013, 2016, and 2017); State Council, Regulation on the Exploitation of Offshore Petroleum Resources in Cooperation with Foreign Entities (CLI.2.1182), 30 January 1982 (amended 2001, 2011, 2013).

23. SOA, Opinions on the Strengthening of the Management of Sea Use for the Construction of Artificial Islands on the Sea (CLI.4.89783), 6 April 2007. PRC Coast Guard Law (CLI.1.351832), 1 February 2021.

24. PRC MFA, "Declaration on the Baselines of the Territorial Sea" (15 May 1996).

25. PRC MFA, "Statement of the Government on the Baselines of the Territorial Sea of Diaoyu Dao and Its Affiliated Islands" (10 September 2012).

26. PRC Note Verbale, CML/8/2011 (11 April 2011). This reference to the whole group of Spratlys with the singular "is" in the official translation is consistent with another set of practices, discussed below, of grouping the various clusters of features into "island groups" that collectively generate entitlements.

27. PRC MFA, "On China's Territorial Sovereignty and Maritime Rights and Interests"; PRC Note Verbale, CML/14/2019 (12 December 2019): "China has [an] EEZ and continental shelf based on Nanhai Zhudao."

28. Jia Yu, "International Law Theory," 26.

29. Jia Yu, "40 Years of Reform," 17.

30. Varied versions of these baselines are widely discussed in PRC expert circles. For a review of some of this writing, see Liu Hongxia, "Study on the Legal Aspects," 15–25. For a State Department approximation of what these baselines might be, see US Dept. of State, "People's Republic of China: Maritime Claims in the SCS," 4, 12, 19.

31. PRC MFA, "Ten Questions on Huangyan Island."

32. PLA Navy, "China Sailing Directions," 172.

33. See chapter 4. For a detailed description of this seizure, see Martinson, "Echelon Defense," 1–2.

34. PRC MFA, "Statement Regarding Huangyan Island." The Philippines officially included the feature in drawing its baselines. Republic of the Philippines, Republic Act 9522, 10 March 2009.

35. PRC MFA, "China's Territorial Sovereignty and Maritime Rights and Interests"; China Society of International Law (CSIL), "Critical Study," para. 546.

36. It was so designated in 1983 by the China Geographical Names Committee, though it has been described as Chinese territory since 1947. China Geographical Names Committee, "Standard Place Names"; Hayton, *The Invention of China*, 237 (for the 1947 inclusion in ROC territory, later adopted by the PRC).

37. All distances were calculated with the US National Oceanic and Atmospheric Administration's "Latitude/Longitude Distance Calculator" (https://www.nhc.noaa.gov/gccalc.shtml).

38. Sina Military, "A Mysterious Giant Ship of Our Navy." This was the largest vessel in PLAN South Sea Fleet at the time.

39. South China Sea Online, "Timeline: 1990–1999."

40. Xinhua, "The Navy South Sea Fleet"; Gan Jun, "Far Seas Training," 1.

41. Asia Maritime Transparency Initiative (AMTI), "China and Malaysia."

42. AMTI, "Island Tracker."

43. PLA Navy, "China Sailing Directions," 179 (noting that Livock [Sanjiao] Reef is above water at high tide and only 21 nautical miles from Mischief Reef; thus Mischief does not lie within the territorial sea of any other feature).

44. The SCS Arbitration consulted this PLAN document as well as other sailing and navigation charts and manuals to determine that "Mischief Reef is a low-tide elevation." *SCS Arbitration*, Award, para. 378.

45. PRC Note Verbale, CML/1/2021 (28 January 2021).
46. PRC MFA spokesman Hong Lei described the dispute as follows: "Suyan Reef is an isolated underwater reef, not territory. There is no territorial dispute between China and South Korea. This is the consensus of China and South Korea. Suyan Reef is located in the overlapping waters of the exclusive economic zone between China and South Korea, and relevant issues can only be resolved through negotiations on the delimitation of the sea." PRC Foreign Ministry Spokespersons' Remarks Database, 9 December 2013 (henceforth "PRC MFA Spokesperson, [date]").
47. Roehrig, "South Korea: The Challenges of a Maritime Nation."
48. PRC MFA Spokesperson, 14 September 2006.
49. Xinhua, "Liu Cigui: The Naming of Our Islands."
50. PRC MFA Spokesperson, 19 January 2010. Similar MFA objections ensued when Japan entered a formal submission to the UN Commission on the Limits of the Continental Shelf claiming a continental shelf extending from the feature (e.g., PRC Note Verbale, CML/2/2009, 6 February 2009).
51. Commission on the Limits of the Continental Shelf (CLCS), "Submission by Japan," PRC communication dated 6 February 2009 and 3 August 2011.
52. PRC MFA, "Position Paper," para. 21.
53. The disputes in the ECS and Yellow Sea also hinge on entitlements, but these do not turn on claimed entitlements from offshore islands and are therefore addressed later in the chapter in the context of maritime boundary delimitation.
54. For states that ratified UNCLOS after 13 May 1999, the deadline is ten years after the treaty's entry into force for that state (UNCLOS, Annex II, Art. 4). The CLCS is an organ established under UNCLOS Art. 76.8.
55. CLCS, "Joint Submission of Malaysia and Viet Nam."
56. Socialist Republic of Vietnam, "Partial Submission."
57. CLCS, "Joint Submission of Malaysia and Viet Nam" (listing each of the ten responses to the joint submission).
58. PRC Note Verbale, CML/17/2009 (7 May 2009), CML/18/2009 (7 May 2009). China issued an identical note to each.
59. Vietnam Note Verbale, No. 86/HC-2009 (8 May 2009).
60. *SCS Arbitration*, Philippines' Memorial—Volume I.
61. *SCS Arbitration*, Award on Jurisdiction and Admissibility, para. 172.
62. Republic of the Philippines, "Why the Philippines Brought This Case," para. 18.
63. *SCS Arbitration*, Award on the Merits, Dispositif, B(7)a.
64. Philippines Note Verbale, No. 000228 (5 April 2011).
65. Indonesia Note Verbale, No. 126/POL-703/V/20 (26 May 2020).
66. Socialist Republic of Vietnam, "Statement Transmitted to the Arbitral Tribunal."
67. Vietnam Note Verbale, no. 22/HC-2020 (30 March 2020).
68. Malaysia Note Verbale, HA 26/20 (29 July 2020).

69. Brunei Darussalam Ministry of Foreign Affairs, "Statement on the SCS."

70. Japan Note Verbale, PM/12/078 (9 April 2012).

71. In 1999, Taiwan drew both straight and normal baselines around the Pratas (Dongsha) Islands and normal baselines around the Scarborough Shoal, but not Macclesfield Bank (Zhongsha). Republic of China, "Territorial Sea Baseline Decree," no. 88.

72. Jia Yu and Zhao Qian, "What Is Measured by Territorial Sea Baselines?" These authors, from the Ministry of Natural Resources, write specifically about the Diaoyu baselines just promulgated, noting that the purpose of the announcement was, in part, to deny Japan's "actual control" (实际控制) of the disputed features and to "help China further improve its territorial waters system."

73. PRC MFA, "Position Paper," para 20.

74. Ma Xinmin, "China and the UNCLOS," 11.

75. CSIL, "Critical Study," provides the most thorough such argument.

76. Zhao Lihai, "Questions on Our Country's Ratification," 56–62.

77. "PRC Working Paper on Sea Area," A/AC.138/SC.II/L.34, at 1.6.

78. See, for example, Jiang Li and Zhang Jie, "A Preliminary Analysis," 167–185; Zhang Hua, "On the Legality," 129–143; Zheng Fan, "State Practice in Archipelagic Waters," 291–300; Hong Nong et al., "The Concept of Archipelagic State," 209–239; Xiao Jun et al., "A Study of State Practice," 27–28; Guo Jing and Liu Dan, "On the Archipelagic Regime," 65–75.

79. Jiang Li and Zhang Jie, "A Preliminary Analysis," 177.

80. Guo Zhongyuan and Zou Ligang, "Study on the Delineation," 136.

81. Zhang Hua, "On the Legality," 140–143: "Based on the practice of international society, the notion that 'straight baselines can be applied to mid-ocean archipelagos' has already become an international customary legal rule, and this type of straight baseline is 'sui generis.'"

82. US Dept. of State, "Straight Baseline Claim: China," 8.

83. Roach, "China's Straight Baseline Claim."

84. See, for example, PRC Letter to UN Secretary General Dated 27 Dec. 1996, UNGA, 51st Session, Item 24(a), A/51/645/Add.1 (30 December 1996).

85. US Central Intelligence Agency, "Spratly Islands." There are many ways these baselines might be drawn, but none appear to meet the water/land ratio requirement. See SCS Arbitration, Merits Award, para. 574: "The ratio of water to land in the Spratly Islands would greatly exceed 9:1 under any conceivable system of baselines."

86. Guo Zhongyuan and Zou Ligang, "Study on the Delineation," 136; Zhou Jiang, "On SCS Sovereignty," 65.

87. PRC MFA, "Position Paper," paras. 20, 25. The US State Department has also begun to factor this impending ("excessive") claim into its objections. See US Dept. of State, "People's Republic of China: Maritime Claims in the SCS."

88. PRC MFA Spokesperson, 8 July 2016.

89. CSIL, "Critical Study," para. 523.

90. US Dept. of State, "Japan: Straight Baseline," 1–28 (with annexes including Japan's law and basepoint chart).

91. CLCS, "Joint Submission of Malaysia and Viet Nam"; Government of Malaysia, "Baselines of Maritime Zones Act," Art. 5.

92. Taiwan's practices are excluded from this analysis by virtue of its undetermined international legal status. The Republic of China, however, has drawn baselines around several of the disputed features: normal baselines around the Diaoyu/Senkaku Islands, one straight and one normal baseline around the Pratas (Dongsha) Islands, and normal baselines around the Macclesfield Bank (including a separate 12nm limit around Scarborough Shoal). See US Dept. of State, "Taiwan's Maritime Claims," 13–14.

93. UN, *Law of the Sea Bulletin,* no. 32, 91. Notably, Vietnam accepted China's straight baselines on the west side of the Leizhou peninsula in its 2000 Gulf of Tonkin boundary agreement. See Zou, "The Sino-Vietnamese Agreement," 14.

94. Kim, "Maritime Boundary Negotiations," 71–73; Van Dyke, "Disputes over Islands," 55.

95. UN, *Law of the Sea Bulletin,* no. 32, 91.

96. Socialist Republic of Vietnam, "Law of the Sea of Vietnam," Art. 2. Notably, Chinese officials from SOA anticipated that this law would strengthen Vietnam's legal position and called for a comparable PRC Basic Ocean Law (as discussed in chapter 2). See Shu Zhenya, "Vietnam Insists on Enacting Legislation."

97. Socialist Republic of Vietnam, "Annex," A/68/980.

98. Japan, "List of Deposited Charts."

99. Japan Note Verbale, PM/12/303 (24 September 2012).

100. Japan, PM/12/303.

101. Vietnam Note Verbale, no. 22/HC-2020 (30 March 2020).

102. Republic of the Philippines, Republic Act No. 9522, Section 2. Art. 121 does not determine baselines, but the evident intent is to propose normal baselines around these features.

103. Republic of the Philippines, Republic Act No. 3046. "The Philippines previously claimed that the territorial borders around the Philippines were provided by the treaty limits established by two international treaties between the United States and Spain (the 1898 Treaty of Paris, the Cession Treaty of 1900) and one treaty between the United States and Great Britain (1930 Treaty of Washington), which form a rectangle around the main archipelago of the Philippines. In 1961 the Philippines enacted straight baseline legislation, which provided that all waters within the baselines are considered inland or internal waters of the Philippines, and that all the waters from the baselines to the international treaty limits form part of the territorial sea of the Philippines." Beckman and Davenport, "CLCS Submissions," 197.

104. Republic of the Philippines, "On the 4th Anniversary."

105. Philippines Note Verbale, no. 00191–2020 (26 May 2020).

106. Indonesia Note Verbale, No. 148/POL-703/VI/20 (12 June 2020).

107. See bilateral diplomatic correspondence in Republic of Indonesia, "Indonesia Protests PRC"; Republic of Indonesia, "RI Reaffirms Rejecting China" (referring to rights "determined based on UNCLOS").

108. Malaysia Note Verbale, HA 26/20 (29 July 2020).

109. Bangladesh v. Myanmar, para. 397.

110. Schofield et al., *The Limits of Maritime Jurisdiction*, 1. A senior Chinese official stated in 2019 that of more than 400 potential maritime boundaries in the world, only about 160 have been delimited. Gao Zhiguo, "Remarks on the Launch," 5.

111. For analysis of this development, see Schofield, "Parting the Waves," 38–58.

112. Evans, "Maritime Boundary Delimitation," 258. See also Churchill and Lowe, *The Law of the Sea*, 191.

113. *Territorial and Maritime Dispute* (Nicaragua v. Honduras), Judgment, 2007 ICJ 659 (8 October), paras. 262–298; *Guyana v. Suriname*, Award, ICGJ 370 (PCA 17 September 2007), paras. 376–392.

114. Evans, "Maritime Boundary Delimitation," 255.

115. See Dutton, "Testing the Boundaries," 1–34.

116. Evans, "Maritime Boundary Delimitation," 255.

117. See *Maritime Delimitation in the Black Sea* (Romania v. Ukraine), Judgment, 2009 ICJ (3 February), para. 120–122. Courts have sometimes employed a "three stage" process, of which Romania v. Ukraine is considered the clearest articulation. The court starts with the median/equidistance line, adjusts for equity, and then verifies that the line so produced does not "lead to an inequitable result by reason of any marked disproportion between the ratio of the respective coastal lengths and the ratio between the relevant maritime area of each State by reference to the delimitation line." (Romania v. Ukraine, para. 122).

118. *Maritime Dispute* (Peru v. Chile), Judgment, General List No. 137 (ICJ, 27 January 2014), para. 180.

119. Nicaragua v. Colombia, Judgment, para. 194.

120. Evans, "Maritime Boundary Delimitation," 261.

121. This recognition of "high seas" is problematic for China's historic rights claims, analyzed in chapter 4.

122. "PRC Working Paper on Sea Area," 2.1.

123. "PRC Working Paper on Sea Area," 3.1.

124. "PRC Working Paper on Sea Area," 2.8, 3.4, 3.5.

125. The exclusion of any reference to adjudication or arbitration is of critical importance to PRC practice on dispute resolution, examined in chapter 6.

126. UN DOALOS, "Declarations and Reservations," 11.

127. "China-Vietnam Maritime Delimitation Agreement."

128. Gao and Jia, "The Nine-Dash Line," 105–106; Zou, "The Sino-Vietnamese Agreement," 15.

129. PRC MFA, "Deputy Foreign Minister Wang Yi." Wang further described the agreement as "a successful practice for both sides to adapt to the new order of the law of the sea." See also *People's Daily*, "Let the China-Vietnam Maritime Border Become a Bond of Peace," 3.
130. Coordinates from "China-Vietnam Maritime Delimitation Agreement," 182; and PRC MFA, "Declaration on the Baselines of the Territorial Sea."
131. Zou, "The Sino-Vietnamese Agreement," 15.
132. Jia Yu, "40 Years of Reform," 26; DeTréglodé, "Maritime Boundary Delimitation," 37.
133. These partial effects have been applied in several court rulings that employ a "disproportionality test" to ensure an equitable result that reflects the lengths of the disputing parties' respective coastlines. For a full discussion of this practice, see Evans, "Maritime Boundary Delimitation," 269–273.
134. DeTréglodé, "Maritime Boundary Delimitation," 36; Fravel, *Strong Borders, Secure Nation*, 267–299, 333.
135. For a thorough and well-documented analysis of the line's origins and meaning, see Chung, "Drawing the U-Shaped Line," 38–72.
136. Gao and Jia, "The Nine-Dash Line," 110.
137. Li Jinming and Li Dexia, "The Dotted Line," 290. On the continental shelf interpretation, see Gao and Jia, "The Nine-Dash Line," 109.
138. Xu Senan, "The Meaning of the Dashed National Boundary Line," 80–81. The quasi-official CSIL "Critical Study" also asserts that "the dotted line indicates a national boundary" (CSIL, "Critical Study," para. 192).
139. US Dept. of State, "China: Maritime Claims in the SCS," 4–5, 15.
140. UN DOALOS, "Declarations and Reservations," 11. This exemption from certain aspects of UNCLOS dispute resolution is examined in detail in chapter 6.
141. Kong Lingjie, "Boundaries with New Era Characteristics," 46.
142. See chapter 4 on "historic rights" for discussion of what these non-territorial claims entail.
143. Quoted in Johnson, "Drawn into the Fray," 155.
144. PRC Note Verbale, CML/46/2020 (2 June 2020).
145. See Su, "The Tiaoyu Islands," 385–421.
146. Tara Davenport, "The China-Japan Dispute," 297–324.
147. CLCS, "PRC Preliminary Information," 6.
148. Davenport, "The China-Japan Dispute," 309.
149. CLCS, "Submission by the PRC Concerning the Outer Limits"; PRC MFA, "Baselines of the Territorial Sea of Diaoyu Dao and Its Affiliated Islands."
150. CLCS, "Submission by the PRC Concerning the Outer Limits," 8. In accordance with Art. 76 of the Convention, these points are 60 nautical miles from the foot of the continental slope as identified by the PRC.
151. CLCS, "Submission by the PRC Concerning the Outer Limits," 2.
152. CLCS, "Submission by the PRC Concerning the Outer Limits," 1–2. These conclusions are based on marine scientific data prepared by China

Geological Survey, the Chinese Academy of Sciences, China Petrochemical Information, and other state institutions, with MFA and SOA "taking the lead" in preparing it for submission.

153. Davenport, "The China-Japan Dispute," 311.

154. However, a 1962 Border Treaty and 1964 Boundary Protocol established their territorial sea boundary in the northern part of the Yellow Sea. See Kong Lingjie, "Boundaries with New Era Characteristics," 46; Qi Huaigao, "Maritime Delimitation," 361–362.

155. Jiang Huai, "Yalu River Mouth," 67: "[China and North Korea] held two informal consultations on the law of the sea in 1996 and formal consultations on the law of the sea since 1997, and have now held 14 rounds of formal consultations on the law of the sea. During these consultations, both sides have comprehensively elaborated their respective positions on issues such as the waters subject to maritime delimitation, and the principles and methods of delimitation. There are obvious differences between the two sides on issues such as the principles of delimitation. The Chinese side advocates a fair and reasonable delimitation result based on equitable principles and taking into account all special circumstances and relevant factors. The Korean side advocates the demarcation of the boundary by the median line. . . . During PRC President Hu Jintao's visit to Korea in August 2008, the two leaders agreed that 'an early resolution of the maritime delimitation issue between China and Korea is important for the long-term stability of relations between the two countries' and that they would expedite negotiations on the maritime delimitation issue between the two countries in the Yellow Sea."

156. CLCS, "Submission by the PRC Concerning the Outer Limits"; CLCS, "Republic of Korea Partial Submission." Curiously, Chinese scholars claim that these submissions are not conflicting, misinterpreting the fixed points to be in different parts of the ECS. See Gao Jianjun, "The Okinawa Trough," 153.

157. Kim, "Maritime Boundary Negotiations," 70, 78–79.

158. Van Dyke, "Disputes over Islands," 56.

159. Bangladesh v. Myanmar, Separate Opinion of Judge Gao, para. 20.

160. Lemonkova, "Mapping the SCS Region," 113.

161. For thorough analyses of the tangle of potential EEZ claims, see Beckman and Schofield, "Defining EEZ Claims," 200.

162. Vietnam Note Verbale, No. 22/HC-2020 (30 March 2020); Malaysia Note Verbale, HA 26/20 (29 July 2020).

163. Gao Zhiguo, "The South China Sea," 351; Johnson, "Drawn into the Fray," 153–161.

164. Quoted in Johnson, "Drawn into the Fray," 154–155.

165. Indonesia Note Verbale, No. 480/POL-703/VII/10 (8 July 2010): "[T]hose remote or very small features in the SCS do not deserve [an] EEZ or continental shelf of their own. Allowing the use of uninhabited rocks, reefs and atolls isolated from the mainland and in the middle of the high sea as a basepoint to generate [entitlements to] maritime space concerns the fundamental prin-

ciples of the Convention and encroaches the legitimate interest of the global community."

166. Indonesia Note Verbale, No. 126/POL-703/V/20 (26 May 2020).

167. PRC Note Verbale, No. CML/46/2020 (2 June 2020).

168. Philippines Note Verbale, No. 000228 (5 April 2011).

169. *SCS Arbitration,* "Note Verbale," No. 13–1878. See also *SCS Arbitration,* Philippines Memorial, vol. I, 4.17.

170. At any rate, the arbitral tribunal lacked jurisdiction for such a delimitation. See *SCS Arbitration,* Jurisdiction and Admissibility Award, para. 157: "In these proceedings, the Philippines has challenged the existence and extent of the maritime entitlements claimed by China in the South China Sea. This is not a dispute over maritime boundaries. The Philippines has not requested the Tribunal to delimit any overlapping entitlements between the two States, and the Tribunal will not effect the delimitation of any boundary."

171. PRC Ministry of Foreign Affairs, "Position Paper," para. 59.

172. Philippines Note Verbale, No. 000191–2020 (6 March 2020).

173. Japan, Law on the Exclusive Economic Zone and the Continental Shelf, Law No. 74 (1996), Arts. 1.2, 2.1.

174. Japan Note Verbale, PM/12/303 (24 September 2012). See also Japan Note Verbale, SC/12/372 (28 December 2012), rejecting China's application of baselines to the disputed Senkaku Islands as "categorically unacceptable."

175. Japan has advocated for this rule since at least 1974, during the UNCLOS Conference negotiations, submitting a draft article stating that delimitation should proceed "taking into account the principle of equidistance," and that "failing such agreement, no State is entitled to extend its sovereign rights over the continental shelf . . . beyond the median line." In Sakamoto, "The Senkaku Islands," 13. See also Japan Note Verbale, SC/09/246 (23 July 2009): "It is indisputable that the establishment of the outer limits of the continental shelf beyond 200nm in an area comprising less than 400nm and subject to the delimitation of the continental shelf between the states concerned cannot be accomplished under the provisions of the Convention."

176. Japan Ministry of Foreign Affairs, "Japan's Legal Position," 1, 2.2.

177. Davenport, "The China-Japan Dispute," 298: "[I]nternational law presently has no clear-cut answer to the question of whether a State is entitled to an extended continental shelf in areas less than 400nm and arguments can be made to support either position."

178. Republic of Korea Note Verbale, MUN/022/13 (23 January 2013).

179. Kim, "Maritime Boundary Negotiations," 78–79.

180. Schofield et al., *The Limits of Maritime Jurisdiction,* 2.

181. *Case Concerning Delimitation of Maritime Areas (St. Pierre and Miquelon)* (Canada v. France). Decision, 10 June 1992, 95 ILR 645, para. 38.

182. Bangladesh v. Myanmar, para. 317.

183. Jia Bingbing, "The Principle of the Domination of the Land," 25.

184. PRC Note Verbale, CML/63/2020 (18 September 2020).

185. "Worldwide, the ratio between the maritime space under a nation's jurisdiction and its land area averages 94:100, yet it is only 30:100 in China's case, less than one-third of the world average." Liu Zhenhuan, "Commentary on 'UN Law of the Sea' Part 2," 14.

CHAPTER 4. RESOURCE RULES

1. Xi Jinping, "Speech on Maritime Power," delivered to the CCP Central Committee Political Bureau.
2. Oxman, "Territorial Temptation," 832: "The effective start of this process [of states succumbing to the 'territorial temptation' at sea]—President Truman's claim to the continental shelf in 1945—was so quickly accepted and emulated by other coastal states that the emergence of the regime of the continental shelf, in derogation of the principle of mare liberum, has been cited as an example of instant customary law." See also Tommy T. B. Koh, *Building a New Legal Order*, 189–190.
3. Posner and Sykes, "Economic Foundations," 569–596.
4. Schatz, "Combating Illegal Fishing," 386; Davenport, "Joint Development in Asia," 131.
5. Koh, *Building a New Legal Order*, 85.
6. *SCS Arbitration*, Merits Award, para. 245.
7. Ma Xinmin, "Merits Award Relating to Historic Rights," 12 (italics added).
8. PRC MFA, "Yang Jiechi Gives Interview to State Media."
9. CSIL, "Critical Study," para. 464.
10. UNCLOS, Art. 56.1: "In the EEZ, the coastal State has: (a) sovereign rights for the purpose of exploring and exploiting, conserving and managing the natural resources, whether living or non-living, of the waters superjacent to the seabed and of the seabed and its subsoil, and with regard to other activities for the economic exploitation and exploration of the zone, such as the production of energy from the water, currents and winds." UNCLOS, Art. 77: "The coastal State exercises over the continental shelf sovereign rights for the purpose of exploring it and exploiting its natural resources. . . . The natural resources referred to in this Part consist of the mineral and other non-living resources of the seabed and subsoil together with living organisms belonging to sedentary species."
11. See ILC, "Draft Articles," 297.
12. Jurisdiction under international law is typically broken down into "jurisdiction to prescribe," which is the state's competence to promulgate law applicable to specified persons or activities (also called "legislative jurisdiction") and a second type, "jurisdiction to enforce," referring to a state's authority to use judicial, executive, administrative, or police action to compel compliance with its law. See Dunoff et al., *International Law*, 355–356.
13. The law also claims exclusive jurisdiction over "security" in the EEZ (Art. 8), addressed in chapter 5.

14. PRC MFA, "Statement on China's Territorial Sovereignty and Maritime Rights," III(i), III(iii).

15. O'Rourke, "Maritime Territorial and EEZ Disputes," 29–31 (citing remarks of Ma Xinmin of the MFA in dialogue with the US State Department).

16. This does not rule out a claim to historic rights in the ECS or Yellow Sea, explored below in the context of "traditional fishing" rights.

17. Franckx and Benatar, "Dots and Lines," 90.

18. PRC Note Verbale, CML/18/2009 (7 May 2009); emphasis added.

19. Socialist Republic of Vietnam, "Statement on the Territorial Sea Baseline."

20. PRC National Administration for Surveying, "Basic Map: National Borders." See Gao and Jia, "The Nine-Dash Line," 110 (citing this as an "authoritative atlas").

21. The surface area of the Mediterranean is 2.5 million square kilometers. NB—the "discontinuous line" (断续线) is a commonly used term in the PRC for describing this map. See, for example, *People's Daily,* "China's Historic Rights in the SCS Discontinuous Line Cannot Be Arbitrarily Discussed or Denied."

22. Light dotted lines also surround certain submerged features in the southwest SCS, at Macclesfield Bank and between Taiwan and the mainland. The only labels aside from country names are the Dongsha, Zhongsha, Nansha, and Xisha "Qundao," or archipelagos.

23. Republic of China, "Location Map." See discussion in Gao and Jia, "Nine-Dash Line," 103.

24. Fravel, *Secure Borders,* 268–269. See chapter 3 on possible status as a provisional boundary.

25. MFA Treaty and Law Director-General Gao Feng, NYU Law, 15 October 2012.

26. Sun Kuan Ming, "Policy of the ROC," 408.

27. Zou Keyuan, "China's U-Shaped Line," 20.

28. Hayton, "The Modern Creation of China's 'Historic Rights' Claim," 7–10; Sun Kuan Ming, "Policy of the ROC," 401–409.

29. Li Zhaoxing, "Explanation on the Draft Law."

30. National People's Congress, "Notes on the EEZ."

31. Cited in Song and Zou, "Maritime Legislation," 332.

32. Geographically specific claims are required under UNCLOS. Art. 74(2) states that "the outer limit lines of the exclusive economic zone and the lines of delimitation drawn in accordance with article 74 shall be shown on charts of a scale or scales adequate for ascertaining their position." Art. 75(1): "Where appropriate, lists of geographical coordinates of points, specifying the geodetic datum, may be substituted for such outer limit lines or lines of delimitation." See also UNCLOS, Arts. 16(2), 47(9), 75(2), 76(9), and 84(2).

33. US Dept. of State, "China: Maritime Claims in the SCS," 4–7.

34. PRC Ministry of Natural Resources, "Notice on 'Problem Maps,'" Art. 3.1.

35. Gao and Jia, "The Nine-Dash Line," 99.

36. One of their claims, widely shared by Chinese commentators, is that the rights survive the Convention because of a doctrine of "intertemporal law": that the law contemporary to the claim should be applied to assess its validity. Chinese officials have also argued for this interpretation; for example, see Shu Zhenya, "Research Overview," 66–77.

37. The authors argue that "[w]hile UNCLOS is a comprehensive instrument of law, it was never intended, even at the time of its adoption, to exhaust international law. On the contrary, it has provided ample room for customary law to develop and to fill in the gaps that the Convention itself was unable to fill in 1982—due to the inherent limitations of a multilateral process of drawn-out negotiations." Gao and Jia, "The Nine-Dash Line," 123.

38. Jia Yu, "China's Historic Rights," 179.

39. Jia Yu, "China's Historic Rights," 203. The ostensible basis for these rights lies in "Chinese domestic law and international law, including the UNCLOS."

40. Li Jian, *China's Historic Rights in the South China Sea and a Catalogue of Evidence*, 19–146. The catalogue was funded by Fujian Province and the Ministry of Education's "Fundamental Research Funds for the Central Universities." It provides nearly 300 pages of bibliographic and archival citations cataloging official and semi-official evidence of historical usage in the SCS.

41. PRC Marine Environmental Protection Law (CLI.1.1367), 23 August 1982, Art. 2.

42. Based on PKU Law database full-text search. Among other key examples of PRC national-level legislation and regulation including this phrase are the Law on Fisheries (CLI.1.2675), 1 July 1986; Law on Surveying and Mapping (CLI.1.6073), 28 December 1992; Special Maritime Procedure Law (CLI.1.24093), 25 December 1999.

43. PRC Supreme People's Court (SPC), "Interpretations on the Application of the Special Maritime Procedure Law."

44. PRC SPC, "Provisions on Several Issues Concerning the Trial of Cases"; PRC SPC, "Opinion on Comprehensively Promoting Foreign-Related Commercial Maritime Trials."

45. CSIL, "Critical Study," paras. 512, 520.

46. CSIL, "Critical Study," para 535.

47. Socialist Republic of Vietnam, "Dispute Regarding the Law," 2.

48. Vietnam Note Verbale, no. 86/HC-2009 (8 May 2009).

49. Socialist Republic of Vietnam, "Vietnam Attends 21st Meeting."

50. Vietnam Note Verbale, no. 22/HC-2020 (30 March 2020).

51. Philippines Note Verbale, No. 000228 (5 April 2011). This note questioned the legal meaning of China's claims to "'the relevant waters as well as the seabed and subsoil thereof' (as reflected in the so-called 9-dash line map)" but stated that if China were to claim resource rights in the Philippines' jurisdictional waters, it "would have no basis under international law, specifically UNCLOS."

52. *SCS Arbitration*, The Philippines Notification and Statement of Claim, paras. 6, 27.

53. Philippines Note Verbale, No. 000191–2020 (26 May 2020).

54. Johnson, "Drawn into the Fray," 153–161. See chapter 3 for further discussion of these dialogues.

55. Indonesia Note Verbale, No. 480/POL-703/VII/10 (8 July 2010).

56. Indonesia Note Verbale, No. 148/POL-703/VI/20 (12 June 2020).

57. Malaysia Note Verbale, HA 26/20 (29 July 2020).

58. Jia Yu, "International Law Theory."

59. Tommy T. B. Koh, "The Exclusive Economic Zone," 1–33.

60. See Mallory, "China's Distant Water Fishing Industry," 106–107 (citing China's "failing scores" on various indicators of IUU fishing).

61. UN, "State of World Fisheries," 2. Asia as a whole, excluding China, produces 34 percent of the world catch.

62. PRC National People's Congress, "Report of the Law Enforcement Inspection Team."

63. This has entailed a growing proportion of distant water fishing catch, much of it IUU fishing. See Mallory, "Appendix G," 117.

64. Not only have fish stocks themselves suffered, but the ecosystems that support their reproduction are severely degraded from environmental damage other than overfishing. According to a PRC fisheries official in 2016, such activities have destroyed 80 percent of the coral reefs and 73 percent of the mangroves present in the 1970s. Li Jing, "Fish and Reefs."

65. Mallory, "China's Distant Water Fishing Industry," 100–101.

66. For a discussion of this mix of top-down and bottom-up initiative, see Martinson, "Catching Sovereignty Fish," 1–11.

67. PRC Fisheries Law (CLI.1.218763), 28 December 2013. Major amendments occurred in 2000, 2004, 2009, and 2013, but implementing regulation and rules have been steadily revised at local levels since 1986.

68. PRC State Council, Regulations for the Implementation of the Fisheries Law (CLI.2.3448772), 29 November 2020 (second revision).

69. Art. 41 notes that "the right to interpret these Regulations rests with the Ministry of Agriculture, Animal Husbandry and Fisheries." Wide interpretive berths granted for administrative agencies are typical of China's legislative and regulatory drafting; these allow the bureaucracy to adjust to policy that varies over space and time.

70. Xue Guifang, "China's Response to International Fisheries Law," 89.

71. PRC SOA, *China Ocean Development Report 2001*, 123.

72. PRC SOA, *China Ocean Development Report 1999*, 11.

73. PRC National People's Congress, "Report of the Law Enforcement Inspection Team."

74. Liu Cigui, "Taking Advantage." The tasks of fisheries law enforcement are often construed in these terms—for example, in the Thirteenth Five-Year Plan (2016–2021), which has been interpreted to require broad social outreach:

"In accordance with the work requirements of 'who enforces the law, popularizes the law,' the organization of fishery law enforcement personnel is to go deep into the fishing areas and villages, and through a variety of actions strengthen the promotion of fishery laws and regulations among the people to achieve strong and warm connection to fishery law enforcement." China Fisheries, "Thirteenth Five-Year Plan," 8.

75. PRC Ministry of Agriculture (MoA), "Ministry of Agriculture Leadership."
76. PRC MoA, "Adjustment of the Summer Fishing Moratorium System" (CLI.4.114542), 1 January 2009, 3.3. "The fishing time in the SCS (including the Beibu Gulf) from 12 degrees north latitude to the 'junction line of Fujian and Guangdong sea areas' is from 12:00 on 16 May to 12:00 on 1 August."
77. PRC MoA, "Adjustment of the Summer Fishing Moratorium System."
78. PRC MoA, China Fisheries Yearbook 2003, 141.
79. PRC MoA, "Press Conference on the Bright Sword Action," 3–5.
80. PRC MoA, "Press Conference on the Bright Sword Action," 5.
81. China Coast Guard, "Bright Sword 2020." Compared to the 4,307 PRC fishing vessels inspected and 1,493 seized, these are not frequent actions in relative terms.
82. PRC MFA Spokesperson, 18 May 2015.
83. Bernini, "Chinese Kidnapping."
84. PRC MoA, "Special Law Enforcement Action Plan," 4.2.4.
85. CCP Central Committee and PRC State Council, "Instructions on Relaxing Policies."
86. Chubb, "PRC Assertiveness," 107.
87. Garver, "China's Push," 1009.
88. Martinson, "Catching Sovereignty Fish," 5, citing an internal distribution fisheries atlas on file with the author.
89. Wu Zhuang, "The Dream of Maritime Power." Wu is also quoted in a Chinese state television program saying that "where there's water there's fish, where there's fish there are fishermen, and where there are fishermen, there are Chinese fisheries law enforcement vessels." China Central Television, "SCS Travel Notes," Part 4.
90. PRC MoA, "Regulations for Managing Spratly Islands Fisheries Production," chapters 2, 4. The special Spratly fishing regulations are unavailable on any PRC government website, unlike the rest of the legal instruments cited in this book; their unavailability likely reflects the sensitivity of this clear incentivization for Chinese fishermen to operate in contested waters. The PKU Law database references but does not include the text of this instrument. The author has the text of the regulations on file.
91. Martinson, "Catching Sovereignty Fish," 6 (citing a faculty member at the China Coast Guard Academy).
92. See, for example, Guangdong Province, "Review and Approval of Nansha Special Fishing License."

93. Martinson, "Catching Sovereignty Fish," 7.

94. Wu Zhuang, "The Dream of Maritime Power."

95. Zhang and Bateman, "Fishing Militia."

96. See Kennedy and Erickson, "China's Maritime Militia," 207–229; Kennedy and Erickson, "China's Third Sea Force," 1–22; and Erickson and Martinson, "Records Expose China's Maritime Militia at Whitsun Reef."

97. Jia Yu, "China's Historic Rights," 184–186, 195. Other PRC officials, including the current foreign minister, Wang Yi, have likewise cited the purported threat to traditional fishing rights posed by the EEZ regime. See PRC MFA, "Deputy Foreign Minister Wang Yi."

98. Cited in Song and Zou, "Maritime Legislation," 332.

99. Wu Zhuang, "The Dream of Maritime Power."

100. Fravel, "Traditional Fishing Grounds."

101. PRC MFA Spokesperson, 25 June 2009.

102. PRC MoA, "China Fisheries Law Enforcement."

103. Martinson, "Catching Sovereignty Fish," 7; Fravel, "Traditional Fishing Grounds"; Connelly, "Indonesia in the SCS."

104. Sina Military, "Chinese Fisheries Law Enforcement."

105. Bentley, "Mapping the Nine-Dash Line"; Connelly, "Indonesia in the SCS," 1–5.

106. See PRC MFA Spokesperson, 21 March 2016, 19 June 2016, 20 June 2016, 14 July 2017.

107. PRC MFA Spokesperson, 31 December 2019.

108. PRC MFA, "Ten Questions on Huangyan Island."

109. For example, Wu Zua "Party Group" under the Ministry of Natural Resources was established in 2020 to combine the "sub-Party groups" from the ECS, SCS, and the Yellow Sea/Beibu (Beihai) and better coordinate facilities construction and law enforcement actions. Ministry of Natural Resources, "Notice of the CCP Group."

110. Applying this parameter disentangles the sovereignty disputes over islands from the disputes over the rules of the law of the sea. No state has relinquished sovereignty claims to any disputed features, meaning that any claimant's fishing activities within 12 nautical miles of them are essentially an expression of their claim to sovereign title over the feature rather than a specific resource right. There is no law of the sea rule at stake in the question of title.

111. Ding Duo and Yang Li, "Exploration of the Legal Status," 52–53 (explaining the necessity of acquiescence by other states).

112. The more consequential disputes involving these states revolve around the question of where their maritime boundaries should be drawn, examined in chapter 3.

113. Lü Tian, "SCS Fishing Ban," 97; Amer, "China, Vietnam," 20–21.

114. Nguyen, "Vietnam's Maritime Militia."

115. The deputy chief of staff of the Vietnam Coast Guard, Senior Captain Dao Ba Viet, describes this trend to "proactively protect sovereignty, sovereign

rights, jurisdiction, and national interests at sea" and instructs the "Coast Guard and Navy to be politically, ideologically, and organizationally strong and absolutely loyal to the Party" (Dao Ba Viet, "Some Solutions for Protecting Sovereignty"). See Morris, "Blunt Defenders," 20–24, for insight on the Vietnam Coast Guard organization and activities. See Chen Qi, "Expansion and Military Deployment," for analysis of Vietnam's garrisons and construction activity in the Spratlys.

116. Republic of the Philippines, "Statement on the Inclusion of Bajo de Masinloc." The Philippines Department of Foreign Affairs was even more expansive in a subsequent statement, noting that the fishing bans "include areas over which the Philippines exercise sovereignty, sovereign rights, and jurisdiction" and invoking the specific elements of the SCS arbitral award (para. 716) as grounds for concluding that "China's annual fishing moratorium extends far beyond China's legitimate maritime entitlements under UNCLOS and is without basis under international law." See Republic of the Philippines, "On the Philippines' Protest of 17 May 2021."

117. *SCS Arbitration,* Philippines Memorial, 6.36.

118. See, for example, Ramos and Quismundo, "PH Ignores China Bid."

119. Ramos and Quismundo, "PH Ignores China Bid."

120. Morris, "Blunt Defenders," 27.

121. Republic of the Philippines, "DFA Deplores Chinese Embassy Response."

122. *SCS Arbitration,* Merits Award, para. 775.

123. *SCS Arbitration,* Merits Award, para. 781.

124. Republic of Indonesia, "RI Reaffirms," 2.

125. Indonesian law enforcement seized a PRC vessel in 2009 and later sank the vessel in a deterrent publicity stunt that also involved seized fishing boats from Vietnam (5 boats), the Philippines (11 boats) and Thailand (2 boats). See Salim, "RI Flexes Muscle."

126. Martinson, "Sovereignty Fish," 4–7.

127. Bentley, "Maritime Fulcrum," 21.

128. Martinson, "Sovereignty Fish," 4.

129. Japan National Institute for Defense Studies (NIDS), "China Security Report 2011," 18–19.

130. Bentley, "Malaysia's Special Relationship."

131. Ng and Moss, "Malaysia Toughens Stance."

132. PRC MFA Spokesperson, 8 June 2015.

133. The report also specifies 89 separate "intrusions" of PLA or CCG vessels into "Malaysian waters," though the nature and locations of these incidents are not disclosed. See *Straits Times,* "Chinese Ships Intruded into Malaysian Waters."

134. For example, Reuters, "Vietnam Opposes Chinese Fishing Ban."

135. Bentley, "Malaysia's Special Relationship," fn 38. NB—Direct observation of all such incidents is impossible, so analysis must rely on public reporting

that varies depending on many unobserved factors, including the diplomatic relationships among the parties.

136. North Korea's activities remain obscure, though analysis of remote sensing data reveals some of its patterns. See Park et al., "Illuminating Dark Fishing," 1–7.

137. PRC MFA, "China-Japan Fisheries Agreement." This agreement replaced a 1975 accord pertaining to territorial seas and high seas fisheries, none of which were disputed (with the important exception of the Diaoyu/Senkaku territorial sea). On prior Sino-Japanese fisheries agreements and practices, see Xue Guifang, "China's Response to International Fisheries Law," 193–199.

138. The western edge of this zone is 52 nautical miles from Chinese baselines, and the eastern edge is 52 nautical miles from Japan's. Those 52 nautical miles are effectively each side's uncontested EEZ entitlement.

139. Jia Yu, "40 Years of Reform," 29.

140. This is the area northeast of 30°40′ N latitude and 124°45′ to 127°30′ E longitude, lying north of the main disputed area, including portions of EEZ claimed by South Korea.

141. PRC MFA, "China-Japan Fisheries Agreement," Annex.

142. Ma Li, "China-Japan Fishery Commission Reached an Agreement"; Japan, "White Paper on Fisheries," 3.

143. Kim, "Illegal Chinese Fishing," 455–477.

144. Several of these incidents have been violent, including the deaths of two Chinese fishermen after a collision with a Korean Coast Guard (KCG) vessel in December 2010, the fatal stabbing of a KCG officer by a Chinese fisherman in December 2011, and the ramming and sinking of a KCG vessel in October 2016 by a fleet of forty Chinese fishing vessels, after which the KCG was authorized to use live-fire ammunition (rather than stun grenades and rubber bullets, as previously approved). See Maritime Awareness Project, "Republic of Korea Profile"; Park, "The Role of Fishing Disputes"; Roehrig, "South Korea: The Challenges of a Maritime Nation."

145. PRC MFA, "Fisheries Agreement Between China and Korea."

146. Another distinction is a "Transitional Waters Zone," which allowed fishermen from the other party to fish a narrow area flanking the "Provisional Measures Zone" closer to their shores; this was phased out after five years.

147. PRC MoA, "Issues Concerning the Implementation of the China-Korea Fishery Agreement."

148. The Sino-Vietnamese agreement also establishes a small "buffer zone" south of the Common Fishery Zone for small vessels that are exempt from detention, arrest, and punishment by the other side's law enforcement (Art. 12).

149. PRC State Council, "National Marine Functional Zoning Plan." These are the "Beibu Gulf North Fishery" (北部湾北部渔场) and the "Beibu Gulf South and Southwest Hainan Island Fishing Ground" (北部湾南部及海南岛西南部渔场).

150. See US Dept. of State, "Straight Baselines: Vietnam," 11–12. Historic bays are typically formed with baselines closing a large bay, with the space landward of the baseline treated as internal waters. See Symmons, *Historic Waters in the Law of the Sea,* 39–44, 301–304. The PRC objected to the Vietnamese historic bay claim in 1979 on the grounds of its sovereignty claims, stating that it "is absurd from the viewpoint of international law and is illogical and self-contradictory." *Beijing Review,* "Speech by Han Nianlong," 17.

151. Wu Zhuang states that "[b]efore the Fisheries Agreement came into effect, 25,000 copies of the 'Notice of Operation in the Waters of the Sino-Vietnamese Beibu Gulf Fisheries Cooperation Agreement,' 28,000 operating charts, 7,000 copies of law enforcement materials and information, and 3,000 copies of posters were distributed to grassroots government units and fishermen. The agreement was publicized and launched in all aspects by opening a column in relevant magazines to explain the relevant provisions of the agreement in detail, holding a press conference, and organizing a large-scale launch ceremony for the effective fisheries law enforcement cruises. At the same time, the fishery administrative departments of the three adjacent provinces [Guangxi, Guangdong, and Hainan] also carried out extensive three-dimensional publicity through radio, television, newspapers, slogans, posters, and propaganda vehicles." Liu Yusong, "Five Years After Implementation of the Fisheries Agreement," 4.

152. Zou Keyuan, "The Sino-Vietnamese Agreement," 16.

153. Some Chinese law enforcement officials have written critically about these decisions and advocated reassertion of those rights; see, e.g., Dong Jiawei, a Shandong province China Marine Surveillance officer, "On the Protection of Traditional Fishing Rights," 35–47.

154. Mallory, "China's Distant-Water Fishing Industry," 99–108.

155. International Energy Agency, "Offshore Energy Outlook," 9.

156. The report claimed "a high probability . . . that the continental shelf between Taiwan and Japan may be one of the most prolific oil reservoirs in the world." Cited in Gao and Wu, "Key Issues in the East China Sea," 32.

157. Convention on the Continental Shelf, 29 April 1958, 499 UNTS 311, Art. 1, defining the continental shelf as referring "(a) to the seabed and subsoil of the submarine areas adjacent to the coast but outside the area of the territorial sea, to a depth of 200 metres, or beyond that limit, to where the depth of the superjacent waters admits of the exploration of the natural resources of the said areas; (b) to the seabed and subsoil of similar submarine areas adjacent to the coasts of islands."

158. See Downs, "Chinese Energy Security," 55–69; Kirshner and Cohen, "The Cult of Energy Insecurity," 146–177; Kardon, "Oil for the Lamps," 305–328.

159. The most comprehensive listing of documents supporting China's claims of historic rights indexes 120 official documents back to the seventh century BCE through 1981. None relates to oil and gas. See Li Jian, *China's Historic Rights in the South China Sea,* 113–129.

160. State Council, Regulation on Offshore Cooperation (CLI.2.1182).

161. Jia Yu, "40 Years of Reform," 6.

162. PRC Mineral Resources Law (CLI.1.2730), 19 March 1986. The 1986 law was amended in 1996 to include "other sea areas under China's jurisdiction" (a 2009 revision also includes this language).

163. These are general areas in which claimants have sought to develop oil and gas resources. For more detailed descriptions of the nine hydrocarbon platforms in the SCS, see Owen and Schofield, "Disputed SCS Hydrocarbons," 813–814; for the ECS, see Guo Rongxing, "Territorial Disputes and Seabed Petroleum," 6–8.

164. China does not recognize Japan's median line and reportedly utilizes a different version of the median line lying further to the east in its negotiations with Japan. See Zhang Xinjun, "Why the 2008 Sino-Japanese Consensus Has Stalled," 55.

165. Manicom, "Sino-Japanese Cooperation," 462–463.

166. Chubb, "PRC Assertiveness," 106–107.

167. Duan Dang, "China's Latest Incursion"; Duan Dang, "What Is Happening in Indonesia's Natuna Sea?"

168. Allard and Lamb, "China Protested Indonesian Drilling." See further detail below on Indonesia's response.

169. Bentley, "Maritime Fulcrum."

170. Hayton, "The Modern Creation of China's 'Historic Rights' Claim," 7.

171. Jiang Sanqiang, "Multi-National Oil Companies," 598. Crestone chairman Randall C. Thompson was quoted saying "I was assured by top Chinese officials that they will protect me with their full naval might. That's what they told me in negotiations—that they'll have the entire full naval fleet out there backing me up, if necessary."

172. PRC MFA Spokesperson, 16 July 1992.

173. *Economist*, "Oil on Troubled Waters."

174. Li Jinrong et al., "Status of Oil and Gas," 12–16. These authors from the PRC State Oceanic Administration detail the extensive oil and gas operations of foreign claimants in waters claimed by the PRC.

175. Fravel, "China's Strategy," 302.

176. Li Jinrong et al., "Status of Oil and Gas," 14; see also map and concession information at Asia Maritime Transparency Initiative (AMTI), "South China Sea Energy Exploration and Development."

177. PRC SOA, *China Ocean Development Report 2008*, 127; see also Martinson, "Echelon Defense," 45. In 2013 China Central Television (CCTV) released a documentary on Chinese MLE activities in the area that publicly confirmed several of these activities, with ship captains declaring that such aggressive acts were authorized and necessary. See CCTV, "South China Sea Travel Notes," Part 4.

178. See Fravel, "China's Strategy," 306.

179. *SCS Arbitration*, Merits Award, para. 663.

180. China National Offshore Oil Company (CNOOC), Ltd., "Notification of Part of Open Blocks in Waters Under Jurisdiction of the PRC."

181. See AMTI, "South China Sea Energy Exploration and Development." Among the firms are Repsol, Talisman Energy, BP, Exxon, Eni SpA, and Murphy Oil Corporation.

182. Reuters, "China CNOOC Invites Foreign Firms."

183. PRC Marine Safety Administration (MSA), "Notice to Mariners," 2 and 27 May 2014. The links to these and subsequent MSA notices during this controversial episode have been removed from the MSA website; the author has retained screenshots of the notices.

184. The author attended a conference at Danang University in June 2014 that included a visit to a shipyard to observe the salvaged Vietnamese fishing vessel.

185. Vietnam Letter to UN Secretary-General, UN Doc. A/68/870 (9 May 2014).

186. PRC Marine Safety Administration, "Notice to Mariners," 27 May 2014. This notice also expanded the "exclusion zone" to 3 nautical miles; on file with author.

187. An engineer from PetroChina states that the Ministry of Land and Resources had approved seismic surveys in 2004 and well site surveys in 2011. This cannot be independently verified as Vietnam did not issue a specific complaint and the purported Ministry of Land and Resources approval has not been made public. See Cui Wenyi, "981 Drilling Platform Operations."

188. MFA officials insisted that this early end of operations went according to plan. See PRC MFA Spokesperson, 16 July 2014.

189. PRC MFA, "The Operation of the HYSY 981 Drilling Rig."

190. Vietnam's Ministry of Foreign Affairs, Coast Guard, and National Border Commission held a press briefing and offered a large amount of information about the episode, including details of the Chinese operation and posture: "The Chinese escort fleet is divided into 3 rings: the inner ring includes 10–15 ships at 1–1.5 nautical miles from the rig, the middle ring consists of 40–45 ships at 4.5–5 nautical miles from the rig and the outer ring includes 25–35 ships at 10–12 nautical miles from the oil rig. China constantly deployed 9 to 12 ships to closely follow Vietnamese vessels, ready to hinder and collide with Vietnamese vessels at 10–12 nautical miles away from the oil rig." Vietnam, "Developments in the East Sea."

191. For a thorough discussion of this operational capability and details of the action in May 2014, see Martinson, "Echelon Defense," 45–55.

192. Chubb, "China's Assertiveness," 79–121.

193. In the ECS, Japan has been more cautious and has restricted its activities to the east side of the provisional median line between the countries. One Chinese maritime analyst reported Korean surveys on the Chinese side of the Yellow Sea median line, but no evident production in disputed waters has occurred. See Zhang Shiping, China's Sea Power, 5.

194. Zhang Shiping, China's Sea Power, 4–9.

195. Allard and Lamb, "China Protested Indonesian Drilling."

196. See AMTI, "South China Sea Energy Exploration and Development." Among the blocks reported as producing in April 2021: Vietnam's 06–01, Indonesia's "South Natuna Sea Block B," and Malaysia's Kumang Cluster Production Area (wholly within the nine-dash line), Blocks D35/D21/J4, MLNG 2, SK310A, SK309/311, G and H.

197. For the most recent active production, see Petronas, "First Deepwater Gas Production from Block H." Murphy Oil, one of the partners at several Malaysian oil and gas blocks, reported to the US Securities and Exchange Commission that it was producing 14,100 barrels of oil and gas liquids in 2016 from Blocks SK 309/3011. (See Murphy Oil Corporation, "Form 10-K.")

198. See, for example, AMTI, "China and Malaysia" (discussing the November 2020 standoff over a Malaysian gas operation near Luconia Shoals).

199. Latiff and Ananthalakshmi, "Malaysian Oil Exploration."

200. Malaysia, "SCS: Press Statement."

201. Long and David, "Malaysia: Chinese Survey Ship Is in Our Waters."

202. AMTI, "China and Malaysia in Another Staredown."

203. *Offshore,* "Partners to Drill Two Wells." In April 2021, an Indonesian firm reported "accelerating development of its offshore Block B in the Natuna Sea," which straddles the nine-dash line (Energy Voice, "Indonesia's Medco Makes Offshore Block B Investment").

204. Fabi, "Indonesia to Step Up Oil Exploration."

205. PRC MFA, "Ambassador Xiao Qian Meets with Indonesian Minister of Energy."

206. Duan Dang, "How Did Indonesia Respond to China's Incursion?"

207. AMTI, "Nervous Energy."

208. Allard and Lamb, "China Protested Indonesian Drilling."

209. Hayton, "The SCS in 2020," 6.

210. Rosneft, "Rosneft Starts Drilling."

211. PXPEnergy Corp., "SC 72 Recto Bank."

212. Storey, "China and the Philippines." Following the encounter, PRC diplomats objected to these "oil and gas exploration activities by any country or company in the waters under China's jurisdiction without permission of the Chinese government."

213. PXPEnergy Corp., "SC 72 Recto Bank"; *Offshore,* "Forum Energy."

214. See Introduction for the origins of this policy line with Deng Xiaoping in the late 1970s.

215. PRC experts report joint development of offshore energy with North Korea beginning in 2005, but no details of this purported agreement have been published or observed in practice. See Gao Jianjun, "A Note on the 2008 Cooperation Consensus," 292, 298.

216. Namely, the 1974 Japan–South Korea JDA, 1982 Vietnam-Cambodia, 1989 Indonesia-Australia JDA, 1990 Malaysia-Thailand JDA, 1992 Malaysia-Vietnam JDA, and 2009 Malaysia-Brunei JDA (see Davenport, "Joint Development," 133–135).

217. PRC MFA, "Oil Companies of China, the Philippines, and Vietnam."

218. Li Jianwei and Chen Pingping, "Joint Development in the SCS," 152–153.

219. Song Xue, "Why JDAs Fail," 423. The "undertaking" also failed due to strong anti-China sentiments emerging in the Philippines at the time, with opposition channeled in part through the constitutional objection to the deal.

220. Constitution of the Republic of the Philippines, Art. XII, Sec. 2: "The exploration, development, and utilization of natural resources shall be under the full control and supervision of the State. The State may directly undertake such activities, or it may enter into co-production, joint venture, or production-sharing agreements with Filipino citizens, or corporations or associations at least sixty *per centum* of whose capital is owned by such citizens."

221. PRC MFA, "Memorandum of Understanding on Cooperation on Oil and Gas Development," III(a-c).

222. Reed and Hille, "Philippines to Restart Oil and Gas Exploration."

223. Rivera, "PXP Energy Hikes Stake in SC72."

224. Jia Yu, *Maritime Development Strategy Anthology*, 140.

225. Japan, "June 2008 Agreement."

226. PRC MFA, "China and Japan Reach a Consensus" (italics added).

227. Zhang Xinjun, "Why the 2008 Sino-Japanese Consensus Has Stalled," 53–65.

228. Japan, "Joint Press Conference."

229. Manicom, "Sino-Japanese Cooperation," 461–463.

230. Japan, "Joint Press Conference."

231. PRC MFA, "Chinese FM Yang Jiechi Meets the Press."

232. Manicom, "Sino-Japanese Cooperation," 470.

233. Zhang Xinjun, "Why the 2008 Sino-Japanese Consensus Has Stalled," 57–61.

234. Japan Ministry of Foreign Affairs, "Maritime Platforms."

235. AMTI, "Over the Line."

236. The most systematic study of these "assertive actions" finds that once initiated, nearly 40 percent have been sustained in perpetuity. See Chubb, "PRC Assertiveness," 94–96.

237. Xu Senan, "We Must Pay Attention to the Studies of Sea Borders," 18–20.

238. Jia Yu, "Reflections on Ocean Power Strategy," 7 (noting the persistence of "foreign plunder" of China's resources).

239. Jia Yu, "International Law Theory."

CHAPTER 5. NAVIGATION RULES

1. US Dept. of State, "Conversation Between President Nixon and His Assistant [National Security Adviser Henry Kissinger]."

2. PRC MFA, "Briefing by Xu Hong."

3. Xi Jinping, "Deepen the Partnership to Build a Beautiful Home in Asia." Speech at the National University of Singapore, 7 November 2015.

4. For a description of the legal controversies attending competition among European powers since the fifteenth century, see O'Connell, *International Law of the Sea*, 1–28.

5. Koh and Jayakumar, "The Negotiating Process," in Nordquist, ed., *UNCLOS 1982: A Commentary*, vol. 1, 79–80.

6. UNCLOS, A/CONF.62/SR.55.

7. Art. 87 establishes the "freedom of the high seas," which includes, inter alia, freedom of navigation, freedom of overflight, freedom to lay submarine cables and pipelines, and freedom to construct artificial islands. The other "relevant provisions" that may affect these freedoms are examined below.

8. For a thorough discussion on these views, see Kwiatkowska, *The 200nm EEZ*; Nordquist, ed., *UNCLOS 1982: A Commentary*, vol 2, 491–823.

9. Zhang Haiwen, "Is It Safeguarding the Freedom of Navigation?" 31.

10. This liberal position is often associated with the judgment in *S.S. Lotus* (France v. Turkey), 1927, Permanent Court of International Justice (ser. A) No. 10 (7 September).

11. These are "(a) the safety of navigation and the regulation of maritime traffic; (b) the protection of navigational aids and facilities and other facilities or installations; (c) the protection of cables and pipelines; (d) the conservation of the living resources of the sea; (e) the prevention of infringement of the fisheries laws and regulations of the coastal State; (f) the preservation of the environment of the coastal State and the prevention, reduction and control of pollution thereof; (g) marine scientific research and hydrographic surveys; (h) the prevention of infringement of the customs, fiscal, immigration or sanitary laws and regulations of the coastal State" (UNCLOS, Art. 21.1).

12. Author database, drawing primarily on US Navy Judge Advocate General's Corps (JAG Corps), *Maritime Claims Reference Manual* (*MCRM*). This number includes states with unclear restrictions or restrictions that apply only to nuclear-powered or -armed vessels.

13. Convention on the Territorial Sea and Contiguous Zone, 29 April 1958, 516 UNTS 206 (effective 10 September 1964).

14. Zou Keyuan, "Innocent Passage for Warships," 199–200.

15. Zou, "Innocent Passage for Warships," 200–202.

16. UNCLOS, A/CONF.62/SR.182.

17. UNCLOS, A/CONF.62/SR.191.

18. UNCLOS, A/CONF.62/SR.182, A/CONF.62/SR.135. The PRC initially claimed this rule in a 1973 working paper submitted to the UN Seabed Committee: "A coastal State may, in accordance with its laws and regulations, require military ships of foreign States to tender prior notification to, or seek prior approval from, its competent authorities before passing through its territorial sea." "PRC Working Paper on Sea Area," A/AC.138/SC.II/L.34, 2.

19. UNCLOS, A/CONF.62/SR.191 (adding that "a considerable number of States, including China, time and again submitted an amendment in this regard").

20. Ministry of Communications, Regulations Governing the Supervision and Control of Foreign Vessels (CLI.2.586), 18 September 1979, Art. 2.
21. PRC Maritime Traffic Safety Law (CLI.1.1754), 2 September 1983, Art. 11.
22. PRC NPC, "Notes on EEZ and Continental Shelf Draft Law."
23. UN, "Declarations and Reservations," 11 (italics added).
24. Zou, "Innocent Passage for Warships," 214.
25. PRC Supreme People's Court, "Understanding and Application."
26. The sole case that might be so construed does not involve innocent passage, per se, and took place outside the limits of the territorial sea. It is nonetheless a notable case. It occurred during the "Second Taiwan Strait Crisis" of August–October 1958. The crisis began when the PLA initiated shelling of Quemoy, a small island near the mainland coastline controlled by the Republic of China (Taiwan). In support of its ally, the US provided naval escorts for ROC supply ships to the 3nm limit of Quemoy (then the ROC's territorial sea claim), prompting the PRC announcement to halt this practice. The agreement to deescalate the crisis allowed the US to continue its naval escort to the edge of the Quemoy "sea area." Although the PRC had established a 12nm territorial sea around Quemoy and other PRC-claimed islands in its Declaration on 4 September 1958, the island was under Taiwanese control and US vessels did not enter Taiwan's territorial sea claim. See Chiu Hung-dah, "China and the Question of the Territorial Sea," 45–47.
27. Muller, *China as a Maritime Power*, 190.
28. US Dept. of State, "Straight Baselines: PRC," 8–9.
29. PRC State Council Regulations for the Administration of Foreign Non-Military Ships Passing Through the Qiongzhou Strait (CLI.2.325), 8 June 1964.
30. From February 1965, the US Navy was involved in combat operations against North Vietnam, during which time aircraft periodically strayed into PRC territorial airspace above Hainan Island and drew fire from anti-aircraft defenses and PLAN fighter jets. Beijing claimed to have shot down twelve American planes in 2,138 combat sorties. Whiting, "China's Use of Force," 113–116.
31. Cohen and Chiu, *People's China and International Law*, 1499.
32. US Dept. of State, "Straight Baselines: PRC," 8–9. Cf. the 2022 State Department *Limits in the Seas* study, which projects hypothetical PRC straight baselines around *all* the South China Sea island groups in order to analyze and critique the ambiguous Chinese claim; US Dept. of State, "People's Republic of China: Maritime Claims," *Limits in the Seas*, No. 150.
33. The US now evidently recognizes Triton as a "rock" generating a 12nm territorial sea. See US Department of Defense statement in LaGrone, "US Destroyer Challenges More Chinese SCS Claims." NB—the Spratlys are not included on the map, given the lack of PRC occupation of any of those features until 1988.
34. A Chinese analyst states that "this incident did not arouse much attention at the time" (Li Yan, "Freedom of Navigation Issues," 23).

35. US Department of Defense, "Annual Freedom of Navigation Report," 1992–1996.
36. PRC MFA, "Briefing by Xu Hong."
37. Kardon, "US-China Maritime Security," 185–190.
38. See, for example, PRC Ministry of National Defense, "Yang Yujun on Unauthorized Entry."
39. *SCS Arbitration,* Merits Award, para. 366.
40. *South China Morning Post,* "More Footage Emerges."
41. PRC MFA Spokesperson, 2 October 2018.
42. Minnie Chan, "China-US Close Encounters."
43. PRC State Council Information Office, "The Diversified Employment of China's Armed Forces." For a comprehensive analysis of PLAN "out of area" operations, see Yung et al., "China's Out of Area Naval Operations"; McDevitt, *China as a Twenty-First Century Sea Power.*
44. LaGrone, "Chinese Warships Made 'Innocent Passage.'"
45. Hayton, "Britain Is Right to Stand Up to China."
46. Dutton, "Scouting, Signaling, and Gatekeeping," 17–21.
47. Cordesman, *Chinese Strategy and Military Modernization,* 325.
48. PRC MFA Spokesperson, 17 June 2016.
49. James Przystup, "No Lack of Dialogue, Results—TBD," 112–113. Japanese officials protested that the PLAN vessel was in territorial seas, not an international strait, and that the intelligence vessel conducted normal operations (i.e., it was not engaged in "expeditious and continuous passage") as required for the right of innocent passage under UNCLOS Art. 39(1)c.
50. See, for example, Zhang Guobin, *Research on the Innocent Passage Regime,* 3: "Our country should promptly start the study of whether the domestic policy and legal amendments for the innocent passage of foreign warships through our country's territorial waters are properly understood, so as to provide for the further improvement of relevant maritime policies and legal systems in the future."
51. This dispute revolves around Japan's formal non-recognition of a sovereignty dispute with China, addressed in chapter 6.
52. *Japan Times,* "Japan Had Plans to Sail MSDF Ship Near Chinese-Held Islet"; *Radio Free Asia,* "Japan Reported to Have Conducted Free Navigation Ops."
53. Socialist Republic of Vietnam, "Law of the Sea of Vietnam," Art. 12.
54. UN DOALOS, "Declarations and Reservations," 22.
55. Republic of the Philippines, "Constitution," Art. 1.
56. *SCS Arbitration,* "Philippines Memorial," vol. 1, 6.133.
57. *Tuoi Tre News,* "Chinese Warship Soldiers Point Guns."
58. *Straits Times,* "Chinese Ships Intruded into Malaysian Waters."
59. See US Dept. of Defense, "Annual Freedom of Navigation (FON) Reports"; US Dept. of State, "Military Operational Issues." The State Department also has a role in coordinating the clearance of US Navy operational challenges.

60. US Dept. of Defense, "Annual Freedom of Navigation Report," 2017–2020.

61. Beckman and Davenport, "The EEZ Regime," 3.

62. US Dept. of State, "Conversation Between President Nixon and His Assistant for National Security Affairs," doc. 395.

63. UNCLOS, Art. 59: "In cases where this Convention does not attribute rights or jurisdiction to the coastal State or to other States within the exclusive economic zone, and a conflict arises between the interests of the coastal State and any other State or States, the conflict should be resolved on the basis of equity and in the light of all the relevant circumstances, taking into account the respective importance of the interests involved to the parties as well as to the international community as a whole."

64. Beckman and Davenport, "The EEZ Regime," 9.

65. O'Connell, *The International Law of the Sea*, 570.

66. Kraska, *Maritime Power and the Law of the Sea*, 8.

67. Kopela, "The 'Territorialisation' of the EEZ," 1–15.

68. For a thorough account of Chinese law and regulation of the zones landward of the EEZ, including river systems, see Zou Keyuan, "Navigation of Foreign Vessels," 355–364.

69. "PRC Working Paper on Sea Area," A/AC.138/SC.II/L.34, 2–3.

70. See Noyes, "The Territorial Sea and Contiguous Zone," 110–113.

71. "PRC Working Paper on MSR," A/AC.138/SC.III/L.34, 1.

72. PRC Survey and Mapping Law (CLI.1.6073), 28 December 1992, Arts. 1–2.

73. A further revision to this law on 27 April 2017 (CLI.1.293713) specifies criminal penalties attached to surveying and mapping "without approval or without cooperating with relevant departments" (Art. 51).

74. SOA, MFA, PLA General Staff, Ministry of State Security, Hong Kong and Macao Affairs Office of the State Council, and Taiwan Affairs of the State Council, Notice on the Strict Implementation of the Regulations of the PRC on Foreign-Related MSR (CLI.4.185081), 10 December 1999; SOA, Notice on Issues Related to Law Enforcement and Supervision of Foreign-Related MSR (CLI.4.69815), 16 May 2000.

75. UNCLOS, A/CONF.62/C.2/SR.30, 228.

76. See Zou Keyuan, "Governing MSR," 1–27; Wang Ying, "Jurisprudential Analysis," 37–48; Ren and Cheng, "A Chinese Perspective," 139–146.

77. PRC Supreme People's Court, "Actively Exercise Maritime Jurisdiction."

78. Sina Military, "US Aircraft Carrier."

79. Song, "Declarations and Statements with Respect to the 1982 UNCLOS," 275.

80. Mann and Pine, "Faceoff Between US Ship, Chinese Sub Is Revealed."

81. Donnelly, "The US-China EP-3 Incident," 25–42.

82. PRC MFA, "Spokesman Zhu Bangzao Gives Full Account."

83. Zou Keyuan, "Peaceful Use of the Sea," 172–173.

84. PRC Survey and Mapping Law (CLI.1.41760), 29 August 2002, Art. 7. An earlier "Notice" from the State Oceanic Administration on law enforcement for

"foreign-related MSR" already suggests the official sensitivity to this specific issue prior to the *Bowditch* incident. It instructs maritime law enforcement agencies and local governments to use their discretion in approving foreign survey activities and "not establish any project which is not conducive to the national defense and security and maritime rights and interests of the PRC. All cooperative research projects to be conducted in disputed sea areas or sea areas which China finds difficult to control at this stage shall be determined according to China's appropriate foreign policies." SOA, Notice on the Law Enforcement Supervision for the Foreign-Related Marine Scientific Research (CLI.4.69815), 16 May 2000.

85. PRC MFA Spokesperson, 26 September 2002.

86. Wang Xinyi, "Cruise Law Enforcement," 61.

87. The Yulin Naval Base is located in Yalong Bay, in the southern part of Hainan Island.

88. Odom, "True Lies," 414–416.

89. Along with official statements, the Pentagon released video from on board the *Impeccable* that illustrates the descriptions rendered above. See YouTube, "USNS Impeccable Harassed by Chinese Vessels."

90. See Odom, "True Lies," 414–420, for a thorough documentation of the official exchange.

91. PRC MFA Spokesperson, 10 March 2009.

92. Ross, "The 1995–1996 Taiwan Strait Confrontation," 87–123.

93. PRC MFA Spokesperson, 4 December 2007.

94. Panda, "Making Sense of China's Reaction."

95. *Hindustan Times,* "Indian Destroyer Warship in Qingdao."

96. PRC MND, "Spokesperson Ren Guoqiang."

97. China Global TV, "China Lodges Solemn Representation."

98. PRC MND, "Defense Ministry's Regular Press Conference 27 June 2019."

99. Pan Shanju, "Two US Ships Sail Through the Taiwan Strait."

100. Reuters, "China Says US Undermining Stability."

101. There are presumably unpublicized incidents, but those that have been reported in open sources include confrontations between Chinese vessels and the following foreign vessels: USNS Bowditch (March 2001); EP-3 Incident (April 2001); USNS Bowditch (2002), USNS Impeccable (March 2009); USNS Victorious (May 2009); USS George Washington (July–November 2010); U-2 Intercept (June 2011); INS [Indian Naval Ship] Airavat (July 2011); INS [Indian Naval Ship] Shivalik (June 2012); USNS Impeccable (July 2013); USNS Spruance (July 2013); USNS Cowpens (December 2013); unsafe P-8 intercept (August 2014); unsafe EP-3 intercept (May 2016). See Congressional Research Service, "China's Actions in South and East China Seas," 9–12.

102. For direct quotations, see O'Rourke, "US-China Strategic Competition," 80–83.

103. Gomez, "Chinese Diplomat Outlines Limits to Freedom of Navigation."

104. Nan Li, "The Evolution of China's Naval Strategy and Capabilities," 122–126.

105. Yung et al. "China's Out of Area Naval Operations," 15–19; McDevitt, *China as a Twenty-First Century Naval Power*, 20–32.
106. US Dept. of Defense, "Annual Report to Congress 2018," 67–69. India issued a formal protest to one such operation conducted by a Chinese Academy of Sciences survey vessel in 2019. See Liu, "Chinese Research Vessel Expelled."
107. Military Excellence, "Chinese Warship 'Visits' the US."
108. LaGrone, "Chinese Spy Ship Monitoring RIMPAC." Another example of uncontested PLAN operations in the US EEZ during exercises occurred in July 2017, when a PLAN task force and intelligence ships arrived in the EEZ surrounding Alaska to monitor a test of theater ballistic missile defenses. Caixin, "Department of Defense Responded That 'Chinese Warships Appeared in Waters Near Alaska.'"
109. Martinson, "China as an Atlantic Naval Power," 24.
110. US Dept. of Defense, "Annual Report to Congress 2018," 16. The following year, the Philippines opted to approve these operations. See Maritime Executive, "Philippines Approves Chinese Research."
111. Dutton and Martinson, "China's Distant-Ocean Survey Activities," 10–13 (detailing some of the organizations and the PLAN utilization of their data).
112. SOA, MFA, and PLA General Staff, Notice on the Strict Implementation of the Regulations of the PRC on Foreign-Related MSR (CLI.4.185081), 10 December 1999.
113. US Navy JAG Corps, *MCRM*, "Malaysia."
114. Socialist Republic of Vietnam, "Law of the Sea of Vietnam," Art. 37. See Art. 14 on contiguous zone security jurisdiction.
115. *Tuoi Tre News*, "Chinese Warship Soldiers Point Guns."
116. Poling, "From Orbit to Ocean," 15.
117. Cambodia claims security jurisdiction in the contiguous zone and a right to control "devices" in its EEZ; Myanmar claims security jurisdiction in the contiguous zone, prior permission for military aircraft overflight in the EEZ, and some undefined "security" jurisdiction across the EEZ; Thailand prohibits military exercises in its EEZ; and North Korea has designated various "military zones" that lie in its claimed EEZ and are off-limits to foreign vessels and aircraft. See US Navy JAG Corps, *MCRM*.
118. Maritime Awareness Project, "Republic of Korea Profile."
119. Lee, "Seoul to Summon Chinese Diplomats."
120. These actions are not correctly interpreted as operations in foreign EEZs; they are analyzed instead in the context of the sovereignty dispute over Diaoyu/Senkaku in chapter 6.
121. See McVadon, "The PLA Navy as an Instrument of Statecraft," 231–232.
122. Japan has also objected to Chinese MSR in its undisputed EEZs, demanding prior notification for such activities—though whether any of these were "military surveys" is not evident from the reported record. See Japan Ministry of Foreign Affairs, "Visit to Japan by Premier Zhu Rongji."

123. Dutton, "Scouting, Signaling, and Gatekeeping," 20.
124. PRC Ministry of National Defense, "Regular Press Conference," 30 April 2020.
125. Kotani, "Can Japan Join U.S. Freedom of Navigation Operations?"
126. *Japan Times*, "Japan Had Plans to Sail MSDF Ship Near Chinese-Held Islet."
127. PRC Ministry of National Defense, "Announcement of the Aircraft Identification Rules of the ECS."
128. For a thorough discussion of the legal issues surrounding the ADIZ, see Dutton, "Caelum Liberum," 691–709.
129. In announcing the ADIZ, China cited the PRC National Defense Law (CLI.1.17009), 14 March 1997; PRC Civil Aviation Law (CLI.1.13135), 30 October 1995; and PRC Basic Flight Regulations (CLI.2.98813), 18 October 2007. See Rinehart and Elias, "China's ADIZ," 7.
130. The US Navy articulates its complaint as follows: "While States are not prohibited from establishing ADIZs, the requirements of China's ADIZ does [sic] not distinguish between aircraft intending to enter China's national airspace and those merely overflying international airspace without an intent to enter China's national airspace" (US Navy JAG Corps, *MCRM*, "China").
131. Rinehart and Elias, "China's ADIZ," 4.
132. US Dept. of Defense, "Annual Freedom of Navigation Report," 2014–2021.
133. Rinehart and Elias, "China's ADIZ," 11–21.
134. PRC MFA Spokesperson, 15 December 2015.
135. Chang Ching, "Why Is There No SCS ADIZ?" See also PRC MFA Spokesperson, 4 February 2014; PRC Ministry of National Defense, "Statement by MND Spokesman Geng Yansheng."
136. The UK, France, Germany, Australia, and Japan have each deposited notes verbales protesting, inter alia, Chinese restrictions on the "freedom of navigation and overflight." See Japan Note Verbale, SC/21/002 (19 January 2021); Australia Note Verbale, no. 20/026 (23 July 2020); UK/France/Germany Note Verbale, UK NV No. 162/20 (16 September 2020).
137. Data from US Dept. of Defense, "Annual Freedom of Navigation Report," 2007–2020.
138. "By conducting this operation, the United States demonstrated that these waters are beyond what China can lawfully claim as its territorial sea, and that China's claimed straight baselines around the Paracel Islands are inconsistent with international law" (US Navy Seventh Fleet, "7th Fleet Destroyer Conducts FONOP in SCS."
139. UK Parliament, "South China Sea: Freedom of Navigation," Remarks of Nigel Adams, UK Minister for Asia.
140. Institute of International Strategic Studies, "Strengthening the Regional Order in the Asia-Pacific: Q&A."
141. Seibt, "France Wades into the SCS."
142. Reuters, "German Warship to Sail Through SCS."
143. Goldrick, "Australia's Naval Presence."

144. US Dept. of State, "Senate Foreign Relations Committee Testimony," 621.

145. See Kraska, *Maritime Power.*

146. Xiao Feng, "Reflections on the US-China Freedom of Navigation Debate," 41.

147. Military analysts draw range rings on maps to indicate the distances within which various weapons systems can strike targets.

148. Chinese law enforcement does interfere in the navigation of foreign vessels seeking to exploit resources in China's claimed sea areas, where such activities are better understood as an exercise of resource rights rather than navigation.

149. Xi Jinping, "Speech at National University of Singapore."

150. See Kaye, *Freedom of Navigation;* Churchill and Lowe, *The Law of the Sea,* 420–430.

CHAPTER 6. DISPUTE RESOLUTION RULES

1. Deng Xiaoping, Remarks to Japanese Prime Minister Takeo Fukuda, 25 October 1978. Wilson Center Digital Archive, "Record of Meeting Between Prime Minister Fukuda and Vice Premier Deng (Second Meeting)."

2. Xi Jinping, "Deepen the Partnership to Build a Beautiful Home in Asia." Speech at the National University of Singapore, 7 November 2015.

3. Ma Xinmin, "China and the UNCLOS," 9.

4. See Weil, "Towards Relative Normativity," 413–442.

5. Oxman, "Courts and Tribunals," 395.

6. Klein, Dispute Settlement in the UNCLOS, 2. Klein includes the UN Charter as a partial third example, which includes a separate instrument (the Statute of the International Court of Justice) that must also be ratified for prior consent to be established, as well as providing for means of dispute resolution under Chapter VII that need not include mandatory arbitration or adjudication. See also Alter, *The New Terrain,* 136 (analyzing all twenty-four standing international judicial bodies, of which just seven have "dispute settlement jurisdiction for specified international agreements," but "unless clearly indicated in a treaty, a court's jurisdiction is presumed to be optional, something both parties must agree to before a case can proceed").

7. See Klein, *Dispute Settlement in the UNCLOS,* 121–123; Oxman, "Courts and Tribunals," 397–408.

8. Xi Jinping, "Deepen the Partnership to Build a Beautiful Home in Asia."

9. Wang Tieya and Wei Min, eds., *International Law,* 611–612.

10. The WTO is the key exception, considered below. On the general pattern of PRC practice regarding international adjudication, see Ku, "China and the Future of International Adjudication," 154–178.

11. Ling Qing, *From Yan'An to the UN,* chapter 7.

12. Ling Qing, *From Yan'An to the UN,* chapter 7 (observing that "it seems that when we first started out, we did not fully investigate how the 200 nautical mile economic zone affected China's own interests. China is partially closed off from the ocean, which is to say that it is a state with unfavorable

geographic conditions. This is because while the South China Sea can be extended, the East China Sea and Yellow Sea are less than 400 nautical miles from neighboring countries and consequently cannot expand outward").

13. UNCLOS, A/CONF.62/SR.112 (italics added).

14. UNCLOS, Art. 309: "No reservations or exceptions may be made to this Convention unless expressly permitted by other articles of this Convention."

15. UN DOALOS, "Declarations and Reservations," 11 (italics added). See chapter 3 on the "equitable principle."

16. UN DOALOS, "Declarations and Reservations," 11.

17. See Cai, *The Rise of China,* 142 (noting that China has "rejected all optional protocols which would subject China to compulsory jurisdictions of human rights bodies"). See also Ku, "China and the Future of International Adjudication," 154–178 (noting China's basic posture of "strictly limiting its exposure to international adjudicatory mechanisms" but also recognizing some increasing acceptance of them in certain forums).

18. *SCS Arbitration,* "Notification of Statement and Claim."

19. After submission of the Notification and Statement of Claim, the arbitral body was formed, and formal procedures were adopted. The Philippines submitted a Memorial setting out fifteen submissions on which they sought relief.

20. The China Society of International Law group that drafted and reviewed the long brief includes sitting officials from the Ministry of Foreign Affairs and the Ministry of Natural Resources as well as international law scholars. CSIL, "Critical Study," 748.

21. PRC MFA Spokesperson, 23 January 2013.

22. "不接受, 不参, 不承认, 不执行." See Kardon, "China Can Say 'No,'" 1–46.

23. PRC MFA Spokesperson, 19 February 2013.

24. PRC MFA, "Position Paper."

25. *SCS Arbitration,* "Procedural Order," no. 4. NB—the Permanent Court of Arbitration is only the registry for the procedure; the tribunal's jurisdiction derives from UNCLOS alone.

26. *SCS Arbitration,* Jurisdiction Award, para. 64 (quoting from a letter to the tribunal from the Chinese ambassador to the Netherlands on 6 February 2015).

27. *SCS Arbitration,* "Procedural Order," no. 4, 1.1.

28. PRC MFA, "Position Paper," para. 3.

29. PRC MFA, "Position Paper," para 14.

30. "Whatever logic is to be followed, only after the extent of China's territorial sovereignty in the South China Sea is determined can a decision be made on whether China's maritime claims in the South China Sea have exceeded the extent allowed in the Convention." PRC MFA, "Position Paper," para. 10.

31. PRC MFA, "Position Paper," para. 25.

32. PRC MFA, "Position Paper," para. 30.

33. PRC MFA, "Position Paper," 33 (italics added).

34. PRC MFA, "Position Paper," para. 35.

35. PRC MFA, "Position Paper," para. 38.

36. "China has been reluctant to sign a legally binding code of conduct with the ASEAN countries." Zou Keyuan, "China's U-Shaped Line," 24.

37. PRC Law on the Procedure for Conclusion of Treaties (CLI.1.4922), 28 December 1990, art. 2.

38. For example, the PRC has determined that the series of bilateral communiques between the US and China are of equal status to treaties. See *Encyclopedia of China*, "Jurisprudence," 195.

39. PRC MFA, "Position Paper," IV.

40. PRC MFA, "Position Paper," para. 65.

41. PRC MFA, "Position Paper," paras. 65, 69.

42. PRC MFA, "Position Paper," para. 92.

43. PRC MFA, "Position Paper," para. 29.

44. Bradford and Posner, "Universal Exceptionalism," 1–54.

45. *SCS Arbitration*, Jurisdiction Award, paras. 271, 369, 370.

46. PRC MFA, "Statement on the Jurisdiction of the SCS Arbitration Tribunal," 3. The statement was released on 24 October 2015 and then re-released on 30 October with no alterations other than the date.

47. PRC MFA, "Statement on the Jurisdiction of the SCS Arbitration Tribunal," 4 and 5.

48. PRC MFA Spokesperson, 30 October 2015.

49. PRC MFA, "Briefing by Xu Hong."

50. PRC MFA, "Minutes of the Meeting Between Vice FM Liu Zhenmin and US Media Delegation."

51. PRC MFA, "Minutes of the Meeting Between Vice FM Liu Zhenmin and US Media Delegation."

52. PRC MFA, "Yang Jiechi Gives Interview to State Media."

53. *People's Daily,* "Shunji Yanai."

54. American Society of International Law, Annual Meeting, remarks of Sienho Yee, 10 April 2015.

55. Many of these statements are analyzed in chapters 3 to 5 in light of their substantive import for boundary, resource, and navigation rules.

56. PRC SCIO, "China Adheres to the Position," para. 120.

57. PRC MFA, "Minutes of the Meeting Between Vice FM Liu Zhenmin and US Media Delegation."

58. *SCS Arbitration*, Merits Award, Dispositif (11). Discussing the traditional fishing regime, the Award observed that "in the EEZ, in contrast [to archipelagic waters and territorial seas], traditional fishing rights are extinguished" (para. 804); it also noted the traditional fishing at the Shoal by China, Taiwan, the Philippines, and Vietnam (para. 805).

59. Hunt and Quiano, "China Allows Philippines Fishermen."

60. Asia Maritime Transparency Initiative, "Fishing in Troubled Waters."

61. *SCS Arbitration*, Merits Award, para. 1201. For a view that this represents weak PRC compliance, see Ku and Mirasola, "Tracking China's Compliance."
62. Xu Hong, "Experiencing the Storm," 36–37.
63. These are Duan Jielong 2020 to the present (former director-general of MFA Treaty and Law Department and ambassador to Singapore), Gao Zhiguo 2008–2020 (formerly director of the Center for International Maritime Affairs at the State Oceanic Administration), Xu Guangjian 2001–2007 (former legal adviser to the MFA), and Zhao Lihai 1996–2000 (formerly a distinguished international law scholar at Peking University).
64. Bangladesh v. Myanmar, "Separate Opinion of Judge Gao," para. 20: "Since . . . the equidistance method 'does not automatically have priority over other methods of delimitation' [Nicaragua v. Honduras, para. 272], there should be no reason whatsoever for any court or tribunal in one case to follow the equidistance method as applied in previous cases. . . . The [tribunal's] interpretation of article 76 of the Convention in general and the concept of natural prolongation in particular is neither correct nor accurate."
65. See Bangladesh v. Myanmar, "Separate Opinion of Judge Gao"; *Case Concerning the Detention of Three Ukrainian Naval Vessels* (Ukraine v. Russia), Provisional Measures, Order, Separate Opinion of Judge Gao, 26 ITLOS (25 May 2019), para. 9.
66. Xu Hong, "Experiencing the Storm," 34.
67. Ma Xinmin, "China and the UNCLOS," 7.
68. Ma Xinmin, "China and the UNCLOS," 8–9.
69. ITLOS, *Arctic Sunrise*.
70. In *Arctic Sunrise*, as in the SCS Arbitration, the tribunal did not consider refusals to accept its jurisdiction as bearing on the objective existence of that jurisdiction: "The fact that a party may contest the jurisdiction of the tribunal is not a basis on which a party can frustrate the effective discharge by that tribunal of its responsibility to adjudicate a dispute brought before it, including determining its own jurisdiction." *Arctic Sunrise Arbitration* (Netherlands v. Russia), Merits Award, Case no. 2014–02 PCA (14 August 2015), para. 368.
71. PRC MFA, "Signed Article by Guangming Daily."
72. See, e.g., *Aegean Sea Continental Shelf* (Greece v. Turkey), 1977 ICJ 3 (19 December); Nicaragua v. US.
73. For example, CSIL, "Critical Study," paras. 152 (*Arctic Sunrise*), 276 (Greece v. Turkey), 953 (Nicaragua v. US).
74. Zhang, "Russia's Non-Appearance in the Arctic Sunrise Case," 20, 29, 32.
75. Wu Shicun, "Will Vietnam Think Twice?"
76. Zheng Zhihua, "Is China Ready for a Second SCS Arbitration?"
77. Jayakumar, Koh, et al., "The South China Sea Arbitration," 1.
78. UNCLOS Art. 296 and Annex VII, Art. 11. On the general lack of *stare decisis*, see Scott and Stephan, *The Limits of Leviathan*, 34–35 (arguing that international court decisions do influence customary international law); Verdier

and Voeten, "Precedent, Compliance, and Change" 419–422 (arguing that "it matters whether international courts are conservative or pathbreaking in their interpretations of customary international law").

79. Lim, "Philippines' Duterte Says SCS Arbitration Case to Take 'Back Seat.'"

80. Madarang, "Duterte on the Constitution."

81. Zhang Feng, "Assessing China's Response," 453. For other formal Philippines' statements on the matter, see Philippines Note Verbale, no. 00191–2020 (26 May 2020); Philippines Note Verbale, no. 0929–2020 (9 October 2020).

82. Republic of the Philippines, "On the Fourth Anniversary."

83. Philippines, "DFA Deplores Chinese Embassy Response."

84. Philippines Note Verbale, no. 00191–2020 (26 May 2020).

85. Philippines, "On the Fourth Anniversary."

86. For example, *Maritime Delimitation in the Area Between Greenland and Jan Mayen* (Denmark v. Norway), 1993 ICJ 41 (14 June); *Maritime Delimitation and Territorial Questions Between Qatar and Bahrain* (Qatar v. Bahrain), 2001 ICJ 40 (16 March); Romania v. Ukraine (2009); Nicaragua v. Honduras (2007); Eritrea v. Yemen (1998). See also McDormand, "The South China Sea Tribunal Awards," 134–145.

87. Schofield, "A Landmark Decision," 341.

88. The Merits Award develops a stringent interpretation of the regime of islands, considering the "historical evidence of conditions on the features— prior to the advent of the exclusive economic zone as a concept or the beginning of significant human modification—to represent a more reliable guide to the capacity of the features to sustain human habitation or economic life" (*SCS Arbitration*, Merits Award, para. 578). Relying on historical evidence of actual human habitation and economic activity, the tribunal found that none of the Spratly Islands warranted status as more than a "rock" with a 12nm territorial sea but no EEZ or continental shelf (paras. 615–626).

89. *SCS Arbitration*, Jurisdiction Award, para. 183. The procedural history of Vietnam's submissions and the Philippines' responses is summarized in paras. 47–49, 54, 57, 61–62, 65, and 67.

90. *SCS Arbitration*, Merits Award, para. 157. Earlier, the court had resolved that "having sought the views of the Parties, the Tribunal agreed to grant Viet Nam access to the Memorial of the Philippines and its annexed documents and noted that the Tribunal would consider in due course Viet Nam's request for access to any other relevant documents" (*SCS Arbitration*, Jurisdiction Award, para. 49).

91. *SCS Arbitration*, Jurisdiction Award, para. 183.

92. Socialist Republic of Vietnam, "Statement on Vietnam's Response to the Award."

93. See chapters 3 and 4 for detail on the boundary delimitation and fishing rights implicated by this ruling.

94. Indonesia Note Verbale, no. 126/POL-703/V/20 (26 May 2020), 2, 3.

95. Republic of China, "ROC Position on the SCS Arbitration." The amicus brief was submitted by a scholarly association rather than the ROC government. See Chinese (Taiwan) Society of International Law, "In the Matter of an Arbitration under Annex VII."

96. Australia Note Verbale, no. 20/026 (23 July 2020); Canada Ministry of Foreign Affairs, "Statement on the SCS Arbitration"; New Zealand Note Verbale, No. 08/21/02 (3 August 2021); UK/France/Germany Note Verbale, UK NV No. 162/20 (16 September 2020); Japan Note Verbale, SC/21/002 (19 January 2021). The US has done so as well in several diplomatic communications. See US Dept. of State, "Digest of US Practice 2016," 519–522; US Note Verbale, A/74/874-S/2020/483 (2 June 2020).

97. See Asia Maritime Transparency Initiative, "Who Is Taking Sides After the SCS Ruling?"

98. PRC MFA Spokesperson, 14 June 2016.

99. Fravel, *Strong Borders*, 3.

100. A typical clause in these agreements reads: "The contracting parties agree that after the official delimitation of the border between the two countries, if any border dispute arises, it shall be settled through friendly consultations between the two parties." PRC MFA, PRC Treaty Database, Sino-Burma Boundary Treaty of 1960, art. 11.

101. Bạch Long Vĩ/Bai Long Wei was unilaterally ceded to Vietnam in 1957.

102. Cohen and Chiu, *People's China and International Law*, 1416.

103. See Tommy T. B. Koh, "The Asian Way."

104. Cohen and Chiu, *People's China*, 1443.

105. Wilson Center, "Main Speech by Premier Zhou Enlai."

106. Asian-African Conference, "Final Communiqué," art. 8 (italics added).

107. Cohen and Chiu, *People's China*, "Note of the MFA to the Indian Embassy in China" (26 December 1959), 1427.

108. Cohen and Chiu, *People's China*, "Text of Chinese Foreign Ministry Note to India" (9 October 1963), 1441–1442.

109. Cohen and Chiu, *People's China*, "Statement of the Government of the PRC" (24 May 1969), 1445.

110. PRC MFA, *PRC Treaty Database*, 1958 Sino-Soviet Treaty of Commerce and Navigation, Art. 11.

111. See Ku, "China and the Future of International Adjudication," 154–178.

112. In author discussions with MFA, SOA, and NPC officials, as well as many PRC law of the sea scholars, the only explanation offered was that the PRC was "studying" the treaty during that decade. Given how adamantly the PRC had opposed compulsory dispute resolution for maritime boundaries at the Conference, this profession of incomplete knowledge of the treaty is surprising and indicative of some bureaucratic failure in claiming an Article 298 exemption.

113. Chiu, "China and the Law of the Sea Convention," 187–215.

114. UNCLOS, A/CONF.62/SR.60 (italics added).

115. PRC MFA, "Statement by Ms. Xue Hanqin."
116. See, e.g., PRC MFA, "Statement by Shen Guofang."
117. PRC MFA, "Statement by Wang Min" (italics added).
118. PRC MFA, "Statement by Liu Jieyi."
119. PRC MFA, "Statement by Wu Haitao."
120. PRC MFA, "Statement on the Rule of Law."
121. See Ku, "China's Definition of 'Peaceful Settlement.'"
122. PRC MFA, "Statement on the Rule of Law."
123. See Foot, "China and the ARF," 425–440.
124. Johnson, "Drawn into the Fray," 153–161. See chapter 3 for discussion of substantive elements of this process.
125. ASEAN, "ASEAN Declaration on the South China Sea."
126. ASEAN, "Chairman's Statement at the First ARF." NB—in addition to China, Russia is also a "consultative partner" with ASEAN. ASEAN consists of Brunei Darussalam, Indonesia, Malaysia, Philippines, Singapore, and Thailand. ASEAN also has "dialogue partners," namely, Australia, Canada, the European Union, Japan, New Zealand, Republic of Korea, and the United States. ASEAN's "observers" are Laos, Papua New Guinea, and Vietnam. See ASEAN, "Chairman's Statement at the First ARF."
127. ASEAN, "Chairman's Statement at the Second ARF," 11.
128. The SCS claimant states' UNCLOS ratification were Philippines (May 1984), Indonesia (February 1986), Vietnam (July 1994), China (June 1996), Malaysia (October 1996), Brunei (November 1996).
129. Buszynski, "ASEAN, the DOC, and the SCS," 350.
130. Foot, "China and the ARF," 430.
131. On prior negotiations, see, e.g., ASEAN, "Joint Statement of the Meeting of Heads of State."
132. ASEAN, "Declaration on the Conduct of Parties in the SCS," 4.
133. ASEAN, "Declaration on the Conduct of Parties in the SCS," 6, 10.
134. PRC MFA, "Wang Yi: 'Dual-Track Approach.'"
135. PRC MFA, "Report of the Secretary-General."
136. ASEAN, "Single Draft Code of Conduct in the South China Sea Negotiating Text," 3. The other parties' views are analyzed in the next section on specially affected states.
137. ASEAN, "Single Draft COC Negotiating Text," 7–8.
138. ASEAN, "Single Draft COC Negotiating Text," 10.
139. PRC MFA, "Statement on Settling Disputes."
140. North Korea is excluded from this analysis, as elsewhere, as an anomalous case—and further, one lacking any public diplomatic record. Chapter 3 relates the sparse facts about consultations between China and North Korea on boundary delimitation since 1997.
141. These meetings have been periodically interrupted or changed in format. See Republic of Korea, "Outcomes of the 12th Korea-China Meeting" (2007); Republic of Korea, "8th ROK-China Director-General Level Meeting" (2021).

For details on the substantive issues under discussion, see Kim, "Maritime Boundary Negotiations," 69–94.

142. Republic of Korea, Ministry of Foreign Affairs Spokesperson's Press Briefing (13 March 2012).

143. Republic of Korea, Ministry of Foreign Affairs Spokesperson's Press Briefing (21 April 2016); PRC MFA Spokesperson, 6 November 2015.

144. PRC MFA, "China and ROK Hold the First Meeting." Meetings have been focused on technical issues involving fisheries law enforcement, environmental protection, and marine science, and they have occasionally included mutual criticisms of Japan. See also Republic of Korea, "Outcome of the 1st Meeting of Korea-China Dialogue (2021)."

145. Because the feature falls within the area of their overlapping EEZ and continental shelf claims, it is a factor in entitlements and delimitation but not a sovereignty dispute.

146. PRC MFA, "China and Japan Hold 12th Round of High-Level Consultations"; see also CSIL, "Critical Study," para. 314.

147. Crises in 1972, 1996, 2010, and 2012 revolved around the Diaoyu/Senkaku dispute, examined in the subsequent section of this chapter.

148. PRC State Council Information Office, "China Adheres to the Position," para. 121.

149. Genba, "Japan-China Relations at a Crossroads."

150. During a Council on Foreign Relations roundtable, another official from the Japanese Ministry of Foreign Affairs commented that "the Government of Japan has never modified Genba's statement and stands by it." See Cohen, "How Dangerous Are Sino-Japanese Tensions."

151. Two months prior to penning the ICJ invitation op-ed, Genba himself had explicitly ruled out Japan initiating an ICJ suit with China on the grounds that "The Senkaku Islands are undoubtedly Japan's inherent territory" (Jiji Press, "Japan Not To Take Senkaku Issue to the ICJ").

152. Japan, "Declarations Recognizing the Jurisdiction of the Court as Compulsory."

153. PRC officials have made no formal statements in this matter, but several have written academic articles. Shu Zhenya, "Research Overview on the Study of the Critical Date," 66–77; Liu Dan, "The 'Critical Date' Factor," 81–90. Notable non-official writing on the matter includes Shaw, "Revisiting the Diaoyutai/Senkaku Islands Dispute," 156; Li Yuling, "Assessment of the Sovereignty Dispute," 10–12.

154. PRC "Declaration on the Territorial Sea" (1958). For details on the Japanese government's assessment of the dispute, see Shaw, "Revisiting the Diaoyutai/Senkaku Islands Dispute," 95–169.

155. ASEAN, "Single Draft COC Negotiating Text," 18.

156. ASEAN, "Single Draft COC Negotiating Text," 17. Vietnam also proposes that an ASEAN "Commission" might make recommendations on maritime issues.

157. ASEAN, "Treaty of Amity and Cooperation," Art. 13. The TAC further provides that "mediation, inquiry or conciliation" may be recommended by the ASEAN "High Council" (Art. 14).

158. ASEAN, "Single Draft COC Negotiating Text," 17; ASEAN, "Treaty of Amity and Cooperation," Art. 17.

159. Chesterman, "Asia's Ambivalence," 16–17: "Asian countries, for example, have by far the lowest rate of acceptance of the compulsory jurisdiction of the International Court of Justice (ICJ) and of membership of the International Criminal Court (ICC); they are also least likely to have signed conventions such as the International Covenant on Civil and Political Rights (ICCPR) or the International Covenant on Economic, Social and Cultural Rights or to have joined the WTO."

160. Chesterman, "Asia's Ambivalence," 30. "Regional cohesion is further complicated by the need to accommodate the great power interests of China, India, and Japan. However, the limited nature of regional bodies is also consistent with a general wariness of delegating sovereignty." Chesterman also observes that "[o]nly fifteen of the fifty-three Asia-Pacific states have ever appeared before the ICJ, which equates to 28%. The corresponding figures for other regions are 48% of Latin American states, 50% of African states, 57% of Eastern European states and 79% of WEOG. Of those fifteen Asian states, six first appeared before the ICJ in 2001 or later."

161. Chesterman, "Asia's Ambivalence," 28. China has the second-most bilateral investment treaties (BITs). Its early BITs tended to permit investor-State arbitration only in very limited circumstances, but those since the late 2000s have included greater recourse to such third-party DRM. See Akande, "Is China Changing Its View?"

162. Koh, "The Asian Way."

163. SCS Arbitration, Jurisdiction Award, para. 148.

164. Mavrommatis Palestine Concessions, Judgment No. 2, 1924 PCIJ, Series A, No. 2, 11.

165. SCS Arbitration, Jurisdiction Award, paras. 149–150.

166. This inference is drawn most clearly in Talmon, "The SCS Arbitration," paras. 12–25.

167. Talmon, "The SCS Arbitration," para. 32.

168. See also Kraska, "The Legal Rationale."

169. For a discussion of the administrative and security functions of Sansha City, see Haver, "Sansha City."

170. For a well-sourced description of the various changes of possession of all or part of these islands, see Tønnesson, "The Paracels," 145–169.

171. For details on this action, see Zhang Wei, "Mao's Last Decision," 38–41; Fravel, Strong Borders, 272–296.

172. See Hayton, The South China Sea, 50–60.

173. PRC MFA, "Memorandum on the Issues of the Paracel and Nansha Islands." See Jia Yu, "International Law Theory," 30–31.

174. Annex to the Letter from PRC to UN Secretary-General, UN Doc. A/69/645 (8 December 2014), 2.

175. UN Doc. A/69/645, 4.

176. Tønnesson, "The Paracels," 146–147.

177. Agreement between the USA and Japan Concerning the Ryukyu Islands and the Daito Islands (Okinawa Reversion Treaty), vol. 841 UNTS 249, no. 12037, signed 17 June 1971, effective 15 May 1972.

178. PRC SCIO, "Diaoyu Dao," Foreword.

179. "Declaration on the Territorial Sea of the People's Republic of China" (4 September 1958), Art. 1.

180. PRC SCIO, "Diaoyu Dao," II. This controversy derives from the 1952 San Francisco Treaty in which Japan "renounce[d] all right, title and claim to Formosa and the Pescadores," which the PRC claims was understood to include the nearby Diaoyu/Senkaku group. Treaty of Peace with Japan, Vol 136 UNTS 45, no. 1832, signed 8 September 1951 (entered into force 28 April 1952).

181. See Downs and Saunders, "Legitimacy and the Limits of Nationalism," 125–126.

182. Yang Dongxiao, "The Historical Process of Nationalization."

183. Wilson Center, "Record of the Third Meeting Between PM Tanaka and Premier Zhou."

184. PRC MFA, "Shelve Disputes and Jointly Develop."

185. Downs and Saunders, "Legitimacy and the Limits of Nationalism," 127–131.

186. Japan Ministry of Foreign Affairs, "Trends in Chinese Vessels."

187. Yu Zhirong, "What Is the Value of the First Territorial Sea Cruise?"

188. For a detailed summary of this sequence of events, see Drifte, "The Japan-China Confrontation." This was one of several administrative steps adopted by organs of the Chinese government. For example, in 2005 the State Council issued a Notice of the Bureau of Surveying and Mapping on Strengthening the Publicity and Education of National Territorial Awareness and the Supervision of the Map Market, noting that some maps were "missing important islands such as Diaoyu Island and Chiwei Island" (23–26), the main features in the Diaoyu group.

189. PRC MFA, "Statement of the MFA on Diaoyu Dao."

190. PRC MFA, "Statement of the PRC on Diaoyu Baselines."

191. Japan Ministry of Foreign Affairs, "Trends in Chinese Vessels" (data derived from chart updated 7 April 2021).

192. Japan Ministry of Foreign Affairs, "Trends in Chinese Vessels."

193. Gu Xiudong, "Upgrading the Diaoyu Islands Situation."

194. Hirose, "Japan's Effective Control."

195. PRC MFA, "China and Japan Reach Four-Point Principled Agreement." For detailed comparison of the Chinese and Japanese statements, see Liff, "Principles Without Consensus."

196. Urano, *Senkaku Islands,* 206–207; Koo, "The Senkaku/Diaoyu Dispute," 229 fn 6.

197. Johnson, "Drawn into the Fray," 155.

198. Republic of Indonesia, "Indonesia Protests PRC Violations."

199. PRC Note Verbale, No. CML/46/2020 (2 June 2020).

200.Vietnam Letter to the UN Secretary-General, A/68/943 (3 July 2014).

201. Republic of Indonesia, "Indonesia Protests PRC Violations" ("[r]eaffirm[ing] that Indonesia does not have overlapping jurisdiction with China").

202.Japan Ministry of Foreign Affairs, "The Basic View on the Sovereignty" (italics added).

203. Japan Note Verbale, no. PM/12/303 (24 September 2012).

204.Miyoshi, "Exercising Enforcement Jurisdiction" (noting a 2012 revision of the Japan Act on Navigation of Foreign Ships that permits Japanese Coast Guard [JCG] vessels to order foreign ships to leave the territorial sea without an onboard inspection).

205. For analysis of the JCG's growing role as a paramilitary force, see Samuels, "New Fighting Power," 84–112.

206.Morris, "Blunt Defenders," 17–20.

207. Japan Ministry of Foreign Affairs, "Takeshima: Definitive Clarifications."

208.Ginsburg, "Eastphalia and Asian Regionalism." But also see Koh, "The Asian Way," for an alternative argument that Southeast Asian states are willing to refer their disputes to formal dispute resolution, including three sovereignty disputes adjudicated by the ICJ: *Request for Interpretation of the Judgment of 15 June 1962 in the Case Concerning the Temple of Preah Vihear* (Cambodia v. Thailand), Judgment, 2013 ICJ Rep 281 (11 November); *Sovereignty over Pulau Ligitan and Pulau Sipadan* (Indonesia v. Malaysia), Judgment, 2002 ICJ 54 (17 December); *Sovereignty over Pedra Branka/Pulau Batu Puteh, Middle Rocks and South Ledge* (Malaysia v. Singapore), Judgment, 2008 ICJ 130 (23 May).

CONCLUSION

1. The nine-dash line is potentially an element of a valid claim to territorial sovereignty over the island, but it is generally not accepted as a valid basis for any claims to jurisdiction or sovereign rights. See *SCS Arbitration,* Merits Award, Dispositif. See also Franckx and Benatar, "Dots and Lines"; Zou, "China's U-Shaped Line"; Chung, "Drawing the U-Shaped Line"; Kraska and Pedrozo, *International Maritime Security Law.*

2. Twenty-nine states require prior authorization and eleven require prior notice (author database). Some Chinese analysts place the aggregate figure as high as fifty-five, though they have not produced evidence of the other fifteen states' practice (Grandview Institution, "Is It Necessary for China to Change?"). A 2020 report by a PRC legal scholar cited forty countries that "believe that the passage of warships in the territorial waters is conditional. Therefore . . . the customary international law has not yet reached a consensus on this issue" (Wang Zelin, "Twelfth China Oceans University Salon").

An Australian law of the sea scholar argues that "when considered in the context of coastal States only, those States seeking restriction or regulation make up 52 percent of the international community. This raises the question as to whether the LOSC in the context of freedom of navigation represents customary international law, and whether such behaviour might serve in the long term to undermine the efficacy of the LOSC in this or other areas" (Kaye, "Freedom of Navigation," 15).

3. See Van Dyke, "The Disappearing Right to Navigational Freedom in the EEZ"; Kaye, "Freedom of Navigation."

4. China has already done so violently against Vietnam (1974, 1988) and more subtly against the Philippines (1994, 2012); further forcible seizures are certainly possible and perhaps even likely. Yet such actions would also clearly breach even China's conception of the rules, which does not accept that territory may be taken by force. As such, the action would not so much challenge the rules as seek a specific exemption for China on the basis of an irredentist justification.

5. While these are not all explicitly documented in law or official statements, they can be inferred from the evidence presented in this study.

6. See Roberts, *Is International Law International?*; Roberts, Stephan, Verdier, and Versteeg, *Comparative International Law.*

7. Ginsburg, "Authoritarian International Law?" 231.

8. Ginsburg, "Eastphalia and Asian Regionalism," 101–119.

9. "Such norms might facilitate cooperation across borders to repress regime opponents, enhancing the security of authoritarian rule. They might discourage freedoms of expression and association. They might also facilitate the dilution of democratic institutions and norms through practices and rhetoric that undermine them, turning general international law more authoritarian." Ginsburg, "Authoritarian International Law?" 231. For a view of international law that is less interactive, see Bradford and Posner, "Universal Exceptionalism."

10. Declaration of the Russian Federation and the PRC on the Promotion of International Law, A/70/982, S/2016/600 (8 July 2016), at 9: "It is of utmost importance that the provisions of this universal treaty [UNCLOS] are applied consistently, in such a manner that does not impair rights and legitimate interest of States Parties."

11. Ginsburg, "Eastphalia as a Return," 27–45. For a critical view on how inviolable Westphalian norms of sovereignty have actually been in practice, see Krasner, *Organized Hypocrisy.*

12. Hakimi, "Making Sense of Customary International Law," 1494.

13. See Harold Koh, "Why Do Nations Obey International Law?" 2599–2659; Slaughter and Burke-White, "The Future of International Law," 327–352.

14. Yang Jiechi, "Conscientiously Study and Publicize."

15. See Ikenberry, *After Victory,* which proposes constitutional orders as ones featuring the rule of law and binding institutions. See also discussion in Schweller, "The Problem of International Order Revisited," 161–186.

16. PRC MFA, "Statement of Duan Jielong."
17. "[A]though the customary international law process sometimes produces norms that have the clarity and stability of rules, most of its normative output is more fragmentary—treated and accepted as customary international by some actors or in certain settings but not by or in others." Hakimi, "Making Sense of Customary International Law," 1504.
18. Ikenberry, *Liberal Leviathan*, 310.
19. For a compelling analysis of how relative power limits the machinery of international law, see Carr, *Twenty Years' Crisis*, 136–206.
20. Goldsmith and Posner, "A Theory of Customary International Law," 1113–1177; Reisman, "The Cult of Custom, 144; Roberts, "Traditional and Modern Approaches," 767; Charney, *Universal International Law*, 537.
21. Gilpin, *War and Change*, 45–49.
22. Hirschman, *Exit, Voice, and Loyalty*. For consideration of conditions that make exit from international order more likely, see Goddard, *When Might Makes Right*.
23. Johnston, "A World of Orders," 18–21.
24. Gilpin, *War and Change*, 47.

Abbott, Kenneth W., Robert O. Keohane, Andrew Moravcsik, Anne-Marie Slaughter, and Duncan Snidal. "The Concept of Legalization." *International Organization* 54, no. 3 (2000): 401–419.

Abbott, Kenneth W., and Duncan Snidal. "Hard and Soft Law in International
Governance." *International Organization* 54, no. 3 (2000): 421–456.

Akande, Dapo. "Is China Changing Its View of International Tribunals?" *EJIL:
Talk*, 4 October 2010. http://www.ejiltalk.org/is-china-changing-its-view-of
-international-tribunals/.

Akehurst, Michael. "Custom as a Source of International Law." *British Yearbook of
International Law* 47, no. 1 (1975): 1–53.

Alagappa, Muthiah, ed. *Asian Security Order: Instrumental and Normative Features.*
Stanford: Stanford University Press, 2003.

Alford, William P. "Of Arsenic and Old Laws: Looking Anew at Criminal Justice
in Late Imperial China." *California Law Review* 72, no. 6 (1984): 1180–1256.

Allard, Tom, and Kate Lamb. "China Protested Indonesian Drilling, Military
Exercises." Reuters, 1 December 2021. https://www.reuters.com/world/asia
-pacific/exclusive-china-protested-indonesian-drilling-military-exercises
-2021–12–01/.

Allott, Philip. "The Concept of International Law." *European Journal of International Law* 10, no. 1 (1999): 31–50.

Amer, Ramses. "China, Vietnam, and the South China Sea: Disputes and Dispute
Management." *Ocean Development and International Law* 45, no. 1 (2014):
17–40.

Anand, R. P. *Origin and Development of the Law of the Sea: History of International
Law Revisited.* The Hague: Martinus Nijhoff, 1983.

Asahi News. "China Coast Guard Vessel Performs On-Site Inspection of Chinese-Flagged Fishing Boat near Senkaku Islands [尖閣諸島沖に中国公船、漁船に立ち入り検査か]." *Asahi News,* 1 August 2015.

Asia Maritime Transparency Initiative (AMTI). "Beijing Keeps Busy in ECS Oil and Gas Fields." *CSIS,* 23 August 2018. https://amti.csis.org/busy-summer-beijings-rigs/.

———. "China and Malaysia in Another Staredown over Offshore Drilling." 25 November 2020. https://amti.csis.org/china-and-malaysia-in-another-staredown-over-offshore-drilling/.

———. "Fishing in Troubled Waters." 7 July 2017. https://amti.csis.org/fishing-troubled-waters/.

———. "Island Tracker." Accessed 5 November 2021. https://amti.csis.org/island-tracker/.

———. "Nervous Energy: China Targets New Indonesian, Malaysian Drilling." 12 November 2021. https://amti.csis.org/nervous-energy-china-targets-new-indonesian-malaysian-drilling/.

———. "Over the Line: Tracking Energy Competition in the East China Sea." 14 October 2016. https://amti.csis.org/energy-competition-east-china-sea/.

———. "Reading Between the Lines: The Next Spratly Legal Dispute." 21 March 2019. https://amti.csis.org/reading-between-lines-next-spratly-dispute/.

———. "South China Sea Energy Exploration and Development." Accessed 5 November 2021. https://amti.csis.org/south-china-sea-energy-exploration-and-development/.

———. "Who Is Taking Sides After the SCS Ruling?" 15 August 2016. https://amti.csis.org/sides-in-south-china-sea/.

———. "Who's Taking Sides on China's Maritime Claims." 30 September 2021. https://amti.csis.org/whos-taking-sides-on-chinas-maritime-claims/.

Asian-African Conference. "Final Communiqué of the Asian-African Conference." *Interventions* 11, no. 1 (1955/2009): 94–102.

Association of Southeast Asian Nations (ASEAN). "Chairman's Statement to the First ASEAN Regional Forum." First ASEAN Regional Forum, Bangkok, Thailand (25 July 1994). https://aseanregionalforum.asean.org/wp-content/uploads/2019/01/First-ARF-Bangkok-25-July-1994.pdf.

———. "Chairman's Statement to the Second ASEAN Regional Forum." Second ASEAN Regional Forum, Brunei Darussalam (1 August 1995). https://aseanregionalforum.asean.org/wp-content/uploads/2019/01/Second-ARF-Bandar-Seri-Begawan-1-August-1995.pdf.

———. "Declaration on the Conduct of Parties in the South China Sea." Adopted in Phnom Penh, Cambodia (4 November 2002). https://asean.org/?static_post=declaration-on-the-conduct-of-parties-in-the-south-china-sea-2.

———. "Declaration on the South China Sea." Adopted in Manila, Philippines (22 July 1992). https://cil.nus.edu.sg/wp-content/uploads/2019/02/1992-ASEAN-Declaration-on-the-South-China-Sea-1.pdf.

———. "Joint Statement of the Meeting of Heads of State/Government of the Member States of ASEAN and the President of the PRC." Meeting on ASEAN-China Cooperation Towards the 21st Century. Kuala Lumpur, Malaysia (16 December 1997). https://asean.org/joint-statement-of-the-meeting-of-heads-of-state-government-of-the-member-states-of-asean-and-the-president-of-the-peoples-republic-of-china-kuala-lumpur-malaysia-16-december-1997/#:~:text=1.,ASEAN%20member%20states%20and%20China.

———. "Single Draft Code of Conduct in the South China Sea Negotiating Text." 27 July 2018. Document on file with the author.

———. "Treaty of Amity and Cooperation in Southeast Asia." Adopted in Indonesia (24 February 1976). https://asean.org/treaty-amity-cooperation-southeast-asia-indonesia-24-february-1976/.

Austin, Greg. *China's Ocean Frontier: International Law, Military Force, and National Development.* Sydney: Allen & Unwin, 1998.

Bao Yinan [包毅楠]. "An Empirical Analysis of the International Law of US Warships Trespassing in the Adjacent Sea Areas of China's South China Sea Islands [美国军舰擅闯我国南海岛礁邻近 海域的国际法实证分析]." *Pacific Journal* [太平洋学报] 27, no. 6 (2019): 52–63.

Beckman, Robert C. "International Law, UNCLOS, and the South China Sea." In *Beyond Territorial Disputes in the South China Sea: Legal Frameworks for the Joint Development of Hydrocarbon Resources,* edited by Ian Townsend-Gault, Clive Schofield, Tara Davenport, and Leonardo Bernard. Cheltenham, UK: Edward Elgar Publishing, 2013, 47–92.

Beckman, Robert C., and Tara Davenport. "CLCS Submissions and Claims in the SCS." In *The South China Sea: Towards a Region of Peace, Security, and Cooperation,* edited by Tran Truong Thuy. Hanoi: The Gioi Publishers, 2011.

———. "The EEZ Regime: Reflections After 30 Years." *Law of the Sea Institute Conference: Securing the Ocean for the Next Generation.* Berkeley, CA: University of California, 2012.

Bellacqua, James, and Josiah Case. "PRC Media Baseline: Evolution of PRC Media, Official Narratives on USN SCS FONOPs (2015–2021). *Center for Naval Analyses,* DIM-2021-U-029153 (March 2021).

Beijing Review. "Speech by Han Nianlong, Head of the Government Delegation of China, at the Fourth Plenary Meeting of the Sino-Vietnamese Negotiations at the Vice-Foreign Minister Level." *Beijing Review* 22, no. 21 (25 May 1979): 17.

Bentley, Scott. "Malaysia's 'Special Relationship' with China and the SCS: Not So Special Anymore." *The ASAN Forum,* 31 July 2015. http://www.theasanforum.org/malaysias-special-relationship-with-china-and-the-south-china-sea-not-so-special-anymore/.

———. "Mapping the Nine-Dash Line: Recent Incidents Involving Indonesia in the SCS." *ASPI The Strategist,* 29 October 2013. https://www.aspistrategist.org.au/mapping-the-nine-dash-line-recent-incidents-involving-indonesia-in-the-south-china-sea/.

———. "Maritime Fulcrum of the Indo-Pacific: Indonesia and Malaysia Respond to China's Creeping Expansion in the South China Sea." *CMSI Red Book*, no. 17 (2022). https://digital-commons.usnwc.edu/cmsi-red-books/17/.

Bernhardt, Rudolf. *Custom and Treaty in the Law of the Sea*, vol. 205, *Collected Courses of the Hague Academy of Law*. Leiden: Nijhoff, 1987.

Bernini, Elana. "Chinese Kidnapping of Vietnamese Fishermen in the SCS: A Primary Source Analysis." *CSIS* Asia Maritime Transparency Initiative, 14 September 2017. https://amti.csis.org/chinese-kidnapping-primary -source/.

Blum, Yehuda Zvi. *Historic Titles in International Law*. The Hague: Martinus Nijhoff, 1965.

Bodansky, David M. "The Concept of Customary International Law." *Michigan Journal of International Law* 16, no. 3 (1995): 667–679.

Bosco, Joseph. "Two US Carriers Through the Taiwan Strait in 48 Years—Time For More." *The Hill*, 21 July 2020. https://thehill.com/opinion/international/ 508167-two-us-carriers-through-the-taiwan-strait-in-48-years-time-for-more.

Bradford, Anu, and Eric Posner. "Universal Exceptionalism in International Law." *Harvard International Law Journal* 52, no. 1 (2011): 1–54.

Brilmayer, Lea, and Natalie Klein. "Land and Sea: Two Sovereignty Regimes in Search of a Common Denominator." *NYU Journal of International Law and Politics*, no. 33 (2001): 703–768.

Brunei Darussalam Ministry of Foreign Affairs. "Statement on the South China Sea." 20 July 2020. http://www.mfa.gov.bn/Lists/Press%20Room/news.aspx ?id=841&source=http://www.mfa.gov.bn/site/home.aspx.

Buga, Irina. "Between Stability and Change in the Law of the Sea Convention: Subsequent Practice, Treaty Modification, and Regime Interaction." In *The Oxford Handbook of the Law of the Sea*, edited by Donald Rothwell et al. New York: Oxford University Press, 2015, 46–68.

Bull, Hedley. *The Anarchical Society: A Study of Order in World Politics*. New York: Columbia University Press, 1977.

———. "The Revolt Against the West." In *The Expansion of International Society*, edited by Hedley Bull and Adam Watson. Oxford: Oxford University Press, 1984, 217–228.

Buszynski, Leszek. "ASEAN, the Declaration on Conduct, and the South China Sea." *Contemporary Southeast Asia* 25, no. 3 (2003): 343–362.

Byers, Michael. *Custom, Power, and the Power of Rules: International Relations and Customary International Law*. New York: Cambridge University Press, 1999.

Cable, James. *Gunboat Diplomacy, 1919–1991*. 3rd ed. Basingstoke, UK: Macmillan, 1994.

Cai Congyan. *The Rise of China and International Law: Taking Chinese Exceptionalism Seriously*. New York: Oxford University Press, 2019.

Cai Dingjian [蔡定剑]. *History and Reform—The Process of New China's Legal Construction* [历史与变革—新中国法制建设的历程]. Beijing: China Politics and Law University Press, 1999.

Caixin. "Department of Defense Responded That 'Chinese Warships Appeared in Waters Near Alaska' During the US Test of THAAD [国防部回应'美国测试'萨德'时中国军舰出现在阿拉斯加附近水域]." Caixin [财新], 24 July 2017. https://international.caixin.com/2017-07-24/101121272.html.

Canada Ministry of Foreign Affairs. "Statement on the SCS Arbitration." 21 July 2016. https://www.canada.ca/en/global-affairs/news/2016/07/canadian-statement-on-south-china-sea-arbitration.html.

Carlson, Allen. Unifying China, Integrating with the World: Securing Chinese Sovereignty in the Reform Era. Stanford: Stanford University Press, 2005.

Carr, Edward Hallett. The Twenty Years' Crisis 1919–1939: An Introduction to the Study of International Relations. Reissue. London: Palgrave Macmillan, 2016.

Carrai, Maria Adele. Sovereignty in China: A Genealogy of a Concept Since 1840. Cambridge: Cambridge University Press, 2019.

Carter, David B., and H. E. Goemans. "The Making of the Territorial Order: New Borders and the Emergence of Interstate Conflict." International Organization 65, no. 2 (2011): 275–309.

Cassel, Par Kristoffer. Grounds of Judgment: Extraterritoriality and Imperial Power in Nineteenth-Century China and Japan. Oxford: Oxford University Press, 2012.

Cassese, Antonio, and Joseph Weiler, eds. Change and Stability in International Law-Making. Berlin: De Gruyter, 1988.

CCP Central Committee. "Decision of the Central Committee of the CCP on Several Major Issues Concerning the Comprehensive Promotion of Governing the Country by Law [中共中央关于全面推进依法治国若干重大问题的决定]." Xinhua [新华], 28 October 2014. http://www.gov.cn/zhengce/2014-10/28/content_2771946.htm.

———. "Opinions of the Central Committee of Political and Legal Affairs on the Implementation of the Education and Training Program for Excellent Legal Talents [中央政法委员会关于实施卓越法律人才教育培养计划的若干意见]." Xinhua [新华], 23 December 2011. http://www.moe.gov.cn/srcsite/A08/moe_739/s6550/201112/t20111223_168354.html.

CCP Central Committee, and PRC State Council. "Instructions of the Central Committee of the Communist Party of China and the State Council on Relaxing Policies and Accelerating the Development of the Fisheries Industry [中共中央、国务院关于放宽政策、加速发展水产业的指示]" (March 1985).

———. "Several Opinions of the Central Committee of the CCP and the State Council on Establishing a Land and Space Planning System and Supervising Its Implementation [中共中央 国务院关于建立国土空间规划体系并监督实施的若干意见]" (May 2019). http://www.gov.cn/zhengce/2019-05/23/content_5394187.htm.

Chan, Minnie. "China-US Close Encounters 'Raise Conflict Risk in SCS.'" South China Morning Post. 16 June 2020. https://www.scmp.com/news/china/military/article/3089312/china-us-close-encounters-raise-conflict-risk-south-china-sea.

Chang Ching. "Why Is There No South China Sea Air Defense Identification Zone?" *South China Sea Probing Initiative*, 23 November 2020.

Charney, Jonathan I. "Central East Asian Maritime Boundaries and the Law of the Sea." *American Journal of International Law* 89, no. 4 (1995): 729–749.

———. "Universal International Law." *American Journal of International Law* 87, no. 4 (1993): 529–551.

Chayes, Abram, and Antonia Handler Chayes. "On Compliance." *International Organization* 47, no. 2 (1993): 175–205.

Chen Caiyun [陈彩云]. "Blue Territory Shout-Out—Analysis of the Meaning and Necessity of Our Country's Present Maritime Rights and Interests Protection [蓝色国土的呼唤———当前我国维护海洋权益的必要性和意义分析]." *Peaceful Society* [和平社会], no. 10 (2009): 147–148.

Chen Degong [陈德恭]. *Modern International Law of the Sea* [现代国际海洋法]. 2nd ed. Beijing: Ocean Press, 2009.

Chen Degong [陈德恭], and Gao Zhiguo [高之国]. "New Development of International Maritime Law [国际海洋法的新发展]." *Maritime Development* [海洋开发], no. 1 (1985): 42–49.

Chen Qi. "Expansion and Military Deployment on Vietnamese-Occupied Features in the Spratly Islands." *South China Sea Strategic Situation Probing Initiative*, 6 April 2021. http://www.scspi.org/sites/default/files/expansion_and _military_deployment_on_vietnamese-occupied_features_in_the_spratly _islands_0.pdf.

Chen, Titus Chih-chieh. "Capped Socialization: How Have International Norms Changed China, 1860–2007." PhD diss., University of California, Irvine, 2008.

Chen Wenhui [陈文辉]. "China's Voice in International Rule-Making [在国际规则制定中发出中国声音]." *People's Daily* [人民日报], 1 April 2015. http://opinion .people.com.cn/n/2015/0401/c1003–26780246.html.

Chen Yixin [陈一新]. "Xi Jinping Thought on Ruling by Law Is the Latest Achievement in the Sinicization of Marxism [习近平法治思想是马克思主义中国化最新成果]." *People's Daily* [人民日报], 30 December 2020. http://sfj.jcgov.gov .cn/sfdt/stxx/202012/t20201230_1327940.shtml.

Cheng Bin. "Custom: The Future of General State Practice in a Divided World." In *The Structure and Process of International Law: Essays in Legal Philosophy, Doctrine, and Theory*, edited by R. St. J. MacDonald and Douglas M. Johnston. The Hague: Martinus Nijhoff, 1983, 513–544.

Cheng Tao. "Communist China and the Law of the Sea." *American Journal of International Law* 63, no. 1 (1969): 47–73.

Chesterman, Simon. "Asia's Ambivalence About International Law." Chapter 2 in *The Oxford Handbook of International Law in Asia and the Pacific*, edited by Simon Chesterman, Hisashi Owada, and Ben Saul. Oxford: Oxford University Press, 2019.

China Academy of Sciences [中国科学院]. *Research Report on Comprehensive Survey of the Spratly Islands and Nearby Maritime Areas* [南沙群岛及其邻近还去综合调查研究报告]. Beijing: China Sciences Press, 1989.

China Central Television. "南海纪行 [South China Sea Travel Notes], Part 4," December 2013. http://news.cntv.cn/special/nhjx/.

China Coast Guard. "Bright Sword 2020: At the End of the Moratorium Season, the Coast Guard's 'Bright Sword' to Protect Resources [亮剑2020 伏休季结束 海警'亮剑'护资源]." *China Coast Guard WeChat* [中国海警微信], 27 September 2020. https://mp.weixin.qq.com/s/Xc6T3HYgWksOZaHKzkOnWQ.

China Fisheries. "The 'China Fisheries Bright Sword 2020' Series of Special Enforcement Action Program Issued [《"中国渔政亮剑2020"系列专项执法行动方案》印发]." *China Fisheries* [中国水产], no. 4 (2020): 16–20.

———. "'Thirteenth Five-Year Plan' Fisheries Law Enforcement Has Been Effective ['十三五' 渔政执法成效显著]." *China Fisheries* [中国水产], no. 2 (2021): 8.

China Geographical Names Committee [中国地名委员会]. "The China Geographical Names Committee Authorized to Publish Some Standard Place Names of the South China Sea Islands [中国地名委员会受权公布我国南海诸岛部分标准地名]." *Bulletin of the State Council of China*, no. 10 (April 1983): 452–463.

China Global Television Network. "China Lodges Solemn Representations over Passage of Canadian Warship Through Taiwan Strait." CGTN, 29 October 2020. https://news.cgtn.com/news/2020–10–29/China-lodges-solemn-representations-over-warship-passing-Taiwan-Strait-UZ3OGNlZAI/index.html.

China National Offshore Oil Company (CNOOC), Ltd. "Annual Report 2019." 25 March 2020. https://www.cnoocltd.com/attach/0/f6a7aa6b93294582889a1b0aec07c8fi.pdf.

———. "Annual Report 2020." 8 April 2021. https://www.cnoocltd.com/attach/0/c63efe2e72b84001bf234fcc38d836ff.pdf.

———. "Notification of Part of Open Blocks in Waters Under Jurisdiction of the PRC Available for Foreign Cooperation in the Year 2012." Press Release, 23 June 2012.

China Ocean News [中国海洋报]. "Forum Marking 10th Anniversary of Our State's Ratification of UNCLOS Held in Beijing [纪念我国批准《联合国海洋法公约》十周年座谈会在京召开]." *China Ocean News* [中国海洋报], 17 May 2006. http://www.cso.org.cn/Xhdt/xuehuitongzhi/2013/0507/969.html.

———. "Pushing China's Blue Economy from Concept to Practice [推动蓝色经济由理念走向实践]." *China Ocean News* [中国海洋报], 5 July 2016. http://epaper.oceanol.com/shtml/zghyb/20160705/61518.shtml.

China Society of International Law (CSIL). "The South China Sea Arbitration Awards: A Critical Study." *China Journal of International Law*, 17, no. 2 (2018): 207–748.

Chinese (Taiwan) Society of International Law. "In the Matter of an Arbitration Under Annex VII to the 1982 United Nations Convention on the Law of the Sea." *Amicus Curiae* submission to PCA Case no. 2013–19 between the Republic of the Philippines and the People's Republic of China, 23 March

2016. http://csil.org.tw/home/wp-content/uploads/2016/03/SCSTF-Amicus -Curiae-Brief-final.pdf.

Chiu Hungdah. "China and the Law of the Sea Convention." In *China in the Global Community*, edited by James C. Hsiung and Samuel S. Kim. New York: Praeger Publishers, 1981: 187–215.

———. "China and the Question of the Territorial Sea." *Maryland Journal of International Law* 1, no. 1 (1975): 29–78.

———. "Chinese Attitudes Toward International Law in the Post-Mao Era, 1978–1987." *International Lawyer* 21, no. 4 (1987): 1127–1165.

Chubb, Andrew. "Chinese Nationalism and the 'Gray Zone.'" *CMSI Red Book*, no. 16 (2021). https://digital-commons.usnwc.edu/cmsi-red-books/16/.

———. "International Law as Driver of Confrontation: UNCLOS and China's Policy in the South China Sea." Working Paper for *China's Quest for Sovereignty: Workshop on International Law in China in a Historical Perspective.* Princeton University, 29 May 2018.

———. "PRC Assertiveness in the South China Sea: Measuring Continuity and Change, 1970–2015." *International Security* 45, no. 3 (2021): 79–121.

———. "Xi Jinping and China's Maritime Policy." *Brookings Institution, 22 January 2019.* https://www.brookings.edu/articles/xi-jinping-and-chinas -maritime-policy/.

Chung, Chris P. C. "Drawing the U-Shaped Line: China's Claim in the South China Sea, 1946–1974." *Modern China* 42, no 1 (2016): 38–72.

Churchill, Robin R. "The 1982 United Nations Convention on the Law of the Sea." In *Oxford Handbook of the Law of the Sea,* edited by Donald Rothwell et al. New York: Oxford University Press, 2015, 24–45.

Churchill, Robin R., and Vaughan Lowe. *The Law of the Sea.* London: Manchester University Press, 1999.

Cohen, Jerome A. "Chinese Attitudes Toward International Law—And Our Own." *Proceedings of the American Society of International Law at Its Annual Meeting,* no. 61 (1967): 108–116.

———. "How Dangerous Are Sino-Japanese Tensions." *ChinaFile,* 1 August 2013. https://www.chinafile.com/conversation/how-dangerous-are-sino-japanese -tensions.

———. "Law and Power in China's International Relations." *New York University Journal of International Law and Politics,* no. 52 (2019): 123–165.

Cohen, Jerome A., and Hungdah Chiu. *China's Practice of International Law: Some Case Studies.* Cambridge: Harvard University Press, 1972.

———. *People's China and International Law: A Documentary Study.* Princeton: Princeton University Press, 1974.

Colgan, Jeff D., and Robert O. Keohane. "The Liberal Order Is Rigged." *Foreign Affairs,* no. 96 (2017): 36–44.

Colson, David. "The Delimitation of the Outer Continental Shelf Between Neighboring States." *American Journal of International Law* 97, no. 1 (2003): 91–107.

Commission on Extraterritoriality in China. "Summary and Recommendations of the Report of the Commission on Extraterritoriality in China." *American Journal of International Law* 21, no. 3 (1927): 58–66.

Commission on the Limits of the Continental Shelf (CLCS). "Joint Submission by Malaysia and the Socialist Republic of Viet Nam" (6 May 2009). https://www.un.org/depts/los/clcs_new/submissions_files/submission_mysvnm_33_2009.htm.

———. "Partial Submission by Malaysia in the South China Sea," 12 December 2019. https://www.un.org/depts/los/clcs_new/submissions_files/submission_mys_12_12_2019.html.

———. "PRC Preliminary Information Indicative of the Outer Limits of the Continental Shelf Beyond 200 Nautical Miles" (13 May 2009). https://www.un.org/Depts/los/clcs_new/submissions_files/preliminary/chn2009preliminaryinformation_english.pdf.

———. "Republic of Korea Partial Submission to the Commission on the Limits of the Continental Shelf: Executive Summary," 26 December 2012. https://www.un.org/depts/los/clcs_new/submissions_files/kor65_12/executive_summary.pdf.

———. "Submission by the PRC Concerning the Outer Limits of the Continental Shelf Beyond 200 Nautical Miles in Part of the East China Sea." Executive Summary (14 December 2012). https://www.un.org/depts/los/clcs_new/submissions_files/chn63_12/executive%20summary_EN.pdf.

———. "Submission of Japan." 12 November 2008. https://www.un.org/depts/los/clcs_new/submissions_files/submission_jpn.htm.

Congressional Research Service. "China's Actions in South and East China Seas: Implications for US Interests—Background and Issues for Congress." *Congressional Research Service Report*, R42784 (31 January 2019).

Connelly, Aaron L. "Indonesia in the South China Sea: Going It Alone." *Lowy Institute*, 5 December 2016: https://www.lowyinstitute.org/publications/indonesia-south-china-sea-going-it-alone.

Cordesman, Anthony. "Chinese Strategy and Military Modernization in 2016." *CSIS*, 5 December 2016. https://csis-website-prod.s3.amazonaws.com/s3fs-public/publication/161208_Chinese_Strategy_Military_Modernization_2016.pdf.

Corne, Peter Howard. "Creation and Application of Law in the PRC." *American Journal of Comparative Law* 50, no. 2 (2002): 369–443.

Creemers, Rogier. "China's Constitutionalism Debate: Content, Context, and Implications." *China Journal*, no. 74 (July 2015): 91–109.

Cui Wenyi [崔文毅]. "981 Drilling Platform Operations [981钻井平台作业]." *Xinhua* [新华], 16 July 2014. http://world.people.com.cn/n/2014/0716/c1002-25290823.html.

D'Amato, Anthony A. *The Concept of Custom in International Law.* Ithaca: Cornell University Press, 1971.

———. "The Concept of Special Custom in International Law." *American Journal of International Law* 63, no. 2 (1969): 211–223.

———. "Groundwork for International Law." *American Journal of International Law* 108, no. 4 (2014): 650–679.

Danilenko, Gennady M. "The Theory of International Customary Law." *German Yearbook of International Law* 31 (1988): 9–47.

Dao Ba Viet. "Some Solutions for Protecting Sovereignty over Sea and Islands in the New Situation." *National Defence Journal* (March 2021). http://tapchiqptd .vn/en/research-and-discussion/some-solutions-for-protecting-sovereignty -over-sea-and-islands-in-the-new-situation/16892.html.

Davenport, Tara. "The China-Japan Dispute over Entitlement in the East China Sea: Legal Issues and Prospects for Resolution." In *The Limits of Maritime Jurisdiction,* edited by Clive Schofield et al. Boston: Martinus Nijhoff, 2014, 297–324.

———. "Joint Development in Asia: Some Valuable Lessons Learned." In *Energy Resources in Asia: Legal Regimes and Cooperation,* edited by Clive Schofield. NBR Special Report, no. 37. Seattle: National Bureau of Asian Research, 2012.

deLisle, Jacques. "China's Approach to International Law: A Historical Perspective." *Proceedings of the Annual Meeting of the American Society of International Law* 94 (2000): 267–275.

———. "Law in the China Model 2.0: Legality, Developmentalism, and Leninism Under Xi Jinping." *Journal of Contemporary China* 26, no. 103 (2017): 68–84.

———. "States of Exception in an Exceptional State." In *Emergency Powers in Asia Exploring the Limits of Legality,* edited by Arun K. Thiruvengadam and Victor V. Ramraj. Cambridge: Cambridge University Press, 2009, 342–390.

DeTréglodé, Benoît. "Maritime Boundary Delimitation and Sino-Vietnamese Cooperation in the Gulf of Tonkin (1994–2016)." *China Perspectives,* no. 3 (2016): 33–41.

Deng Zhihui [邓志慧], and Zhong Zhuo [钟焯]. "On World Oceans Day, Feel Xi Jinping's 'Blue Faith' in Building a Maritime Power [世界海洋日感受习近平建设海洋强国'蓝色信念']." *People's Daily,* 7 June 2020. http://politics.people .com.cn/n1/2020/0607/c1001-31738010.html.

Ding Duo [丁铎], and Yang Li [杨力]. "Exploration of the Legal Status of Traditional Fishing Rights in the International Law of the Sea [国际海洋法上传统捕鱼权法律地位探析]." *International Law Research* [国际法研究], no. 1 (2020): 44–64.

Dong Jiawei [董加伟]. "On the Protection of Traditional Fishing Rights Under the Framework of China-Korea and China-Japan Fisheries Agreements [论中韩、中日渔业协定框架下的传统捕鱼权保障]." *Northeast Asia Forum* [东北亚论坛], no. 4 (2020): 35–47.

Donnelly, Eric. "The United States–China EP-3 Incident: Legality and Realpolitik." *Journal of Conflict & Security Law* 9, no. 1 (2004): 25–42.

Downs, Erica S. "The Chinese Energy Security Debate." *China Quarterly* 37, no. 4 (2004): 55–69.

Downs, Erica, and Phillip C. Saunders. "Legitimacy and the Limits of Nationalism: China and the Diaoyu Islands." *International Security* 23, no. 3 (1999): 114–146.

Downs, George W., David M. Rocke, and Peter N. Barsoom. "Is the Good News About Compliance Good News About Cooperation?" *International Organization* 50, no. 3 (1996): 379–406.

Drifte, Reinhard. "The Japan-China Confrontation over the Senkaku/Diaoyu Islands—Between 'Shelving' and 'Dispute Escalation.'" *Asia-Pacific Journal* 12, no. 30 (2014): 1–61.

Duan Dang. "China's Latest Incursion into Malaysia's Waters." *South China Sea Brief,* 25 September 2021. https://scsbrief.substack.com/p/chinas-latest -incursion-in-malaysias.

———. "How Did Indonesia Respond to China's Incursion into the Natuna Sea?" *South China Sea Brief,* 19 September 2021.

———. "What Is Happening in Indonesia's Natuna Sea?" *South China Sea Brief,* 18 September 2021. https://scsbrief.substack.com/p/what-is-happening-in -indonesias-natuna.

Duan Zhaoxian [段昭显]. "On the Strategic Objectives of Turning China into a Maritime Power [论建设海洋强国的 战略目标]." *China Military Science* [中国军事科学], no. 3 (2013): 24.

Dunoff, Jeffrey L., and Mark A. Pollack. *Interdisciplinary Perspectives on International Law and International Relations: The State of the Art.* New York: Cambridge University Press, 2013.

Dunoff, Jeffrey L., Steven R. Ratner, and David Wippman. *International Law: Norms, Actors, Process. A Problem-Oriented Approach.* 2nd ed. New York: Aspen Publishers, 2006.

Dutton, Peter A. "Caelum Liberum: Air Defense Identification Zones Outside Sovereign Airspace." *American Journal of International Law* 103, no. 4 (2009): 691–709.

———, ed. "Military Activities in the EEZ: A US-China Dialogue on Security and International Law in the Maritime Commons." *CMSI Red Book,* no. 3 (2010). https://digital-commons.usnwc.edu/cmsi-red-books/3/.

———. "Scouting, Signaling, and Gatekeeping: Chinese Naval Operations in Japanese Waters and the International Law Implications." *CMSI Red Book,* no. 2 (2009): 1–32.

———. "Testing the Boundaries: When Are International Institutional Dispute Resolution Mechanisms Effective to Resolve Maritime Disputes?" *NYU Law School US-Asia Law Institute* (2020).

———. "Three Disputes and Three Objectives." *Naval War College Review* 64, no. 4 (2011): 42–67.

Dutton, Peter A., and Ryan D. Martinson. "Beyond the Wall: Chinese Far Seas Operations." *CMSI Red Book,* no. 14 (2015): https://digital-commons.usnwc .edu/cmsi-red-books/14/.

———. "China's Distant-Ocean Survey Activities: Implications for US National Security." *CMSI China Maritime Report,* no. 3 (2018).

Economist. "Oil on Troubled Waters: Two Case Studies in a Disputed Sea." *Economist,* 24 January 2015.

Encyclopedia of China (Editorial Board). *Encyclopedia of China: Jurisprudence* [中国大百科全: 法学]. Beijing: Encyclopedia of China Publishing House, 1982.

Endicott, Timothy A. O. *Vagueness in Law.* Oxford: Oxford University Press, 2000.

Energy Voice. "Indonesia's Medco Makes Offshore Block B Investment." *Energy Voice,* 14 April 2021. https://www.energyvoice.com/oilandgas/asia/314662/indonesias-medco-makes-offshore-block-b-investment/.

Erickson, Andrew S., and Lyle J. Goldstein. "Chinese Perspectives on Maritime Transformation." Introduction in *China Goes to Sea: Maritime Transformation in Comparative Perspective,* edited by Andrew S. Erickson, Lyle J. Goldstein, and Carnes Lord. Annapolis, MD: Naval Institute Press, 2009.

Erickson, Andrew S., and Ryan D. Martinson. "Records Expose China's Maritime Militia at Whitsun Reef." *Foreign Policy,* 29 March 2021. https://foreignpolicy.com/2021/03/29/china-militia-maritime-philippines-whitsunreef/.

Evans, Malcolm D. "Maritime Boundary Delimitation." In *The Oxford Handbook of the Law of the Sea,* edited by Donald Rothwell et al. New York: Oxford University Press, 2015, 254–279.

Fabi, Randy. "Indonesia to Step Up Oil Exploration, Fishing in SCS Waters." Reuters, 29 June 2016. https://www.reuters.com/article/us-southchinasea-indonesia/indonesia-to-step-up-oil-exploration-fishing-in-south-china-sea-waters-idUSKCN0ZF10Y.

Fairbank, John King. "Chinese Diplomacy and the Treaty of Nanking, 1842." *Journal of Modern History* 12, no. 4 (March 1940): 585–588.

———. *The Chinese World Order: Traditional China's Foreign Relations.* Cambridge: Harvard University Press, 1968.

———. "Maritime and Continental in China's History." Introduction in *The Cambridge History of China,* vol. 12, *Republican China (1912–1949).* Cambridge: Cambridge University Press, 1983.

———. *Trade and Diplomacy on the China Coast: The Opening of the Treaty Ports, 1842–1854.* Cambridge: Harvard University Press, 1964.

Fan Xiaoting [范晓婷], and Lin Tingting [罗婷婷]. "Analysis of the Legal Basis of Maritime Rights Protection Law Enforcement [海洋维权执法的法律依据质变]. *Administration and Law* [行政与法], no 12 (2009): 77–81.

Fang Baoyu [方宝宇], and Wang Junjie [王俊杰]. "The Navy Provides Fuel and Resource Guarantees to Coast Guard Maritime Law Enforcement Vessels [海军为海景海上执法船只提供油科保障]." *People's Navy* [人民海军], 21 June 2014, 1.

Fang Xiao [方晓]. "China Strengthens Coordination of Maritime Rights Maintenance [中国加强海洋维权统筹协调]." *Oriental Morning Post* [东方早报], 5 February 2013. http://news.sina.com.cn/c/2013-02-05/063926206544.shtml.

Feinerman, James V. "Chinese Participation in the International Legal Order: Rogue Elephant or Team." *China Quarterly,* no. 141 (1995): 186–210.

Feng Liang [冯梁], and Duan Tingzhi [段延志]. "The Characteristics of China's Sea Geosecurity and Maritime Security Strategy in the New Century [中国海洋地缘安全特征与新世纪海上安全战略]." *China Military Science* [中国军事科学], no. 1 (2007): 22–29.

Feng Liang [冯梁], and Zhang Xiaolin [张晓林]. "On the Navy's Strategic Use in Peacetime [论和平时期海军的战略运用]." *China Military Science* [中国军事科学], no. 3 (2001): 77–84.

Foot, Rosemary. "China in the ASEAN Regional Forum: Organizational Processes and Domestic Modes of Thought." *Asian Survey* 38, no. 5 (1998): 425–440.

Finnemore, Martha, and Stephen J. Toope. "Alternatives to 'Legalization': Richer Views of Law and Politics." *International Organization* 55, no. 3 (2001): 743–758.

Fitzmaurice, G. "Vae Victis or Woe to the Negotiators—Your Treaty or Our Interpretation of It." *American Journal of International Law* 65, no. 2 (1971): 358–373.

Franck, Thomas M. *The Power of Legitimacy Among Nations.* New York: Oxford University Press, 1990.

Franck, Thomas M., and Arun K. Thiruvengadam. "International Law and Constitution-Making." *Chinese Journal of International Law* 2, no. 2 (2003): 467–518.

Franckx, Erik, and Marco Benatar. "Dots and Lines in the South China Sea: Insights from the Law of Map Evidence." *Asian Journal of International Law* 2, no. 1 (2011): 89–118.

Fravel, M. Taylor. "China's Strategy in the South China Sea." *Contemporary Southeast Asia* 33, no. 3 (2011): 292–319.

———. "Explaining Stability in the Senkaku (Diaoyu) Islands Dispute." In *Getting the Triangle Straight: Managing China-Japan-US Relations,* edited by Gerald Curtis, Ryosei Kokubun, and Wang Jisi. Washington, DC: Brookings Institution Press, 2010, 144–164.

———. *Strong Borders, Secure Nation: Cooperation and Conflict in China's Territorial Disputes.* Princeton: Princeton University Press, 2008.

———. "Traditional Fishing Grounds and China's Historic Rights Claims in the SCS." NBR Maritime Awareness Project, 11 July 2016. https://www.nbr.org/publication/traditional-fishing-grounds-and-chinas-historic-rights-claims-in-the-south-china-sea/.

———. "Xi Jinping's Overlooked Revelation on China's Maritime Disputes." *Diplomat,* 15 August 2013. http://thediplomat.com/2013/08/xi-jinpings-overlooked-revelation-on-chinas-maritime-disputes/?all=true.

Frieden, Jeffry, David A. Lake, and Kenneth Schultz. *World Politics: Interests, Interactions, Institutions.* New York: W.W. Norton, 2018.

Friedheim, Robert L. *Negotiating the New Ocean Regime.* Columbia, SC: University of South Carolina Press, 1993.

Fu Kuenchen [傅崐成]. *Research on the Legal Status of the South (China) Sea* [南中國海法律地位之研究]. Taipei: Sanmin Agency Press, 1995.

Fulton, Thomas W. *The Sovereignty of the Sea: An Historical Account.* Clark, NJ: Lawbook Exchange, 2010.

Gan Jun [甘俊]. "A Far Seas Training Formation from the South Sea Fleet Returns to Port, Deputy Political Commissar of the Navy Wang Sentai Meets Them Pierside and Gives a Speech [南海舰队远海训练编队返港, 海军副政委王森泰到码头迎接并讲话]." *People's Navy* [人民海军], 12 February 2014, 1.

Gao Jianjun. "A Note on the 2008 Cooperation Consensus Between China and Japan in the East China Sea." *Ocean Development and International Law* 40, no. 3 (2009): 291–292.

———. "The Okinawa Trough Issue in the Continental Shelf Delimitation Disputes within the East China Sea." *Chinese Journal of International Law* 9, no. 1 (2010): 143–177.

Gao Zhiguo [高之国]. "China and the Law of the Sea." In *Freedom of Seas, Passage Rights, and the 1982 Law of the Sea Convention,* edited by Myron H. Nordquist, John Norton Moore, and Tommy T. B. Koh. Leiden: Martinus Nijhoff Publishers, 2009, 265–307.

———. "Remarks on the Launch of the Journal of Boundary and Ocean Studies [《边界与海洋研究》发刊词]." *Journal of Boundary and Ocean Studies* [边界与海洋研究] 1, no. 1 (2016): 5–6.

———. "The South China Sea: From Conflict to Cooperation?" *Ocean Development and International Law* 25, no. 3 (1994): 345–359.

Gao Zhiguo, and Jia Bingbing. "The Nine-Dash Line in the South China Sea: History, Status, and Implications." *American Journal of International Law* 107, no. 1 (2013): 98–124.

Gao Zhiguo [高之国], Jia Yu [贾宇], and Zhang Haiwen [张海文], eds. *Research on the Development Trends in the International Law of the Sea* [国际海洋发展趋势研究]. Beijing: Ocean Press, 2007.

Gao, Zhiguo, and Jilu Wu. "Key Issues in the East China Sea: A Status Report and Recommended Approaches." In *Seabed Petroleum in Northeast Asia: Conflict or Cooperation?* edited by Selig S. Harrison. Washington, DC: Woodrow Wilson International Center for Scholars, 2005, 32–38.

Garver, John W. "China's Push Through the South China Sea: The Interaction of Bureaucratic and National Interests." *China Quarterly,* no. 132 (1992): 999–1028.

Genba Koichiro. "Japan-China Relations at a Crossroads." *International Herald Tribune,* 20 November 2012. https://www.nytimes.com/2012/11/21/opinion/koichiro-genba-japan-china-relations-at-a-crossroads.html?_r=0.

Gilpin, Robert. *War and Change in World Politics.* Cambridge: Cambridge University Press, 1981.

Ginsburg, Tom. "Authoritarian International Law?" *American Journal of International Law* 114, no. 2 (2020): 221–260.

———. "Eastphalia and Asian Regionalism." *University of California, Davis Law Review* 44, no. 2 (2010): 101–119.

———. "Eastphalia as a Return to Westphalia." *Indiana Journal of Global Legal Studies* 17, no. 1 (2010): 27–45.

Goddard, Stacey. *When Might Makes Right: Rising Powers and World Order*. Ithaca, NY: Cornell University Press, 2018.

Goldrick, James. "Australia's Naval Presence in the South China Sea Is Nothing New." *Australian Strategic Policy Institute,* 5 February 2021. https://www .aspistrategist.org.au/australias-naval-presence-in-the-south-china-sea-is -nothing-new/.

Goldsmith, Jack L., and Eric A. Posner. *The Limits of International Law*. Oxford: Oxford University Press, 2006.

———. "A Theory of Customary International Law." *University of Chicago Law Review* 66, no. 4 (1999): 1113–1177.

Gomez, Jim. "Chinese Diplomat Outlines Limits to Freedom of Navigation." *Military Times,* 12 August 2015. https://www.militarytimes.com/news/ your-military/2015/08/12/chinese-diplomat-outlines-limits-to-freedom-of -navigation/.

Grandview Institution [国观智库]. "Is It Necessary for China to Change Its Domestic Legislation on Innocent Passage for Warships in Territorial Waters [中国是否有必要改变外国军舰领海无害通过国内立法]?" 15 August 2019. https://www.sohu.com/a/333845596_100124379.

Greenfield, Jeannette. *China's Practice in the Law of the Sea*. Oxford: Clarendon, 1992.

Gu Xiudong [贾秀东]. "Upgrading the Diaoyu Islands Situation, Japan Will Eat Its Own Fruit [升级钓鱼岛事态 日本将自食其果]." *People's Daily* [人民日报], 14 January 2016. http://www.81.cn/rd/2016–01/14/content_6856721.htm.

Guangdong Province. "Review and Approval of Nansha Special Fishing License [南沙专项捕捞许可证审核、审批]." Guangdong Department of Agriculture and Rural Affairs, 29 November 2019. http://gjzwfw.www.gov.cn/art/2019/ 11/29/art_4_92275106.html.

Guo Jing [郭静], and Liu Dan [刘丹]. "On the Archipelagic Regime and the Practice of Continental States in Outlying Archipelagos [论群岛制度与大陆国家远洋群岛的实践]." *Journal of South China Sea Studies* [南海学刊] 2, no. 2 (2016): 65–75.

Guo Rongxing. "Territorial Disputes and Seabed Petroleum Exploitation: Some Options for the East China Sea." Brookings Institution CNAPS Visiting Fellow Working Paper (Spring 2010): 1–36.

Guo Zhongyuan [郭中元], and Zou Ligang [邹立刚]. "Study on the Delineation of Straight Baseline from Mid-Ocean Archipelagos [洋中群岛划定直线基线问题研究]." *Hebei Legal Science* [河北法学] 37, no. 9 (September 2019): 130–139.

Guzman, Andrew. "Saving Customary International Law." *Michigan Journal of International Law* 27 (2005): 115–176.

Hakimi, Monica. "Making Sense of Customary International Law." *Michigan Law Review* 118, no. 8 (2020): 1487–1538.

———. "The Work of International Law." *Harvard International Law Journal* 58, no. 1 (2017): 1–46.

Han Depei, and Stephen Kanter. "Legal Education in China." *American Journal of Comparative Law* 32, no. 3 (1984): 543–582.

Hao Yen-ping, and Wang Erh-min. "Changing Chinese Views of Western Relations, 1840–1895." In *The Cambridge History of China*, vol. 11, edited by John King Fairbank. London: Cambridge University Press, 1978, 142–201.

Hart, HLA. *The Concept of Law.* New York: Oxford University Press, 1960.

Hathaway, Oona A. "Between Power and Principle: An Integrated Theory of International Law." *University of Chicago Law Review* 72, no. 2 (2005): 469–536.

———. "Why Do Countries Commit to Human Rights Treaties?" *Journal of Conflict Resolution* 51, no. 4 (2007): 588–621.

Haver, Zoe. "Sansha City in China's South China Sea Strategy: Building a System of Administrative Control." *CMSI China Maritime Report*, no. 12 (2021). https://digital-commons.usnwc.edu/cmsi-maritime-reports/12/.

Hayton, Bill. "Britain Is Right to Stand Up to China over Freedom of Navigation." *Chatham House*, 1 June 2018. https://www.chathamhouse.org/2018/06/britain-right-stand-china-over-freedom-navigation.

———. *The Invention of China.* New Haven: Yale University Press, 2020.

———. "The Modern Creation of China's 'Historic Rights' Claim in the South China Sea." *Asian Affairs* 49, no. 3 (2018): 370–382.

———. "The South China Sea in 2020." Statement Before the US-China Economic and Security Review Commission Hearing, 9 September 2020. https://www.uscc.gov/sites/default/files/2020–09/Hayton_Testimony.pdf.

———. *The South China Sea: The Struggle for Power in Asia.* New Haven: Yale University Press, 2014.

He Rong [贺荣]. "China's Participation in the Making of International Economic Rules [论中国司法参与国际经济规则的制定]." *International Legal Research* [国际法研究], no. 1 (2016): 3–15.

He Zhipeng. "International Law Debates in China: Traditional Issues and Emerging Fields." *Pacific Review* 33, nos. 3–4 (2020): 550–573.

Hindustan Times. "Indian Destroyer Warship in Qingdao to Help Chinese Navy Plan Mega Parade." *Hindustan Times*, 21 April 2019.

Hirose Hajime. "Japan's Effective Control of the Senkaku Islands." *SPF Review of Island Studies* (June 2013). https://www.spf.org/islandstudies/research/a00005.html.

Hirschman, Albert. *Exit, Voice, and Loyalty: Responses to Decline in Firms, Organizations, and States.* Cambridge: Harvard University Press, 1970.

Hollick, Ann L. *US Foreign Policy and the Law of the Sea.* Princeton: Princeton University Press, 1981.

Hong Nong, Li Jianwei, and Chen Pingping. "The Concept of Archipelagic State and the South China Sea: UNCLOS, State Practice, and Implication." *China Oceans Law Review* 1, no. 1 (2013): 209–239.

Howson, Nicholas C. "Can the West Learn from the Rest? The Chinese Legal
    Order's Hybrid Modernity." *Hastings International and Comparative Law
    Review* 2, no. 2 (2009): 815–830.
Hsü, Immanuel C. Y. *China's Entrance into the Family of Nations: The Diplomatic
    Phase, 1858–1880.* Cambridge: Harvard University Press, 1960.
Hu Bo [胡波]. *Chinese Maritime Power in the 21st Century: Strategic Planning, Policy,
    and Predictions,* edited by Geoffrey Till. New York: Routledge, 2020.
———. "On China's Important Maritime Interests [论中国的重要海洋利益]."
    Asia-Pacific Security and Maritime Affairs [亚太安全与海洋研究], no. 3 (2015):
    14–28.
———. "Sino-US Competition in the South China Sea: Power, Rules and Legiti-
    macy." *Journal of Chinese Political Science* 26 (2021): 485–504.
Hu Bo [胡波] and Zhu Feng [朱锋]. "Future Stability in the South China Sea De-
    pends on the Establishment of Regional Rules [未来南海局势稳定有赖区域
    规则的建立]." *World Knowledge* [世界知识], no. 16 (2018): 18–21.
Hu Jintao. "Work Report at the 18th Party Congress." Xinhua, 17 November
    2012. http://news.xinhuanet.com/english/special/18cpcnc/2012–11/17/
    c_131981259.htm.
Huang Huikang [黄惠康]. "Developments in International Law and Frontier
    Issues Worthy of Attention [国际法的发展动态及值得关注的前沿问题]."
    International Law Studies [国际法研究], no. 1 (2019). https://www.gmw.cn/
    xueshu/2020–03/31/content_33703044.htm.
———. "Ten Issues Worthy of Attention at the Forefront of the International Law
    of the Sea [国际海洋法前沿值得关注的十大问题]." *Journal of Boundary and
    Ocean Studies* 4, no. 1 (2019): 5–24.
Hunt, Katie, and Kathy Quiano. "China Allows Philippines Fishermen Access to
    Disputed Shoal in South China Sea." *CNN,* 31 October 2016. https://www
    .cnn.com/2016/10/31/asia/philippines-china-scarborough-shoal-fishermen/
    index.html.
Hurd, Ian. *How To Do Things with International Law.* Princeton: Princeton Univer-
    sity Press, 2017.
Ikenberry, G. John. *After Victory: Institutions, Strategic Restraint, and the Rebuilding
    of Order After Major Wars.* Princeton: Princeton University Press, 2001.
———. *Liberal Leviathan: The Origins, Crisis, and Transformation of the American
    World Order.* Princeton: Princeton University Press, 2011.
Ikenberry, G. John, and Daniel H. Nexon. "Hegemony Studies 3.0: The Dynamics
    of Hegemonic Orders." *Security Studies* 28, no. 3 (2019): 395–421.
International Energy Agency. "Offshore Energy Outlook." World Energy Outlook
    Series (May 2018). https://www.iea.org/reports/offshore-energy-outlook
    -2018.
International Institute for Strategic Studies. "Strengthening the Regional Order
    in the Asia-Pacific: Q&A." *IISS Shangri-la Dialogue,* 31 May 2015. https://www
    .iiss.org/events/shangri-la-dialogue/shangri-la-dialogue-2015.

International Law Association (ILA). "Baselines Under the International Law of the Sea: Final Report" (2018). https://www.ila-hq.org/images/ILA/DraftReports/DraftReport_Baselines.pdf.

———. "Statement of the Principles Applicable to the Formation of General Customary International Law." Final Report of the Committee on the Formation of Customary (General) International Law. London Conference (2000).

International Law Commission (ILC). "Draft Articles Concerning the Law of the Sea, with Commentaries." In *Yearbook of the International Law Commission,* vol. 2. UN Doc. A/3159 (1956).

———. "Identification of Customary International Law." *Analytical Guide to the Work of the ILC* (2018). http://legal.un.org/ilc/guide/1_13.shtml.

Ioffe, Olympiad S., and Peter B. Maggs. *Soviet Law in Theory and Practice.* New York: Oceana, 1983.

Japan. "Declarations Recognizing the Jurisdiction of the Court as Compulsory." International Court of Justice (6 October 2015). https://www.icj-cij.org/en/declarations/jp.

———. "Joint Press Conference by Minister for Foreign Affairs Masahiko Koumura and Minister of Economy, Trade, and Industry Akira Amari (Regarding Cooperation Between Japan and China in the East China Sea)." 18 June 2008. https://www.mofa.go.jp/announce/fm_press/2008/6/0618.html.

———. "June 2008 Agreement: Cooperation Between Japan and China in the East China Sea." Japan-China Joint Press Statement, 18 June 2008. https://www.mofa.go.jp/files/000091726.pdf.

———. Law on the Exclusive Economic Zone and Continental Shelf. Law No. 74. In *Law of the Sea Bulletin,* no. 35: 94–96.

———. "List of Deposited Charts." M.Z.N.61.2008.LOS, 14 March 2008: https://www.un.org/Depts/los/LEGISLATIONANDTREATIES/STATEFILES/JPN_Deposit_MZN61.html.

———. "White Paper on Fisheries: FY2016 Trends in Fisheries, FY2017 Fisheries Policy." Ministry of Agriculture, Forestry, and Fisheries (2017). https://www.maff.go.jp/e/data/publish/attach/pdf/index-68.pdf.

Japan Ministry of Foreign Affairs. "The Basic View on the Sovereignty over the Senkaku Islands." 8 May 2013. https://www.mofa.go.jp/region/asia-paci/senkaku/basic_view.html.

———. *Diplomatic Bluebook 2019.* https://www.mofa.go.jp/policy/other/bluebook/2019/html/index.html.

———. "Japan's Legal Position on the Development of Natural Resources in the East China Sea." 6 August 2015. https://www.mofa.go.jp/a_o/c_m1/page3e_000358.html.

———. "Maritime Platforms (x14 locations)." 22 July 2015. https://www.mofa.go.jp/files/000091724.pdf.

———. "Senkaku Islands Q&A." 13 April 2016. https://www.mofa.go.jp/region/asia-paci/senkaku/qa_1010.html.

———. "Status of Activities by Chinese Government Vessels and Chinese Fishing Vessels in Waters Surrounding the Senkaku Islands." 26 August 2016. https://www.mofa.go.jp/files/000180283.pdf.

———. "Takeshima: Definitive Clarifications as to Why Takeshima Is Japan's Territory!" Northeast Asia Division, Asian and Oceanian Affairs Bureau. March 2014.

———. "Trends in Chinese Government and Other Vessels in the Waters Surrounding the Senkaku Islands, and Japan's Response." 7 April 2021. https://www.mofa.go.jp/region/page23e_000021.html.

———. "Visit to Japan by Premier Zhu Rongji of the PRC, Overview and Evaluation." 17 October 2000. https://www.mofa.go.jp/region/asia-paci/china/pv0010/overview.html.

Japan Times. "Japan Had Plans to Sail MSDF Ship Near Chinese-Held Islet in the SCS." *Japan Times,* 21 November 2020. https://www.japantimes.co.jp/news/2020/11/21/national/japan-msdf-south-china-sea/.

Ji Guoxing [李国兴]. *China's Maritime Security and Maritime Jurisdiction* [中国的海洋安全和海域管辖]. Shanghai: Shanghai People's Press, 2009.

Jia Bingbing [贾兵兵]. "The Notion of Natural Prolongation in the Current Regime of the Continental Shelf: An Afterlife?" *Chinese Journal of International Law* 12, no. 1 (2013): 79–103.

———. "The Principle of the Domination of the Land over the Sea: A Historical Perspective on the Adaptability of the Law of the Sea to New Challenges." *German Yearbook of International Law,* no. 57 (2014): 1–32.

———. *Public International Law: Theory and Practice* [国际公法：理论与实践]. Beijing: Tsinghua University Press, 2015.

———. "The Relations Between Treaties and Custom." *Chinese Journal of International Law* 9, no. 1 (2010): 81–109.

———. "A Synthesis of the Notion of Sovereignty and the Ideal of the Rule of Law: Reflections on the Contemporary Chinese Approach to International Law." *German Yearbook of International Law,* no. 53 (2010): 11–61.

Jia Yu [贾宇]. "40 Years of Reform and Opening in Chinese Maritime Law Development [改革开放 40 年中国海洋法治的发展]." *Journal of Boundary and Ocean Studies* [边界与海洋研究] 4, no. 4 (2019): 5–33.

———. "China's Historic Rights in the South China Sea [中国在南海的历史性权利]." *China Legal Science* [中国法学], no. 3 (2015): 179–203.

———. "Implications of Historic Rights and the South China Sea Dashed Line—A Refutation of the US State Department's Report on the South China Sea Discontinuity Line [历史性权利的意涵与南海断续线———对美国国务院关于南海断续线报告的批驳]." *Legal Studies Forum* [法学论坛], no. 3 (2016): 85–94.

———. "International Law Theory of South China Sea Issues [南海问题的国际法理]." *China Legal Science* [中国法学], no. 6 (2012): 26–35.

———, ed. *Maritime Development Strategy Anthology* [海洋发展战略文集]. Beijing: Oceans Press, 2017.

———. "Reflections on Ocean Power Strategy [关于海洋强国战略的思考]." *Pacific Journal* [太平洋学报] 26, no. 1 (2018): 1–8.

Jia Yu, and Wu Jilu. "The Outer Continental Shelf of Coastal States and the Common Heritage of Mankind." *Ocean Development and International Law* 42, no. 4 (2011): 317–328.

Jia Yu [贾宇], and Zhang Xiaoyi [张小奕]. "The Maritime Strategy of Mao Zedong, Deng Xiaoping, and Xi Jinping [毛泽东、邓小平和习近平的海洋战略思想初探]." *Journal of Boundary and Ocean Studies* [边界与海洋研究] 3, no. 3 (2018): 5–17.

Jia Yu [贾宇], and Zhao Qian [赵骞]. "What Is Measured by Territorial Sea Baselines? [领海基线量出什么?]." *China Business News* [中国经营报], 22 October 2012. http://www.cimamnr.org.cn/info/362.

Jiang Huai [江淮]. "Yalu River Mouth: View of the Yellow Sea [鸭绿江口 眺望黄海]." *World Affairs* [世界知识], no. 23 (2009): 67.

Jiang Li, and Zhang Jie. "A Preliminary Analysis of the Application of Archipelagic Regime and the Delimitation of the South China Sea." *China Oceans Law Review*, no. 1 (2010): 167–185.

Jiang Sanqiang. "Multinational Oil Companies and the Spratly Dispute." *Journal of Contemporary China* 6, no. 16 (1997): 591–601.

Jiji Press. "Japan Not to Take Senkaku Issue to ICJ." Jiji Press English News Service, 21 September 2012.

Johnson, Douglas. "Drawn into the Fray: Indonesia's Natuna Islands Meet China's Long Gaze South." *Asian Affairs* 24, no. 3 (1997): 153–161.

Johnston, Alastair Iain. "China in a World of Orders: Compliance and Challenge in Beijing's International Relations." *International Security* 44, no. 2 (2019): 429–455.

———. "China's Militarized Interstate Dispute Behaviour 1949–1992: A First Cut at the Data." *China Quarterly*, no. 153 (1998): 1–30.

———. "How New and Assertive Is China's New Assertiveness?" *International Security* 37, no. 4 (2013): 7–48.

———. "Is China a Status Quo Power?" *International Security* 27, no. 4 (2013): 5–56.

———. *Social States: China in International Institutions, 1980–2000*. Princeton: Princeton University Press, 2008.

Kardon, Isaac B. "China Can Say 'No': Analyzing China's Rejection of the South China Sea Arbitration." *University of Pennsylvania Asian Law Review* 13 (2018): 1–46.

———. "China's Maritime Rights and Interests: Domesticating Public International Law." In *China's Socialist Rule of Law Reforms*, edited by John Garrick and Yan Bennett. London: Routledge, 2016, 179–196.

———. "Oil for the Lamps of China: Managing Uncertainty and Vulnerability in World Energy Markets." *Journal of Global Policy and Governance* 2, no. 2 (2013): 305–328.

———. "The Other 'Gulf of Tonkin Incident.'" *CSIS* Asia Maritime Transparency Initiative, 21 October 2015. https://amti.csis.org/the-other-gulf-of-tonkin-incident-chinas-forgotten-maritime-compromise/.

———. "US-China Maritime Security Flashpoints in a New Era." In *US-China Foreign Relations: Power Transition and Its Implications for Europe and Asia,* edited by Robert S. Ross, Øystein Tunsjø, and Dong Wang. London: Routledge, 2021, 178–193.

Katzenstein. Peter J. "Alternative Perspectives on National Security." Introduction in *The Culture of National Security: Norms and Identity in World Politics,* edited by Peter J. Katzenstein. New York: Columbia University Press, 1996: 1–32.

———, ed. *Sinicization and the Rise of China: Civilizational Processes Beyond East and West.* New York: Routledge, 2012.

———. *A World of Regions: Asia and Europe in the American Imperium.* Ithaca: Cornell University Press, 2005.

Kayaoglu, Turan. *Legal Imperialism: Sovereignty and Extraterritoriality in Japan, the Ottoman Empire, and China,* Cambridge: Cambridge University Press, 2010.

Kaye, Stuart. "Freedom of Navigation in the Indo-Pacific Region." *Sea Power Centre Papers in Australian Maritime Affairs,* no. 22 (2008).

Kelly, J. Patrick. "The Twilight of Customary International Law." *Virginia Journal of International Law* 40, no. 2 (2000): 450–544.

Kennedy, Conor M., and Andrew S. Erickson. "China's Maritime Militia." Appendix II in *China as a Twenty-First Century Naval Power,* edited by Michael McDevitt. Annapolis, MD: Naval Institute Press, 2020: 207–229.

———. "China's Third Sea Force, The People's Armed Forces Maritime Militia: Tethered to the PLA." *CMSI China Maritime Report,* no. 1 (2017). https://digital-commons.usnwc.edu/cmsi-maritime-reports/1/.

Kennedy, David B. "One, Two, Three, Many Legal Orders: Legal Pluralism and the Cosmopolitan Dream." *NYU Review of Law and Social Change* 31, no. 3 (2007): 641–659.

Kent, H. S. K. "The Historical Origins of the Three-Mile Limit." *American Journal of International Law* 48, no. 4 (1954): 537–553.

Keohane, Robert. *After Hegemony: Cooperation and Discord in the World Political Economy.* Princeton: Princeton University Press, 1984.

———. "The Demand for International Regimes." *International Organization* 36, no. 2 (Spring 1982): 325–355.

Keohane, Robert, and Joseph Nye. *Power and Interdependence: World Politics in Transition.* Boston: Little, Brown, 1977.

Kim, Samuel S. "China and the United Nations." In *China Joins the World: Progress and Prospects,* edited by Elizabeth Economy and Michel Oksenberg. New York: CFR Press, 1999, 42–89.

———. "The Development of International Law in Post-Mao China: Change and Continuity." *Journal of Chinese Law* 1, no. 2 (1987): 117–160.

———. "The People's Republic of China and the Charter-Based International Legal Order." *American Journal of International Law* 72, no. 2 (1978): 317–349.

Kim, Suk-Kyoon. "Illegal Chinese Fishing in the Yellow Sea: A Korean Officer's Perspective." *Journal of East Asia and International Law* 5, no. 2 (2012): 455–477.

———. "Maritime Boundary Negotiations Between China and Korea: The Factors at Stake." *International Journal of Marine and Coastal Law* 32, no. 1 (2017): 69–94.

Kirshner, Jonathan, and Danielle Cohen. "The Cult of Energy Insecurity." Chapter 6 in *Nexus of Economics, Security, and International Relations in East Asia*, edited by Avery Goldstein and Edward Mansfield. Stanford: Stanford University Press, 2012, 144–176.

Klein, Natalie. *Dispute Settlement in the UN Convention on the Law of the Sea*. New York: Cambridge University Press, 2005.

Koh, Harold. "Why Do Nations Obey International Law?" *Yale Law Journal*, no. 106 (1997): 2599–2659.

Koh, Tommy T. B. "The Asian Way to Settle Disputes." *Straits Times*, 15 June 2015. https://www.straitstimes.com/opinion/the-asian-way-to-settle-disputes.

———. *Building a New Legal Order for the Oceans*. Singapore: National University of Singapore Press, 2020.

———. "The Exclusive Economic Zone." *Malaya Law Review* 30 (1988): 1–33.

Koh, Tommy T. B., and S. Jayakumar. "Negotiating Process of UNCLOS III." In *UNCLOS 1982: A Commentary*, vol. 1., edited by Myron Nordquist. Boston: Martinus Nijhoff, 1985, 29–134.

Kong Lingjie [孔令杰]. "Boundaries with New Era Chinese Characteristics and Maritime Foreign Policy: Foundation, Content, and Challenges [新时代中国特色边界与海洋外交政策: 基础、 内涵与挑战]." *Journal of Boundary and Ocean Studies* [边界与海洋研究] 3, no. 1 (2018): 36–55.

Kopela, Sophia. *Dependent Archipelagos in the Law of the Sea*. Leiden: Martinus Nijhoff, 2013.

———. "The 'Territorialisation' of the Exclusive Economic Zone: Implications for Maritime Jurisdiction." Paper presented at 20th Anniversary Conference of the International Boundaries Research Unit on the State of Sovereignty, Durham University, UK, 2009. http://eprints.kingston.ac.uk/16418/.

Koskenniemi, M. *From Apology to Utopia: The Structure of International Legal Argument*, Helsinki: Finnish Lawyers' Publishing Company, 1989.

———. "International Law and Hegemony: A Reconfiguration." *Cambridge Review of International Affairs* 17, no. 20 (2004): 197–218.

Kotani, Tetsuo. "Can Japan Join U.S. Freedom of Navigation Operations in the SCS?" *CSIS Asia Maritime Transparency Initiative*, 2 November 2015. https://amti.csis.org/can-japan-join-u-s-freedom-of-navigation-operations-in-the-south-china-sea/.

Kraska, James. "Indian Ocean Security and the Law of the Sea." *Georgetown Journal of International Law* 43 (2012): 433–493.

———. "The Legal Rationale for Going Inside 12." *CSIS* Asia Maritime Transparency Initiative, 11 September 2015. https://amti.csis.org/the-legal-rationale-for-going-inside-12/.

———. *Maritime Power and the Law of the Sea: Expeditionary Operations in World Politics.* New York: Oxford University Press, 2011.

Kraska, James, and Raul Pedrozo. *International Maritime Security Law.* Boston, MA: Brill Academic Publishers, 2013.

Krasner, Stephen. *Sovereignty: Organized Hypocrisy.* Princeton: Princeton University Press, 1999.

———. *Structural Conflict: The Third World Against Global Liberalism.* Berkeley: University of California Press, 1985.

Ku, Julian. "China and the Future of International Adjudication." *Maryland Journal of International Law* 27 (2012): 154–178.

———. "China's Definition of the 'Peaceful Settlement of International Disputes' Leaves Out International Adjudication." *Opinio Juris,* 15 October 2013. http://opiniojuris.org/2013/10/15/obligation-seek-peaceful-settlement-international-disputes-include-international-adjudication/.

Ku, Julian, and Chris Mirasola. "Tracking China's Compliance with the SCS Arbitral Award." *Lawfare,* 3 October 2016. https://www.lawfareblog.com/tracking-chinas-compliance-south-china-sea-arbitral-award.

Kwiatkowska, Barbara. *The 200 Mile Exclusive Economic Zone in the New Law of the Sea.* Leiden: Martinus Nijhoff, 1989.

LaGrone, Sam. "Chinese Spy Ship Monitoring RIMPAC Exercise, Again." US Naval Institute News, 13 July 2018. https://news.usni.org/2018/07/13/navy-chinese-spy-ship-monitoring-rimpac-exercise.

———. "Chinese Warships Made 'Innocent Passage' Through US Territorial Waters Off Alaska." US Naval Institute News, 3 September 2015. https://news.usni.org/2015/09/03/chinese-warships-made-innocent-passage-through-u-s-territorial-waters-off-alaska.

———. "US Destroyer Challenges More Chinese South China Sea Claims in New Freedom of Navigation Operation." US Naval Institute News, 30 January 2016. https://news.usni.org/2016/01/30/u-s-destroyer-challenges-more-chinese-south-china-sea-claims-in-new-freedom-of-navigation-operation.

Lasswell, Harold D., and Abraham Kaplan. *Power and Society: A Framework for Political Inquiry.* New Haven: Yale University Press, 1950.

Latiff, Rozanna, and A. Ananthalakshmi. "Malaysian Oil Exploration Vessel Leaves SCS Waters After Standoff." Reuters, 12 May 2020. https://www.reuters.com/article/us-china-security-malaysia/malaysian-oil-exploration-vessel-leaves-south-china-sea-waters-after-standoff-idUSKBN22O1M9.

Lee Tae-hoon. "Seoul to Summon Chinese Diplomats over Ieodo Remarks." *Korea Times,* 11 March 2012. http://www.koreatimes.co.kr/www/nation/2012/03/113_106688.html.

Lemonkova, Polina. "Mapping the South China Sea Region by GMT for Marine Geological Analysis." *Analele Universității din Oradea*, Seria Geografie 30, no. 1 (2020): 107–121.

Lenin, Vladimir. "A Letter to a Comrade on Our Organizational Tasks." In *Collected Works of Vladimir Lenin*, vol. 6, edited by Clemens Dutt and Julian Katzer. Moscow: Progress Publishers, 1964, 231–252.

Li Baojun [李宝俊]. *Treatise on Contemporary Chinese Foreign Policy* [当代中国外交概论]. Beijing: Renmin University Press, 1999.

Li Buyun [李步云], and Wang Yongqing [王永庆]. *The Basic Theory and System of China's Legislation* [中国立法的基本理论和制度]. Beijing: Chinese Legal Press, 1998.

Li Jian [利剑]. *China's Historic Rights in the South China Sea and a Catalogue of Evidence* [中国在南海的历史性权利及证据目录]. Xiamen: Xiamen University Press, 2018.

Li Jianwei, and Chen Pingping. "Joint Development in the South China Sea: Is the Time Ripe?" *Asian Yearbook of International Law* 22 (2016): 131–158.

Li Jing. "The Chinese Communist Party and the People's Courts: Judicial Dependence in China." *American Journal of Comparative Law* 64 (2016): 37–74.

———. "Fish and Reefs Under Siege as Feuding SCS Claimants Refuse to Cooperate." *South China Morning Post*, 10 June 2016. http://www.scmp.com/news/china/policies-politics/article/1961538/fish-and-reefs-under-siege-feuding-south-china-sea.

Li Jinming, and Li Dexia. "The Dotted Line on the Chinese Map of the South China Sea: A Note." *Ocean Development & International Law* 34, no. 3–4 (2003): 287–295.

Li Jinrong [李金蓉], Zhu Ying [朱瑛], and Fang Yinxia [方银霞]. "Status of Oil and Gas Resources Exploration and Development in the Southern South China Sea and Suggestions for Countermeasures [南海南部油气资源勘探开发状况及对策建议]." *Ocean Development and Management* [海洋开发与管理], no. 4 (2014): 12–16.

Li Lingqun. *China's Policy Towards the South China Sea: When Geopolitics Meets the Law of the Sea*. New York: Routledge, 2018.

Li Shujun [李树军], Xu Chunming [许春明], and Wang Rui [王瑞]. "Research on Ocean Mapping and Implementation of Maritime Diversification Support Tasks [海洋测绘履行海上多样化保障任务研究]." *Military Operations Research and Systems Engineering* [军事运筹与系统工程] 24, no. 1 (2010): 13–16.

Li Tiansheng [李天生]. "Fully Understand the Important Meaning of Strengthening Maritime Judicial Sovereignty [充分认识强化海事司法主权的重要意义]." *People's Court News* [人民法院报], 3 August 2016. https://www.chinacourt.org/article/detail/2016/08/id/2048089.shtml.

Li Xiaonian [李肖年], and Chen Liejing [陈列兢]. "Will the South China Sea Become a Second Persian Gulf? [南中国海会成为'第二波斯湾'吗?]" *Modern Navy* [当代海军], no. 4 (2003): 8–11.

Li Yan [李岩]. "Freedom of Navigation Issues in Sino-US Relations [中美关系中的航行自由问题]." *Modern International Relations* [现代国际关系], no. 11 (2016): 22–28.

Li Yuling [李玉玲]. "Assessment of the Sovereignty Dispute over the Diaoyu Islands Under International Law [国际法下钓鱼岛主权争端的评估]." *China Oceans Law Review* [中国海洋法学评论], no. 2 (2013): 1–30.

Li Yunquan [李云泉]. *Historical Theory of the Tributary System: Research on China's Classical Foreign Relations System* [朝贡制度史论: 中国古代对外关系体制研究]. Beijing: Xinhua Publishing House, 2004.

Li Zhaojie. "China." Chapter 12 in *The Oxford Handbook of International Law in Asia and the Pacific*, edited by Simon Chesterman, Hisashi Owada, and Ben Saul. Oxford: Oxford University Press, 2019, 299–319.

Li Zhaoxing. "Explanation on the Draft Law on the Exclusive Economic Zone and the Continental Shelf of the People's Republic of China." *Gazette of the Standing Committee of the National People's Congress of the PRC*. 23rd Session of the Standing Committee of the 8th National People's Congress, 24 December 1996.

Liang Qichao [梁启超]. *On Rights Consciousness* [论权利思想]. Beijing: China Publishing House, 1903.

Liff, Adam. "Principles Without Consensus: Setting the Record Straight on the 2014 Sino-Japanese 'Agreement to Improve Bilateral Relations.'" Working Paper. Indiana University (8 November 2014). http://www.adamphailliff.com/documents/Liff2014_PrinciplesWithoutConsensus.pdf.

Lim, Benjamin Kang. "Philippines Duterte Says South China Sea Arbitration Case To Take 'Back Seat.'" Reuters, 19 October 2016. https://www.reuters.com/article/us-china-philippines/philippines-duterte-says-south-china-sea-arbitration-case-to-take-back-seat-idUSKCN12J10S.

Ling Qing [凌青]. "The Third United Nations Convention on the Law of the Sea." Chapter 7 in *From Yan-an to the UN: The Diplomatic Career of Ling Qing* [从延安到联合国: 凌青外交生涯]. Fuzhou: Fujian People's Press, 2008. Translated by China Maritime Studies Institute, US Naval War College.

Liu Cigui [刘赐贵]. "Some Considerations on Building a Maritime Power [关于建设海洋强国的若干思考]." *Ocean Development and Management* [海洋开发与管理], no. 12 (2012): 8–10.

———. "Striving to Realize the Historical Leap from Being a Large Maritime Country to Being a Maritime Power." State Oceanic Administration. 9 June 2014.

———. "Taking Advantage of Opportunities to Achieve Additional Victories in Maritime Strategy Initiatives [乘势而上再夺海洋工作新胜利]." *China Oceanology Review* [中国海洋报], 11 January 2013.

Liu Dan [刘丹]. "The 'Critical Date' Factor in Territorial Settlement Jurisprudence and Implications for the Diaoyu Islands Dispute [领土争端解决判例中的"关键日期"因素及对钓鱼岛争端的启示]." *Pacific Journal* [太平洋学报] 21, no. 7 (2013): 81–90.

Liu Fengming [刘丰名]. *Essentials of International Law* [现代国际法纲要]. Beijing: People's Publishing House, 1982.

Liu Hongxia [刘红霞]. "Study on the Legal Aspects of the Delineation of the Baselines of the Territorial Sea of the Spratly Islands [南沙群岛领海基线划定的法律问题研究]." MA Thesis. China Oceans University, 2015.

Liu Kefu [刘刻福]. "Push Forward the Construction of Maritime Power with Threefold Efforts [以三重保护力度推进海洋强国建设]." *China Ocean News* [中国海洋报], 17 September 2013.

Liu Nanlai [刘楠来]. "Liu Nanlai's View on the Legal Status of the 'U' Shaped Line from the International Law of the Sea [刘楠来 从国际海洋法看'U'形线的法律地位]." *China Oceans Report* [中国海洋报], no. 1 (2005): 1–3. https://www.nansha.org.cn/study/9.html.

———. "Safeguard Maritime Rights and Interests, Build A Strong Maritime Nation [维护海洋权益，建设海洋强国]. Paper presented at the High Level Roundtable on Constructing a Strong Maritime Power Strategy, 18 May 2013. http://www.iolaw.org.cn/showArticle.aspx?id=3672.

———. "Third Conference on the Law of the Sea and China's Protection of Its Maritime Rights and Interests." *Journal of Boundary and Ocean Studies* 4, no. 5 (2019): 38–41.

Liu Yusong [刘禹松]. "Five Years After the Implementation of the Fisheries Agreement [《渔业协定》实施后的这5年]." *China Fisheries* [中国水产], no. 7 (2009): 4–6.

Liu Zhen. "Chinese Research Vessel Expelled by Indian Warship for Operating near Andaman and Nicobar Islands." *South China Morning Post*, 4 December 2019. https://www.scmp.com/news/china/diplomacy/article/3040638/chinese-research-vessel-expelled-indian-warship-operating-near.

Liu Zhenhuan [刘振环]. "Commentary on UNCLOS, Part II [《联合国海洋法公约》评述(下)]." *National Defense* [国防], no. 11 (1996): 14–16.

Long, Drake, and Nisha David. "Malaysia: Chinese Survey Ship Is in Our Waters." *Radio Free Asia*, 17 April 2020. https://www.rfa.org/english/news/china/southchinasea-malaysia-survey-04172020190602.html.

Lü Tian [吕田]. "South China Sea Fishing Ban Gives Rise to Controversial International Disputes [南海禁渔令引争议 国际纷争难解决]." *China Food* [中国食品], no. 11 (2013): 97–99.

Lubman, Stanley B. *Bird in a Cage: Legal Reform in China After Mao*. Stanford: Stanford University Press, 1999.

Ma Kai [马凯]. "Restructure State Oceanic Administration, Establish High-Level Coordinating Agency State Oceanic Commission [重新组建国家海洋局 设立高层次一是协调机构国家海洋委员会]." Xinhua News Agency, 10 March 2013.

Ma Li [马丽]. "China-Japan Fishery Commission Reached an Agreement on the Number of Fishing Vessels Operating in the EEZ [中日渔业委员会就专属经济区作业渔船数量达成协议]." *Global Times* [环球时报], 25 November 2016. https://world.huanqiu.com/article/9CaKrnJYPhP.

Ma Xinmin. "China and the UNCLOS: Practices and Policies." *Chinese Journal of Global Governance* 5, no. 1 (2019): 1–20.

———. "Merits Award Relating to Historic Rights in the South China Sea Arbitration: An Appraisal." *Asian Journal of International Law* 8, no. 1 (2018): 12–23.

Madarang, Catalina Ricci S. "Duterte on the Constitution as 'Toilet Paper': Controversial or Out of Context?" *Interaksyon*, 3 July 2019. https://interaksyon .philstar.com/politics-issues/2019/07/03/151335/duterte-constitution-toilet -paper/.

Malaysia. Baselines of Maritime Zones Act, no. 660 (2006). http://faolex.fao.org/ docs/texts/mal70074.doc.

———. "South China Sea: Ministry of Foreign Affairs Press Statement." YB Dato' Seri Hishammuddin Tun Hussein, Minister of Foreign Affairs. Wisma Putra (23 April 2020).

Mallory, Tabitha G. "Appendix G: Chinese Distant Water Fishing Activities." In "Trade in Fishing Services: Emerging Perspectives on Foreign Fishing Arrangements." *World Bank Report*, no. 92622-GLB (2014).

———. "China, Global Governance, and the Making of a Distant Water Fishing Nation." PhD Dissertation, Johns Hopkins SAIS, 2013.

———. "China's Distant Water Fishing Industry: Evolving Policies and Implications." *Marine Policy*, no. 38 (2013): 99–108.

Manicom, James. "Sino-Japanese Cooperation in the ECS: Limitations and Prospects." *Contemporary Southeast Asia* 30, no. 3 (2008): 455–478.

Mann, Jim, and Art Pine. "Faceoff Between US Ship, Chinese Sub Is Revealed." *Los Angeles Times*, 14 December 1994. https://www.latimes.com/archives/la -xpm-1994-12-14-mn-8896-story.html.

Maritime Awareness Project. "Republic of Korea Country Profile." NBR Maritime Awareness Project (2020). https://www.nbr.org/publication/republic-of -korea/.

Maritime Executive. "Philippines Approves Chinese Research at Benham Rise." Maritime Executive, 15 January 2018. https://www.maritime-executive.com/ article/philippines-approves-chinese-research-at-benham-rise.

Martinson, Ryan. "Catching Sovereignty Fish: Chinese Fishers in the Southern Spratlys." *Marine Policy* 125 (March 2021).

———. "China as an Atlantic Naval Power." *RUSI Journal* 164, no. 7 (2019): 18–31.

———. "Early Warning Brief: Introducing the 'New, New' China Coast Guard." *Jamestown China Brief* 21, no. 2 (2021).

———. "Echelon Defense: The Role of Sea Power in Chinese Maritime Dispute Strategy," *CMSI Red Book*, no. 15 (February 2018).

———. "From Words to Actions: The Creation of the China Coast Guard." Paper presented at the Center for Naval Analyses Conference on Maritime Power. 28 July 2015. https://www.cna.org/cna_files/pdf/creation-china-coast-guard.pdf.

———. "*Jinglue Haiyang:* The Naval Implications of Xi Jinping's New Strategic Concept." *Jamestown China Brief* 15, no. 1 (2015). https://jamestown.org/

program/jinglue-haiyang-the-naval-implications-of-xi-jinpings-new-strategic
-concept/.

———. "Shepherds of the South Seas." *Survival* 58, no. 3 (2016): 187–212.

Mastanduno, Michael. "Partner Politics: Russia, China, and the Challenge of Extending US Hegemony After the Cold War." *Security Studies* 28, no. 3 (2019): 479–504.

McDevitt, Michael, ed. "Becoming a Great 'Maritime Power': A Chinese Dream." *Center for Naval Analyses Report* (June 2016). https://www.cna.org/cna_files/pdf/IRM-2016-U-013646.pdf.

———. *China as a Twenty-First Century Naval Power.* Annapolis, MD: Naval Institute Press, 2020.

McDorman, Ted L. "The South China Sea Tribunal Awards: A Dispute Resolution Perspective." *Asia-Pacific Journal of Ocean Law and Policy* 3, no. 1 (2018): 134–145.

McVadon, Eric. "The PLA Navy as an Instrument of Statecraft." In *The Chinese Navy: Expanding Capabilities, Evolving Roles,* edited by Phillip C. Saunders, Christopher Yung, and Andrew Nien-Dzu Yang. Washington, DC: National Defense University Press, 2011, 215–246.

Military Excellence [卓越军事]. "Chinese Warship 'Visits' the US, the US Protests [中国军舰'访'美，美国抗议]." NetEase [网易], 29 July 2017. https://www.163.com/dy/article/CQHLKOL20515H4SR.html.

Miyoshi, Masahiro. "Exercising Enforcement Jurisdiction Around the Senkaku Islands." *Review of Island Studies* (October 2014). https://www.spf.org/islandstudies/research/a00013.html.

Morris, Lyle J. "Blunt Defenders of Sovereignty: The Rise of Coast Guards in East and Southeast Asia." *Naval War College Review* 70, no. 2 (2017): 75–112.

Muller, David G. *China as a Maritime Power—The Formative Years: 1945–1983.* 2nd ed. Lexington, VA: Rockbridge Books, 2016.

Murphy Oil Corporation. "Form 10-K." US Securities and Exchange Commission, file no. 1–8590 (2016). https://www.sec.gov/Archives/edgar/data/717423/000071742317000005/mur-20161231x10k.htm.

Nan Li. "The Evolution of China's Naval Strategy and Capabilities: From 'Near Coast' and 'Near Seas' to 'Far Seas.'" In *The Chinese Navy: Expanding Capabilities, Evolving Roles,* edited by Phillip C. Saunders, Christopher Yung, and Andrew Nien-Dzu Yang. Washington, DC: National Defense University Press, 2011, 109–140.

Nanjing University. "Collaborative Innovation Center of South China Sea Studies [中国南海研究协商创新中心]." https://nanhai.nju.edu.cn/main.htm.

National Institute for Defense Studies, Japan (NIDS). "NIDS China Security Report 2011." February 2012. http://www.nids.mod.go.jp/publication/chinareport/pdf/china_report_EN_web_2011_A01.pdf.

Ng, Jason, and Trefor Moss. "Malaysia Toughens Stance with Beijing over South China Sea." *Wall Street Journal,* 8 June 2015. https://www.wsj.com/articles/malaysia-toughens-stance-with-beijing-over-south-china-sea-1433764608.

Nguyen The Phuong. "Vietnam's Maritime Militia Is Not a Black Hole in the SCS." Maritime Transparency Initiative, 22 May 2020. https://amti.csis.org/vietnams-maritime-militia-is-not-a-black-hole-in-the-south-china-sea/.

Niu Tao [牛涛]. "Naval Organs Held 'Navy Hall' Tutorial Lectures—Central Committee of Political and Legal Affairs Commission Secretary General Chen Yixin Gave a Tutorial Lecture [海军机关举行"海军大讲堂"辅导讲座—中央政法委秘韦长陈一新作辅导授课]." People's Navy [人民海军], 31 December 2020: 1.

Nordquist, Myron, ed. UNCLOS 1982: A Commentary, vol. 1. Boston: Martinus Nijhoff, 1985.

———. UNCLOS 1982: A Commentary, vol. 2. Boston: Martinus Nijhoff, 1993.

Noyes, John E. "The Territorial Sea and Contiguous Zone." In Oxford Handbook of the Law of the Sea, edited by Donald Rothwell et al. New York: Oxford University Press, 2015: 91–113.

NPC Observer. "Annotated Translation: 2018 Amendment to the PRC Constitution (Version 2.0)." Translated and annotated by Wei Chenhao and Hu Taige. NPC Observer, 11 March 2018. https://npcobserver.com/2018/03/11/translation-2018-amendment-to-the-p-r-c-constitution/.

O'Connell, D. P. The Influence of Law on Sea Power. Annapolis, MD: Naval Institute Press, 1975.

———. The International Law of the Sea. Oxford: Clarendon Press, 1982.

Odom, Jonathan G. "True Lies of the Impeccable Incident." Michigan State University College of Law Journal of International Law 18, no. 3 (2010): 411–452.

Official Records of the Third United Nations Conference on the Law of the Sea. United Nations Diplomatic Conferences: Official Records, vols. 1–17 (1973–1982). http://legal.un.org/diplomaticconferences/lawofthesea-1982/Vol1.html.

Offshore. "Forum Energy Confirms Force Majeure for Philippines SC 72." Offshore Magazine, 4 March 2015. https://www.offshore-mag.com/regional-reports/article/16764856/forum-energy-confirms-force-majeure-for-philippines-sc-72.

———. "Partners to Drill Two Wells on Tuna Offshore Indonesia." Offshore Magazine, 26 January 2021. https://www.offshore-mag.com/regional-reports/asia/article/14196196/partners-to-drill-two-wells-on-tuna-offshore-indonesia.

O'Rourke, Ronald. "Maritime Territorial and Exclusive Economic Zone (EEZ) Disputes Involving China: Issues for Congress." Congressional Research Service Report, 7–5700 (R42784). 24 May 2018.

Oxman, Bernard H. "An Analysis of the Exclusive Economic Zone as Formulated in the Informal Composite Negotiating Text." In Law of the Sea: State Practice in Zones of Special Jurisdiction, ed. Thomas A. Clingan. Honolulu, HI: Law of the Sea Institute, 1982, 57–78.

———. "Courts and Tribunals: The ICJ, ITLOS, and Arbitral Tribunals." In The Oxford Handbook of the Law of the Sea, edited by Donald Rothwell et al. New York: Oxford University Press, 2015, 394–415.

———. "Territorial Temptation: A Siren Song at Sea." American Journal of International Law 100, no. 4 (2006): 830–851.

Paler, Laura. "China's Legislation Law and the Making of a More Orderly and Representative Legal System." *China Quarterly* 182 (2005): 301–318.

Pan Shanju [潘珊菊]. "Two US Ships Sail Through Taiwan Strait and China's Ministry of Defense and Ministry of Foreign Affairs Make Strong Statements [美军双舰穿航台湾海峡,中国国防部,外交部相继强硬发声]." *Southern Metropolis Daily* [南方都市报], 31 December 2020. https://www.sohu.com/a/441765934_161795.

Panda, Ankit. "Making Sense of China's Reaction to the French Navy's Taiwan Strait Transit." *Diplomat*, 26 April 2019.

Park, Jaeyoon, et al. "Illuminating Dark Fishing Fleets in North Korea." *Science Advances* 6, no. 30 (2020). https://advances.sciencemag.org/content/6/30/eabb1197.

Park, Young Kil. "The Role of Fishing Disputes in China–South Korea Relations." NBR Maritime Awareness Project, 23 April 2020. https://www.nbr.org/publication/the-role-of-fishing-disputes-in-china-south-korea-relations/.

Peking University. "PKU Law Database [北大法宝]." www.pkulaw.cn.

People's Daily [人民日报]. "Chairman Mao's Theory of the Differentiation of the Three Worlds Is a Major Contribution to Marxism-Leninism." 1 November 1977.

———. "China's Historic Rights in the SCS Discontinuous Line Cannot Be Arbitrarily Discussed or Denied." 23 May 2016. http://opinion.people.com.cn/n1/2016/0523/c1003–28369833.html.

———. "Editorial." 4 May 1982.

———. "The Five Principles of Peaceful Coexistence [和平共处五项原则]." 30 April 1954.

———. "The Healthy Road of Ruling the Nation Through Law [依法治国的康庄大道]." 3 February 2015.

———. "HYSY-981 Drilling Platform Successfully and Efficiently Completed Operations in the Waters near Xisha's Zhongjian Island [海洋石油-981钻井平台顺利高效完成西沙中建岛附近海域作业]." 16 July 2014. http://env.people.com.cn/n/2014/0716/c1010–25288551.html.

———. "Let China-Vietnam Maritime Border Become a Bond of Peace, Friendship, and Cooperation [让中越海上边界成为和平友好与合作的纽带]." 1 July 2004, 3.

———. "Shunji Yanai, Manipulator Behind Illegal South China Sea Arbitration." 17 July 2016. http://en.people.cn/n3/2016/0717/c90000–9087223.html.

———. "Speech by the Chairman of the Delegation of the PRC, Deng Xiaoping, at the Sixth Special Session of the UN General Assembly." 11 April 1974.

———. "Study Xi Jinping's 'Four Comprehensives' Strategic Thought [学习习近平"四个全面"战略思想]." http://politics.people.com.cn/GB/8198/394083/.

———. "Why Does China Need to Declare Its Core Interests? [中国为什么要宣示核心利益?]." *People's Daily* [人民日报]. 27 July 2010.

———. "Xi Jinping at the 8th Study Session of the Central Committee Political Bureau." 1 August 2013. http://paper.people.com.cn/rmrb/html/2013–08/01/nw.D110000renmrb_20130801_2–01.htm.

———. "Xi Jinping Sets Out Requirements to Build a Maritime Power [建设海洋强国，习近平从这些方面提出要求]." 11 July 2018. http://cpc.people.com.cn/n1/2019/0711/c164113-31226894.html.

People's Liberation Army Navy [中国人民解放军海军]. "China Sailing Directions: South China Sea [中国航路指南：南海海区]." Navigation Guarantee Department of the Chinese Navy Headquarters [司令部航海保证部] (2011). Reproduced as Annex 232 in the *SCS Arbitration*. "Memorial of the Philippines—Volume VII Annexes." 30 March 2014. https://pca-cpa.org/en/cases/7/.

Petronas. "First Deepwater Gas Production from Block H Offshore Malaysia Augments Malaysia's Investment Potential." 16 February 2021. https://www.petronas.com/media/press-release/first-deep-water-gas-production-block-h-offshore-malaysia-augments-malaysias.

———. "Petronas and CNOOC to Pursue Energy Security, Cleaner Energy Solutions." 15 March 2021. https://www.petronas.com/media/press-release/petronas-and-cnooc-pursue-energy-security-cleaner-energy-solutions.

Poling, Greg. "The Conventional Wisdom on China's Island Bases Is Dangerously Wrong." *War on the Rocks*. 10 January 2020. https://warontherocks.com/2020/01/the-conventional-wisdom-on-chinas-island-bases-is-dangerously-wrong/.

———. "From Orbit to Ocean—Fixing Southeast Asia's Remote Sensing Bind." *Naval War College Review* 74, no. 1 (2021): 1–21.

Posner, Eric A., and Alan O. Sykes. "Economic Foundations of the Law of the Sea." *American Journal of International Law* 104 (2010): 569–596.

Potter, Pittman. *China's Legal System*. Cambridge: Polity Press, 2013.

———. "The Chinese Legal System: Continuing Commitment to the Primacy of State Power." *China Quarterly*, no. 159 (1999): 673–683.

PRC Ministry of Agriculture (MoA). "Announcement on the Adjustment of the Summer Fishing Moratorium System [农业部关于调整海洋伏季休渔制度的通告]." Ministry of Agriculture, Notice no. 1, 27 February 2009.

———. "China Fisheries Law Enforcement: Protector of Blue Territory [中国渔政，蓝色国土的保护者]." *China Fisheries Report* [中国渔业报], 21 February 2011.

———. "Issues Related to the Implementation of the China-Korea Fisheries Agreement in 2017 [关于2017年实施中韩渔业协定有关问题]." General Office of the Ministry of Agriculture Notice [农业部办公厅的通知], 20 April 2017. http://www.moa.gov.cn/nybgb/2017/dsiqi/201712/t20171230_6133450.htm.

———. "Ministry of Agriculture Leadership Answers Questions About the Relevant Regulations of the Summer Fishing Moratorium [农业部有关负责人就海洋伏季休渔有关规定答问]." Central People's Government of the PRC. 6 April 2009. http://www.gov.cn/gzdt/2010-04/06/content_1574596.htm.

———. "Press Conference on the Bright Sword Action of China's Fishery Administration [农业农村部举行 中国渔政亮剑行动新闻发布会]." 2019. *China Fisheries* [中国水产], no. 4: 3–6.

———. Regulations for Managing Spratly Fisheries Production [南沙渔业生产管理规定]. Document 50. 22 December 2003.

———. "Special Law Enforcement Action Plan for the 'China Fishery Policy Bright Sword 2020' ["中国渔政亮剑2020"系列专项执法行动方案]." Notice of the Ministry of Agriculture and Rural Affairs. 5 March 2020. http://www.moa.gov.cn/gk/tzgg_1/tz/202003/t20200306_6338386.htm.

PRC Ministry of Agriculture, and PRC State Administration of Worker Safety. "Urgent Notice on Further Strengthening the Supervision and Administration of Fishery Production Safety [农业部,国家安全生产监督管理总局关于进一步加强渔业安全生产监督管理工作的紧急通知]." Agriculture and Fisheries Law, no. 40. 2007.

PRC Ministry of Civil Affairs. "Approving Hainan Province Sansha City to Establish City Jurisdiction Districts [民政部关于国务院批准海南省三沙市设立市辖区的公告]." China Government Net [中国政府网], 18 April 2020. https://perma.cc/XU9X-CKE5.

———. "Establishment of Prefecture-Level Sansha City [民政部关于国务院批准设立地级三沙市的公告]." China Government Net [中国政府网], 21 June 2012. https://perma.cc/3Q23-SQGA.

PRC Ministry of Foreign Affairs (MFA). "Ambassador Xiao Qian Meets with Indonesian Minister of Energy and Minerals Ariffin [驻印度尼西亚大使肖千会见印尼能源和矿产部长阿里芬]." 25 November 2019. https://www.fmprc.gov.cn/web/zwbd_673032/wshd_673034/t1718675.shtml.

———. Briefing by Xu Hong, Director-General of the Department of Treaty and Law on the South China Sea Arbitration Initiated by the Philippines. 12 May 2016. www.fmprc.gov.cn/mfa_eng/wjdt_665385/zyjh_665391/t1364804.shtml.

———. "China and Japan Hold 12th Round of High-Level Consultations on Maritime Affairs." 4 February 2021. https://www.fmprc.gov.cn/mfa_eng/wjbxw/t1852040.shtml.

———. "China and Japan Reach a Principled Consensus on the ECS Issue." Joint Press Statement with the Ministry of Affairs of Japan, 18 June 2008. https://www.fmprc.gov.cn/123/xwfw/fyrth/1056/t466568.htm.

———. "China and Japan Reach Four-Point Principled Agreement on Handling and Improving Bilateral Relations—State Councilor Yang Jiechi Meets National Security Advisor of Japan Shotaro Yachi." Beijing, 7 November 2014. https://www.fmprc.gov.cn/ce/cebe/eng/mhs/t1208360.htm.

———. "China and ROK Hold the First Meeting of Dialogue and Cooperation Mechanism of Maritime Affairs." 14 April 2021. https://www.fmprc.gov.cn/mfa_eng/wjbxw/t1869273.shtml.

———. China-Japan Fisheries Agreement [中华人民共和国和日本国渔业协定]. 11 November 1997: https://www.fmprc.gov.cn/web/ziliao_674904/tytj_674911/tyfg_674913/t556672.shtml.

———. "China's Territorial Sovereignty and Maritime Rights and Interests in the South China Sea." 12 July 2016. https://www.fmprc.gov.cn/nanhai/eng/snhwtlcwj_1/t1379493.htm.

———. "Chinese Foreign Minister Yang Jiechi Meets the Press on ECS Issue." 24 June 2008. https://www.fmprc.gov.cn/mfa_eng/wjb_663304/zzjg_663340/yzs_663350/gjlb_663354/2721_663446/2724_663452/t469127.shtml.

———. Declaration of the Government of the PRC on the Baselines of the Territorial Sea. 15 May 1996. http://www.un.org/depts/los/LEGISLATIONANDTREATIES/PDFFILES/CHN_1996_Declaration.pdf.

———. "Declaration on the Territorial Sea of the People's Republic of China." *Peking Review* 1, no. 28, 9 September 1958.

———. "Deputy Foreign Minister Wang Yi Accepts an Interview with Reporters on the Entry into Force of the China-Vietnam Beibu Gulf Demarcation Agreement and Fishery Cooperation Agreement [王毅副外长就中越北部湾划界协定和渔业合作协定生效接受记者专访]." 30 June 2004. https://www.fmprc.gov.cn/ce/cemx/chn/xw/t141537.htm.

———. "Fisheries Agreement Between China and the Republic of Korea [中华人民共和国政府和大韩民国政府渔业协定]." Signed 11 November 2000; effective 30 June 2001.: https://www.fmprc.gov.cn/web/wjb_673085/zzjg_673183/bjhysws_674671/bhfg_674677/t556669.shtml.

———. "Memorandum of Understanding on Cooperation on Oil and Gas Development Between the PRC and the Republic of the Philippines." 27 November 2018. https://www.fmprc.gov.cn/mfa_eng/wjdt_665385/2649_665393/t1616644.shtml.

———. "Memorandum on the Issues of the Paracel and Nansha Islands [关于西沙群岛、南沙群岛问题的备忘录]." *Xinhua* [新华], 12 May 1988. http://www.thesouthchinasea.org.cn/2016-06/28/c_52677.htm.

———. Minutes of the Meeting Between Vice-Foreign Minister Liu Zhenmin and US Media Delegation on the SCS Issue. 3 June 2016. https://www.fmprc.gov.cn/mfa_eng/wjdt_665385/zyjh_665391/t1369249.shtml.

———. "Oil Companies of China, the Philippines, and Vietnam Signed Agreement on South China Sea Cooperation." Embassy of the PRC in the Republic of the Philippines, 15 March 2005. http://ph.china-embassy.org/eng/zt/nhwt/t187333.htm.

———. "The Operation of the HYSY 981 Drilling Rig: Vietnam's Provocation and China's Position." 8 June 2014. https://www.fmprc.gov.cn/mfa_eng/zxxx_662805/t1163264.shtml.

———. "Position Paper of the Government of the PRC on the Matter of Jurisdiction in the South China Sea Arbitration Initiated by the Republic of the Philippines." 7 December 2014. https://www.fmprc.gov.cn/nanhai/eng/snhwtlcwj_1/201606/t20160602_8527277.htm.

———. *PRC Treaty Database* [中国人民共和国条约数据库]. http://treaty.mfa.gov.cn/Treaty/web/index.jsp.

———. "Remarks by Chinese Foreign Minister Wang Yi on the Award of the So-Called Arbitral Tribunal in the SCS Arbitration." 12 July 2016. https://www.fmprc.gov.cn/mfa_eng/wjdt_665385/zyjh_665391/t1380003.shtml.

———. Remarks by Head of the Chinese Delegation Ambassador Wang Min. Meeting in Commemoration of the 20th Anniversary of the Entry into Force of the UNCLOS, 9 June 2014. http://chnun.chinamission.org.cn/eng/chinaandun/legalaffairs/hyf/t1163776.htm.

———. "The Report of the Secretary-General." Statement by Ambassador Wu Haitao. 28th Meeting of States Parties to the UNCLOS. 12 June 2018. http://chnun.chinamission.org.cn/eng/chinaandun/legalaffairs/hyf/t1569738.htm.

———. "Shelve Disputes, Jointly Develop [搁置争议，共同开发]." 7 November 2000. mfa.gov.cn/ce/cohk//chn/topic/zgwj/wjlshk/t8958.htm.

———. "Signed Article in Guangming Daily: It Is a Just Move for China to Reject the SCS International Arbitration [光明日报署名文章：我拒绝南海国际仲裁是正义之举]." 17 December 2015. http://archive.today/5sqKR.

———. "Spokesman Zhu Bangzao Gives Full Account of the Collision Between the US and Chinese Military Planes." 4 April 2001. https://www.fmprc.gov.cn/ce/cegv/eng/premade/11437/spokesman040401.htm.

———. Statement by Duan Jielong. 61st Session of the UNGA, Agenda Item 80 (17 October 2006). https://www.mfa.gov.cn/ce/ceun//eng/chinaandun/legalaffairs/sixthcommittee1/t349635.htm.

———. Statement by Liu Jieyi. 69th Session of the UNGA, Agenda Item 74 (9 December 2014). http://chnun.chinamission.org.cn/eng/chinaandun/legalaffairs/hyf/t1217930.htm.

———. Statement by Liu Zhenmin, 62nd Session of the UNGA (10 December 2007). https://www.fmprc.gov.cn/ce/ceun/eng/gywm/czdbt/liuzhenminhuodong/t388772.htm.

———. Statement by Shen Guofang. 65th Plenary of the 56th Session of the UNGA, Item 30 (28 November 2021). http://chnun.chinamission.org.cn/eng/chinaandun/legalaffairs/hyf/t28539.htm.

———. Statement by Wang Min. 65th Session of the UNGA (9 December 2010). http://chnun.chinamission.org.cn/eng/chinaandun/legalaffairs/hyf/t775597.htm.

———. Statement by Wu Haitao. 72nd Session of the UNGA, Item 77 (5 December 2017). http://chnun.chinamission.org.cn/eng/chinaandun/legalaffairs/hyf/t1516979.htm.

———. Statement by Xue Hanqin. UNGA Agenda Item 34 (26 October 2000). http://chnun.chinamission.org.cn/eng/chinaandun/legalaffairs/hyf/t28565.htm.

———. Statement of the Government of the PRC on the Baselines of the Territorial Sea of Diaoyu Dao and Its Affiliated Islands. 10 September 2012. http://www.fmprc.gov.cn/mfa_eng/topics_665678/diaodao_665718/t968769.shtml.

———. Statement of the MFA on Diaoyu Dao. 10 September 2012. https://www.fmprc.gov.cn/diaoyudao/chn/xwdt/t967820.htm.

———. Statement on Settling Disputes Between China and the Philippines in the South China Sea Through Bilateral Negotiation. 8 June 2016. https://www.fmprc.gov.cn/nanhai/eng/snhwtlcwj_1/t1370476.htm.

———. Statement on the Jurisdiction and Admissibility of the South China Sea Arbitration Tribunal Established at the Request of the Republic of the Philippines. 24 October 2015. https://www.fmprc.gov.cn/ce/cgny/chn/xw/t1380161.htm.

———. Statement on the Rule of Law at the National and International Levels by H. E. Ambassador Wang Min. 68th Session of the UNGA, 10 October 2013. https://www.fmprc.gov.cn/mfa_eng/wjb_663304/zwjg_665342/zwbd_665378/t1087085.shtml.

———. Statement Regarding Huangyan Island. 22 May 1997.

———. "Ten Questions on Huangyan Island [黄岩岛十问]." Embassy of the PRC in the Republic of the Philippines. 15 June 2012. https://www.fmprc.gov.cn/ce/ceph/chn/zgxw/t941671.htm.

———. "Wang Yi Delivers a Speech at the Opening Ceremony of the Lanting Forum on International Order and Global Governance in the Post-COVID-19 Era." 28 September 2020. https://www.fmprc.gov.cn/mfa_eng/zxxx_662805/t1820459.shtml.

———. Wang Yi: "Dual-Track Approach" Is the Most Practical and Feasible Way to Resolve the South China Sea Issue." 21 April 2016. https://www.fmprc.gov.cn/mfa_eng/zxxx_662805/t1358167.shtml.

———. "Yang Jiechi Attends Work Symposium on International Law Marking the 40th Anniversary of Reform and Opening Up." 28 December 2018. https://www.fmprc.gov.cn/mfa_eng/zxxx_662805/t1626488.shtml.

———. "Yang Jiechi Gives Interview to State Media on the So-Called Award by the Arbitral Tribunal for the South China Sea Arbitration." 15 July 2016. https://www.fmprc.gov.cn/nanhai/eng/wjbxw_1/t1381740.htm.

PRC Foreign Ministry Spokesperson. *PRC Foreign Ministry Spokesperson's Remarks Database* 1997–2021 [外交部发言人言论数据库1997–2021]. Archives of the Chinese Government [中国政府资料库]. Oriprobe Information Services, Inc.

PRC Ministry of National Defense (MND). Announcement of the Aircraft Identification Rules of the East China Sea Air Defense Identification Zone of the PRC. 23 November 2013. http://www.mod.gov.cn/affair/2013–11/23/content_4476910.htm.

———. Defense Ministry's Regular Press Conference. *China Military Online,* 27 June 2019. http://eng.chinamil.com.cn/view/2019–06/27/content_9541430.htm.

———. Regular Press Conference. 30 April 2020. http://eng.mod.gov.cn/news/2020–05/04/content_4864650.htm.

———. "Spokesman Ren Guoqiang Answers Questions About US Ships Passing Through the Taiwan Strait [国防部发言人任国强就美舰过航台湾海峡答问]." 26 March 2019. http://www.mod.gov.cn/topnews/2019–03/26/content_4838204.htm.

———. Statement by MND Spokesman Geng Yansheng on China's Air Defense Identification Zone. 3 December 2013. https://www.fmprc.gov.cn/ce/cebe/eng/zt/dhfksbq13/t1109762.htm.

———. "Yang Yujun on the Unauthorized Entry of US Warships into Our Xisha Territorial Waters [国防部新闻发言人杨宇军就美国军舰擅自进入我西沙领海发表谈话]." *MND Spokesperson*, 30 January 2016. http://news.mod.gov.cn/headlines/2016–01/30/content_4638192.htm.

PRC Ministry of Natural Resources. "Notice of the CCP Group of the Ministry of Natural Resources on the Establishment of Sub-Party Groups of Beihai Bureau, East China Sea Bureau, and South China Sea Bureau of the Ministry of National Resources [中共自然资源部党组关于成立自然资源部北海局、东海局、南海局分党组的通知]. Ministry of Natural Resources Party Law, no. 14 (2020).

———. "Notice of the Ministry of Land and Resources and the National Bureau of Surveying, Mapping, and Geographic Information on Launching a Special Action to Investigate and Remediate 'Problem Maps' [国土资源部、国家测绘地理信息局关于开展全覆盖排查整治"问题地图"专项行动的通知]." *National Resources Publication* [国土资发], no. 99 (21 August 2017).

———. "Notice of the CCP Group of the Ministry of Natural Resources on the Establishment of Sub-Party Groups of Beihai Bureau, East China Sea Bureau, and South China Sea Bureau of the Ministry of National Resources [中共自然资源部党组关于成立自然资源部北海局、东海局、南海局分党组的通知]. Ministry of Natural Resources Party Law, no. 14 (2020).

PRC National People's Congress (NPC). *The Effective Laws and Administrative Regulations of the People's Republic of China* [中华人民共和国啊现行法律行政法规汇编]. Legislative Work Commission. Beijing: People's Press, 2014.

———. Eleventh PRC Five-Year Plan for Economic and Social Development (2006). http://news.xinhuanet.com/misc/2006–03/16/content_4309517_5.htm.

———. Exclusive Economic Zone and Continental Shelf Law. 3rd Meeting of the 9th National People's Congress, 26 June 1998. https://www.un.org/Depts/los/LEGISLATIONANDTREATIES/PDFFILES/chn_1998_eez_act.pdf.

———. National Law and Regulation Database [国家法律法规数据库]. https://flk.npc.gov.cn/.

———. "Notes on the EEZ and Continental Shelf Law of the PRC (Draft) [关于《中华人民共和国专属经济区和大陆架法（草案）》的说明]." Standing Committee of the Eighth National People's Congress, 23rd Meeting. 24 December 1996. http://www.npc.gov.cn/wxzl/gongbao/2000–12/17/content_5003953.htm.

———. "Plan for Structural Reform and Functional Transformation of the State Council [国务院机构改革和职能转变方案]." 15 March 2013. http://www.gov.cn/2013lh/content_2354443.htm.

———. "PRC Constitutional Amendment [中国人民共和国宪法修正案]." 1st Session of the 13th National Party Congress, 11 March 2018. http://www.xinhuanet.com/politics/2018lh/2018–03/11/c_1122521235.htm.

———. "Report of the Law Enforcement Inspection Team of the NPC Standing Committee on the Inspection of the Implementation of the Fishery Law of

the PRC [全国人民代表大会常务委员会执法检查组关于检查《中华人民共
和国渔业法》实施情况的报告].” Thirteenth National People’s Congress, Fifteenth Meeting of the Standing Committee of the NPC, 24 December 2019.

———. Tenth PRC Five-Year Plan for Economic and Social Development (2001).
http://www.gov.cn/gongbao/content/2001/content_60699.htm.

———. Territorial Sea and Contiguous Zone Law. 24th Meeting of the Standing
Committee of the NPC, 25 February 1992. https://www.un.org/depts/los/
LEGISLATIONANDTREATIES/PDFFILES/CHN_1992_Law.pdf.

PRC Permanent Mission to the United Nations. “Speech by An Chih-Yuan,
Representative of the PRC at the UN Committee on the Peaceful Uses of
the Seabed and the Ocean Floor Beyond the Limits of National Jurisdiction.”
International Legal Materials 11, no. 3 (1972): 654.

PRC State Council. National Marine Economic Plan [全国海洋经济发展规划纲
要]. National Law, no. 13 (2003). http://www.gov.cn/gongbao/content/2003/
content_62156.htm.

———. National Marine Functional Zoning Plan [全国海洋主体功能区规划]. National Law, no. 42 (2014). http://www.gov.cn/zhengce/content/2015–08/20/
content_10107.htm.

PRC State Council Information Office (SCIO). “China Adheres to the Position
of Settling Through Negotiation the Relevant Disputes Between China
and the Philippines in the South China Sea.” 13 July 2016. http://english
.www.gov.cn/state_council/ministries/2016/07/13/content_281475392503075
.htm.

———. “China’s Military Strategy.” 26 May 2015. https://www.chinadaily.com.cn/
china/2015–05/26/content_20820628.htm.

———. “China’s National Defense in the New Era.” 24 July 2019. http://www
.xinhuanet.com/english/2019–07/24/c_138253389.htm.

———. “Diaoyu Dao, an Inherent Territory of China [钓鱼岛是中国的固有
领土].” 25 September 2012. http://www.scio.gov.cn/zfbps/ndhf/2012/
Document/1225271/1225271.htm.

———. “The Diversified Employment of China’s Armed Forces.” 16 April 2013.
http://english.www.gov.cn/archive/white_paper/2014/08/23/content
_281474982986506.htm.

PRC State Oceanic Administration (SOA). *China Fisheries Yearbook* [中国渔业年
纪], vols. 1–20. Beijing: Oceans University Press, 1999–2019.

———. *China Ocean Development Report* [中国海洋发展报告], vols. 1–20. Beijing:
China Oceans Press, 2000–2020.

———. *China Oceans Agenda 21* [中国海洋21世纪议程]. 31 October 1996. http://
www.npc.gov.cn/zgrdw/huiyi/lfzt/hdbhf/2009–10/31/content_1525058.htm.

———. *China Oceans Yearbook* [中国海洋年鉴], vols. 1–20. Beijing: China Oceans
Press, 1999–2019.

———. *Collection of the Sea Laws of the People’s Republic of China* [中华人民共
和国海洋法规选编]. SOA Department of Policy Legislation and Planning.
Beijing: Oceans Press, 2012.

———. "Twelfth Five-Year Plan for Marine Development [国家海洋事业发展'十二五'规划]." 2 September 2014. http://www.gov.cn/guoqing/2014-09/02/content_2744175.htm.

PRC Supreme People's Court. "Actively Exercise Maritime Jurisdiction in Accordance with the Law to Unify the Criteria for Adjudication of Maritime-Related Cases [依法积极行使海上司法管辖权统一涉海案件裁判尺度]." August 2016.

———. "Interpretations on the Application of the Special Maritime Procedure Law of the People's Republic of China." Adopted at the 1259th meeting of the Adjudication Committee of the Supreme People's Court, 3 December 2002, *Supreme People's Court,* No.3 Interpretation, effective 1 February 2003.

———. "Opinion on Comprehensively Promoting Foreign-Related Commercial Maritime Trials [全面推进涉外商事海事审判精品战略为构建开放型经济体制和建设海洋强国提供有力司法保障的意见]". 14 July 2015.

———. "Provisions of the Supreme People's Court on Several Issues Concerning the Trial of Cases Occurring in Waters Under the Jurisdiction of the People's Republic of China [最高人民法院关于审理发生在我国管辖海域相关案件若干问题的规定]," Nos. 1–2. 2 August 2016.

———. "Understanding and Application of the Provisions on Certain Issues Concerning the Trial of Cases Occurring in the Marine Areas Under Our Jurisdiction [《关于审理发生在我国管辖海域相关案件若干问题的规定》的理解与适用]." *People's Justice (Application)* [人民司法（应用）], no. 31 (2016): 27.

Przystup, James. "No Lack of Dialogue, Results—TBD." *Comparative Connections* (September 2016): 105–118.

PXP Energy Corporation. "SC 72 Recto Bank." Service Contracts. 2014. https://www.pxpenergy.com.ph/service-contracts/sc-72/.

Qi Huaigao. "Maritime Delimitation Between China and North Korea in the North Yellow Sea." *Ocean Development and International Law* 51, no. 4 (2020): 358–385.

Radio Free Asia. "Japan Reported to Have Conducted Free Navigation Ops in South China Sea." *Radio Free Asia,* 12 January 2022. https://www.rfa.org/english/news/china/japan-southchinasea-01122022144855.html.

Ramos, Marlon, and Tarra Quismundo. "PH Ignores China Bid to Free Poachers." *Philippine Daily Inquirer,* 9 May 2014. https://globalnation.inquirer.net/103840/ph-ignores-china-demand-to-free-fishermen.

Reed, John, and Kathrin Hille. "Philippines to Restart Oil and Gas Exploration in South China Sea." *Financial Times,* 17 October 2020. https://www.ft.com/content/b361afe9-9aa2-461a-b8ea-d8fc8850ddfa.

Reisman, W. Michael. "The Cult of Custom in the Late 20th Century." *California Western International Law Journal* 17 (1987): 133–145.

Ren Xiaofeng [任筱锋]. *Handbook on the Law of Naval Operations* [海上军事行动法手册]. Beijing: Haichao Press, 2009.

Ren Xiaofeng, and Cheng Xizhong. "A Chinese Perspective." *Marine Policy* 29, no. 2 (2005): 139–146.

Republic of China (Taiwan). "Location Map of the South China Sea Islands [南海诸岛位置图]." Ministry of the Interior, Department of Regional Affairs (February 1948). http://www.thesouthchinasea.org.cn/2016–07/19/c_53237.htm.

———. "Republic of China Position on the South China Sea Arbitration." Statement by the Ministry of Foreign Affairs. No. 002, 12 July 2016. https://en .mofa.gov.tw/News_Content.aspx?n=1330&s=34146.

———. Territorial Sea Baseline Decree (No. Tai 88 Nei Tze 06161). *ROC Executive Yuan Gazette* 5, no. 6 (10 February 1999): 36–37.

Republic of Indonesia. "Indonesia Protests PRC Violations in Indonesia's EEZ [Indonesia Protes Pelanggaran RRT di ZEE Indonesia]." Ministry for Foreign Affairs of the Republic of Indonesia, 30 December 2019. https://kemlu.go .id/portal/id/read/931/siaran_pers/indonesia-protes-pelanggaran-rrt-di-zee -indonesia.

———. "RI Reaffirms Rejecting China's Unilateral Claims on Indonesia's EEZ [RI Kembali Tegaskan Tolak Klaim Unilateral RRT atas ZEE Indonesia]." Ministry for Foreign Affairs of the Republic of Indonesia, 1 January 2020. https://kemlu.go.id/portal/id/read/933/siaran_pers/ri-kembali-tegaskan -tolak-klaim-unilateral-rrt-atas-zee-indonesia.

Republic of Korea. "8th ROK-China Director-General-Level Meeting on Delimitation of Maritime Boundaries Takes Place (5 March 2021). https://www.mofa .go.kr/eng/brd/m_5676/view.do?seq=321562.

———. Ministry of Foreign Affairs Spokesperson's Press Briefings. https://www .mofa.go.kr/eng/brd/m_5679/list.do.

———. "Outcomes of the 12th Korea-China Meeting of the Director-Generals for Maritime Boundary." 16 December 2007.

Republic of the Philippines. Constitution of the Republic of the Philippines (17 January 1973). https://www.un.org/Depts/los/ LEGISLATIONANDTREATIES/PDFFILES/PHL_1973_Constitution.pdf.

———. "DFA Deplores Chinese Embassy Response to Secretary of Defense's Statement." Department of Foreign Affairs (5 April 2021). https://dfa.gov .ph/dfa-news/statements-and-advisoriesupdate/28811-dfa-deplores-chinese -embassy-response-to-secretary-of-defense-s-statement.

———. "On the Fourth Anniversary of the Issuance of the Award in the SCS Arbitration." Statement of the Secretary of Foreign Affairs Teodoro L. Locsin, Jr. (12 July 2020). https://dfa.gov.ph/dfa-news/statements-and -advisoriesupdate/27140-statement-of-secretary-of-foreign-affairs-teodoro-l -locsin-jr-on-the-4th-anniversary-of-the-issuance-of-the-award-in-the-south -china-sea-arbitration.

———. "On the Philippines' Protest of 17 May 2021 against China's Moratorium on Fishing in the South China Sea." Department of Foreign Affairs (18 May 2021). https://dfa.gov.ph/dfa-news/statements-and-advisoriesupdate/

28982-statement-on-the-philippines-protest-of-17-may-2021-against-china-s
-moratorium-on-fishing-in-the-south-china-sea.

———. Republic Act No. 3046 (17 June 1961). https://www.un.org/Depts/los/
LEGISLATIONANDTREATIES/PDFFILES/PHL_1961_Act.pdf.

———. Republic Act No. 9522. Fourteenth Congress, Second Regular Session
(10 March 2009). https://lawphil.net/statutes/repacts/ra2009/ra_9522
_2009.html.

———. "Statement on the Inclusion of Bajo de Masinloc and the Philippine EEZ
in China's Fishing Ban." *Official Gazette of the Government of the Philippines*
(14 May 2012). https://www.officialgazette.gov.ph/2012/05/14/philippine
-statement-on-the-inclusion-of-bajo-de-masinloc-and-the-philippine-exclusive
-economic-zone-in-chinas-fishing-ban-may-14-2012/.

———. "Why the Philippines Brought This Case to Arbitration and Its Importance to the Region and the World." Statement Before the Permanent Court
of Arbitration of Hon. Albert F. Del Rosario, Secretary of Foreign Affairs (7
July 2015). https://dfa.gov.ph/dfa-news/dfa-releasesupdate/6795-statement
-before-the-permanent-court-of-arbitration.

Reus-Smit, Christian. *The Moral Purpose of the State: Culture, Social Identity, and
Institutional Rationality in International Relations.* Princeton: Princeton University Press, 1999.

———, ed. *The Politics of International Law.* New York: Cambridge University
Press, 2004.

Reuters. "China CNOOC Invites Foreign Firms to Bid for SCS, Bohai Blocks."
Reuters, 27 June 2019. https://www.reuters.com/article/uk-china-cnooc-oil/
china-cnooc-invites-foreign-firms-to-bid-for-south-china-sea-bohai-blocks
-idUKKCN1TS12M.

———. "China Says US Undermining Stability After US Warship Sails Through
the Taiwan Strait." Reuters, 24 February 2021. https://www.reuters.com/
article/us-usa-china-taiwan-warship/china-says-u-s-undermining-stability
-after-u-s-warship-sails-through-taiwan-strait-idUSKBN2AP0AO.

———. "German Warship to Sail Through South China Sea, Officials Say."
Reuters, 2 March 2021. https://www.reuters.com/article/uk-germany-china
-frigate-idUKKCN2AU2B9.

———. "Philippines Sentences 12 Chinese Fishermen to Jail." Reuters, 5 August
2014. https://www.reuters.com/article/philippines-china/philippines
-sentences-12-chinese-fishermen-to-jail-idINKBN0G50EN20140805.

———. "Vietnam Opposes Chinese Fishing Ban in Disputed Sea." Reuters,
17 May 2015. http://www.reuters.com/article/us-vietnam-china-fish
-idUSKBN0O20PF20150517.

Riesenfeld, S. A. *Protection of Coastal Fisheries Under International Law.* Washington: Carnegie Endowment for International Peace, 1942.

———. "The Third UN Conference on the Law of the Sea: What Was Accomplished? A Comment on T. T. B. Koh." *Law and Contemporary Problems* 46,
no. 2 (1983): 11–15.

Rinehart, Ian, and Bart Elias. "China's Air Defense Identification Zone (ADIZ)." *Congressional Research Service Report,* 7–5700 (R43894). 30 January 2015.

Rivera, Danessa. "PXP Energy Hikes Stake in SC72." PhilStar, 7 August 2020. https://www.philstar.com/business/2020/08/07/2033388/pxp-energy-hikes -stake-sc-72.

Roach, J. Ashley. "China's Straight Baseline Claim: Senkaku (Diaoyu) Islands." *ASIL Insights* 17, no. 7 (2013). https://www.asil.org/insights/volume/17/ issue/7/china%E2%80%99s-straight-baseline-claim-senkaku-diaoyu-islands #_edn26.

———. "Offshore Archipelagos Enclosed by Straight Baselines: An Excessive Claim?" *Ocean Development and International Law* 49, no. 2 (2018): 176–202.

———. "Today's Customary International Law of the Sea." *Ocean Development and International Law* 45, no. 3 (2014): 239–259.

Roach, J. Ashley, and Robert M. Smith. *Excessive Maritime Claims,* 4th Ed. Publications on Ocean Development, no. 93. The Netherlands: Brill Nijhoff, 2021.

Roberts, Anthea Elizabeth. *Is International Law International?* Oxford: Oxford University Press, 2017.

———. "Traditional and Modern Approaches to Customary International Law: A Reconciliation." *American Journal of International Law* 95, no. 4 (2001): 757–791.

Roberts, Anthea, Paul B. Stephan, Pierre-Hugues Verdier, and Mila Versteeg. "Exploring Comparative International Law: Framing the Field." *American Journal of International Law* 109, no. 3 (2015): 467–474.

———, eds. *Comparative International Law.* Oxford: Oxford University Press, 2018.

Rocha, Euan. "CNOOC Closes $15.1bn Acquisition of Canada's Nexen." Reuters, 25 February 2013. http://www.reuters.com/article/us-nexen-cnooc -idUSBRE91O1A420130225.

Roehrig, Terence. "Caught in the Middle: South Korea and the South China Sea Arbitration." *Asian Yearbook of International Law* 21 (2015): 96–120.

———. "South Korea: The Challenges of a Maritime Nation." National Bureau of Asian Research, 23 December 2019. https://www.nbr.org/publication/south -korea-the-challenges-of-a-maritime-nation/#_ftn10.

Rosneft. "Rosneft Starts Drilling Offshore Production Wells in Vietnam." Rosneft Information Division, 18 May 2018. https://www.rosneft.com/press/news/ item/190909/.

Ross, Robert S. "The 1995–96 Taiwan Strait Confrontation: Coercion, Credibility, and the Use of Force." *International Security* 25, no. 2 (2000): 87–123.

Ruggie, John Gerard. *Multilateralism Matters: The Theory and Praxis of Institutional Form.* New York: Columbia University Press, 1993.

Sakamoto Shigeki. "China's New Coast Guard Law and Implications for Maritime Security in the East and South China Seas." *Lawfare,* 16 February 2021. https://www.lawfareblog.com/chinas-new-coast-guard-law-and-implications -maritime-security-east-and-south-china-seas.

———. "The Senkaku Islands as Viewed Through Chinese Law." *Review of Island Studies* (September 2016). https://www.spf.org/islandstudies/research/a00017r.html.

Salim, Tama. "RI Flexes Muscle, Sinks Chinese Boat, A Big One." *Jakarta Post,* 20 May 2015. http://www.thejakartapost.com/news/2015/05/20/ri-flexes-muscle-sinks-chinese-boat-a-big-one.html.

Samuels, Merwyn. *Contest for the South China Sea.* London: Routledge, 2013.

Samuels, Richard J. "'New Fighting Power!': Japan's Growing Maritime Capabilities and East Asian Security." *International Security* 32, no. 3 (2008): 84–112.

Scharf, Michael P. *Customary International Law in Times of Fundamental Change: Recognizing Grotian Moments.* New York: Cambridge University Press, 2014.

Schatz, Valentin J. "Combating Illegal Fishing in the Exclusive Economic Zone." *Goettingen Journal of International Law* 7, no. 2 (2016): 383–414.

Scheppele, Kim Lane. "Law in a Time of Emergency: States of Exception and the Temptations of 9/11." *University of Pennsylvania Journal of Constitutional Law* 5, no. 6 (2004): 1001–1085.

Schofield, Clive. "A Landmark Decision in the South China Sea: The Scope and Implications of the Arbitral Tribunal's Award." *Contemporary Southeast Asia* 38, no. 3 (2016): 339–348.

———. "Parting the Waves: Claims to Maritime Jurisdiction and the Division of Ocean Space." *Penn State Journal of Law & International Affairs* 1, no. 1 (2013): 38–58.

Schweller, Randall L. "Managing the Rise of Great Powers." In *Engaging China: The Management of an Emerging China,* edited by Alastair Iain Johnston and Robert S. Ross. New York: Routledge, 1999, 1–31.

———. "The Problem of International Order Revisited: A Review Essay." *International Security* 26, no. 1 (2001): 161–186.

Scott, Robert E., and Paul B. Stephan. *The Limits of Leviathan: Contract Theory and the Enforcement of International Law.* Cambridge: Cambridge University Press, 2016.

Seibt, Sebastian. "France Wades into the South China Sea with a Nuclear Attack Submarine." *France24,* 12 February 2021. https://www.france24.com/en/france/20210212-france-wades-into-the-south-china-sea-with-a-nuclear-attack-submarine.

Shan Xu [山旭]. "China's Participation in the Negotiations of the UN Convention on the Law of the Sea [我国参与联合国海洋法公约谈判始末]." *Oriental Outlook* [东方周刊], 10 December 2012. http://news.sina.com.cn/c/sd/2012–12–10/141125774618.shtml.

Shaw Han-yi. "Revisiting the Diaoyutai/Senkaku Islands Dispute: Examining Legal Claims and New Historic Evidence Under International Law and the Traditional East Asian World Order." *Chinese Yearbook of International Law* 26 (2008): 95–169.

Shearer, Ivan. "The Limits of Maritime Jurisdiction." In *The Limits of Maritime Jurisdiction*, edited by Clive Schofield, Seokwoo Lee, and Moon Sang Kwon. Leiden: Brill Nijhoff, 2014, 51–63.

Shen Manhong [沈满洪], and Yu Xuan [余璇]. "Research on Xi Jinping's Important Exposition on Building Maritime Power [习近平建设海洋强国重要论述研究]." *Journal of Zhejiang University* [浙江大学学报] 48, no 6. (2018): 5–17.

Shi Yuanhua [石源华]. "'Diplomacy on Hold': Sovereignty Is Ours, Shelve Disputes and Pursue Joint Development ['搁置外交'：主权在我，搁置争议，共同开发]." *World Affairs* [世界知识], no. 4 (2014): 22–23.

Shi Yulong [史育龙]. "Give Full Play to the Strategic Leading Role of Land and Sea Coordination [充分发挥陆海统筹的战略引领作用]." *People's Daily* [人民日报], 1 July 2018. http://theory.people.com.cn/n1/2018/0701/c40531–30097800.html.

Shu Zhenya [疏震娅]. "Research Overview on the Study of the Critical Date in International Law [国际法上关键日期问题的理论研究考察]." *Journal of Boundary and Ocean Studies* [边界与海洋研究] 3, no. 3 (2018): 66–77.

———. "Vietnam Insists on Enacting Legislation for Xisha and Nansha, Which Seriously Violates China's Sovereignty [越南执意为西沙和南沙立法 严重侵犯中国主权]." PRC State Oceanic Administration, Center for International Marine Affairs [国家海洋局海洋发展战略研究所], 5 July 2012. http://www.cimamnr.org.cn/info/348.

Simmons, Beth A. *Mobilizing for Human Rights*. New York: Cambridge University Press, 2009.

———. "Rules over Real Estate: Trade, Territorial Conflict, and International Borders as Institution." *Journal of Conflict Resolution* 49, no. 6 (2005): 823–848.

Sina Military [新浪军事]. "Chinese Fisheries Law Enforcement Vessels Have Rescued Captured Chinese Fishing Boats in Spratlys 7 Times [中国渔政船曾7次在南沙现场解救被抓扣中方渔船]." *Sina News* [新浪新闻], 22 November 2011. http://mil.news.sina.com.cn/2011–11–22/1455674661.html.

———. "A Mysterious Giant Ship of Our Navy Retired After Only 10 Years of Service and Went to Nansha to Declare Sovereignty [我海军一神秘巨舰仅服役10年便退役 曾赴南沙宣示主权]." *Sina News* [新浪新闻], 5 September 2018. http://mil.news.sina.com.cn/jssd/2018–09–05/doc-ihiixzkm4813155.shtml.

———. "US Aircraft Carrier Entered China's Territorial Waters to Provoke and Was Intercepted by Our J8 Su-27 Warplanes [美航母曾进中国领海挑衅遭我军歼8苏27战机拦截]." *Sina News* [新浪新闻], 4 January 2015. http://mil.news.sina.com.cn/2015–01–04/0831816887.html.

Slaughter, Anne-Marie, and William Burke-White. "The Future of International Law." *Harvard International Law Journal* 47, no. 2 (2006): 327–352.

Socialist Republic of Vietnam. "Developments in the East Sea." Ministry of Foreign Affairs, National Border Commission, and Vietnam Coast Guard International Press Conference, 5 June 2014. https://www.mofa.gov.vn/en/tt_baochi/tcbc/ns140609024213.

———. "Dispute Regarding the Law on the EEZ and Continental Shelf of the PRC Which Was Passed on 26 June 1998." Diplomatic Note of 6 August 1998. *Law of the Sea Bulletin*, no. 38: 54–55.

———. Law of the Sea of Vietnam. The National Assembly, Law No. 18/2012/QH13, 21 June 2012. https://vanbanphapluat.co/law-no-18–2012-qh13-on -vietnamese-sea.

———. Partial Submission in Respect of Vietnam's Extended Continental Shelf: North Area (VNM-N). Executive Summary. 7 May 2009. https:// www.un.org/Depts/los/clcs_new/submissions_files/mysvnm33_09/mys _vnm2009excutivesummary.pdf.

———. Statement on the Territorial Sea Baseline of Vietnam (12 November 1982). https://www.un.org/Depts/los/LEGISLATIONANDTREATIES/PDFFILES/ VNM_1982_Statement.pdf.

———. "Statement on Vietnam's Response to the Final Judgment Issued by the Arbitral Tribunal Established Under Annex VII of the 1982 UNCLOS on the Basis of the Claim of the Philippines." 12 July 2016. http://www.mofa.gov.vn/ vi/tt_baochi/pbnfn/ns160712171301.

———. Statement Transmitted to the Arbitral Tribunal in the Proceedings Between the Republic of the Philippines and the People's Republic of China. Ministry of Foreign Affairs of the Socialist Republic of Vietnam, 14 December 2014. https://www.un.org/depts/los/clcs_new/submissions_files/vnm37 _09/vnm2009n_executivesummary.pdf.

———. "Vietnam Attends 21st Meeting of UNCLOS States Parties." Embassy of the Socialist Republic of Vietnam in the USA. 20 June 2011. http:// vietnamembassy-usa.org/news/2011/06/vietnam-attends-21st-meeting -unclos-states-parties.

Solum, Lawrence B. "On the Indeterminacy Crisis: Critiquing Critical Dogma." *University of Chicago Law Review* 54, no. 2 (1987): 462–503.

Song Xue. "Why Joint Development Agreements Fail: Implications for the South China Sea Dispute." *Contemporary Southeast Asia* 41, no. 3 (2019): 418–446.

Song Yann-huei. "Declarations and Statements with Respect to the 1982 UN-CLOS: Potential Legal Disputes Between the United States and China After US Accession to the Convention." *Ocean Development & International Law* 36, no. 3 (2005): 261–289.

———. "The July 2016 Arbitral Award, Interpretation of Article 121(3) of the UNCLOS, and Selecting Examples of Inconsistent State Practices." *Ocean Development and International Law* 49, no. 3 (2018): 247–261.

———. "Peaceful Proposals and Maritime Cooperation Between Mainland China, Japan, and Taiwan in the East China Sea: Progress Made and Challenges Ahead." *Asian Yearbook of International Law* 22 (2016): 20–49.

Song Yann-huei, and Zou Keyuan. "Maritime Legislation of Mainland China and Taiwan: Developments, Comparisons, Implications, and Potential Challenges for the United States." *Ocean Development & International Law* 31 (2000): 303–345.

South China Morning Post. "More Footage Emerges from 2018 Near Collision of US and China Warships in the SCS." 4 November 2018. https://www .scmp.com/video/china/2171609/newly-released-video-shows-near-collision -between-us-and-chinese-warships-south.

South China Sea Arbitration (SCS Arbitration). The Republic of Philippines v. The People's Republic of China. Case 2013–9. Permanent Court of Arbitration. 12 July 2016. (All awards, memorials, and documents cited from this case can be retrieved at https://pca-cpa.org/en/cases/7/.)

South China Sea Online [中国南海网]. "1948 New Map of the Nanyang Islands [1948 南洋群岛新地图]." 19 July 2016. http://www.thesouthchinasea.org.cn/ 2016–07/19/c_53239.htm.

———. "Timeline: 1990–1999." 22 July 2016. http://www.thesouthchinasea.org .cn/2016–07/22/c_53607.htm.

Steinberg, Richard H., and Jonathan M. Zasloff. "Power and International Law." *American Journal of International Law* 100, no. 1 (2016): 64–87.

Storey, Ian. "China and the Philippines: Implications of the Reed Bank Incident." *Jamestown China Brief* 11, no. 8 (2011). https://jamestown.org/program/china -and-the-philippines-implications-of-the-reed-bank-incident/.

Straits Times. "Chinese Ships Intruded into Malaysian Waters 89 Times in Four Years: Report." *The Straits Times,* 14 July 2020. https://www.straitstimes .com/asia/se-asia/chinese-ships-intruded-into-malaysian-waters-89-times-in -four-years-report.

Su, Steven Wei. "The Tiaoyu Islands and Their Possible Effect on the Maritime Boundary Delimitation Between China and Japan." *Chinese Journal of International Law* 3 (2004): 385–421.

Sun Hang [孙航]. "Zhou Qiang Puts Forward Requirements on Maritime Trial Work [周强对海事审判工作提出要求]." *People's Court News* [人民法院新闻], 22 October 2020. http://www.court.gov.cn/fabu-xiangqing-265411.html.

Sun Jisheng [孙吉胜]. "The Path of Shaping and Enhancing China's International Discourse [中周国际话语权的 塑造马提升路]." *World Economics and Politics* [世界经济与政治], no. 3 (2019): 19–43.

Sun Kuan Ming. "Policy of the Republic of China Towards the South China Sea: Recent Developments." *Marine Policy* 19, no. 5 (1995): 401–409.

Sun Yundao [孙运道]. "Iron Warriors Able to Win Victory [能大胜站的铁军]." *China Ocean News* [中国海洋报], 10 May 2013. http://epaper.oceanol.com/ shtml/zghyb/20130510/32701.shtml.

Symmons, Clive R. *Historic Waters in the Law of the Sea: A Modern Re-Appraisal.* Publications on Ocean Development 61. Leiden: Brill, 2008.

Talmon, Stefan. "The South China Sea Arbitration: Observations on the Award on Jurisdiction and Admissibility." *Chinese Journal of International Law,* no. 15 (2016): 309–391.

Tanaka, Yoshifumi. *The International Law of the Sea*. Cambridge: Cambridge University Press, 2012.

———. *The South China Sea Arbitration: Toward an International Legal Order in the Oceans*. Oxford: Bloomsbury, 2019.

Tang Zhengrui [唐正瑞]. *The Taiwan Issue in the US-China Chess Game* [中美棋局中的台湾问题]. Shanghai: Shanghai People's Press, 2000.

Tanner, Murray Scot. *The Politics of Lawmaking in Post-Mao China: Institutions, Processes, and Democratic Prospects*. New York: Oxford University Press, 1999.

Tønnesson, Stein. "The Paracels: The 'Other' South China Sea Dispute." *Asian Perspective* 26, no. 4 (2002): 145–169.

Tobin, Liza. "Wind in the Sails: China Accelerates Its Maritime Strategy." *War on the Rocks*, 9 May 2018. https://warontherocks.com/2018/05/wind-in-the-sails -china-accelerates-its-maritime-strategy.

Tuoi Tre News. "Chinese Warship Soldiers Point Guns at Vietnamese Supply Boat in Vietnam's Waters." *Tuoi Tre News*, 27 November 2015. https:// tuoitrenews.vn/news/society/20151127/chinese-warship-soldiers-point-guns -at-vietnamese-supply-boat-in-vietnam%E2%80%99s-waters/14351.html.

United Kingdom Parliament. "South China Sea: Freedom of Navigation." *United Kingdom House of Commons*, vol. 679 (3 September 2020). https:// hansard.parliament.uk/commons/2020–09–03/debates/99D50BD9 –8C8A-4835–9C70–6E9A38585BC4/SouthChinaSeaFreedomOfNavigation.

United Nations Division for Ocean Affairs and the Law of the Sea (DOALOS). "Declarations and Reservations." XXI United Nations Convention on the Law of the Sea 6. https://treaties.un.org/doc/Publication/MTDSG/Volume %20II/Chapter%20XXI/XXI-6.en.pdf.

United Nations Food and Agriculture Organization. "The State of World Fisheries and Aquaculture: Sustainability in Action." Rome, 2020. http://www.fao.org/ 3/ca9229en/CA9229EN.pdf.

United States Central Intelligence Agency. "Coastline." *The World Factbook*. https://www.cia.gov/the-world-factbook/field/coastline/.

———. "Spratly Islands." *The World Factbook*. Updated 15 March 2021. https:// www.cia.gov/the-world-factbook/countries/spratly-islands/.

United States Department of Defense. Annual Freedom of Navigation Reports. 1991–2020. Office of the Under Secretary of Defense for Policy, Oceans Policy Advisor. https://policy.defense.gov/OUSDP-Offices/FON/.

———. "Military and Security Developments Involving the People's Republic of China." Office of the Secretary of Defense, Annual Report to Congress. 2016–2021.

United States Department of State. "Agreement on Establishing a Consultation Mechanism to Strengthen Military Maritime Safety." US Department of Defense and PRC Ministry of National Defense, 19 January 1998. https://www .state.gov/wp-content/uploads/2019/02/12924-China-Maritime-Matters-Misc -Agreement-1.19.1998.pdf.

———. "China: Maritime Claims in the South China Sea." *Limits in the Seas,* No. 143, 5 December 2014. https://www.state.gov/wp-content/uploads/2019/10/LIS-143.pdf.

———. "Conversation Between President Nixon and His Assistant for National Security Affairs (Kissinger)." *Foreign Relations of the United States, 1969–1976,* vol. E-1, Documents on Global Issues, 1969–1972, Document 395, 29 May 1971. https://history.state.gov/historicaldocuments/frus1969–76ve01/d395.

———. *Digest of the United States Practice in International Law 2016.* Office of the Legal Advisor. Edited by CarrieLyn D. Guymon. https://2017–2021.state.gov/wp-content/uploads/2019/05/2016-Digest-United-States.pdf.

———. "A Foreign Policy for the American People." Office of the Spokesperson, 3 March 2021. https://www.state.gov/a-foreign-policy-for-the-american-people/.

———. "Japan: Straight Baseline and Territorial Sea Claims." *Limits in the Seas,* No. 120, 30 April 1998. https://2009–2017.state.gov/documents/organization/57684.pdf.

———. "Maritime Boundary: Chile–Peru." *Limits in the Seas,* No. 86, 2 July 1979. http://www.state.gov/documents/organization/58820.pdf.

———. "Military Operational Issues." *US Department of State Archive 2001–2009.* https://2001–2009.state.gov/t/pm/iso/c21539.htm#fon.

———. "People's Republic of China: Maritime Claims in the South China Sea." *Limits in the Seas,* No. 150, January 2022. https://www.state.gov/wp-content/uploads/2022/01/LIS150-SCS.pdf.

———. "Secretary Antony J. Blinken, National Security Advisor Jake Sullivan, Director Yang and State Councilor Wang at the Top of Their Meeting." *Office of the Spokesperson,* 18 March 2021. https://www.state.gov/secretary-antony-j-blinken-national-security-advisor-jake-sullivan-chinese-director-of-the-office-of-the-central-commission-for-foreign-affairs-yang-jiechi-and-chinese-state-councilor-wang-yi-at-th/.

———. Senate Foreign Relations Committee Testimony of Asst. Sec. State in Office of the Legal Adviser, 27 September 2007. *Digest of US Practice in International Law.* Washington, DC: International Law Institute, 2008: 614–624.

———. "Spain: Maritime Claims and Boundaries." *Limits in the Seas,* No. 149, 23 November 2020. https://www.state.gov/wp-content/uploads/2020/11/LIS149-Spain.pdf.

———. "Straight Baseline Claim: China." *Limits in the Seas,* No. 117, 9 July 1996. http://www.state.gov/documents/organization/57692.pdf

———. "Straight Baselines: People's Republic of China." *Limits in the Seas,* No. 43, 2 July 1972.: http://www.state.gov/documents/organization/58832.pdf.

———. "Straight Baselines: Vietnam." *Limits in the Seas,* No. 99, 12 December 1983. https://www.state.gov/wp-content/uploads/2019/12/LIS-99.pdf.

———. "Taiwan's Maritime Claims." *Limits in the Seas,* No. 127, 15 November 2005. https://www.state.gov/wp-content/uploads/2019/12/LIS-127.pdf.

———. "US Responses to Excessive National Maritime Claims." *Limits in the Seas*, No. 112, 9 March 1992. https://www.state.gov/wp-content/uploads/2019/12/LIS-112.pdf.

United States Navy Judge Advocate General's (JAG) Corps. *Maritime Claims Reference Manual.* Updated 22 March 2021. https://www.jag.navy.mil/organization/code_10_mcrm.htm.

United States Navy Seventh Fleet. "7th Fleet Destroyer Conducts FONOP in the South China Sea." *7th Fleet Public Affairs.* 5 February 2021. https://www.cpf.navy.mil/news.aspx/130803.

Urano, Tatsuo. *Senkaku Islands, Okinawa Islands, and China* [尖閣諸島、沖縄諸島、そして中国]. Tokyo: Sanwa Shoseki, 2005.

Vagts, Alfred, and Detlev F. Vagts. "The Balance of Power in International Law: A History of an Idea." *American Journal of International Law* 73, no. 4 (1979): 555–580.

Vagts, Detlev F. "Hegemonic International Law." *American Journal of International Law* 95, no. 4 (2001): 843–848.

———. "International Relations Looks at Customary International Law: A Traditionalist's Defence." *European Journal of International Law* 15 (5): 1031–1040.

Van Dyke, Jon M. "The Disappearing Right to Navigational Freedom in the Exclusive Economic Zone." *Marine Policy* 29, no. 2 (2005): 107–121.

———. "Disputes over Islands and Maritime Boundaries in East Asia." In *Maritime Boundary Disputes, Settlement Processes, and the Law of the Sea,* edited by Seoung-Yong Hong and Jon M. Van Dyke. Leiden: Martinus Nijhoff, 2009, 39–75.

———. "Military Ships and Planes Operating in the Exclusive Economic Zone of Another Country." *Marine Policy* 28, no. 1 (2004): 29–39.

Verdier, Pierre-Hugues, and Erik Voeten. "Precedent, Compliance, and Change in Customary International Law: An Explanatory Theory." *American Journal of International Law* 108, no. 3 (2014): 389–434.

Wang Chen [王晨]. "Actively Participate in Foreign-Related Legal Struggles and Counter Suppression [积极参与涉外法治斗争，反制打压]." *Observer* [观察], 9 December 2020. https://www.guancha.cn/politics/2020_12_09_574071.shtml.

———. "Xi Jinping Thought on Rule by Law Is a New Development and Leap in the Sinicization of Marxist Rule by Law Theory [习近平法治思想是马克思主义法治理论中国化的新发展新飞跃]." *People's Daily (Theory)* [人民日报(理论)], 20 April 2021. http://theory.people.com.cn/n1/2021/0420/c40531-32083076.html.

Wang Chenguang. "From the Rule of Man to the Rule of Law." In *China's Journey Toward the Rule of Law: Legal Reform 1978–2008,* edited by Cai Dingjian and Wang Chenguang. Leiden: Brill, 2010, 1–50.

Wang Dong. *China's Unequal Treaties: Narrating National History.* New York: Lexington Books, 2005.

———. "The Discourse of Unequal Treaties in Modern China," *Pacific Affairs* 76, no. 3 (2003): 399–425.

Wang Kan [王看]. "Analysis of International Legal Research on the Philippines' South China Sea Arbitration [菲律宾南海仲裁案国际法研究文献述评]." *Journal of Boundary and Ocean Studies* [边界与海洋研究] 3, no. 3 (2018): 31–53.

Wang Shumei [王淑梅]. "Build an International Maritime Judicial Center to Help Build Maritime Power [打造国际海事司法中心 助推海洋强国建设]." *People's Court News* [人民法院报], 3 August 2018. http://aoc.ouc.edu.cn/2a/9b/c9821a207515/page.psp.

Wang Tieya [王铁崖]. "International Law in Ancient China." In *International Law in China: Historical and Contemporary Perspectives*. Leiden: Martinus Nijhoff, 1990, 205–225.

———. "International Law in Modern China." In *International Law in China: Historical and Contemporary Perspectives*. Leiden: Martinus Nijhoff, 1990, 226–249.

———. "Present Trends of International Law." *Peking University Journal* [北京大学学报] 2, no. 17 (1980).

———. "The Sources of International Law [国际法的渊源]." *Great Encyclopedia of China: Law* [中国大百科全书：法学]. Beijing: People's Press, 1984.

———. "Teaching and Research of International Law in Present Day China." *Columbia Journal of Transnational Law* 22, no. 1 (1983): 77–82.

Wang Tieya [王铁崖], and Wei Min [魏敏]. *International Law* [国际法]. Beijing: Legal Press, 1981.

Wang Xinyi [王新艺]. "Cruise Law Enforcement: The Changed Pattern of China's Rights Protection [巡航执法:改变了的中国海洋维权格局]." *Modern Navy* [当代海军], no. 8 (2011): 60–61.

Wang Ying [王莹]. "Jurisprudential Analysis of 'Other Countries' Attitudes' on the Formation of Historic Rights [他国的态度"在历史性权利构成中的法理分析]." *Journal of Boundary and Ocean Studies* [边界与海洋研究] 4, no. 3 (2019): 54–68.

Wang Zelin [王泽林]. "Twelfth 'Oceans University International Law Academic Salon' Was Successfully Held in 2020 [2020年第十二期'中国还大国际法学术沙龙'成功举办]." *Oceans University of China Law School*, 7 July 2020. http://law.ouc.edu.cn/2020/0709/c17230a292545/page.htm.

Watts, Arthur. "The International Rule of Law." *German Yearbook of International Law* 36 (1993): 15–45.

Weil, Prosper. "Towards Relative Normativity in International Law?" *American Journal of International Law* 77, no. 3 (1983): 413–442.

Weiss, Jessica Chen. *Powerful Patriots: Nationalist Protest in China's Foreign Relations*. New York: Oxford University Press, 2014.

Weiss, Jessica Chen, and Jeremy L. Wallace. "Domestic Politics, China's Rise, and the Future of the Liberal International Order." *International Organization* 75, no. 2 (2021): 635–664.

White House. "Remarks by President Obama and President Xi of the PRC in Joint Press Conference." 25 September 2015. https://obamawhitehouse .archives.gov/the-press-office/2015/09/25/remarks-president-obama-and -president-xi-peoples-republic-china-joint.

———. "Remarks by the President in Meeting on the Trans-Pacific Partnership." Office of the Press Secretary. 13 November 2015. https://obamawhitehouse .archives.gov/the-press-office/2015/11/13/remarks-president-meeting-trans -pacific-partnership.

Whiting, Allen S. "China's Use of Force, 1950–1996, and Taiwan." *International Security* 26, no. 2 (2001): 103–131.

Wilson Center Digital Archive. "Main Speech by Premier Zhou Enlai, Head of the Delegation of the People's Republic of China, Distributed at the Plenary Session of the Asian-African Conference, April 19, 1955." *History and Public Policy Program Digital Archive*. Translation from China and the Asian-African Conference (Documents). Peking: Foreign Languages Press, 1955: 9–20.

———. "Record of Meeting Between Prime Minister Fukuda and Vice Premier Deng (Second Meeting, 25 October 1978)." *History and Public Policy Program Digital Archive, Diplomatic Archives of the Ministry of Foreign Affairs of Japan,* 01–935–2, 016–027. Contributed by Robert Hoppens and translated by Stephen Mercado. https://digitalarchive.wilsoncenter.org/document/120019.

———. "Record of the Third Meeting Between Prime Minister Tanaka and Premier Zhou Enlai, 27 September 1972." *History and Public Policy Program Digital Archive*, no 2001–42. Translated by Ryo C. Kato. https://digitalarchive .wilsoncenter.org/document/121228.

Wu Shicun. "Will Vietnam Think Twice Before Filing an Arbitration in the South China Sea?" *South China Sea Probing Initiative*, 12 June 2020. http://www .scspi.org/en/dtfx/1591971010.

Wu Zhuang [吴壮]. "The Dream of Maritime Power Has Never Been So Close: Director of the Nanhai District Fisheries Bureau, Ministry of Agriculture [农业部南海区渔政局局长：海洋强国梦从未这么近]." *People's Daily* [人民日报], 20 December 2012. http://politics.people.com.cn/n/2012/1220/ c1001–19959400.html.

Xi Jinping. "Carry Forward the Five Principles of Peaceful Coexistence to Build a Better World Through Win-Win Cooperation." Address at the Meeting Marking the 60th Anniversary of the Initiation of the Five Principles of Peaceful Coexistence. 28 June 2014. http://www.china.org.cn/world/2014–07/07/ content_32876905.htm.

———. "Deepen the Partnership to Build a Beautiful Home in Asia [深化合作 伙伴关系共建亚洲美好家园]." Speech at the National University of Singapore. 7 November 2015. http://www.china.org.cn/chinese/2015–11/12/content _37046980.htm.

———. "Secure a Decisive Victory in Building a Moderately Prosperous Society in All Respects and Strive for the Great Success of Socialism with Chinese Characteristics for a New Era." Speech at 19th National Party Congress.

18 October 2017. http://www.xinhuanet.com/english/download/Xi_Jinping
's_report_at_19th_CPC_National_Congress.pdf.

———. "Speech on Building Maritime Power—Comrade Xi Jinping's speech at
the Eighth Collective Study of the Political Bureau of the CPC Central Committee [习近平关于建设海洋强国的讲话—近平同志在中共中央政治局第
八次集体学习时的讲话]." *Pacific Journal* [太平洋学报], 30 July 2013. http://
www.pacificjournal.com.cn/CN/news/news263.shtml.

———. "We Must Further Care About the Ocean, Be Aware of the Ocean, and
Strategically Manage the Ocean [要进一步关心海洋、认识海洋、经略
海洋]." Xinhua [新华], 31 July 2013. http://www.xinhuanet.com//politics/
2013–07/31/c_116762285.htm.

Xiao Feng [肖锋]. "Reflections on the US-China Freedom of Navigation Debate
[对中美航行自由之争的思考]." *Journal of Boundary and Ocean Studies* [边界
与海洋研究] 5, no. 4 (2020): 32–43.

Xiao Jun [肖君], Gao Hengsheng [高恒生], Guo Zhiwei [郭志伟], Zhang Yan
[张琰], and Jiang Meichen [姜美辰]. "A Study of State Practice in the Outlying Archipelagic Regime [远洋群岛制度的国家实践研究]." *Rule of Law and
Society* [法制与社会], no. 6 (2017): 27–28.

Xiao Xunlong [肖勋龙], and Li Shouqi [李寿其]. "Considering Countermeasures
of Public Opinion Warfare in the Struggle for Maritime Rights." *National
Defense Science & Technology* [国防科技] 34, no. 5 (2013): 99–102.

Xiao Yongping [肖永平]. "Revolution in Teaching and Studying Law [法律的教与
学之革命]." *Jurisprudence Review* [法学评论], no. 3 (2003): 153–160.

Xinhua. "The Central Committee of the Communist Party of China Issued the
'Deepening Party and State Institutional Reform Plan' [中共中央印发'深
化党和国家机构改革方案']." Xinhua [新华社]. 21 March 2018. http://www
.xinhuanet.com/2018–03/21/c_1122570517.htm.

———. "Chinese Representative Speaks at the Sub-committee of UN Seabed
Committee." *Xinhua Weekly* [新华周刊], no. 15 (9 April 1973), 18.

———. "Li Peng Sends Motion on New Law on Exclusive Economic Zone."
24 December 1996.

———. "Liu Cigui: The Naming of Our Islands by the SOA Is Normal [刘赐
贵：国家海洋局对我海岛命名属正常工作]." Xinhua [新华], 4 March 2012.
https://china.huanqiu.com/article/9CaKrnJusxl.

———. "The Navy's SCS Fleet Open Sea Training Formation Held an Oath-
Taking Ceremony at James Shoal [海军南海舰队远海训练编队在曾母暗沙举
行宣誓仪式]." 26 March 2013. http://www.gov.cn/jrzg/2013–03/26/content
_2362922.htm.

———. "Strive to Start a New Journey of Building a Rule of Law in China [奋力
开启法治中国建设新征程]." Xinhua [新华], 19 March 2021. http://www
.xinhuanet.com/politics/2021–03/19/c_1127230039.htm.

Xu Hong [徐宏]. "Experiencing the Storm of International Law and Praising
China's Contribution [亲历国际法风云点赞中国贡献]." *Wuhan University
Law Review* [武大国际法评论], no. 1 (2019): 29–40.

Xu Senan [许森安]. "The Meaning of the Dashed National Boundary Line in the SCS [南海断续国界线的内涵]." In *Seminar on SCS Issues and the Way Forward in the 21st Century* [21世纪的南海问题与前瞻"研讨会文选]. Hainan, PRC: Hainan South China Sea Research Center, 2000, 80–82.

———. "We Must Pay Attention to the Studies of Sea Borders [要重视海邻研究]." *Historical and Geographic Studies of China's Borders* [中国边疆史地研究], no. 4 (1988): 18–20.

Xue Guifang. "Bilateral Fisheries Agreements for the Cooperative Management of the Shared Resources of the China Seas: A Note." *Ocean Development and International Law* 36, no. 4 (2005): 363–374.

———. "China and the Law of the Sea: An Update." *International Law Studies Series US Naval War College* 84 (2008): 97–110.

———. "China's Response to International Fisheries Law and Policy: National Action and Regional Cooperation." PhD Dissertation, University of Wollongong, 2004.

Xue Hanqin. *Chinese Contemporary Perspectives on International Law.* Leiden: Brill Nijhoff, 2012.

Xue Hanqin, and Jin Qian. "International Treaties in the Chinese Domestic Legal System." *Chinese Journal of International Law* 8, no. 2 (2009): 299–322.

Yang Dongxiao [杨东晓]. "The Historical Process of Nationalization of the Diaoyu Islands by the Japanese Government [日本政府将钓鱼岛"国有化"的历史过程]." *Sina History* [新浪历史], 13 August 2013. http://history.sina.com.cn/his/bk/2013–08–13/162051361.shtml.

Yang Jiechi [杨洁篪]. "Conscientiously Study and Publicize the Spirit of the 19th Party Congress [推动构建人类命运共同体]." *People's Daily* [人民日报], 19 November 2017. http://cpc.people.com.cn/n1/2017/1119/c64094–29654801.html.

———. "Deeply Understand and Make Good Use of International Law [深刻认识和用好国际法]." *Seeking Truth* [求是], no. 20 (2020). http://www.qstheory.cn/dukan/qs/2020–10/16/c_1126613584.htm.

———. "Firmly Uphold and Practice Multilateralism and Persist in Promoting the Building of a Community with a Shared Future for Mankind [坚定维护和践行多边主义 坚持推动构建人类命运共同体]." *People's Daily* [人民日报], 21 February 2021. http://paper.people.com.cn/rmrb/html/2021–02/21/nw.D110000renmrb_20210221_1–06.htm.

Yang Wenhua [杨文华], and Li Yunwei [李韫伟]. "The Promotion of National Ideology of the International Right to Speak [国家意识形态国际话语权的提升]." *Journal of Chongqing University of Posts and Telecommunications* 31, no. 2 (2019): 1–7.

Yang Xiaodan [杨晓丹], and Yang Zhirong [杨志荣]. "Maintain Maritime Rights and Build a Maritime Power [维护海洋权益建设海洋强国]." *People's Daily* [人民日报网], 21 September 2017. http://theory.people.com.cn/n1/2017/0921/c40531–29549318.html.

Yee, Sienho. "AALCO Informal Expert Group's Comments on the ILC Project on 'Identification of Customary International Law': A Brief Follow-up." *Chinese Journal of International Law* 17, no. 1 (March 2018): 187–194.

YouTube. "USNS Impeccable Harassed by Chinese Vessels." 25 March 2009. https://www.youtube.com/watch?v=hQvQjwAE4w4&ab_channel=dvidshub.

Yu Mincai [余民才]. "China and the UN Convention on the Law of the Sea [中国籍联合国海洋法公约]." *Contemporary International Relations* [现代国际关系], no. 10 (December 2012): 55–62.

Yu Zhirong [郁志荣]. "What Is the Value of the First Territorial Sea Cruise in the Diaoyu Islands? [首次钓鱼岛领海巡航的价值何在?]." Chahar Institute [察哈尔学会]. 9 December 2019. http://www.charhar.org.cn/newsinfo.aspx?newsid=15572.

Yung, Christopher, Ross Rustici, Isaac Kardon, and Joshua Wiseman. "China's Out of Area Naval Operations: Case Studies, Trajectories, Obstacles, and Potential Solutions." *INSS China Strategic Perspectives*, no. 3 (December 2010).

Zhang Dengyi [张登义]. "Properly Manage and Use the Oceans, Build a Maritime Great Power [管好用好海洋建设海洋强国]." *Seeking Truth* [求是], no. 11 (2001): 46–48.

Zhang Feng. "Assessing China's Response to the South China Sea Arbitration Ruling." *Australian Journal of International Affairs* 71, no. 4 (2017): 440–459.

Zhang Guobin [张国斌], ed. *Research on the Innocent Passage Regime* [无害通过制度研究]. Shanghai: Jiaotong University Press, 2019.

Zhang Haiwen. "Is It Safeguarding the Freedom of Navigation or Maritime Hegemony of the United States?—Comments on Raul (Pete) Pedrozo's Article on Military Activities in the EEZ." *Chinese Journal of International Law* 9, no. 1 (2010): 31–47.

———. *The UN Convention on the Law of the Sea and China.* Beijing: China International Press, 2014.

Zhang Hongzhou, and Sam Bateman. "Fishing Militia, the Securitization of Fishery, and the South China Sea Dispute." *Contemporary Southeast Asia* 39, no. 2 (2017): 288–314.

Zhang Hua [张华]. "On the Legality of Applying Straight Baselines to China's Mid-Ocean Archipelagos: A Perspective from Customary International Law [中国洋中群岛适用直线基线的合法性: 国际习惯法的视角]." *Foreign Affairs Review* [外交评论], no. 2 (2014): 129–143. Translated by China Maritime Studies Institute, US Naval War College.

———. "Russia's Non-Appearance in the Arctic Sunrise Case and Its Implications for China [俄罗斯不应诉'北极日出号'案 及其对中国的启示]." *Russian Studies* [俄罗斯研究], no. 6 (2014): 19–35.

Zhang Qi [张琦]. "The Contradiction Between Localization and Internationalization of Maritime Law and Its Reconciliation [海商法本土化与国际化之矛盾及其协调]." *Oceans University Law Review* [海洋大学法律评论], no. 1 (2020).

Zhang Shiping [张士平]. *China's Sea Power* [中国海权]. Beijing: *People's Daily Press*, 2009.

Zhang Taisu, and Tom Ginsburg. "China's Turn Toward Law." *Virginia Journal of International Law* 59, no. 2 (2019): 278–361.

Zhang Wei [张伟]. "A General Review of the History of China's Sea-Power Theory Development [中国特色海权理论发展历程综述]." *Frontiers* [学术前沿], no. 7 (2012): 28–35. Translated by China Maritime Studies Institute, US Naval War College.

———. "Mao's Last Decision for Battle: The Battle of the Xisha Islands [毛泽东—声中决策的最后一仗—西沙群岛保卫战]." *Party History* [党史博采], no. 10 (2008): 38–41.

Zhang Wenmu [张文木]. *On China's Sea Power* [论中国海权]. Beijing: Ocean Press, 2010.

Zhang Xinjun. "Why the 2008 Sino-Japanese Consensus on the East China Sea Has Stalled: Good Faith and Reciprocity Considerations in Interim Measures Pending a Maritime Boundary Delimitation." *Ocean Development & International Law* 42, no. 1–2 (2011): 53–65.

Zhang Zhaoyin [张兆垠]. "Effective Safeguard Maritime Rights and Interests in the South China Sea [切实有效维护南海海洋权益]." *People's Navy* [人民海军], 19 March 2014.

Zhao Jianwen [赵建文]. "The UN Convention on the Law of the Sea and China's Residual Rights in the South China Sea [联合国海洋法公约与中国在南海的既得权利]." *Legal Studies* [法学研究], no. 2 (2003): 147–160.

Zhao Jing [赵精]. "Peking University Maritime Strategy Center Established [北京大学海洋战略重心成立]." *China Oceans Report* [中国海洋报], 30 June 2014.

Zhao Lihai [赵理海]. "Questions on Our Country's Ratification of UNCLOS [我国批准《联合国海洋公约》问题]." *Ocean Development and Management* [海洋开发与管理], no. 1 (1994): 56–62.

Zheng Fan [郑凡]. "State Practice in Archipelagic Waters Conference Summary [群岛水域国家实践研讨会综述]." *China Oceans Law Review* [中国海洋法学论坛], no. 1 (2013): 291–300.

Zheng Zhihang [郑智航]. "A Study of the Mechanisms by Which the Party System Shapes Justice [党政体制塑造司法的机制 研究]." *Global Law Review* [环球法律评论], no. 6 (2020). https://mp.weixin.qq.com/s/EJ1h2IjXRFNsgPvxubK8fQ.

Zheng Zhihua. "Is China Ready for a Second South China Sea Arbitration?" *South China Sea Probing Initiative*, 15 June 2020. http://www.scspi.org/en/dtfx/1592210057.

Zhou Gengsheng [周鲠生]. *International Law* [国际法]. Beijing: Legal Press, 1981.

Zhou Jiang [周江]. "On South China Sea Sovereignty in 'Surrounding Waters' Claimed by China [论我国南海主权主张中的'附近海域']." *Journal of Chongqing University of Technology* [重庆理工大学学报], no. 9 (2011): 60–67.

Zhou Qiang [周强]. "Deepen the Reform of Maritime Trial Work and Strive to Build an Influential International Maritime Judicial Center [深入推进海事审

判工作改革 努力建设具有影响力的国际海事司法中心]." Supreme People's Court [最高人民法院]. 4 December 2016. http://www.court.gov.cn/zixun -xiangqing-16238.html.

———. "Supreme People's Court Work Report [最高人民法院工作报告]." Fourth Session of the Twelfth National People's Congress. 13 March 2016. http:// www.gov.cn/xinwen/2016–03/20/content_5055629.htm.

Zhou Zhonghai [周忠海]. *International Law* [国际法]. Beijing: University of Politics and Law Press, 2004.

———. "Maritime Law and National Maritime Security [海洋法与国家海洋安全]." *Henan Cadre Management College of Politics and Law* [河南省政法管理干部学院学报] 24, no. 2 (2009): 60–67.

Zhu Qiwu [朱奇武]. "Warships Should Not Enjoy the Right of Innocent Passage [论军舰不应享有无害通过权]." *Journal of the Beijing Academy of Political Science and Law* [北京政法学院学报], no. 2 (1983): 44–67.

Zou Keyuan. "China's Exclusive Economic Zone and Continental Shelf: Developments, Problems, and Prospects." *Marine Policy* 25 (2001): 71–81.

———. "China's Governance over Offshore Oil and Gas Development and Management." *Ocean Development & International Law* 35, no. 4 (2004): 339–364.

———. *China's Marine Legal System and the Law of the Sea.* Boston: Martinus Nijhoff, 2005.

———. "China's Ocean Policymaking: Practice and Lessons." *Coastal Management* 40, no. 2 (2012): 145–160.

———. "China's U-Shaped Line in the SCS Revisited." *Ocean Development & International Law* 43 (2012): 18–34.

———. "The Chinese Traditional Maritime Boundary Line in the South China Sea and Its Legal Consequences for the Resolution of the Dispute over the Spratly Islands." *International Journal of Marine and Coastal Law* 14, no. 1 (1999): 27–55.

———. "Governing Marine Scientific Research in China." *Ocean Development & International Law* 34, no. 1 (2003): 1–27.

———. "Innocent Passage for Warships: The Chinese Doctrine and Practice." *Ocean Development and International Law* 29, no. 3 (1998): 195–223.

———. "The International Tribunal for the Law of the Sea: Procedures, Practices, and Asian States." *Ocean Development & International Law* 41, no. 2 (2010): 131–151.

———. "Joint Development in the South China Sea: A New Approach." *International Journal of Marine and Coastal Law* 21, no. 1 (2006): 83–110.

———. "Peaceful Use of the Sea and Military Intelligence Gathering in the EEZ." *Asian Yearbook of International Law* 22 (2016): 161–176.

———. "The Sino-Vietnamese Agreement on Maritime Boundary Delimitation in the Gulf of Tonkin." *Ocean Development & International Law* 36, no. 1 (2005): 13–24

INDEX

Italic page numbers indicate illustrations.